# A History of the Frenc<br>through Texts

# Related titles

**The French Language Today**
*Adrian Battye and Marie-Anne Hintze*

**A History of the French Language**
*Peter Rickard*

**Thinking Translation**
A course in translation method: French to English
*Sándor Hervey and Ian Higgins*

# A History of the French Language through Texts

Wendy Ayres-Bennett

London and New York

First published 1996
by Routledge
11 New Fetter Lane, London EC4P 4EE

Simultaneously published in the USA and Canada
by Routledge
29 West 35th Street, New York, NY 10001

The publisher has made every effort to trace copyright holders and would be
glad to hear from any who have not been traced.

Typeset in Times by Florencetype Ltd, Stoodleigh, Devon
Printed and bound in Great Britain by
TJ Press (Padstow) Ltd, Padstow, Cornwall

The author asserts the moral right to be identified
as the author of this work.

*British Library Cataloguing in Publication Data*
A catalogue record for this book is available from the British Library

*Library of Congress Cataloguing in Publication Data*
A catalogue record for this book has been requested

ISBN 0–415–09999–4 (hb)
ISBN 0–415–10000–3 (pb)

# Contents

# Symbols

> : 'becomes'

< : 'comes from'

* : placed before a word indicates that the form is unattested; this may be a form posited on the basis of evidence such as comparative data from other Romance languages.

# Figures

# Acknowledgements

Three people – Rebecca Posner, Glanville Price and Peter Rickard – deserve my heartfelt thanks both for the constant support and encouragement they have offered me over the years and for undertaking the onerous task of reading the complete manuscript of this work and offering detailed comments on it. Others have generously helped with individual commentaries, and especially Clive Sneddon (text 8), Tony Hunt (text 10), Frank Lestringant (text 26), John N. Green (text 36) and Francis Nolan (text 44); mention should also be made of colleagues in the French Department, Cambridge, and in particular, Peter Bayley and Sarah Kay. I would also like to thank Simon Bell and his team at Routledge and the staff at the Cambridge University Library for their practical assistance, and my sons Matthew and Luke Bennett for their tolerance and good humour. Finally, my greatest debt goes to my husband, Andrew Bennett, whose roles in the completion of this project are far too numerous to mention, and to whom this book is dedicated.

# Introduction

## Texts and why we should study them

What is the point of a history of French *through texts*? There are, after all, a number of good readable general histories of the language available which make relatively little use of texts or relegate them to an appendix. Peter Rickard's *A History of the French Language* (1974, ²1989) provides an excellent introduction in English for students to the subject, and there is also an impressive selection of one-volume surveys in French, including those by Picoche and Marchello-Nizia (1989), Cohen (1947, ⁴1973), or Wartburg (1934, ¹⁰1971), all of which have their merits.[a] Is not philology, the study of texts, somewhat out of date?

But what if we want to adopt a less passive approach and try to discover for ourselves how the French language has evolved? How can we find out about the history of any language? It is, of course, impossible for us, except in respect of the recent past, to turn to recordings or interrogate native speaker informants about their usage, as would a linguist describing and analysing the contemporary French system. Rather, the historian is dependent on textual material, on written sources, with all the difficulties that we shall see this implies. These texts must provide us with information about the linguistic usage of earlier ages; subsequent comparison of the usage in texts of different periods may then provide clues as to how the language has evolved.

In this volume, therefore, texts are central. Whereas in the past collections of texts have tended to concentrate almost exclusively on the Old and Middle French periods (see, for example, Aspland (1979) or Studer and Waters (1924)), and especially the earliest extant monuments of the French language, here texts dating from the earliest examples in the ninth century up to the late twentieth century have been included, so that the evolution of French up to the present day can be traced. For each period a range of texts is given, including a number of longer core or key texts. The texts are accompanied by detailed linguistic commentaries and not

---

a   For further bibliographic references, see Appendix III.

merely notes on difficult or unusual usages or textual variants; this includes detailed descriptions of the sound system (phonology), spelling (orthography), forms or internal structure of words (morphology), construction and word order (syntax), vocabulary (lexis), meanings (semantics) and discourse type of the key texts; briefer, more specific, comments about interesting features of the other texts are given.

The collection thus allows the history of the French language to be viewed both synchronically and diachronically. These concepts are perhaps best understood through Saussure's well-known analogy of a chess-board. One can either stop a game of chess at any moment in the game and describe the position and the relationship of the pieces to each other in terms of the structure of the game: such would be a synchronic description. Alternatively one could trace the moves, or history of a particular piece, say a knight, throughout a game: this would give a historical or diachronic description of that piece. In providing synchronic analyses of French at different points in its history, the danger is avoided of viewing Old French, for instance, as merely a stepping stone in the history from Vulgar Latin to Modern French. Thus, from a historical point of view it may be interesting to know that negative *pas* and the noun *le pas* ('step') derive from the same Latin term, *passum*. For a synchronic description of Modern French, however, this is less relevant, since for most speakers they are now discrete items.

## Texts of different discourse types

Two basic characteristics are shared by most standard, traditional accounts of the history of French. First, as the very name, the history of *the* French language, implies, traditional surveys have tended to see the language as a *monolithic* structure and ignore or marginalize variation. Many, for instance, chart the evolution of French in terms of the emergence of a unified standard language, itself characterized by the suppression or elimination of dialectal variation.[b] Typical of this approach is the statement by Picoche and Marchello-Nizia (1989: 3) in the introduction to their history of French: 'Ce livre a l'ambition d'être une histoire de ce *trésor commun* qu'est la LANGUE française, non des styles, créations individuelles que cette langue a permis d'engendrer'. Second, most histories of the French language have been based on predominantly *literary* texts. Let us look at the implication of each of these features in turn.

The assumption of homogeneity has, in many ways, been essential, since it has allowed philologists to provide synchronic descriptions of the structure of French at various points in its history. Indeed, as Suzanne Romaine has suggested (1982: 10), without such a sound descriptive basis, subsequent studies of variation would have been impossible. Nevertheless,

b   See, however, Lodge (1993).

as we shall see, the marginalization of variation clearly furnishes an artificial picture of the richness and diversity of linguistic usage which characterized the usage of earlier periods just as much as it does French today.

Approaches to the history of languages have, however, begun to change in the wake of sociolinguistic research and notably the variationist paradigm of sociolinguistics, associated above all with the work of William Labov, from the early 1960s on; this attempts to account for the productive and regular patterns of linguistic behaviour in a systematic way. Although there had previously been accounts of individual examples of past variation, it was really only in the 1980s that a theoretical framework was considered for looking systematically at variation of earlier periods. Thus in 1982 Suzanne Romaine coined the term *socio-historical linguistics*, the aim of which is to reconstruct a language in its social context and whose basic working principle is that there is no reason to assume that language did not vary in the same patterned way in the past as has been observed today.

The French themselves have, however, been somewhat reluctant to embrace sociolinguistics perhaps for two main reasons. First, they have long been preoccupied with the study of one specific kind of variation, namely dialectology. The focus of these dialect studies has, however, been upon the collection of phonological or lexical data, often with a view to compiling linguistic atlases. Second, the strength of the normative tradition in France has led to the widespread condemnation of anything considered non-standard or alien to *le bon usage* and a reluctance to consider it as an object worthy of study. This is not to say that non-literary texts have been totally neglected in France – far from it. Godefroy, for instance, used them extensively in his *Dictionnaire* (1881–1902), and there have been a number of important collections of charters and other non-literary documents. As early as 1829 J.-J. Champollion-Figeac commented in the following terms on Raynouard's use of almost exclusively verse texts: 'Les pièces en prose sont aussi des monuments de la [langue romane], des productions intéressantes à la fois et pour l'histoire de son perfectionnement, et pour l'histoire de l'état moral des peuples qui la parlèrent; peut-être même pourrait-on ajouter que les pièces en prose d'un certain ordre, les actes publics, comme toute autre composition réfléchie, peuvent, autant au moins que les pièces en vers, servir à l'étude approfondie et chronologique de cet idiome' (Monfrin 1974: xi). Cerquiglini (1989: 50) has made the telling point that in medieval manuscripts (e.g. Harley 978; see text 10, pp. 84–85) texts of different types – anthological, literary and factual – are found side by side. The full theoretical implications of such insights have not, however, always been appreciated, nor have they necessarily had an impact on the way histories of French have been written.

There are signs of a growing awareness that, even in the case of a language like French, on which the pressures of standardization and codification have been immense, the language of the past was not homogeneous; we may note for instance the very valuable contributions made by members of the Groupe Aixois de Recherches en Syntaxe (GARS). Yet it has often fallen to non-French linguists and notably Germans such as Bodo Muller, Günter Holtus, Franz Josef Hausmann and Gerhard Ernst to work, especially since the 1970s, on variation in French both in its contemporary form and for earlier periods of its history.

The assumption of homogeneity of development is allied to my second consideration, the hitherto almost exclusive concentration on literary texts in readers on the history of French. Histories of French have been primarily histories of the literary language and have tended to neglect other texts which might reflect other discourse types, such as legal, scientific or medical texts, or journals. Once again the description of French has tended to be conservative in this respect. We may note for the study of English the recent publication of a number of collections of texts which have tried to embrace a broader sociolinguistic perspective as reflected in a wider range of texts of different discourse types: John Fisher and Diane Bornstein, *In Forme of Speche is Chaunge: Readings in the History of the English Language* (University Press of America, 1984), David Burnley, *The History of the English Language: A Source Book* (Longman, 1992) or Dennis Freeborn, *From Old English to Standard English* (Macmillan, 1992).

The fact that previous anthologies of Old French texts have tended to focus almost exclusively on literary texts may have produced a rather distorted image of the language of earlier times, and indeed of contemporary French. For instance, statements to the effect that the dropping of pre-verbal negative *ne* in contemporary spoken French is a relatively recent phenomenon can be challenged, for, if we consider earlier texts which aim to transcribe *spoken* rather than literary usage, constructions of the type 'je sais pas' can be found at least as far back as the seventeenth century. Similarly Rothwell's work (1993) has shown that the study of Anglo-Norman literary texts tends to yield a predictable and restricted vocabulary, but that wider lexicographical horizons are opened up when a broader range of texts, whether legal, political, scientific, or administrative, are included in the analysis.

It is, moreover, vital to take the discourse type of each text into consideration if one is to try to make general statements on the basis of these texts about the state of the language at a given time. When considering, for instance, the only two extant texts from the ninth century, the Strasbourg Oaths (AD 842) and the *Sequence of Saint Eulalia* (*c.* AD 880), as sources of information on early Old French, it is crucial to bear in mind that the first is a legal–political document and the second religious verse incorporated within a liturgical framework, otherwise a skewed vision of the early history of French is produced. Perhaps an analogy may clarify my point: the situation is the same as if, ten centuries hence, a characterization of twentieth-century French had to be based on only two extant texts, a parliamentary act and an item from a modern hymnal. Or imagine that at the end of the present century all texts excepts two fragments of literature were destroyed, say a piece of Proust and a piece of Gide. Valuable though these texts would undoubtedly be, it would be essential to take account of their discourse type, register, audience, milieu, etc. to appreciate their status, and they could not illustrate the full richness and diversity of the possible uses of twentieth-century French. To make the point from a slightly different angle, it is essential when comparing texts of different periods to try, wherever possible, to compare like with like. To this end, texts concerned with similar themes, such as medicine, have been included for different periods to enable a more genuine comparison. Fleischman (1990a: 22–23) has shown convincingly that apparent 'idiosyncrasies' of Old French grammatical notation and text structure bear striking resemblance to 'disconcerting phenomena confronting modern linguists whose object of study is likewise a spoken idiom'; she therefore concludes: 'the New Philologist must ... recontextualize the texts as acts of communication, thereby acknowledging the extent to which linguistic structure is shaped by the pressures of discourse' (37).

The texts in this collection are therefore designed to illustrate a wide range of different usages of French whether in, for instance, legal, scientific, epistolary, literary, administrative, or liturgical documents or in more popular domains, including attempts to represent, albeit imperfectly, spoken usage. Texts illustrating the use of French outside France have also been included (see texts 36 and 45). The inclusion of non-literary as well as literary texts serves not only to illustrate some of the many varieties of French throughout the ages: an additional bonus is that this approach also allows the reader to note key points when the use of French, rather than that of Latin or indeed of a local dialect, spreads to new domains. While some of the texts may be very familiar or 'great' texts, less familiar texts, not generally considered by philologists, are also included.

**Difficulties and problems**

The adoption of a socio-historical approach and the use of textual sources are not, of course, without their problems and pitfalls. A primary difficulty concerns the selection and choice of edition of the texts. Fashions in textual editing have changed since the 1860s, when Gaston Paris, following Lachmann's principles, attempted to produce a 'correct' version of Old French texts, a hybrid based on the manuscripts thought to be closest to the hypothetical original and excluding any idiosyncrasies or 'mistakes', for example in the non-observation of the two-case declension system for nouns. At the other end of the spectrum is the approach associated with Cerquiglini and his school which views the plurality of variants between Old French manuscripts as a positive feature symptomatic of the richness and lack of fixity of texts composed before the advent of printing. There are thus difficulties dealing with variation between different manuscripts of a text: which, if any, is the 'correct' version? is an idiosyncratic spelling a 'mistake' or an alternative regional form? how 'accurate' were the scribes in their copying? All these questions are very difficult to answer, especially in those cases where a presumed original version has not survived.

Since it is not my principal objective to provide new editions or interpretation of variants, etc., such questions will be largely neglected. For works written before the advent of printing, the extracts are simply taken, wherever possible, from a modern edition. Such a policy is, of course, problematic and readers should bear in mind that the version included is just one of many possibilities and one which has been subjected to the interpretation of one or more editors. These passages will be presented in modern typography, but may occasionally be accompanied by a reproduction of four or five lines of the original manuscript or printed edition in order to discuss interesting features of this aspect of the text. For texts written after the introduction of printing into France we have generally selected the first edition or the last version published during the author's lifetime; this permits discussion of the evolution of typographical and orthographical practices.

A second challenge concerns the interpretation of written records which are often sparse or incomplete. From these not only must a plausible system be created but also a social context. In the case of contemporary French, sociolinguists try to guarantee that their data reflect a representative sample of users by, for instance, a judicious choice of informants and a careful use of statistical computer programs. This is obviously impossible to achieve for earlier periods. The historian of French therefore has to make decisions, sometimes on the basis of scant evidence, about what constitute reliable sources of *français populaire* or *français parlé* for earlier periods. A major obstacle is knowing how representative a particular text is of linguistic usage of the time. If the earliest stages of the history of French are fairly thinly documented, for more modern periods the opposite problem may arise: trying to find texts representative of the diversity of usages of French from the plethora available.

A third difficulty resides in how to interpret any perceived variation, and especially what the relationship is between variation and change. Unless we can be sure that we are comparing texts which are alike in all respects, differences perceived between texts of different periods may reflect sociolinguistic variation rather than change. Moreover, when considering the past, the problems of trying to separate off and analyse the different parameters of variation are heightened. The parameters of variation that we might be interested in for studies of earlier periods are no different from those which are relevant today. These are, to use

Coseriu's terminology, *diatopisch* (or in Muller's (1985) terms, *la perspective diatopique*), that is geographical or regional variation; *diastratisch* (*perspective diastratique*) or social variation according to the speaker's 'preverbal constitution' (Offord 1990: 47), and embracing such factors as sex, age, socio-economic status (or SES); *diaphasisch (perspective qualitative)* or variation according to the communicative situation, thus introducing notions of style and register. If we add to these the question of medium, whether we are dealing with the oral or the graphic code, we can see that there is a complicated network of values to assess. Even with studies of contemporary French there are difficulties in trying to distinguish, for example, *français populaire* and *français familier*, or questions of medium are wrongly equated with differences in register, so that spoken French is incorrectly considered to be the same as *français populaire*. These problems are intensified when studying past periods because we often lack precise information about the speakers or the context.

Finally, since we are dealing with written texts, there are difficulties in interpreting their orthography. We know that modern French orthography is grossly inconsistent, with the same sound being represented in different ways (e.g. [s] in *ration, passion, science, face, français, semer*, etc.) and the same symbol being employed to represent different sounds or no sound at all (e.g. 's' in *sauvage, close, pas*, etc.). At different periods in its history French spelling has represented phonological reality with greater or less fidelity. Early scribes were faced with the problems of transcribing a newly emerging language and new sounds with the existing Latin orthographic system.

For all these problems, there is a clear value in studying texts. Many studies of modern usage suffer from taking examples out of context or using invented examples. In using texts we have authentic material and language used in context.

## A brief summary of the history of French

The main linguistic features of each period will be described in the commentaries on the texts and summarized in Appendix I. It is perhaps appropriate here to provide a framework for these changes by giving a brief external history of French, concentrating on those historical and socio-cultural factors which have had an impact on the evolution of the language. It is important to remember that the history of French is a continuum, but for convenience we may divide it into broad periods, using a combination of external factors and key linguistic changes.

The history, or prehistory, of French begins with the colonization of France by the Romans in the first two centuries BC. Before that, Gaul was mainly occupied by the Celtic-speaking Gauls. However, it is possible that by the fifth century AD the Gaulish tongue had given way to Latin, the language of the military garrisons, administration, trade, education and of Christianity. The term 'Latin' embraces a whole range of different varieties including the 'classical' Latin of Cicero and Caesar and what is commonly referred to as 'Vulgar Latin', embracing the spoken language of the legionaries, and popular and late written forms which in their differences from classical norms are thought to be closest to speech and the common ancestor of the modern Romance languages. Changes observed over time in Latin, such as the simplification of the declension of nouns and the formation of new compound tenses, point the way to the new Romance vernaculars.

While pre-fifth-century texts suggest little difference between the Latin of Gaul and that of the rest of the Empire, the Celtic tongue did not disappear without leaving its mark on the language of the conquerors. This substrate influence is most easily detected in the lexicon, especially in words for agricultural and domestic life such as *bruyère, chêne, if* or *mouton*. In the fifth century, with the decline of the Roman Empire, Germanic-speaking tribes invaded Gaul, with the Visigoths establishing themselves south of the Loire, the Burgundians in the Rhône and Saône valleys (i.e. the eastern central area), and the Franks, the most powerful of the tribes, in the north and north-east of France. This tribe later expanded its territory, notably under their powerful king Clovis (*c.* 465–511), and conquered land further south, thus extending its rule over most of Gaul.

With the breakup of the Roman Empire came the loss of the relative unity of language of the Vulgar Latin period. At first sight it may seem surprising that the Germanic conquerors should abandon their native tongue and, after a period of some centuries of bilingualism, adopt the Romance speech. Nevertheless, there are clear reasons for this: while the Franks were the ruling class, they were a minority and adopted much of the Roman system of administration; the cultural prestige of Latin was great and the conversion of Clovis to Christianity in AD 496 was also significant. However, the Franks, in speaking Latin, retained some of their German speech habits and this superstrate influence caused the language of Gaul to change rapidly. Here again, the most obvious influence is lexical, with terms clustering particularly in areas in which the Franks excelled such as military matters (*heaume, baron*), country life (*gerbe, jardin, gazon*), as well as in the general lexicon (*honte, orgueil, haine*). Already by the late eighth century there is textual evidence in the Glossary of Reichenau for these changes. This text lists approximately 1,200 words from the Vulgate considered to be in need of explanation. While the equivalents of the Latin lexemes are generally also Latin words, there are some 'latinized' Germanic ones; thus *pignus* is glossed by the Germanic *wadius* from which Modern French *gage* derives. There is much debate about when it is appropriate to speak of the French vernacular as distinct from Latin. Roger Wright (1982) has argued that the conceptual distinction between the Latin of France and Romance can only have been the result of a deliberate innovation in a particular historical context, that of the Carolingian renewal of Christian intellectual life. While his thesis remains controversial, it is certain that the gap between the Latin of everyday speech and Classical Latin was emphasized by the Carolingian Reforms, which were an attempt by Charlemagne to restore the language of the Church and administration to its classical purity. The recognition of a purer form of Latin for administrative purposes meant that the vernacular began to be recognized as something different; this consciousness is also reflected in the decision of the Council of Tours (AD 813) to instruct the French clergy to translate their sermons 'in rusticam Romanam linguam aut Thiotiscam' ('into the Romance speech of the countryside, or into the Germanic language'), so as to be comprehensible to the people. It is for these reasons that it is generally thought to be appropriate to speak of French from about the middle of the ninth century, the period from which the two earliest extant vernacular texts date (texts 1 and 2).

Although the period from the Strasbourg Oaths to the end of the eleventh century is generally referred to as 'Early Old French', it was not a single undifferentiated language which emerged in Gaul. Rather, the Gallo-Romance area was divided into two main zones – in the North the *langue d'oïl* area, roughly that occupied by the Franks, and the ancestor of Modern French, and in the South the Occitan-speaking *langue d'oc* region (*oïl* and *oc* were the words for 'yes' in each region) – and a third, smaller wedge-shaped area in central eastern France (*franco-provençal*). Usage in the Occitan area, which developed its own literary language, was generally more conservative, with the Latin vocalic system undergoing fewer changes and intervocalic and final consonants remaining more stable than in the North. Within each area, as yet lacking a strong sense of nation or a centralized government, there was a network of dialects which sometimes gradually shaded into each other, sometimes changed abruptly either side of a geographical barrier. Thus within the *langue d'oïl* region the principal dialects of Old French which clustered around the central dialect of Francien (the name is a nineteenth-century invention), the language of the Île-de-France, included other central dialects such as Orléanais and Champenois; the northern dialects of Picard and Walloon; Lorrain and Burgundian in the east; Norman[c] and Angevin in the west; Poitevin, Saintongeais and Angoumois in the south-west; as well as Anglo-Norman, the northern French taken to Britain at the Norman Conquest (see Figure 1).

The 'heyday' of Old French in the twelfth and thirteenth centuries witnesses a number of important developments. First, by the twelfth century conditions were becoming more favourable for greater standardization with increased intermarriage between different regions and

c   In the early period the dialect of North Norman more closely resembled the northern dialects.

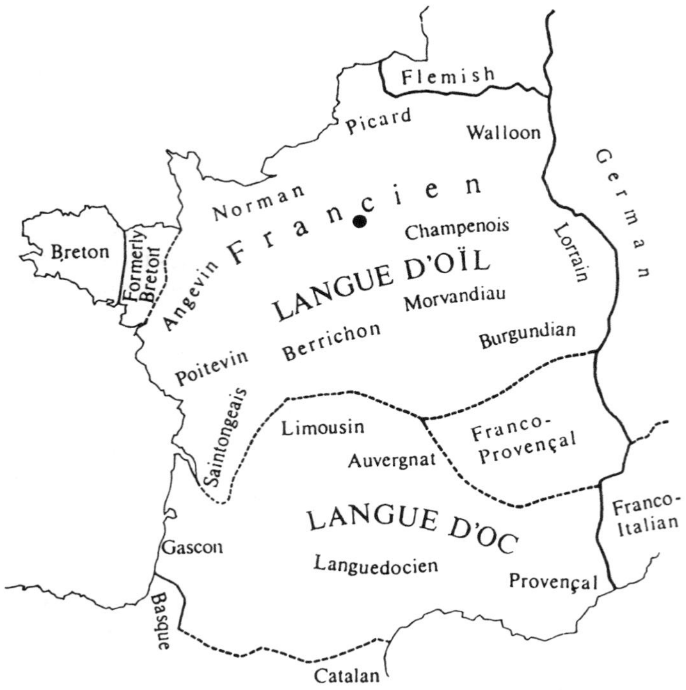

*Figure 1*   Dialect map of France, *c.* AD 1200.

*Source:*   P. Rickard, *A History of the French Language* (London, Unwin Hyman, 1989), p. 40.

minstrels moving between courts, anxious not to pepper their language with pronounced dialect features. The question of which dialect would predominate was quickly settled in favour of Francien, the language of the capital, of the royal and law courts, and of St-Denis, the nation's spiritual centre. There the Bible was translated, royal charters written and men of learning gathered. Moreover, occupying a fairly central position in the *langue d'oïl* area, Francien was less different from other dialects than those on the periphery. The prestige of Francien is witnessed in the much-quoted twelfth-century boast by Garnier de Pont-Saint-Maxence: 'Mes langages est buens, car en France [i.e. the Île-de-France] fui nez'. Île-de-France usage was, however, adopted only very gradually throughout France. The abundant literary texts in the vernacular display a mixture of dialect and supraregional features; all texts written in *langue d'oïl* have dialectal features at least until the end of the thirteenth century, but they also share a large number of common features. The usual explanation of this has been that scribes tried to use the language of prestige but, given their regional origins, 'faults' in the form of dialectal features intruded; alternatively it may be that the 'common' forms were none the less a vital part of their own regional usage allowing intercommunication between regions. By the end of the thirteenth century, Francien had made considerable progress as the written norm, even before Paris became an important literary centre in the following century. The supremacy of Francien was never really challenged except towards the end of the twelfth century by Picard, which had a flourishing literary tradition, and by Champenois, notably during the time of Chrétien de Troyes (*fl.* 1165–85). In the South of France, the situation was a different one, entailing the replacement of one language (Occitan) by another. The role of Occitan as a literary language was diminished by the Albigensian Crusade (1209–13) which led to the demise of the Toulousain dynasty and the eventual submission of the South to the Crown. Nevertheless Occitan continued to be used for everyday purposes in the South, just as in the North many dialects continued to be spoken.

Throughout its history the 'standard' language has had to compete not only with other dialects but also with Latin. During the thirteenth century French was used in some measure in local documents in Picardy and from 1254 it was employed alongside Latin in the royal chancellery. Latin remained common, however, in a number of areas right up to the sixteenth century: there was thus a diglossic situation with the vernacular being used for poetry and fiction, for instance, but Latin generally employed in scientific and religious works.

Of all the period labels, 'Middle French' is the most controversial both in terms of its chronological limits and the unfortunate connotations which imply that it is merely a transitional phase between Old and Modern French. Usually a date in the first half of the fourteenth century is taken as its starting point, but there is less agreement about its end-point, or whether the sixteenth century should be considered a separate period of 'Renaissance French'.

Politically, the early Middle French period was one of unrest with a series of French kings involved in disputes both with their own subjects and with the English. Normandy, Guyenne and Gascony came under French rule with the end of the Hundred Years' War in 1453, Provence and Anjou under Louis XI, and Brittany in 1491. The growing national consciousness of the period has important linguistic repercussions.

The literature of the late Middle Ages is composed in French, which in the fourteenth century generally means Francien with a light Picard colouring. While Latin still held sway as the language of the university, by the Middle French period it no longer had the monopoly in official records and legal texts. In the South, Occitan continued to be the usual spoken language, but either French or Latin was used for written purposes. Beyond France, however, French lost its influence in southern Italy, Sicily and Cyprus.

Despite the unrest caused by wars with Italy and the Holy Roman Empire and outbreaks of civil war the political unification of France proceeded in the sixteenth century. In the South, French gained ground with the literate minority, albeit very slowly; in the North, French increasingly rivalled Latin in official documents. A series of royal edicts from 1490 on promoted the use of French in legal proceedings, the best-known of which, the Ordonnances of Villers-Cotterêts (1539), prescribed that from then on all deeds and court proceedings should be kept 'en langue maternel françois et non aultrement'.

The Middle French period also saw the dawn of the Humanist revival of Latin; the realization by clerks that the Latin they used in administration, science or religion was no longer that of the classical period led to a renewed desire to restore it to its former purity. Once revised, however, this Latin became a less suitable medium for expressing certain contemporary needs. The sixteenth century thus witnessed the spread of French to new domains such as theology, science, mathematics and dialectic, as well as early attempts to analyse and describe it in the first vernacular grammars of French. Early discussions focused on the need to give French the stability of a codified grammar and the need to 'improve' it through lexical innovation, thereby giving it the means to compete with Latin. Other factors helping to promote the cause of French include the advent of printing, the Reformation, and the fashion for translations of classical texts.

The seventeenth and eighteenth centuries are the period of Classical and Neo-Classical French. The rise of absolutism, culminating in the reign of Louis XIV, who consolidated territorial gains and held the nobility in check through a system of privileges, is paralleled by increased control and codification of language in the seventeenth century as typified in the work of François Malherbe and Claude Favre de Vaugelas. This movement is also reflected by the founding in 1635 of the French Academy whose aim was to regulate and 'purify' French usage as well as furnish it with a dictionary and grammar (the former appeared in its first edition in 1694, the latter in . . . 1932). Throughout the period every aspect of the language was codified and very high demands were made on French usage in terms of clarity of expression and choice of the *mot juste*. In the eighteenth century, with the decline of the influence of the court and the rise of the bourgeoisie during a period of wars and financial crises under Louis XV, there came something of a relaxation of linguistic control, particularly as regards the lexicon, but on the whole the entire period is characterized by the establishment of the written norms of standard French. For all the fixing of norms, however, there is still much evidence of variation, as for example the text by Héroard (text 35) shows. And if the essentials of Modern French written usage date from this period, the spoken language has continued to change, with the gap between the two media widening.

With the promotion of French in the Classical period came a further decline in the influence of Latin and a criticism of dialect speakers. In the North of France the upper classes normally spoke French, whilst the lower classes either spoke French with a regional colouring or were bilingual in French and dialect. From 1714 French was adopted in international treaties and its prestige abroad is well reflected in the essay subject set for a prize offered by the Berlin Academy in 1782: 'Qu'est-ce qui a rendu la langue française universelle?'. The seventeenth century was also the first period of French colonization with settlement in Canada, Louisiana, the West Indies, the Antilles, Africa and on the Indian continent.

The period from the Revolution to 1945 was characterized by increased standardization and the loss of many dialects. With the Revolution came the idea that France should be unified linguistically and the belief that local dialects and regional languages were an impediment to achieving political unity of a Republic 'une et indivisible'. In 1790 the Abbé Grégoire was commissioned to carry out a survey of the linguistic situation in France; he found that of a population of some 25 million, only 3 million could apparently speak French fluently, while 6 million, mainly in the South, knew no French at all. As a result it was decreed in 1794 that French must be spoken and use of the regional languages was declared undesirable. Since then linguistic unification has been dramatic. The schools proposed by Grégoire may have taken longer to establish than he envisaged, but in the 1880s a significant step was taken when state primary education became free and compulsory. Other factors facilitating standardization include improved communication, conscription and the advent of universal male suffrage in 1848. Since the recording of the dialects by Gilliéron and Edmont in their *Atlas linguistique de la France* (1902–10) further loss has occurred. With this has come the rise of regional varieties of French, French which is essentially standard in its morphology and syntax but which is influenced by former dialect usage in the form of regional pronunciations and local terms. Of course French is not the only language spoken in France: there are also speakers of Breton, Basque, Catalan, Occitan, Corsican, German (i.e. Alsatian) and Dutch (i.e. Flemish) who are more or less militant in the promotion of their tongue. In 1951 the *loi Deixonne* went some way towards facilitating the study of Basque, Breton, Occitan and Catalan by introducing them as optional subjects for the *baccalauréat*; in 1974 Corsican was added.

A second great period of French colonization from 1830 to 1918 saw the establishment of a considerable Empire in Africa, the Far East and Oceania and the widespread introduction of the French language. If since then much of this Empire has been lost, the demise of French has not necessarily followed. Today, French is one of a few languages spoken on all six continents, although very few speakers remain, for instance, in the Indian subcontinent. The number of French speakers is notoriously difficult to estimate – not least since this depends on how we define a speaker of French – but we may perhaps think of some 90–100 million native speakers and some 200 million using it as a second language. Its status ranges from being the official language but only used by an elite (as in the 22 countries of Black Africa south of the Sahara), through being widely used, but not the official language (as in Algeria, Tunisia and Morocco), to being the native tongue (as in Quebec and parts of Belgium and Switzerland). While French is strong in Europe and in Quebec, elsewhere, for example, in Louisiana, the Lebanon, Syria and Indochina, usage is on the wane. In some countries, notably Haiti, the Seychelles, Mauritius and the *Départements d'outre-mer* (*DOM*) such as Martinique, Réunion and Guadeloupe, French exists alongside a 'French' creole.

While the speed of linguistic evolution has been inhibited by the restraining forces of normative grammar and codification in France, the language has changed since the Revolution and continues to change. In the nineteenth century, for example, the literary language was enriched by a variety of terms whether scientific or commercial, archaic, regional or borrowed. Contemporary French is usually said to date from the end of the Second World War, a period when the French have increasingly felt the need to protect their language from Anglicisms and casual usage (including the use of legislation as in the *loi Bas-Lauriol* (1975); further proposals for legislation were made in 1994 by Jacques Toubon), and to assert its role as a world language through the promotion of *la francophonie*. Yet if the forces of linguistic purism and conservatism remain strong in France, so does the vitality of the language in all its many varieties and usages.

## Use of this book

Since it is hoped that this book will be of use to non-specialists as well as specialists in French philology, help is given with Latin forms and constructions, selected technical terms are glossed in Appendix II and there is also a guide to the International Phonetic Alphabet (IPA) as used in the commentaries. Appendix III contains a guide to the relevant reference materials available, such as dictionaries of Old French, as well as suggestions for further reading. The extracts have been translated fairly literally so as to facilitate the understanding of the original; where, however, a strictly accurate rendering would result in very awkward English – for example in translating the tenses of the Old French verse extracts – a slightly freer approach has been adopted. More precise details of the editorial procedures adopted for each text may be found in the source cited at the end of the extract.

Note that the following conventions have been used throughout: numerical superscripts denote edition numbers of references; alphabetical superscripts denote footnotes.

# I    The language of the earliest texts

AD 842 to the end of the eleventh century

Very few French vernacular texts for the period up to about AD 1100 are extant. From the ninth century only two texts remain, the Strasbourg Oaths and the *Sequence of Saint Eulalia*, and from the tenth century only three, including some Notes for a Sermon on Jonah, the precarious survival of which, as the binding for another manuscript, testifies to the often chance nature of evidence becoming available to philologists. Given the sparseness of the documentation, it is perhaps especially important to bear in mind the type of texts with which we are dealing, whether as regards their discourse type, function and intended audience, or their region and dating, although evidence about these factors is lamentably lacking. Moreover, as we shall see in the discussion of the Oaths, it is often difficult clearly to distinguish these different parameters of variation, especially regional and chronological considerations. In no case do we have clear knowledge of the author. Nevertheless some general observations may usefully be made. For instance, it is striking that two of our four texts (1, 3) are non-literary in nature and use prose rather than verse (cf. Beer 1992). Whilst the *Eulalia*, Jonah Fragment, and *Life of Saint Alexis* all stem from a religious context, the notes for the sermon are clearly different in being preparatory rather than a final product, and intended only for the eyes of the writer. Again, all the texts bear witness to the close relationship between writing and speech, but in the case of *Eulalia* and *Alexis* we have a written version of a text intended for oral performance, with the Jonah Fragment notes in preparation for the giving of a sermon, and as regards the Oaths perhaps a citation of spoken oaths, perhaps a version reworked for polemical purposes (see below). All four texts emphasize equally the close relationship between Latin and French during this period and the predominance of the classical language for writing, since they survive in manuscripts which are principally devoted to Latin texts.

# 1 The Strasbourg Oaths (842): the earliest vernacular text

The Strasbourg Oaths are the earliest surviving piece of prose in the vernacular of Gaul, and indeed in any Romance language. Because of their special status as the earliest extant monument of the written *lingua romana*, they appear in virtually all collections of Old French texts, sometimes placed alongside otherwise exclusively literary texts, although clearly they belong to a different discourse type, since they derive from a legal–political context. The text records oaths sworn in Strasbourg on 14 February AD 842 by two of Charlemagne's grandsons, Charles the Bald and Louis the German, who had formed an alliance against their brother Lothair with whom they had been in dispute over the division of the Carolingian Empire. These oaths, sworn following the defeat of Lothair at Fontenay-en-Puisaye near Auxerre in 841, mark a stage towards the partitioning of the Empire established by the Treaty of Verdun the following year (see Figure 2). Traditional accounts suggest that the first oath of mutual support (*sacramentum firmitatis*) was sworn in French by Louis the German and in German by the French-speaking Charles so as to be comprehensible to the other man's followers; each man's followers then swore a different oath (*sacramentum fidelitatis*) in their own language. However, scholars have now challenged this view, arguing that the supporters of Louis the German and Charles the Bald were not exclusively Germanic and Romance speakers respectively, and that their armies were much more heterogeneous in origin and character. Equally, the leaders are attributed one language although it is generally thought that Hugh Capet (crowned AD 987) was the first king to speak only Romance. The use of language is therefore deliberately symbolic and political in nature: the unity of each army and difference from the other could be stressed by attributing a different language to each party, but equally their mutual support for each other underlined by their leaders swearing in the other language. Here are the two parts of the oaths sworn in the vernacular of Gaul:

> **The text of the oath taken by Louis the German:**
> **Pro Deo amur et pro christian poblo et nostro commun**
> **salvament, d'ist di in avant, in quant Deus**
> **savir et podir me dunat, si salvarai eo**
> **cist meon fradre Karlo et in aiudha**
> **et in cadhuna cosa, si cum om per dreit son** 5
> **fradra salvar dift, in o quid il mi altre-**
> **si fazet. Et ab Ludher nul plaid nunquam**
> **prindrai qui, meon vol, cist meon fradre**
> **Karle in damno sit.**

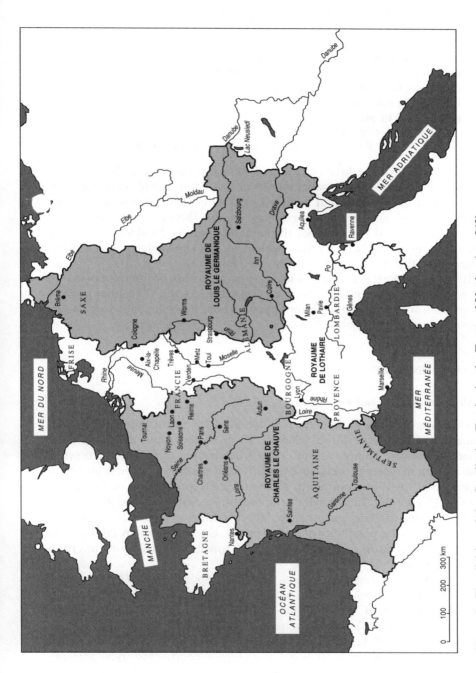

*Figure 2* The division of the Carolingian Empire by the Treaty of Verdun (AD 843)

*Source:* L. Theis, '843: La Première France', *L'Histoire*, Jan 1987, vol. 96, p. 89.

### The text of the oath taken by the followers of Charles the Bald:

**Si Lodhu-**           10
**uigs sagrament, que son fradre Karlo**
**jurat, conservat, et Karlus meos sendra**
**de suo part non los tanit, si io returnar non**
**l'int pois, ne io ne neuls, cui eo returnar**
**int pois, in nulla aiudha contra Lodhu-**     15
**uuig nun li iu er.**

(From C.W. Aspland, *A Medieval French Reader* (Oxford, Clarendon Press, 1979), p. 2, by permission of Oxford University Press.)

[Translation: For the love of God and for the protection of the Christian people and our common salvation, from this day forward, in as much as God gives me wisdom and power, I shall help this my brother Charles both with aid and in all other things, as one should rightly help one's brother, provided that he does the same for me. And I shall never enter into an agreement with Lothair which, to my knowledge, will be detrimental to this my brother Charles.

[10] If Louis keeps the oath which he swore to his brother Charles and Charles my lord for his part does not keep it (his oath), if I cannot prevent him from so doing, neither I nor anyone whom I can dissuade from it will give him any help against Louis.]

## COMMENTARY

### Authors, scribes and editors ...

Whenever we look at an early text, we must be aware that we are often dealing with at least three different levels of recording and reworking. Such texts were composed and written down by a scribe, often recopied in a later manuscript version by a different scribe or scribes, and then 'processed' by a modern editor (compare the reproduction of the manuscript (Figure 3), Tabachovitz's 'diplomatic' edition (Figure 4) and the version with modern punctuation, abbreviations expanded, etc. above). There is thus the possibility of scribal errors, changes made by later scribes and modern editorial intervention, all of which we must try to interpret and evaluate.

The Oaths are recorded in a closely contemporary text, *De dissensionibus filiorum Ludovici Pii* or *The History of the Sons of Louis the Pious* written by Nithard, who died in AD 844. Nithard, a cousin of Lothair, Louis and Charles, had been requested by Charles to write the work as a justification of his political strategy, in which Nithard himself had played a significant role. It is not therefore a neutral historical account, but a work of propaganda or, to use Cerquiglini's (1991: 86) terms, a 'témoignage engagé'.

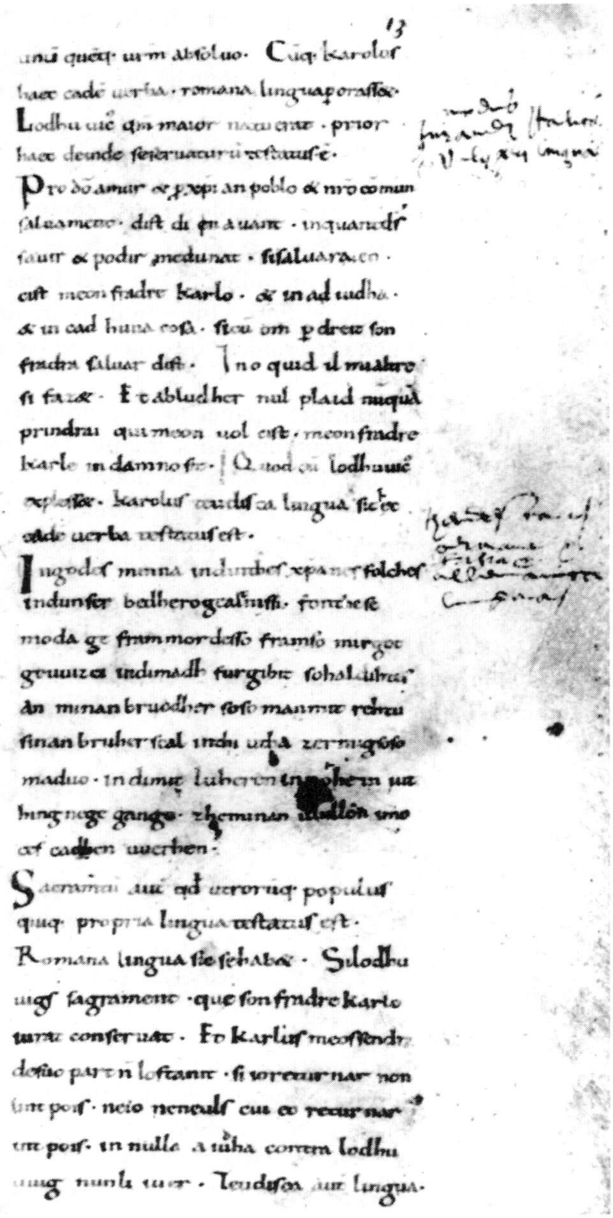

*Figure 3*  Manuscript of the Strasbourg Oaths

*Source:*  Bibliothèque nationale, lat. 9768, fol. 13ʳ, col. 2. © cliché Bibliothèque Nationale de France Paris.

While Nithard's account is closely contemporary to the swearing of the oaths, the work survives today in only one manuscript from the Abbaye de Saint-Médard de Soissons kept in the Bibliothèque nationale in Paris (BN lat. 9768) and dating from the end of the tenth century, that is, some 150 years later, with all the hazards that implies.

## Texte diplomatique.

Pro dõ amur & ,p xp̃ian poblo & nrõ cõmun | ſalvament. diſt di ɇn auant. inquantdſ | ſavir & podir medunat. ſiſalvaraieo. | ciſt meon fradre karlo. & in aḍ iudha. | & in cad huna coſa. ſicũ om p dreit ſon | fradra ſalvar diſt. Ino quid il mialtre|ſi faz&. Et abludher nul plaid nũquã | prindrai qui meon vol ciſt meon fradre | karle in damno ſit.

(Ingodeſ minna indintheſ xp̃aneſ folcheſ | indunſer bedhero gealᵗ-niſſi. fontheſe|moda ge frammordeſſo framſo mirgot | geuuizci indi-madh furgibit ſohaldihteſ|an minan bruodher ſoſo manmit rehtu | ſinan bruher ſcal inthi utha zermigſoſo|maduo. indimit luheren innȯhein iut|hing nege gango. zheminan uuillon imo | ceſ cadhen uuerhen.)

Silodhu|uigſ ſagrament. quę ſon fradre karlo | iurat conſervat. Et karluſ meoſ ſendra | deſuo partñ loſtanit. ſi ioreturnar non | lint poiſ. neio neneulſ cui eo returnar | int poiſ. in nulla a iu͘ha contra lodhu|uuig nun li iuer.

(Oba karl theneid. then er ſine n obruodher | ludhuuuige geſuor geleiſtit. indilud|huuuig min herro thenerimo geſuor forbrih|chit. obi hina neſ iruuen denne mag. noh | ih noh theronoh hein theni-heſ iruuendenmag | uuidhar karle imoce folluſ tine uuirdhit.)

*Figure 4* Tabachovitz's diplomatic edition of the Strasbourg Oaths

*Source:* A. Tabachovitz, *Étude sur la langue de la version française des Serments de Strasbourg* (Uppsala, Almqvist & Wiksells Boktryckeri-A.-B., 1932), p. 1. Reproduced by permission of the Syndics of Cambridge University Library.

There is much debate about the circumstances surrounding the drafting and recording of the Oaths. Some have suggested that the Oaths were first drafted in Latin for perusal and approval by the two parties. Such a hypothesis might help explain the large number of latinisms and the rather archaic flavour of the language of the text. Others have maintained that the short, formulaic and archaizing style is rather typical of the adminis-trative milieu (as a comparison think of the language of modern-day legislative documents and see text 42) and that it is this fact that best explains the apparently radical differences between this text and our next one, the *Sequence of Saint Eulalia*. It is quite possible in this view that some at least of the constructions were modelled on the Latin forms commonly in use in the Court and Chancery, Latin being the usual language of administration and law for some centuries to come. It is indeed possible that Nithard himself was involved in the drafting of the Oaths. Again there is no consensus as to whether this is a pure citation of the actual words spoken or a reworking by Nithard for his polemical purposes. The former is certainly a possibility given the deliberately innovative use of spelling to record the speech and the symbolic importance of the language used as noted already. Ewert (1935), on the other hand, has suggested that perhaps the Oaths were 'retouched' by Nithard and therefore contain some non-original elements; this has been suggested for 'et in aiudha et in cadhuna cosa' (ll. 4–5) and for the problematic line 13 (see below). A final factor to bear in mind when analysing the use of the *lingua romana* is possible influence from the Germanic part of the Oaths, for example in the choice of word order.

**But is it French?**

Given the short, formulaic and, as we shall see, somewhat conservative use of language, due probably primarily to the type of text we are dealing with and perhaps also to the influence of a projected Latin original, we might ask ourselves whether we are justified in considering this the earliest example of the vernacular. De Poerck (1963), for instance, sees it as much as the end of the line of Merovingian and Carolingian *Formulae*, and Price (1990) likewise prefers to see the *Eulalia* as the first French text, since the Oaths are profoundly influenced by Latin judicial texts. We may note the high instance of such latinisms as *Deus* (l. 2), *in damno sit* (l. 9), *conservat* (l. 12), or semi-latinisms such as *in quant* (l. 2) modelled on Latin *in quantum*. The Oaths have therefore featured prominently in the debate, renewed over the past decade by Roger Wright, about the correct dating for the distinction between Latin and Romance. Despite the latinisms, however, even a cursory glance shows it to be very different not only from Classical Latin (see Ewert's reconstruction of a possible Latin version, Figure 5) but also from Vulgar Latin texts, as we shall see when we come to look in detail notably at the phonology and morphology of the text.

**The language of the text**

Much consideration has been given to the question of the region of the language of the text, without any consensus having been reached. Various possible hypotheses have been put forward using either external or internal evidence to support them: for instance, an eastern dialect (Alsace/Lorraine) has been suggested on the basis of Strasbourg's location

1.  \*Ad Dei voluntatem et ad populi christiani
    In Godes minna ind in thes christanes folches
    Pro Deo amur et pro christian poblo

2.  \*et nostrum commune salvamentum,
    ind unser bedhero gealtnissi,
    et nostro commun salvament,

3.  \*de isto die inantea, in quantum mihi Deus
    fon thesemo dage frammordes, so fram so mir Got
    d'ist di in avant, in quant Deus

4.  \*scire et posse donaverit, $\left\{\begin{array}{l}\text{adjutor ero} \\ \text{sic salvabo}\end{array}\right.$

    gewizci indi madh furgibit, so hald ih
    savir et podir me dunat, si salvarai eo

5.  \*isti fratri meo $\left.\begin{array}{l} \\ \end{array}\right\}$ n̄
    istum fratrem meum
    tesan minan bruodher
    cist meon fradre Karlo et in adjudha et in cadhuna cosa

6.  \*sicut homo per drictum esse debet fratri suo,
    soso man mit rehtu sinan bruher scal,
    si cum om per dreit son fradra salvar dift,

7.  \*in hoc ut ille mihi similem promissionem faciat,
    in thiu thaz er mig so sama duo (*MS.* soso maduo),
    in o quid il mi altresi fazet,

8.  \*et ab Lodhario nullum placitum inibo
    indi mit Luheren in nohheiniu thing ne gegango
    et ab Ludher nul plaid numquam prindrai

9.  \*quod, per meam voluntatem, isti fratri meo n̄
    the (*MS.* zhe), minan willon imo
    qui, meon vol, cist meon fradre Karle

10. \*in damno sit.
    ce scadhen werhen.
    in damno sit.

11. \*Si n̄ sacramentum, quod fratri suo n̄ juravit,
    Oba Karl then eid, then er sinemo bruodher Ludhuwige gesuor,
    Si Lodhuuigs sagrament, quę son fradre Karlo jurat,

12. \*conservat, et n̄ meus senior,
    geleistit, indi Ludhuwig min herro
    conservat, et Karlus meos sendra

13. \*quod suo fratri n̄ juravit, infrangit,
    then er imo gesuor, forbrihchit,
    de suo part non (*MS.* n̄) lostanit,

14. \*si ego illum inde retornare non possum,
    ob ih inan es irwenden ne mag,
    si io returnar non l'int pois,

15. \*nec ego nec nullus quem ego inde retornare possum,
    noh ih noh thero nohhein then ih es irwenden mag,
    ne io ne neuls eo returnar int pois,

16. \*auxilio contra n̄ illi non ero.
    widhar Karle imo ce follusti ne wirdhit.
    in nulla ajudha contra Lodhuwig nun li iv er.

*Figure 5* Ewert's reconstruction of a possible Latin version of the Strasbourg Oaths, together with the French and German texts

*Source:* A. Ewert, 'The Strasbourg Oaths', *Transactions of the Philological Society*, 1935, pp. 22–23.

or Poitiers as the seat of Charles's court; on the grounds of internal evidence Castellani (1969, 1978) has made strong claims for Poitevin, a south-western dialect, but Lyonnais or Picard have also been proposed. It is therefore agreed in general that the language is of the North of France, but that no more precise localization can be made with certainty. This uncertainty over the location leads inevitably to interpretative difficulties; features typical of south-western texts such as the absence of diphthongization of tonic free vowels, use of -*a* as the supporting vowel or non-occurrence of the second wave of palatalization (see below) may equally well be conservative or archaic features. One hypothesis is that the language of the Carolingian Court and Chancery at which the text was written was coloured by dialectal traits typical of south-west France, but that it also showed the restraining influence of Latin. On the other hand it has equally been argued, notably by Hilty (1978), that even in these earliest of texts there is evidence of some sense of supra-regionalism or of an emerging *scripta gallo-romane*, following in the Merovingian orthographic tradition.

**Problematic lines**

A number of lines are particularly obscure, and notably 'de suo part non los tanit' (l. 13) over which a great deal of effort has been spent.[a] If we accept this as the correct reading of the manuscript, we may perhaps interpret 'non los tanit' as comprising *lo* plus the enclitic *se* plus *tanit* as a dialectal subjunctive of *tenir* (< *teneat*; Tabachovitz) or perhaps derived from the imperfect indicative *těnēbat* (Cornu). A major problem of interpretation seems to be that *los* refers back to Louis's oath rather than to that sworn by Charles. This may explain why Drašković for instance suggested that *los* is rather derived from *laus* 'honour' so that the phrase has the sense 'to keep honour' and thus 'to keep one's word'. However, various other readings of the manuscript have also been proposed, including *non lo-stanit* (Ph. Aug. Becker, Castellani) as a mistake for *non lo tanist* (< *tenuisset*) or *lof tañit* (Hilty) from *locum tenere* in the sense of 'to hold good'. Since the German version has an affirmative construction here, it has been suggested by Lindner that the line originally read *de suo partem lo fraint*; this may have been later misread as *los tanit* which conveyed the opposite of what was required, and consequently the abbreviated negative *ñ* was introduced after *part* to remedy the difficulty. An additional problem lies in *de suo part* since *part* is feminine, but *suo* is masculine; one suggestion is that the final *o* of *suo* represents [ə]. Let us consider briefly two of the other problems posed by the text. First, *ab* (l. 7). On the one hand it has been suggested (for example by Hilty 1978)

---

a   The debates over this line and other textual problems are well summarized in Tabachovitz (1932) and Hilty (1978).

that it represents *a* falsely latinized as *ab* rather than *ad*. On the other hand, and perhaps less convincingly, Castellani (1969) argued that *ab* is a form typical of southern Poitou derived from *apud*. Second, also in line 7, how should we interpret *nunquam*? Generally this has been thought of as another pure latinism, but De Poerck (1956) has asserted that it is rather composed of *nunqua* with the enclitic *me* giving the sense 'never as far as I am concerned'.

## Orthography

Another problem is determining how well the spelling reflects the pronunciation of the text. If we look, however, at the representation of final unstressed [ə], we can clearly see that there is not a one-to-one correspondence between sound and letter. Note, for example, that both *fradre* (1. 4) and *fradra* (1. 6) and *Karlo* (1. 4) and *Karle* (1. 9) occur, showing the same sound represented by *e*, *a* and *o*. Frequently where the scribe apparently hesitates, the form chosen is the one closest to the Latin etymon, so that for feminines *-a* (= [ə]) is preferred (*in cadhuna cosa, in nulla aiudha*, etc.). This is not at all surprising given the situation in which the scribe found himself, having to transcribe an emerging language, not yet standardized but rather in a state of flux, and having to deal with sounds new to the vernacular with naturally only the Latin alphabet at his disposal. Given this, one should not underestimate the ingenuity of the scribe in employing the diagraph 'dh' as in *cadhuna* (< *cata una*), *aiudha* (< *ajutare*) to notate the dental fricative [ð] or in using 'z' to mark the affricate [ts] in *fazet* (1. 7) from *faciat*.

## Phonology

*Vowels*

The strong stress accent of the Frankish speakers when using the Latin of Gaul had a profound influence on the sound system of French. As a broad generalization we may say that unstressed vowels tended to weaken and fall, whilst stressed vowels in open syllables tended to lengthen and break, thereby creating diphthongs.

Final unstressed vowels

All final unstressed vowels in general disappeared (*amur, christian, om, di*) with two exceptions. Final [a] weakened to [ə] written here as *-a*, and [ə] was also used as a 'supporting vowel' for the consonant clusters [tr], [dr], [pl], [bl], [vr], [zn], etc. which otherwise would have occurred in final position but which did not form part of the phonological structure of French, e.g. *sendra, poblo, fradre, nostro*.

Penultimate unstressed vowels

These similarly fell. When the loss of the vowel created a combination of [mr], [ml], [nr], [lr], [sr], or [zr], a so-called 'glide' consonant was introduced facilitating pronunciation. Here then we have *senior* > *sen're* > *sendra* (l. 12), where in anticipation of the [r] the nasal passage is closed early leaving the latter part of the [n] denasalized, so that a [d], the corresponding non-nasal stop, is heard.

Tonic free vowels

Spontaneous diphthongization is not well indicated in this text. Diphthongization occurred in two waves in the history of French: whilst the diphthongization of [ɛ] and [ɔ] occurs widely in other Romance languages, the diphthongization of [e] and [o] is a characteristically French phenomenon, and must therefore have taken place after the breakup of the Empire. It is difficult to account in a satisfactory way for the first wave of diphthongization; the second wave has, however, traditionally been attributed to the speech habits of the Frankish invaders who, through giving tonic syllables far greater stress, caused vowels when tonic and free to lengthen and diphthongize (see Price 1971: 64–65). More recently other possible explanations have been offered; see, for instance, Zink 1986: 52–60. Since evidence of diphthongization is present in the next text and it is difficult to believe that such a major change could have occurred in the forty years separating these two texts, the absence of such diphthongs here appears to be an example of the scribe being conservative (others might prefer a regional explanation). The diphthongs that are indicated are formed not by the diphthongization of tonic free [e, ɛ, o, ɔ], but as a result of palatalization; thus we have *plaid* < *placitum* and *dreit* < *directum*, where the [j] resulting from palatalization joins with the preceding vowel to form a diphthong. Also conservative is the preservation of stressed [a] in tonic free syllables, e.g. *fradre* in contrast to the *Eulalia* where *spatha* is shown as having changed to *spede*. Again an alternative explanation of this lies in a possible south-western regional influence.

In those syllables where diphthongization is not shown, tonic [e] and [o] are represented by *i* and *u*, regardless of the original vowel (*sapere* – *savir, potere* – *podir; amorem* – *amur, donat* – *dunat*). There is also evidence of the simplification of the last remaining Latin diphthong [au] > [ɔ] in *cosa* (l. 5).

*Consonants*

In very general terms we may say that initial consonants were strong and tended to remain intact (e.g. *podir, savir*), final consonants tended to weaken and then fall, and medial consonants tended to modify through the assimilatory influence of the neighbouring vowels.

## Intervocalic consonants

One or, in some cases, two stages of the modification of intervocalic consonants are illustrated. Through assimilation, voiceless intervocalic stops became voiced (a process known as lenition when a fortis consonant which is made with a relatively high degree of muscular effort and breath force becomes a lenis) giving for example *populum > poblo* (l. 1), *potere > podir* (l. 3), *sacramentum > sagrament* (l. 11) etc. In other items the next stage of the assimilatory process is also indicated, that is when the tongue is no longer raised enough to make a complete closure in the oral cavity thereby producing a fricative: *cata una > cadhuna* [ð] (l. 5), *sapere > savir* (l. 3); *adjutare > aiudha* (l. 4). This suggests that the spellings of the first group may be conservative. In the case of *ego > eo, io* the intervocalic *g* has completely disappeared.

## Final consonants

When consonants fell into final position through the loss of a following unstressed vowel, they tended to become voiceless (e.g. *inde > int*, l. 14). Whereas final -*m* fell silent in most words very early on, it became [n] in a few monosyllables as indicated here by *meum > meon* (l. 8).

## Palatalization

Palatalization, the assimilatory process whereby a sound shifts to the palate either, say, back from the teeth or forward from the velum is represented to some extent in this text. The two main factors causing palatalization in French are the presence of yod ([j]), attracting a neighbouring consonant to its point of articulation, and a front vowel following velar [k, g]. The modification of medial [k] either before palatal [j] or a consonant is shown in *fazet (fakjat > k′ > ts* spelt 'z') and *dreit, plaid* respectively. However, as far as we can tell from the orthography – and there is again dispute whether it is conservative here or not, especially since there was no easy means of representing [tʃ] – the second wave of palatalization, that of [k] followed by [a], which is a typically central French change, is not indicated. Thus we find the [k] maintained in *cosa, cadhuna, Karle* rather than becoming [tʃ] > [ʃ] as in *chose, chacun, Charles*, etc.

## Morphology

*Noun morphology*

The interrelation of phonetic and morphological change is clearly illustrated by the evolution of noun morphology between Latin and Old French. The loss of final unstressed vowels meant that the Latin six-case noun inflections had been greatly reduced leaving only a two-case system for the majority of masculine nouns, a form derived from the nominative fulfilling the subject and vocative functions, and an oblique form fulfilling all other functions. For the vast majority of feminine nouns, only one singular and one plural form remained, giving the modern pattern for feminines from the earliest texts on:

|            | singular | plural |
|------------|----------|--------|
| nominative | *dame*   | *dames* |
| oblique    |          |        |

Occasionally feminines derived from Latin third declension nouns had a final -s in the nominative singular form, either because this existed in the etymon or on the analogy of the main class of masculine nouns:

*floris* (Classical Latin (CL) *flos*) > *flors*    *flores* > *flors*

*flore*(*m*)                            > *flor*

A small number of imparisyllabic feminines – nouns which had an extra syllable in all forms other than the nominative singular – had three distinctive forms in Old French:

*sóror*   > *suer*     *soróres* > *serors*

*sorórem* > *seror*

If the main class of feminines had simply one singular and one plural form, this was not true of the main masculine class which declined in the following way:

| *murus* | > *murs* | *muri* | > *mur* |
|---------|----------|--------|---------|
| *murum* | > *mur*  | *muros* | > *murs* |

The two-case system for this class of masculine substantives is well illustrated in this earliest of French texts: for example, we have the masculine subjects *Deus* (l. 2) and *Karlus* (l. 12), showing the distinctive masculine singular ending in 's', contrasting with the oblique forms *Deo* (l. 1) and *Karlo* (l. 11). A second masculine class, derived from Latin third declension, lacked a final -s in the nominative singular because it did not have one in Latin; the nominative plural form, however, already suggests analogical influence from class 1 (*fratres* having been replaced by *\*fratri*):

| | | | |
|---|---|---|---|
| *frater* | > *frere* | **fratri* | > *frere* |
| *fratrem* | > *frere* | *fratres* | > *freres* |

There were also masculine imparisyllabic nouns which had a distinctive masculine nominative form; sometimes this went together with a change of stress (*ber*, *baron*), sometimes not (*cuens*, *conte*):

| | | | |
|---|---|---|---|
| *báro* | > *ber* | **baróni* | > *baron* |
| *barónem* | > *baron* | *barónes* | > *barons* |
| *cómes* | > *cuens* (*quens*, *cons*) | **cómiti* | > *conte* |
| *cómitem* | > *conte* | *cómites* | > *contes* |

Two imparisyllabic forms used in the Strasbourg Oaths are worthy of special mention: *sendra* (l. 12) is a unique occurrence of this form, and the nominative henceforth appears as *sire* with *seignor* as the oblique; second, Latin *hominem* regularly gave the noun *ome* (> *homme*), but unusually the nominative form *homo* also survived and was specialized in usage as the indefinite pronoun *on* (*om*, l. 5), perhaps through the influence of Germanic *Mann/man*. Both masculine and feminine nouns with a stem ending in -*s* or -*z* were indeclinable in Old French (*passum* > *pas*, *mensum* > *mois*). Also indeclinable were a few nouns derived from Latin neuters ending in -*us* which did not assimilate to the main class of masculines (as the majority did), but rather retained their identical form in the nominative and oblique singular and further extended this to the plural, thereby eliminating the etymological plural forms (*pectus* > *piz*, *corpus* > *cors*).

Hand-in-hand with the reduction of the case system goes the increased use of prepositions to mark the function of the nouns as we can see in, for example, *d'ist di in avant* (l. 2), *per dreit* (l. 5), *de suo part* (l. 13), etc., although this is not invariably true since there is also the use of some vestigial 'cases' without a preposition, that is where an oblique form is used as though it were still showing its original Latin case form and function. Thus we find a 'genitive' or possessive use of the oblique in line 1, *Pro Deo amur* (a modern relic of this survives in *Hôtel-Dieu*), a 'dative' or indirect object use without a preposition in lines 11–12, *que son fradre Karlo jurat* ('which he swore to his brother Charles'), and an 'absolute' use of the oblique in the expression *meon vol* (l. 8). Finally we may note that there is no evidence here of the use of articles which was to become very much a feature of the new Romance vernacular.

*Personal pronouns*

Whereas in Classical Latin the distinctive verb endings had sufficed to mark the person of the verb, in Old French personal pronouns became increasingly used to fulfil this function. In the Oaths there are already several instances of the use of subject pronouns both personal (*eo*, *io* (ll. 3, 13, 14), *il* (l. 6)) and the indefinite personal pronoun *om* (l. 5), although not surprisingly there are still clauses without a subject overtly expressed (e.g. *que son fradre Karlo jurat*, ll. 11–12). The relatively high incidence of subject pronouns in the Oaths may be partly due to the legalistic nature of the formulae. Incidentally we may note the use of *si* < *sic* which is frequently used in Old French either to introduce a clause where no overt subject is expressed or where there is inversion of the finite verb and subject pronoun, as in line 3 *si salvarai eo* (it is generally not necessary to translate it in this usage). This use of *si* should not be confused with other uses of *si* in this text: *si cum* (< *sic quomo*, l. 5) meaning 'as', or *si* (< *si*, l. 10) meaning 'if'.

Personal pronouns used in other functions also appear in the Oaths. Thus we have *me* (l. 3) and *mi* (l. 6), probably a contracted form of the Latin dative form *mihi*, *l'int* 'from it' (l. 14) and *li* (l. 16), the dative unstressed pronoun.

### Possessives

Two forms are worthy of comment. In line 12 *meos* is the sole example of the intermediary stage between Latin *meus* and the usual Old French subject form *mes*. Similarly, *meon* (ll. 4, 8) is a unique attestation of the intermediate stage in the transition from Latin *meum* to *mien*. We may perhaps also note here the construction *cist meon fradre Karle* (ll. 8–9) which continued to be used right up to the sixteenth century but was condemned by Vaugelas in the following century. In the nineteenth century Littré still described constructions of the type *un mien ami*, etc. as 'familier', but today they are considered rather as archaisms.

### Demonstratives

Two sets of demonstratives occurring in Old French are attested here, the one derived from simple Latin forms (e.g. *iste/isto(m) die* > *ist di* (l. 2), or *hoc* > *o* (l. 6)), the other derived from a compound structure in which *iste* or *ille* is reinforced by the deictic *ecce* meaning 'lo!' or 'behold!' (e.g. *ecce iste* > *cist* (l. 8)).

### Verb morphology

Already in Vulgar Latin there is considerable evidence of simplification of Classical Latin verb morphology and a change from synthetic to analytic forms (e.g. *fecit* v. *habet factum*). The new future typical of the Romance language formed on the infinitive + *habeo* is represented here by *salvarai* (l. 3) < *salvarajo* < *salvare habeo* and *prindrai* (l. 8) < *prehendere habeo*, although there is one vestigial occurrence of the synthetic future in *er* (l. 16) < *ero*. Comparison with the Germanic version of the oaths makes it clear that *jurat* is a preterite < *jurávit* in contrast to, for instance, *conservat* where the 'a' represents the [ə] of the present tense.

## Word order

The word order of the Oaths is probably heavily affected by Latin and German influence, so that indeed some have argued that it is Latino-French in this respect. As we can see from the following two examples, there is a strong tendency for the verb to appear in final position:

ll. 2–3   in quant Deus        savir et podir        me dunat
                  S[ubject]     O[bject]              V[erb]

ll. 10–11 Si Lodhuuigs sagrament, que son fradre Karlo jurat, conservat
                  S            O       [I[ndirect] O[bject] V]     V

There is, however, also an example of a clause with the verb in second position (*si salvarai eo*), which is the favoured positioning of the verb in Old French, and for which Germanic influence is likely. Furthermore, the position of the dependent genitive is conservative, although not uncommon in early texts; *Deo amur* (l. 1) thus gives way to *amur Deo*.

## Vocabulary

There is not much variety in the vocabulary and, as we have seen, there is a high proportion of latinisms or semi-latinisms. We may, however, note the use of infinitives as substantives as in *savir, podir* (l. 3), a common means of forming new nouns in Old French, and the creation of the post-verbal noun *aiudha* (l. 4) < *adjutare*. Of interest too is the use of *di* from *diem* which was later replaced by *jour* from *diurnum* but which still survives in *midi* and the names of the days of the week (*samedi, jeudi,* etc.). Aside from the proper names all the vocabulary is of Latin origin. Finally it has been observed that the vocabulary, however limited, is significant in that it contains some key terms associated with feudalism and chivalry, such as *sendra* and *aiudha*.

## The earliest French text

In view of all the features we have noted which are typical of the new vernacular of Gaul we can conclude with Hilty (1978: 126–27) that, despite the conservative elements of orthography, lexis and word order and its brevity and formulaic nature, related to the discourse type, the text nevertheless represents 'le premier échelon de la tradition des textes français'.

## 2 The *Sequence of Saint Eulalia* (*c.* 880–82)

Not surprisingly, there are a significant number of common features between the Strasbourg Oaths and the only other extant ninth-century French text, the *Sequence of Saint Eulalia*. For example, in the *Eulalia* the two-case system for nouns is similarly rigidly observed, the loss of unstressed syllables is evident (e.g. *pulcella* < *pulicella* (l. 1)), and the vocabulary is exclusively Latin in origin. Here too we find a large number of latinisms and semi-latinisms (e.g. *rex* (l. 12), *post* (l. 28), but see also below), suggesting a scribe still unfamiliar with writing in French as opposed to Latin. However, we shall focus here on a number of new features which are at least partially explained by reference to the different temporal and regional circumstances of the text, and its different discourse type and form.

Buona pulcella fut Eulalia,                                                 1 - 10
Bel auret corps, bellezour anima.
Voldrent la veintre li Deo inimi,
Voldrent la faire diaule servir.
Elle no'nt eskoltet les mals conselliers,                                    5
Qu'elle Deo raneiet, chi maent sus en ciel,
Ne por or ned argent ne paramenz
Por manatce regiel ne preiement;
Niule cose non la pouret omque pleier
La polle sempre non amast lo Deo menestier.                                 10
E por o fut presentede Maximiien,                                            —
Chi rex eret a cels dis soure pagiens.
Il li enortet, dont lei nonque chielt,
Qued elle fuiet lo nom christiien.
Ell'ent adunet lo suon element;                                             15
Melz sostendreiet les empedementz
Qu'elle perdesse sa virginitét;
Por os furet morte a grand honestét.
Enz enl fou lo getterent com arde tost;
Elle colpes non auret, por o nos coist.                                     20
A czo nos voldret concreidre li rex pagiens;
Ad une spede li roveret tolir lo chieef.
La domnizelle celle kose non contredist:
Volt lo seule lazsier, si ruovet Krist;
In figure de colomb volat a ciel.                                           25
Tuit oram que por nos degnet preier
Qued auuisset de nos Christus mercit
Post la mort et a lui nos laist venir
    Par souue clementia.

(This is essentially Ewert's version, quoted here from
R. Sampson, *Early Romance Texts: An Anthology* (Cambridge,
Cambridge University Press, 1980), pp. 109–10.)

[Eulalia was a good girl,
She had a beautiful body, a soul more beautiful still.
The enemies of God wanted to overcome her,
they wanted to make her serve the devil.
She does not listen to the evil counsellors,                    5
(who want her) to deny God, who lives up in heaven.
Not for gold, nor silver, nor jewels,
not for the king's threats or entreaties,
nothing could ever persuade the girl
not to love continually the service of God.                    10
And for this reason she was brought before Maximian,
who was king in those days over the pagans.
He exhorts her – but she does not care –
to abandon the name of Christian;
She gathers up her strength.                                    15
She would rather endure torture
than lose her (spiritual) purity.
For this reason she died with great honour.
They threw her into the fire, so that she would burn quickly.
She was without sin, for that reason she did not burn.         20
The pagan king would not tolerate this;
he ordered her head to be cut off with a sword.
The girl did not oppose this;
she wants to leave this earth, she calls upon Christ.
In the semblance of a dove she flies to heaven.                25
Let us all pray that she will deign to intercede for us
that Christ will have mercy on us
after our death and bring us to himself
through his mercy.]

## COMMENTARY

### Dating of the text

The date of composition of the text can be ascertained with a fair degree of certainty. The cult of Eulalia had been revived in France after the supposed discovery of the saint's bones in Barcelona in AD 878. In the manuscript, which is closely contemporary to the date of composition, the French poem is placed between a Latin sequence on the same theme and a German poem that celebrates the battle of Saucourt which took place on 3 August 881 and speaks of the victor (Louis III, †882) as still being alive, thereby narrowing down with some precision the chronology. We thus have none of the problems associated with the 150-year gap between the composition and the surviving manuscript of the Strasbourg Oaths.

## Region

We also have fairly precise information about the provenance of the manuscript (Valenciennes, Bibliothèque municipale 150, formerly 143, fol. 141ᵛ), which comes from the monastery at Saint-Amand-les-Eaux, near Valenciennes. This was a major centre of scholarship in the ninth century and is also the likely place of composition of the text. As we shall see, the Sequence clearly contains certain north and north-eastern linguistic features, making its interpretation less problematic than the Oaths, although there are equally some features which cannot be localized to the Picard-Walloon region and may therefore suggest that even in this earliest period there existed a supra-regional *scripta* (see Introduction, pp. 10–11).

## Discourse type

Although the *Eulalia* dates from only forty years after the Oaths, it comes from a different milieu, being a hymn in praise of the saint incorporated within a liturgical framework; it is therefore an ecclesiastic or clerical text, from a monastic rather than an administrative context. The liturgical setting of the text helps explain certain of its features. First, despite the brevity of the text and the inclusion of latinisms, it appears that the churches were more in touch with the ordinary people and that this is perhaps therefore a more faithful record of ninth-century usage than the Oaths; this is evident, for example, in the recording of diphthongs (see below). Second, the latinisms (e.g. *anima* (1. 2), *Christus* (1. 27), *clementia* (1. 29)) and semi-latinisms (*menestier* (1. 10), *colpes* (1. 20), *virginitét* (1. 17)) often occur in words used in a theological sense, perhaps suggesting direct borrowing from the Latin liturgy. Finally, the content is not merely intended to be factual or informative, but is also designed for reflection, which implies greater care of expression and more syntactic variety; in this respect it therefore has more in common with our fourth text, *La Vie de Saint Alexis*, which is an example of medieval hagiographical literature.

## Form

There is much dispute as to what the precise form of this 29-line hymn is; in the manuscript two of our lines are written side by side with a point separating them. Some scholars, following Lote (1949), maintain that the sequence is composed in semi-poetic prose comprised of fourteen assonating couplets, in which the number of syllables per line and the position of the caesura vary from line to line. De Poerck (1964) argues that, following Latin models, the author wrote in decasyllables, while Meunier (1933) maintains he uses a system which never triumphed in France being based not on counting syllables but on the number of accents: thus each hemistich has two accents and in general pairs of lines assonate (have the same final stressed vowel). Whatever the case, we must always bear in mind when faced with verse that the metre may influence the use of language. Thus, for example, the large number of words with preserved unstressed syllables (latinisms) might equally be explained by the demands of metre.

## Regional features

Coming from the north of France, the text displays certain features typical of the Picard-Walloon dialect. There are therefore elements which are typical of the north-eastern region as well as certain northern features (see Pope 1952: 486–93). Phonological features which are characteristic of the north-east include:

(a) absence of conditioned diphthongs and triphthongs derived from stressed [ɛ, ɔ] followed by a palatal; we find here then, for example, *melz* (1. 16) rather than *mielz < melius*, or *seule* (1. 24) rather than *\*sieil < seculum*;
(b) lowering of pretonic *en* to *an* as in *raneiet* (1. 6), *manatce* (1. 8);
(c) a labial glide developed between vowels in hiatus, perhaps due to Germanic influence, giving here *souue* (1. 29 = *sowe*) for central *soe*; note also *auuisset* (1. 27) for Francien *oüst*;
(d) loss of final unsupported *t* as in *perdesse* (1. 17) and *arde* (1. 19).

These are supported by certain morphological features typical of the north-east:

(a) the first person plural of the imperative, *oram* (1. 26), has a north-eastern ending;
(b) *lei* (1. 13) is a north-eastern form for the feminine singular stressed pronoun.

As regards northern features, we may note:

(a) retention of [k] before [a], thus *chieef* (1. 22), *chielt* (1. 13), *kose* (1. 23), *cose* (1. 9) all begin with an initial [k] and not [tʃ] > [ʃ];
(b) vocalization of *b* before *l* as in *diaule* (1. 4) < *diabolem* (Fr. *deable*).

In line 19 we find *lo* where we might expect *la*; this is probably best explained as a simple slip rather than as a regional feature.

It is not at all surprising to find such regional colouring occurring in a text of this period; what is more interesting from our point of view is the fact that there is also a suggestion of supra-regionalism, in that we find, for instance, presence of a glide *d*, as in *sostendreiet* (1. 16), *voldrent* (1. 3) (< *volvr'unt < voluerant*) which is not a feature of either northern or north-eastern texts.

In short we do not have a homogeneous use of language, but one which is essentially Walloon, with some northern and central features. In other words the language is of a composite nature at both the phonological and morphological levels.

## Problematic lines

Severe difficulties are posed by the reading and interpretation of line 15 which we have given here as:

Ell'ent adunet lo suon element

First, there is the difficulty as to whether the verb form should read *adunet*, *aduret* or *adonet*, and then what it means. This combines with uncertainty as to the meaning of *element*, and the role of *ent* which seems to have little precise meaning in this context. Barnett (1961) has suggested that *element* refers to a god and that *aduret* is a present subjunctive (< *adorare*) giving the reading '(exhorted her ...) that she adore his own god'. Hilty (1990), on the other hand, suggests *son element* refers to the fire and *aduret* means 'suffer' giving 'she suffers the fire'. The reading *adunet* is favoured here: while it has been the generally held opinion that the second downstroke of the *n* is an accidental and therefore insignificant addition, Price (1993b) argues that the stroke is deliberate and, on the basis of the tone of the ink, maintains that this correction was probably made by the original scribe. If we accept this reading, *element* perhaps means 'strength' and the whole line reads 'she gathers up her strength'. Several other interpretations of varying degrees of credibility have also been proposed (e.g. that the last word is, in fact *lenement* < *linamentum* meaning 'drap de lin', 'vêtement de lin').

## Orthography

As with the previous text we find a combination of conservative spellings with ingenious solutions to accommodate changing pronunciations. For instance, the representation of [ə] in final position is still conservative in *buona* (l. 1), *pulcella* (l. 1), whereas in *manatce* (l. 8), *spede* (l. 22), *domnizelle* (l. 23), etc., the same sound is written as *-e* in final position (but still as *a* in the pretonic unstressed position). Hilty (1990) has suggested that in the case of the first line the final 'a's are deliberately retained to give *alleluia* in anagram in the line (*buonA puLcELla fUt EulalIA*) since this immediately preceded all Sequences. [ts] is represented by *tc* in *manatce* (l. 8), but by *c* in *ciel* (l. 6), *pulcella* (l. 1), *cels* (l. 12), by *z* in *domnizelle* (l. 23), *bellezour* (l. 2), and by *cz* in *czo* (l. 21); in this last case *co* would not be possible since in the scribe's system *c* + *o* = [k] as in *cose*. [k] before *e, i* is represented as *ch*. Further evidence of a lack of standardization of orthography is afforded by *Krist* (l. 24)/*Christus* (l. 27).

**Phonology**

*Vowels*

The most striking difference between this text and the previous one is the fact that here we have clear evidence that the diphthongization of tonic free vowels has occurred, indication of which was noticeably absent from the Oaths. So, for instance, the diphthongization of tonic free *o* > *uo* is represented in *ruovet* (l. 24), *buona* (l. 1) and the evolution of tonic free *a* in *maent* (l. 6) and *spede* < *spatha* (l. 22) (cf. Oaths: *fradre*, *salvar*, etc.). The diphthongization does not occur in monosyllables such as *por* (l. 7); in any case this was unlikely to occur as a stressed syllable. An example of metathesis is furnished by *por* < *pro* (l. 20). Note also the absence of prosthetic *e*; early on (in the first century AD) a faint on-glide had developed before words beginning with *s* + consonant, which later became [e]. In these early texts this only occurs when the preceding word ended in a consonant, thus *une spede* (l. 22) rather than *espede* (Modern French *épée*).

*Consonants*

There is further evidence here of the modification of Latin intervocalic consonants: the evolution of medial k, g (> γ which then either becomes [j] or is completely absorbed if following a velar vowel) is represented by *plicare* > *pleier* (l. 9), or *precamentum* > *preiement* (l. 8). The palatalizing effect of yod ([j]) is indicated by *minacia* > *manatce* [ts] (l. 8), *bellationem* > *bellezour* [ts] (l. 2), *fugiat* > *fuiet* (l. 14) and *consiliarios* > *conselliers* [λ] (l. 5). Finally, note that in *eskoltet* (l. 5), the preconsonantal *l* is not yet shown as having vocalized.

**Morphosyntax**

*Adjective morphology*

We have noted that the declension of substantives is strictly observed. This is also true of adjectives, of which there are two main classes in Old French, those derived from Latin first and second declensions, of the type *bonus, bona, bonum*, giving the following pattern:

|  |  | masculine | feminine | neuter (used only to qualify neuter pronouns, phrases and clauses, e.g. *ce est bon*) |
|---|---|---|---|---|
| singular | subject | *bons* | } *bone* | } *bon* |
|  | oblique | *bon* |  |  |

|  |  | masculine | feminine | neuter |
|---|---|---|---|---|
| plural | subject | *bon* | *bones* |  |
|  | oblique | *bons* | | |

and those derived from Latin third declension (e.g. *grandis, grandis, grande*) for which the following system was observed:

|  |  | masculine | feminine | neuter |
|---|---|---|---|---|
| singular | subject | *granz* | *grant* | *grant* |
|  | oblique | *grant* | | |
| plural | subject | *grant* | *granz* | |
|  | oblique | *granz* | | |

In other words the masculine and feminine forms of the oblique were identical and the feminine lacked a final *e*, as is illustrated in *grand honestét* (1. 18); this *e* was later added to feminine adjectives of this class on the analogy of the first class. Also concerning adjectives, the new Romance analytic comparative is not here attested; rather there is a relic of the Latin synthetic comparative form: *\*bellatiorem > bellezour* (1. 2).

*Articles*

Both the definite and the indefinite article are attested in this text for the first time. The definite article, derived from the Latin demonstrative *ille, illa*, patterns in the following way in Old French:

|  | singular | | plural | |
|---|---|---|---|---|
|  | masculine | feminine | masculine | feminine |
| subject | *li* | *la* | *li* | *les* |
| oblique | *le (lo)* | | *les* | |

So in line 3 we find the masculine plural nominative, *li Deo inimi*, in line 5 the masculine plural oblique, *les mals conselliers*, in line 21 the masculine singular nominative form, *li rex pagiens*, and in line 10 the masculine singular oblique form, *lo Deo menestier*. The indefinite article, derived from the Latin numeral 'one', *unus, una*, is likewise attested here for the first time in *ad une spede* (1. 22).

In general the definite article was used in Old French only to define or specify a particular individual or individuals (e.g. *la polle* (1. 10), refers to a specific girl, already mentioned in the text); similarly, the indefinite article was employed to pick out an individual or individuals, and had the value 'a certain (one)'. Thus the article is not used invariably with all nouns here, and the usage of the first two lines, for instance, is quite typical of the period (for further discussion of the use of the article, see text 4).

*Verbs*

There are a number of interesting verb forms in this text. Perhaps most striking to the modern reader are the forms *auret* (l. 2) < *habuerat, pouret* (l. 9) < *potuerat, furet* (l. 18) < *fuerat, voldret* (l. 21) < *voluerat, roveret* (1. 22) < *rogaverat*. While these are derived from Latin pluperfect forms, they are used here with a simple past sense (the function of the Latin pluperfect having been taken over by a new compound tense). In that respect they duplicate the function of the French simple past forms derived from the Latin perfect, and this perhaps explains why these are very rare forms, no longer attested after the middle of the eleventh century.

There is also evidence of the new Romance preference for analytic rather than synthetic forms. Parallel to the new future form which we saw in the Oaths (formed from the infinitive and the present tense of *habere*), there is here the new French conditional formed from the infinitive and the imperfect tense of *habeo*, thus *sustinere habebat* > *sostendreiet* (l. 16). Another analytic formation is evidenced in the passive structure *fut presentede* (l. 11). We may also note the early example of a pronominal structure unknown to Latin in *nos coist* (= *non se coist*, l. 20), used here with a passive sense (see Stefanini 1962: 584–87).

There are a number of subjunctive forms. The French imperfect subjunctive is derived from Latin pluperfect forms, so *amavisset* > *amast* (l. 10), *perdidisset* > *perdesse* (l. 17); *habuisset* > *auuisset* (l. 27); in the last case we might logically expect a present subjunctive. A variety of reasons called for use of the subjunctive: for instance *arde* (l. 19) is used in a clause of purpose introduced by *com* < *quomo(do)*, while the verb of advising governing the use of the subjunctive *raneiet* (l. 6) has to be understood from the sense of the noun *conselliers* (cf. *fuiet* in l. 14).

Finally the use of *fut* in line 1 of the text to describe Eulalia is typical of the Old French period when the imperfect is relatively seldom used; this contrasts with the use of *eret*, derived from the Latin imperfect, in line 12. The use of tenses will be further discussed in the commentaries on *Alexis* and *Roland*.

*Enclitics*

Various enclitics or contracted forms are used in Old French. Where two monosyllables occur in succession, the final unstressed vowel of the second monosyllable may be dropped before a following consonant, and the remaining consonant cliticized to the preceding syllable; e.g. *enl* (l. 19) < *en le*; *nos* (l. 20) < *non se*. Similarly *no'nt* (l. 5) < *non inde*, with reduction of *ent*.

**Construction and word order**

The structuring of clauses is more complex here than in the previous text, as, for example, in lines 9–10:

Niule cose non la pouret omque pleier
La polle sempre non amast lo Deo menestier.

In line 9 the *non* is expletive (that is, it has no semantic value and was probably inserted to fill up the line of verse), whereas it is negative in the main clause. The clauses are simply juxtaposed (parataxis) and the subordination of *non amast* is only suggested through the use of the subjunctive.

There are two possible syntactic readings for lines 26–27, depending whether both of the *que* are taken to depend on *tuit oram*, i.e.

tuit oram     –     que degnet
              –     qued auuisset . . . Christus

Or, perhaps more likely, the second subordinate clause depends on the first, i.e. *tuit oram – que degnet – qued auuisset . . . Christus.*

The word order demonstrates Old French flexibility, a feature which will be discussed in greater detail later. Note here, for instance, the use of V[erb] O[bject] in line 2 with no subject explicitly expressed and separation of the adjective from its substantive, V C[omplement] S[ubject] in line 3, SOV in line 20, and VSO in line 27. In Old French it is usual for direct objects to precede infinitives as in *diaule servir* (l. 4) and object pronouns to show clitic climbing and therefore appear not before the infinitive but the finite verb as in *la pouret . . . pleier* (l. 9); *li roveret tolir* (l. 22). The more unusual ordering in *voldrent la veintre* (l. 3) seems to be explained by a desire to avoid beginning a line with an unstressed pronoun.

**Vocabulary**

Much of the vocabulary comes from the devotional sphere and contrast is made between body and soul (*corps/anima*). One or two lexical items merit comment. The use of *fou* (l. 19) reflects the loss of *ignis* in Vulgar Latin and its replacement in all the Romance languages by reflexes of *focus*, meaning 'hearth'. On the other hand *chieef* (l. 22) < *caput* is still employed for 'head' and not the reflex of the metaphorical *testa* ('pot'). *Chielt* (l. 13) < *calet*, literally 'grows hot', is commonly used in Old French with a dative pronoun of interest, having the sense 'care about, matter to'.

## 3  Extract from the Bilingual Sermon on Jonah (*c.* 937–52)

While this text shares a common religious context with texts 2 and 4, it differs from them in a number of very important ways. First, to use Zumthor's (1960) terminology, it is a *document historique* rather than a *monument historique*; this perhaps explains its omission from many chrestomathies and anthologies of Old French. In fact what we have here are some bilingual Latin and French notes made by the preacher in preparation for a sermon, a rough draft, and not a polished final version. This means that the intended audience of the text is also different, since, to use De Poerck's terms (1963: 139), it is a 'spécimen d'écriture personnelle', jottings intended for the preacher's own private use. It is not then, as the *Alexis* is, a text intended for oral performance, but a draft in preparation for orality; Cerquiglini (1991: 66) describes it thus: 'liée à l'actualité donc, et sans intention de répéter, cette séquence hybride d'écriture ne relève pas de l'écrit. Elle renvoie plus à la communication orale, à ses contraintes énonciatives, et à son inspiration locale et temporelle ... '. Moreover, once the sermon had been given, the notes became redundant, and it is only through extreme chance that the manuscript survives, since it was used as a binding for another manuscript and only discovered accidentally in the 1840s by Bethmann.

What is perhaps most striking about the text is the mixing of Latin and French, providing a first-class illustration of the resolution of the Council of Tours of AD 813 that preachers should address their congregation in the *rustica romana lingua* in order to allow general comprehension. We may suppose that the anonymous writer of the notes – who must himself have been bilingual – had before him his Latin biblical text and the late-fourth-century commentary on it by Saint Jerome and equipped himself with some key phrases in French on which to base his sermon. Broadly speaking then the biblical text is in Latin and the notes for the sermon in the vernacular interspersed with Latin. Sometimes the preacher simply provides a translation of the Latin text, as lines 7–8 gloss the first two lines. In other cases, the French text is much more elaborate and expands upon and explains the Latin original (as in lines 27–34). The natural coexistence of French and Latin at this period has been termed *colinguisme* by Balibar (1985: 14).

This section of the sermon relates to Jonah, Chapter 4, verses 6–9:

**Et preparauit Dominus ederam super caput Ione**
**ut faceret ei umbram. laborauerat**
**<enim dunc> Ionas propheta habebat mult laboret e**
**mult penet a cel populum co dicit. e faciebat grant**
**jholt. et eret mult las**                                              5

&lt;et preparauit Dominus&gt; **un edre sore sen cheve**
**qet umbre li fesist.e repauser si podist.**
Et letatus est Ionas super **edera**
&lt;letitia magna.dunc fut Jonas m&gt;**ult** letus co dicit. **por**
**qe Deus cel edre li donat a sun souev. et a sun**     10
**repausement. Et** precepit Dominus
&lt;uermi ut percuteret ederam&gt; **et exaruit.** et parauit
Deus uentum calidum super caput Ione et dixit.melius est
mihi mori quam uiuere.
&lt;----------------------------&gt; ... **surrede dunc** co dicit     15
si rogat Deus **ad un verme . qe percussist cel**
**edre sost qe cil** sedebat ec
&lt;-----------------------------------------&gt; **cilge edre fu se-**
**che si vint grancesmes jholt la** super caput
Ione et dixit. melius est mihi mori quam uiuere Et dixit Do-     20
minus
&lt;ad Ionam Putasne bene i&gt;**rasceris tu super edera?**
et dixit.bene **irascor ego** usque ad mortem.Postea per
**cel edre dunt cil tel**
&lt;dolor ave&gt;**iet.** si debetis intelligere **les Iudeos . chi sic-**     25
**ci et aridi** permanent. negantes filium Dei.
**les Iudeos porqet il en cele durecie et en cele**
**encredulitet permessient.**et etiam **plora les** si
cum dist e le euangelio
------------------ **m'eum en avant dist.**     30
**e por els**
&lt;si erat Ionas prophet&gt;**es doliants . car** co uidebat
per spiritum prophete. **qe cum gentes uenirent ad fidem. si**
**astreient li Iudei perdut.** si cum **il ore sunt.**

(From Guy de Poerck, 'Le Sermon bilingue sur Jonas du ms. Valenciennes
521 (475)', *Romanica gandensia*, 4 (1955), 31–66 (pp. 42–44).[a])

[And the Lord prepared an ivy (and it came up) over Jonah's head to give him shade. For Jonah the prophet had greatly laboured, he had worked hard and made great exertions for this people, it says. And it was very hot, and he was very tired and the Lord prepared an ivy over his head which gave him shade and he could rest there. [8] And Jonah was glad about the ivy, with a great happiness; then Jonah was very glad, it says, because God gave him this ivy for his comfort and for his rest. And God made a worm to bore through the ivy and it withered. And the Lord prepared a hot wind over Jonah's head and he said: 'It is better for me to die than to live' [15] ... then it says God asked a worm to pierce through the ivy under which he was sitting ... that ivy was dry and there came a very great heat there over the head of Jonah and he said, 'it is

a The layout of the lines of De Poerck's edition has been retained.

better for me to die than to live'. And the Lord said to Jonah, 'Do you think you have reason to be angry over the ivy? And he said, 'I am angry with reason even unto death'. Now for the ivy which gave him such distress, you are to understand the Jews who remain dry and arid, denying the son of God; [27] the Jews because they remain in this stubbornness and state of disbelief. And even weep for them as it says in the gospel. . . . [?] said it to me before. And then Jonah the prophet was sorrowful for them. For it was seen through the spirit of the prophet that when the people came to faith, the Jews would be lost, as indeed they now are.]

## COMMENTARY

### Dating and provenance

This is one of only three extant texts dating from the tenth century, and the only one in prose. The text makes reference to a period of difficulty and De Poerck has convincingly hypothesized that this must refer to the occupation by the pagan Norsemen which occurred between AD 937 and 952, and probably nearer the beginning of this time than the end. It is likely that the sermon was given at Saint-Amand-les-Eaux on the occasion of a three-day fast intended to safeguard the monastery against the threat of the Norsemen. The manuscript is a rare early example of the survival of an author's manuscript in his own hand and is located in the Bibliothèque de Valenciennes (521 (475)).

### Manuscript difficulties

Two major difficulties are presented by the manuscript. First, when the manuscript was used to bind the later manuscript a horizontal band was removed from the top and a vertical band on the right-hand side of the recto; this means that the text is discontinuous all the way down and there are some complete lines missing in places.

Second, the author used a sort of short-hand system known as Tironian notes. These abbreviations were usually reserved for Latin and it is unusual to have them applied to the vernacular as here. I have followed De Poerck in presenting the parts of the manuscript given in full in slightly larger type. Where the Tironian notes refer to Latin words, they are unproblematic, but De Poerck illustrates well some of the difficulties when they are equally applied to French: e.g. should *C(on)R-EMent* be transcribed as *conrovement*, as the French form *corrovement*, as the (unattested) Latin form *corrogamentum* or as the hybrid *corrog-ement*? Does *R-at* refer to the Latin *rogat* or French *rova*? On the whole De Poerck has adopted a conservative approach and retained the Latin forms, while admitting the possibility that *rogat*, for example, might have been 'read' as *rova*.

**Medium**

Another important feature of this text is the use of prose which does not become common in literary texts until the thirteenth century; we thus have here an interesting example of usage where the word order and constructions are not constrained by considerations of metre or assonance, although we must, of course, consider possible influence from the Latin text.

**Region**

The regional origin of the text is generally agreed to be Walloon on the basis of such north-eastern forms as *foers* < *foris* and the eastern ending of the imperfect in *-evet* etc. as in *auardevet*, both of which occur in the lines immediately preceding our extract. Here we find the northern form of the possessive *sen* (1. 6), and the lowering of countertonic *e* > *a* as in *astreient* (1. 34) for the conditional of *estre*. It is possible that the form *cilge* (1. 18) is a regional variant for the feminine singular demonstrative adjective.

**Phonology**

*Vowels*

Unstressed vowels

The loss of all final unstressed vowels (except *-a* > *-e* [ə]) is well attested here (*mult* (1. 3) < *multum*; *las* (1. 5) < *lassum* etc.). In general, internal (intertonic) unstressed syllables have also disappeared (*edre* (1. 6) < *hedera*) or been modified (*eret* (1. 5) < *erat*), but there are some semi-learned forms such as *encredulitet* (1. 28) < *incredulitas, -atis*. The form *verme* (1. 16) with a final *-e* is used rather than the expected *verm*, perhaps on the analogy of those forms where a supporting vowel was necessary for the pronunciation of the consonant cluster.

Tonic free vowels

Diphthongization of tonic free *e* > *ie* is not shown, thus we find *edre* < *(h)edera*. *Letus* < *laetus* is employed here rather than the usual Old French form *lié*.

*au*

Of the three Latin diphthongs *oe*, *ae* and *au*, *au* remained the longest, becoming [ɔ] during the Gallo-Roman period. Whereas in the Strasbourg

Oaths we saw this change represented in *cosa* < *causa*, here the Latin diphthong is retained in the spelling of *repauser, repausement*.

## Consonants

### Palatalization

The palatalization of *k* followed by *a* is regularly shown in this extract, giving *seche* < *sicca, cheve* < *caput*. The spelling of *jholt* < *calidum* is intriguing. It may be a simple variant for [ʃ] or alternatively a dialectal [ʒ] (cf. *Jhesus*).

### Final consonants

Unsupported final *-t* is mostly present, as in *encredulitet* and the verbs *laboret, penet*.

### Latin *h*

There is evidence of the loss of Latin *h*, for instance in *edre*.

## Morphology

### Noun morphology

There appear already to be some occasional instances of non-observance of the two-case system even in this very early text. Here then we might expect to find *jholt* (l. 19) with a distinctive nominative ending.

There was variation regarding the gender of *edre* in Old French: sometimes the feminine gender was used in line with the gender of the Latin etymon (*cilge edre fu seche*, ll. 18–19), elsewhere the masculine was preferred. In the case of *cel edre* (l. 10), the use of *cel* is probably a simple elision rather than an example of use of the masculine gender. Later the article becomes agglutinated to the noun giving the modern French term *lierre*.

### Adjective morphology

The form *grancesmes* (l. 19), perhaps a variant for *grantesmes* or *grandesmes*, is an example of a synthetic superlative form, which perpetuates the Latin method of forming comparatives and superlatives rather than employing the new analytic Romance structures.

*Verb morphology*

In the case of verb morphology, however, the juxtaposition of Latin with the vernacular highlights the replacement of Latin synthetic forms with Romance analytic forms; thus the Latin pluperfect *laboraverat* becomes *habebat laboret* in the French gloss. The form *permessient* (1. 28) is difficult to account for satisfactorily. It may be a north-eastern variant of the past simple of *permaindre* (more usually *permes(s)ent*); others have preferred to substitute the reworked subjunctive form *permesissent*.

## Word order

Frequently even in this early text the Old French preference for having the verb in the second position is illustrated; for example, *dunc fut Jonas mult letus* (1. 9), *si vint grancesmes jholt* (1. 19). Equally, there is a tendency for the verb to appear in final position in subordinate clauses, as in *qet umbre li fesist. e repauser si podist* (1. 7), although other possibilities are also exploited (*qe percussist cel edre sost qe cil sedebat* (ll. 16–17)).

# 4 *La Vie de Saint Alexis* (mid-eleventh century)

This poem of 625 lines differs from our previous texts in that we have here a more sustained example of French being used for literary purposes. Nevertheless, the content is still religious, the text constituting part of the Old French hagiographical tradition. The poem was probably intended to be chanted in church on the saint's day, and this emphasis on orality influences the use of language in some respects, for example, in the rather formulaic and repetitive style. Biblical allusions are also evident, notably in *Com felix cels ki par feit l'enorerent!* (l. 35). The extract here is of lines 466–540. Following Saint Alexis's death, we have the lament of his wife; she is rebuked for this by the Pope, and he and the people express their joy at the event.

Entre le dol del pedra e de la medre
Vint la pulcele que il out espusede.
'Sire', dist ela, 'cum longa demurede
Ai atendude an la maisun tun pedra,
Ou tum laisas dolente ed eguarede.                    5

Sire Alexis, tanz jurz t'ai desirrét,
[E tantes lermes pur le tuen cors plurét,]
E tantes feiz pur tei an luinz guardét.
Si revenisses ta spuse conforter,
Pur felunie nïent ne pur lastét.                      10

O kiers amis, de ta juvente bela!
Ço peiset mai que purirat [en] terre.
E! gentils hom, cum dolente puis estra!
Jo atendeie de te bones noveles,
Mais or les vei si dures e si pesmes!                 15

O bele buce, bel vis, bele faiture,
Cum est mudede vostra bela figure!
Plus vos amai que nule creature.
Si grant dolur or m'est apar[e]üde!
Melz me venist, amis, que morte fusse.                20

Se jo[t] soüsse la jus suz lu degrét
Ou as geüd de lung' amfermetét,
Ja tute gent ne m'en soüst turner
Qu'a tei ansemble n'oüsse conversét:
Si me leüst, si t'oüsse guardét.                      25

Or sui jo vedve, sire', dist la pulcela,
'Ja mais ledece n'avrai, quar ne pot estra,
Ne ja mais hume n'avrai an tute terre.

Deu servirei, le rei ki tot guvernet:
Il nem faldrat, s'il veit que jo lui serve'.                    30

Tant i plurat e le pedra e la medra,
E la pulcela, que tuz s'en alasserent.
En tant dementres le saint cors conreerent
Tuit cil seinor e bel l'acustumerent:
Com felix cels ki par feit l'enorerent!                        35

'Seignors, que faites?' ço dist li apostolie.
'Que valt cist crit, cist dols ne cesta noise?
Chi chi se doilet, a nostr'os est il goie,
Quar par cestui avrum boen adjutorie;
Si li preiuns que de tuz mals nos tolget'.                     40

Trestuz le prenent ki pourent avenir;
Cantant enportent le cors saint Alexis,
E tuit li preient que d'els aiet mercit.
N'estot somondre icels ki l'unt oït:
Tuit i acorent, li grant e li petit.                          45

Si s'en commourent tota la gent de Rome,
Plus tost i vint ki plus tost i pout curre.
Par mi les rues an venent si granz turbes,
Ne reis ne quons n'i poet faire entrarote,
Ne le saint cors ne pourent passer ultra.                     50

Entr'els an prennent cil seinor a parler:
'Granz est la presse, nus n'i poduns passer.
[Pur] cest saint cors que Deu nus ad donét
Liez est li poples ki tant l'at desirrét.
Tuit i acorent, nuls ne s'en volt turner'.                    55

Cil an respondent ki l'ampirie bailissent:
'Mercit seniurs! nus en querreums mecine.
De nos aveirs feruns granz departies
La main menude, ki l'almosne desiret:
S'il nus funt presse, dunc an ermes delivres'.                60

De lur tresors prenent l'or e l'argent
Sil funt jeter devant la povre gent:
Par iço quident aver discumbrement;
Mais ne puet estra, cil n'en rovent nïent:
A cel saint hume trestut est lur talent.                       65

Ad une voiz crient la gent menude:
'De cest aveir, certes, nus n'avum cure.
Si grant ledece nus est apar[e]üde

**D'icest saint cors, que avum am bailide;**
**Par lui avrum, se Deu plaist, bone aiude'.**    70

**Unches en Rome nen out si grant ledice**
**Cum out le jurn as povres ed as riches**
**Pur cel saint cors qu'il unt en lur bailie:**
**Ço lur est vis que tengent Deu medisme;**
**Trestut le pople lodet Deu e graciet.**    75

(From *La Vie de Saint Alexis: Texte du Manuscrit de Hildesheim (L).*
*Publié avec une Introduction historique et linguistique, un Commentaire et un*
*Glossaire complet par Christopher Storey* (Geneva, Droz, 1968), pp. 117–20.)

[While the father and mother were grieving in this way, there came the girl that he had married. 'Sir', she said, 'how long a wait I have kept in your father's house, where you left me grieving and lost.
[6] 'Lord Alexis, so many days have I longed for you, and shed so many tears over you, and looked into the distance for you so many times. If you had come back to comfort your wife, it would not have been out of disloyalty (to the oath) or weariness.
[11] 'O dear lord, alas for your fair youth! It grieves me that it will rot in the ground. Ah noble man, what may be my grief! I was hoping for good news of you, but now the news is sad and very hard (to bear).
[16] 'Oh fair mouth, fair face, fair form, how your beautiful face has changed! I loved you more than any other creature. Such great grief has now come to me. It would be better for me, lord, if I were dead.
[21] 'If I had known you were there under the stairs, where you have lain ill for so long, never would any man on earth have been able to prevent me from living there with you. If it had been allowed to me, I would have looked after you.
[26] 'Now I am a widow, sir', said the maiden, 'never again will I have any joy, for it cannot be. Nor will I ever again have a husband in all this world. God will I serve, the king who rules all: he will not fail me if he sees that I serve him'.
[31] The father and mother and the girl wept so much that they all grew weary. Meanwhile all the lords prepared the body and robed it magnificently. How blessed they who sincerely honoured him!
[36] 'Lords, what are you doing?', said the Pope, 'What is the meaning of this crying, this grief and this noise? Whoever may grieve, as far as we are concerned, it is a matter for joy. For by this man we shall have good aid; so let us pray that he will deliver us from all evils'.
[41] All of them who could reach him pick him up; chanting they carry away Saint Alexis's body, and all pray to him to have mercy on them. There is no need to summon those who have heard it (the news): all come running there, both great and small.
[46] All the people of Rome were touched by it; whoever could run fastest came there first. Such great crowds of people come through the streets

that neither king nor count could gain a passage nor could they pass beyond the holy body.

[51] These lords begin to talk the matter over among themselves: 'The throng is great, we cannot get through it. On account of this holy body that God has granted to us the people are joyful, for they have greatly desired it. They are all running up to it, none of them will turn away'.

[56] They reply who have the empire in their guard: 'Mercy, lords, we will seek a remedy to the situation. We will make great gifts of our wealth to the common people, who desire alms: if they crowd around us now, afterwards we will be free of them'.

[61] From their treasuries they take gold and silver, and have it thrown before the poor people. By this means they think to disencumber themselves, but it cannot be so, for the people want nothing of it. All their desire is for this holy man.

[66] With one voice the common people cry: 'Indeed we do not care at all about this wealth. Such great joy has come to us by this holy body, (that we have in our possession); Through him we shall have, if it please God, good help'.

[71] Never in Rome was there such rejoicing as there was that day among poor and rich alike on account of that holy body that they have in their keeping. It seems to them as if they are holding God himself. All the people praise God and give him thanks.]

## COMMENTARY

### Date and place of composition and base manuscript

Two alternative hypotheses have been offered as regards the dating of this text. The best surviving manuscript is that known as L (Lamspringe), formerly in the monastery library in Lamspringe in Hanover, but now in the library of the church of St Godoard at Hildesheim. This manuscript, dating from the first half of the twelfth century, forms part of the St Alban's Psalter. It has been argued that the manuscript contains the original version of the text which was composed in Anglo-Norman *c.* 1119–23. However, it is more generally thought that the poem was composed in the mid- to late eleventh century (one suggestion is *c.* 1040–50, others favour a somewhat later date), probably in Normandy, perhaps even by a canon of Rouen called Tedbalt de Vernon, and that the manuscript L contains a later, Anglo-Norman copy, perhaps made as early as 1115–19, perhaps as late as 1150. Whatever the precise dating, the text is clearly coloured by the Anglo-Norman writing habits of the scribe.

**Verse form**

The poem comprises 125 strophes, each containing five decasyllabic lines with a common assonance. The assonances may be masculine where the common final stressed vowel is in the final syllable, or feminine when the common stressed vowel is followed by an unstressed [ə]. Most lines are self-contained, that is, there is little use of *enjambement* or *rejet*, and they have a caesura after the fourth syllable in one of four patterns: 4 + 6 (e.g. l. 22); 4 + 6 (+e) (e.g. l. 1); 4 (+e) + 6 (e.g. l. 52); 4 (+e) + 6 (+e) (l. 2). Storey has calculated that 40 of the 625 lines of the poem have, however, either 9 or 11 syllables. The assonance is valuable to philologists since it may furnish information about the usage of the original poet as opposed to information about the scribe's usage afforded by the orthography.

**Problematic lines**

There are a number of problematic readings in this extract: for instance, line 7 is missing from L and is supplied from another twelfth-century manuscript (A), while l. 10, not found in a number of the other surviving manuscripts, is also not entirely satisfactory. Line 69 of our passage is especially vexatious because the reading given here from L does not appear to assonate with the other lines of the strophe. For this reason some editors prefer to supply the reading *n'avum soin d'altre mune* from manuscript A.

**Anglo-Norman features**

Since the majority of the mercenaries who came to England at the Conquest originated from Normandy and Maine, the French introduced into England was primarily western in character with some northern elements. During the period immediately following the Conquest, Anglo-Norman differed relatively little from western French, but in the late twelfth and early thirteenth centuries the language began to evolve more rapidly due to the combined influence of English usage and separation from continental French. Anglo-Norman had a flourishing literary tradition, and many of our early texts survive in Anglo-Norman manuscripts. It is impossible to give a full survey of Anglo-Norman here, and we shall only mention a few key characteristics which feature in our extract (for a fuller description of Anglo-Norman, see Pope (1952)). Anglo-Norman will be discussed again when we look at *La Chanson de Roland*.

*Anglo-Norman phonological features*

Vowels

(a) A striking feature of Anglo-Norman is that both tonic and pretonic *o* are frequently noted as *u*; so, for example, *dolur* (l. 19), *maisun* (l. 4); *plurét* (l. 7), *turner* (l. 23). Related is the use of *o*, *oe* for *ue*, as in *pot* (l. 27), *poet* (l. 49); *ou* is also found for *ue* (so here both *pout* (l. 47) and *puet* (l. 64)).

(b) A second characteristic tendency of Anglo-Norman is to reduce certain diphthongs, so, for instance, *ei* is sometimes reduced to *e* (*aver* (l. 63); but *aveir* (l. 67), *tei* (l. 8)). In the case of *mai* (l. 12) we find *ai* for *ei*. *ie* is also frequently levelled to *e* in Anglo-Norman (compare *ermes* l. 60 with *graciet* l. 75).

(c) *an*, *am* are found for *en*, *em* in both tonic and pretonic positions: *amfermetét* (l. 22), *ampirie* (l. 56), alongside *enportent* (l. 42).

(d) *-a* is found for final [ə], thus *pedra* (l. 1), *tota* (l. 46).

Consonants

(a) [k] before [a] is not palatalized in this region, so *cantant* (l. 42), *buce* (l. 16), *riches* (l. 72). The [k] sound is variously notated as *c*, *ch*, *qu*.

(b) [ʎ] and [ɲ] depalatalize, giving *il*, *in*: here both *seinor* (l. 34) and *seignors* (l. 36) are employed.

(c) Unsupported final *t* and *d* remain in the spelling: *desiret* (l. 59), *mercit* (l. 57), *ad* (l. 53), *geüd* (l. 22).

(d) Intervocalic dentals ceased to be pronounced later in Anglo-Norman than in other dialects, possibly not falling until the first half of the twelfth century; here then they remain in the spelling of *pedra* (l. 1), *medisme* (l. 74), *aiude* (l. 70), etc.

*Anglo-Norman morphosyntactic features*

Nouns

In Anglo-Norman there is early disintegration of the two-case system, something which also happens in western dialects. In the large majority of cases it is a question of obliques being used instead of the expected subject forms, and indeed it is the oblique forms which in general survive into Modern French. So in this extract we find *Trestut le pople lodet Deu e graciet* (l. 75) where *le pople* is in the oblique rather than the expected nominative (cf. l. 54). Likewise *le pedra* (l. 31), *cist crit* (l. 37) are not in the anticipated nominative form; this is also true of the pronoun *cels* (l. 35) for masculine nominative plural *cil*. Note how the oblique still continues to be used in a range of functions, including the marking of possessive (*la maisun tun pedra*, l. 4), and indirect object (*la main menude*, l. 59). The vocative is expressed by both the nominative (l. 11 *O kiers amis*; l. 6 *Sire Alexis*, here with a distinctive imparisyllabic form) and by the oblique (l. 36 *Seignors, que faites?*).

### Adjectives

In Anglo-Norman feminine adjectives derived from the Latin third declension sometimes show an early analogical final *e*: *dolente* (ll. 5, 13). Certain common adjectives were much slower to acquire the analogical *e*, so it is not surprising to find *si grant dolur* (l. 19), *granz est la presse* (l. 52)[a], *si granz turbes* (l. 48), *granz departies* (l. 58), *si grant ledece* (l. 68, etc.).

### Verb morphology

In Anglo-Norman and western dialects the first person plural endings are typically *-ums, -uns, -um*, so that here we find: *avrum* (l. 39), *poduns* (l. 52), *feruns* (l. 58), etc. Present subjunctive forms of verbs in *-ge* are equally characteristic of Anglo-Norman: *tolget* (l. 40), *tengent* (l. 74).

## Phonology

### *Germanic [w]*

Latin [w] had early become [v]. [w] re-entered the language, however, in Germanic borrowings and then underwent the following changes: [w] > [gw] > [g]: *\*wardôn* > *\*gward-* > *garder*; here the stage *guardét* ([gw], l. 8) has been reached.

### *Unstressed vowels in monosyllabic clitics*

These weakened to [ə], giving *me*, *te*, etc. Here *jo* (l. 26) represents the reduction of unstressed *ego*, the vowel of which subsequently further weakened to [ə].

### *Elision*

The articles and pronouns *le* (masc. sing. oblique) and *la* (fem. sing. nominative and oblique) elide, as in Modern French, before a vowel (*l'ampirie* (l. 56), *l'almosne* (l. 59)), but masculine nominative singular *li* never elides in this text: *li apostolie* (l. 36).

---

a   A final *-s* is occasionally found in the nominative singular feminine form of this class of adjectives.

## Morphology

### Comparative and superlative adjectives and adverbs

There is some evidence here of the new Romance synthetic comparative and superlative forms (*plus tost*, l. 47) being used alongside forms derived from Latin synthetic formations (*melz*, l. 20). Note that in Old French it was not necessary to distinguish formally between comparative and superlative adjectives, so that *plus tost* could mean either 'faster' or 'fastest'. *Pesmes* (l. 15), derived from the Latin synthetic superlative, *pessimus*, is used here as an emphatic positive with the meaning 'very bad', 'terrible'.

### Adverbs

Alongside adverbs derived from simple Latin forms (e.g. *plus* (l. 18) < *plus*), other types of adverb formation were used in Old French including those using the suffix *-ment*, destined to become the principal means of adverb formation in Modern French. Here we have a number of examples of final *-s* being used as an adverbial marker, on the analogy of those adverbs for which the final *s* was etymological (e.g. *tres*, *plus*). Thus we find *En tant dementres* (l. 33) < *dum interea* plus adverbial 's'; *unches* (l. 71) < *umquam* + s.

### Verbs

There is a remnant of the Latin synthetic future in *ermes* < *erimus* (l. 60).

## Syntax

### Articles

The function of the definite article in Old French was to mark determination; *la pulcele* therefore meant 'the girl, that girl, the said girl, the girl in question'. As a result – unlike the situation in Modern French when, in general, every noun has a determiner – if the noun was employed in a vague or non-specific sense, or had an abstract meaning or referred to the names of individuals, peoples or countries, no article was used. It was commonly omitted too after prepositions (*par feit*, l. 35). Where used, the definite article thus had a semi-demonstrative force, and indeed could even retain a full demonstrative meaning (as in l. 72 *le jurn*). This means that the partitive article was rare in Old French and was never used when expressing part of an indefinite collective whole. As we shall see, by the thirteenth century the definite article began to be more widely used, its semantic value weakened and it was increasingly used as a nominal marker which in addition showed the number and gender of the following noun.

Similarly, the indefinite article was employed in Old French to introduce or particularize a noun not already mentioned. Thus if the noun was not particularized, or had an abstract meaning or if it featured in comparative, negative, interrogative or conditional clauses, the indefinite article was generally not used: *ne reis ne quons n'i poet faire entrarote* (l. 49); *nus en querreums mecine* (l. 57). Again, if the noun was already distinguished by some other means, such as *tel*, *autre* or an adjective, the article was superfluous (*si grant dolur*, l. 19). The indefinite article was also rare in the plural unless used to denote a pair or where the plural had a different meaning from the corresponding singular noun (e.g. *unes cisoires*).

### Use of pronouns

The pronouns *tu* and *vous* were commonly used interchangeably in Old French to refer to an individual (compare ll. 11–15 with ll. 16–20).

### Verb usage

#### Use of tenses

We find a mixing of tenses in the narrative of Old French texts, especially those destined for oral performance, unknown to the modern written language (see the commentary on the *Chanson de Roland*). Here there is a predominance of present tenses together with past historics, and the occasional imperfect form. Just as the imperfect was relatively rare in the early period, so the past anterior dominated over the pluperfect (e.g. *la pulcele que il out espusede*, l. 2).

#### Use of the subjunctive

The usual means of expressing an unfulfilled condition in Old French was to have an imperfect subjunctive in both the *si* clause and the main clause; there is an extended example of this in lines 21–25. In lines 9–10 there is a condensed version of the construction with the verb omitted from the main clause. The subjunctive was typically employed in Old French to indicate unreality, as in *Ço lur est vis que tengent Deu medisme* (l. 74). It is also employed after the indefinite pronoun *chi chi* ('whoever') in line 38.

#### Impersonal verbs

Impersonal verbs do not require an impersonal subject pronoun *il* in Old French; so in line 44: *N'estot somondre icels ki l'unt oït*. Sometimes *ço* is used with a deictic sense, as in *Ço lur est vis que* (l. 74), where *ço*, filling the sentence-initial slot, anticipates the following subordinate clause. Indeed this deictic usage of *ço* is fairly common in Old French in a range of constructions (cf. *ço dist li apostolie*, l. 36).

## Agreement

There are a number of interesting examples of agreement in this extract. First, it was possible in Old French when the subject was composed of a number of co-ordinated singular nouns, either to have a plural agreement as in Modern French, or, as here, to make a singular agreement with the nearest singular noun: *Tant i plurat e le pedra e la medra, E la pulcela* (ll. 31–32). Second, in the case of collective nouns, agreement could either be made in the singular, which is grammatically regular (*tute gent ne m'en soüst turner* (l. 23)), or in the plural according to the sense (*Ad une voiz crient la gent menude*, l. 66, cf. l. 46). In the seventeenth century grammarians ruled in favour of the former option, leaving *la plupart* as a notable exception. Third, there was flexibility as regards past participle agreement; in lines 2 and 4 agreement is made with the preceding direct objects *pulcele*, *demurede*, but in line 7 *plurét* remains invariable and plural agreement is not made with *lermes*.

## Negation

In Old French *ne(n)* alone served to mark negation (see, for example, ll. 23, 44, 52, etc.). Unstressed or half-stressed *nen* (l. 71) contracted to *ne* before a word beginning with a consonant, and could also further contract to *n'* before a vowel. *Ne* could, however, be reinforced by various adverbs, nouns or pronouns, which initially had an emphatic sense, but which gradually weakened. Here we find the adverbs *ja mais* (l. 27), *unches* (l. 71), and the pronoun *nuls* (l. 55). *Nïent* (l. 10), the origin of which is uncertain (< ? *nec* + *entem*, ? *ne* + *gentem*) was the only one of the reinforcers which had a negative value on its own. Note that *ne* can act as a co-ordinator of both positive (l. 37) and negative (ll. 49–50) phrases or clauses.

## Other constructions

Two other constructions are worth mentioning briefly. First, there is an example of an elliptical exclamation in line 11. Second, line 47 exemplifies a common structure in Old French where the clause in the second half of the line acts as the subject of *vint*.

*Word order*

Evidence of the variation possible in Old French word order is afforded by this extract. Of the six possible permutations of the elements S[ubject] – finite V[erb] – C[omplement] (where C embraces a wide range of categories including direct and indirect object, predicative adjectives and nouns, adverbs and adverbial phrases, participles or infinitives), the two most common in Old French were SVC and CVS. In other words, Old French appears to have favoured the verb in second position in the clause. SVC is illustrated by line 75, and there are a wide range of examples of CVS including where the C is a direct object (*ço dist li apostolie*, l. 36), an adverb (l. 66), or a predicative adjective (*liez est li poples*, l. 54). Since the subject pronoun may frequently be omitted in Old French, it is not always possible, of course, to distinguish with certainty which type is being represented (e.g. *mais or les vei si dures e si pesmes!*, l. 15). SCV, favoured in poetry, is especially found in subordinate clauses where the subject is a relative pronoun (e.g. *ki l'ampirie bailissent*, l. 56). VSC can be used in Old French in affirmative clauses but gradually becomes associated with interrogative structures. CSV is rather rare in Old French and is not used in *Alexis*; likewise, VCS, mainly found in older texts, is unusual. For a stimulating account of Old French as a verb-second language (V2), see Roberts (1993); he, along with a number of other linguists, relates this characteristic of Old French to other structural features of the medieval language and particularly to the fact that subject pronouns were not obligatory in Old French (or, to use modern terminology, that Old French – unlike Modern French – was a pro-drop language).

**Vocabulary**

Learned and semi-learned lexical items continue to occur, especially for those words from the theological domain (*apostolie, felix*). There is evidence here of the assimilation of Germanic words into the French lexicon in *guardét* (l. 8) < *\*wardôn* and *conreerent* (l. 33) which probably entered French via a popular Latin form, *\*conredare*. One or two items are of interest. *Degrét* (l. 21), literally 'step', is used here with the meaning of 'staircase'. Modern French *escalier* did not enter the lexicon until the sixteenth century when it was borrowed from Provençal. In Old French two other words are used to refer to stairs: *viz*, which is usually reserved for a stone spiral staircase, and *eschiele*, used for a wooden, insubstantial staircase (> *échelle*). *Degré* is, of course, no longer used in this concrete sense, but occurs in figurative expressions such as 'le plus bas degré de la hiérarchie sociale', 'avancer par degrés'. In line 6 we find *jurz* (< *diurnus*) rather than *di*, the form used in the Oaths and *Eulalia*. *Conversét* (l. 24) < *conversare*, 'to frequent, live', still retains its Latin meaning, as indeed it was destined to do until the early modern period; the modern meaning is first recorded in Richelet's dictionary of 1680. *Ledece* (l. 27) is a regular development from *laetitia*; the more commonly used Old French noun *liesse* is formed from the adjective *lie* < *laetus*.

# II  The 'heyday' of Old French
## French in the twelfth and thirteenth centuries

The twelfth century witnessed the flowering of literature in the vernacular in France and the experimentation with new genres; here we have examples of an epic (text 5) and a verse romance (text 6). While these are both great works of their kind, they are also typical of literary usage of the period in being in verse and displaying that mixture of heterogeneity and homogeneity of linguistic usage discussed in the introduction, that is, the co-existence of dialectal and supra-regional features. In many cases, too, there is a difference of time and place between the date of composition and the date of the base manuscript: many manuscripts survive in an Anglo-Norman hand as in the case of *Roland*; many date from the thirteenth or even the fourteenth century, so that we are faced with 'une diachronie interne' (Andrieux and Baumgartner 1983: 9). Furthermore, comparison of these literary texts with those of other discourse types suggests that they were probably written in a rather conservative language, in terms both of their morphology and their syntax. An example of a thirteenth-century *fabliau* has been included as an example of a more popular literary form (text 7).

If the literature of the twelfth century was almost exclusively in verse (there are some early prose *romans* which become more important in the thirteenth century), prose was nevertheless used in other domains. It has been estimated that for the twelfth century some fifty prose texts in the vernacular survive, as yet in a fairly circumscribed set of discourse types. In the period up to 1210 prose was used especially in translations – which, as yet, had a primarily religious content and included versions of parts of the Bible – but also in charters and laws, texts of a utilitarian or practical nature, sketches and notes.

Woledge and Clive (1964: 24) suggest that the period 1190–1210 marked an important stage in the expansion of prose into new domains and in particular to secular spheres, notably in its use in historiography. It is thus in the thirteenth century that prose really came into its own. Bible translations and commentaries continued to appear (text 8), but prose was also used for historical texts and chronicles (text 9), in texts with a didactic or moral theme,[a] and in early popular medical documents (text 10). The number of charters and legal documents extant in French increases dramatically during this period (text 11), from which also dates the earliest surviving letter in French (text 12).

What is the significance of the rise of French texts written in prose? Many of the eleventh- and twelfth-century verse texts had displayed a primarily oral quality and were intended to be performed; in this respect they shared features with modern spoken usages. Prose texts, however, were intended for silent, solitary reading and indeed re-reading; often, the authorial voice is less obviously present, the tone more objective. If verse was associated with the dramatic and emotive telling of stories, the rise of prose went hand in hand with the spread of French to new objective and factual domains. The texts in this section bear witness to this evolution and to the multiplication of the uses of the vernacular.

a   See, for example, *Les Quatre Ages de l'homme*. Traité moral de Philippe de Navarre [= Philippe de Novare] publié pour la première fois d'après les manuscrits de Paris, de Londres et de Metz par Marcel de Fréville (Paris, Firmin Didot, 1888).

## 5 *La Chanson de Roland* (early twelfth century)

The *Song of Roland* is the oldest and probably the best example of an Old French *chanson de geste*, a verse epic destined for oral performance by *jongleurs* or minstrels who wandered from court to court. Its oral qualities are evident at a number of different levels: at the microtextual level we find use of repetition of epithets, formulaic expressions and *vers similaires*; at the textual level we find symmetry and parallelism of episodes, and the use of *laisses similaires* (sequences of two or three *laisses* or stanzas of unequal length that repeat the same basic information with some differences of detail) especially at moments of high pathos. It is significant that features such as the use of parataxis and tense-switching (see below), which are typical of Old French texts performed orally, are equally shared with modern conversational usage (see Fleischman 1990b and text 35 below).

This poem is generally thought to be both the culmination of an oral tradition telling a well-known story and the work of a highly talented individual. It is pointless with this sort of text to think in terms of an archetype, since each new performance probably brought with it some modification and involved some degree of 're-creation' of the text. The extract here is of lines 1842–68: heavy defeats have been suffered at the hands of the Saracens by the French rearguard which includes Roland, Oliver and the twelve Peers. Roland, seeing the battle is lost, has reluctantly sounded his horn, and, in so doing, sustains a fatal injury. Hearing the distress signal Charlemagne returns to aid them.

> Par grant irur chevalchet li reis Charles,
> Desur sa brunie li gist sa blanche barbe.
> Puignent ad ait tuit li barun de France;
> N'i ad icel ne demeint irance
> Que il ne sunt a Rollant le cataigne,     5
> Ki se cumbat as Sarrazins d'Espaigne;
> Si est blecét, ne quit que anme i remaigne.
> Deus, quels seisante humes i ad en sa cumpaigne!
> Unches meillurs nen out reis ne ca[ta]ignes. AOI.
>
> Rollant reguardet es munz e es lariz.     10
> De cels de France i veit tanz morz gesir,
> E il les pluret cum chevaler gentill:
> 'Seignors barons, de vos ait Deus mercit,
> Tutes voz anmes otreit il pareïs,
> En seintes flurs il les facet gesir!     15
> Meillors vassals de vos unkes ne vi.
> Si lungement tuz tens m'avez servit,
> A oes Carlon si granz païs cunquis!
> Li empereres tant mare vos nurrit!
> Tere de France, mult estes dulz païs,     20

**Oi desertét a tant ruboste exill!**
**Barons franceis, pur mei vos vei murir,**
**Jo ne vos pois tenser ne guarantir.**
**Aït vos Deus ki unkes ne mentit!**
**Oliver frere, vos ne dei jo faillir,** 25
**De doel murra[i], se altre ne m'i ocit.**
**Sire cumpainz, alum i referir.'**

(From *La Chanson de Roland*, edited by F. Whitehead (Oxford, Blackwell, [2]1946, reprinted 1988), pp. 54–55, by permission of Duckworth.)

[In great wrath rides king Charles; his white beard lies on his cuirass. All the warriors of France gallop in haste; there is not one that does not display anger at not being with Roland the captain, who is fighting the Saracens of Spain; [?] he is (so) wounded, I do not think there is any life left in him.[a] God, what men are the sixty he has in his company! Never did king or captain have better.

[10] Roland looks at the mountains and the hillsides. He sees so many of the men of France lying dead, and he mourns them in the fashion of a noble knight: 'My lord barons, God have mercy on you! May he grant paradise to all your souls, and give them rest among holy flowers! Better vassals than you I never saw. [17] Such a long time you have served me constantly, conquered such extensive lands to Charles's profit! Alas that the emperor maintained you in his household! Land of France, you are a very sweet country, made desolate today by such dreadful suffering! Barons of France, it is on my account that I see you die, I cannot protect you or defend you. [24] May God, the all-truthful, help you! Oliver brother, you I must not fail. I shall die of grief if another does not slay me here. Sir companion, let us go and strike again!']

## COMMENTARY

### Dating

While it is impossible to provide a precise dating for this text, its composition is generally placed in the first quarter of the twelfth century (*c.* 1100–20). The manuscript used here, Digby 23, now in the Bodleian Library in Oxford, dates from only slightly later, with a date between 1140 and 1170 in general being proposed.

### Region

The language of the text displays a number of Norman and central features, but the manuscript is Anglo-Norman, which gives the text certain

---

a   A difficult line. The alternative reading, 'If he is hurt, I think none other lives', has also been offered.

peculiarities of phonology and morphology (see *Life of Saint Alexis*, and below). It is necessary to proceed with some caution when commenting on the regional features of the manuscript, since the vast majority of manuscripts of literary texts surviving from the twelfth century are either Norman or Anglo-Norman in character, and we have relatively little evidence of other dialects to place in comparison.

## Verse form

We have the usual form for a *chanson de geste*: decasyllabic lines, grouped in *laisses*, each *laisse* having a uniform assonance. No two consecutive *laisses* assonate on the same vowel. Note that here [a] followed by a nasal consonant assonates with [a] followed by a non-nasal consonant, although there is evidence elsewhere in the poem to suggest that [a] had already nasalized to [ã] by this period through the assimilatory influence of a following nasal consonant. As in the *Life of Saint Alexis*, there is a caesura after the fourth syllable (with the same four-syllable patterns available), and there is relatively little use of *enjambement*.

## Anglo-Norman features

Many of the same phonological features that we saw in the commentary on *La Vie de Saint Alexis* are also evident here. As regards vowels:

(a) Close *o* is mostly written *u*, but also sometimes *o* and the two are allowed to assonate together in the poem. In this extract we find *sunt* (l. 5), *cumpainz* (l. 27), *barun* (l. 3), etc.; also *oi* for *ui* in *pois* (l. 23).
(b) There is some evidence of the characteristic levelling of diphthongs, notably *e* for *ie*: *chevaler* (l. 12), *tenser* (l. 23). *ei* remains undifferentiated, and does not go to *oi*: *li reis* (l. 1), *dei* (l. 25).

Note also that *l* in the preconsonantal position is not shown as vocalized: *altre* (l. 26), *chevalchet* (l. 1). The interpretation of such orthographies is problematic: while the change [l] > [u] is thought to have been accomplished by the beginning of the ninth century, both the orthography and indeed the assonance of early twelfth-century texts often do not appear to take account of it.

As regards consonants:

(a) [k] before [a] remains and is not palatalized: *cataigne* (l. 5) < *capitaneum*, *Carlon* (l. 18).
(b) *r* is weak and unstable, and is either reduced to a single consonant or lost before another consonant: *tere* (l. 20).
(c) Unsupported final *-t* and *-d* [θ, ð] are common, especially in monosyllables and verb endings: *ad* (l. 4), *reguardet* (l. 10), *pluret* (l. 12). The versification is unable to offer conclusive proof as to whether the

final *-t* or *-d* was pronounced or not, since, for example, when followed by a word beginning with a consonant, the [ə] would have syllabic value regardless of this.

(d) Intervocalic dentals are usually no longer written, although they do occasionally appear elsewhere in the text. Here we have: *pareïs* (l. 14), *frere* (l. 25) for earlier *paredis*, *fredre*.

Once again we find early evidence of the non-observance of the case system for nouns typical of Anglo-Norman manuscripts. Indeed Bédier (1927: 248) goes as far as to maintain: 'si l'on met à part les plus anciens textes, ceux du IXᵉ et du Xᵉ siècle, comme *Sainte Eulalie* ou *Saint Léger*, les règles de la déclinaison n'apparaissent en toute leur pureté que dans les grammaires modernes de l'ancien français'. A number of factors, often acting in combination, apparently encouraged the use of the oblique where strictly speaking the nominative should have been used, including when the noun was used without a determiner, when it appeared in a negative or comparative clause, when it featured in post-verbal position or in a formulaic expression, etc. (see Woledge and others 1967–69). Here the oblique is used after *i ad* (l. 4, l. 8) and in the comparative clause *Et il les pluret cum chevaler gentill* (l. 12). The proper name *Rollant* is generally abbreviated in the manuscript as *Roll'*; where it is written in full, it is always spelt *Rollant*, suggesting a tendency to make proper names invariable. The two-case system is usually well maintained for imparisyllabics (*sire*, l. 27), although the use of the oblique may afford an extra syllable in verse or offer a different assonance. In the case of *empereres* (l. 19), however, the 'regular' nominative form *emperere* has acquired an analogical *s*. Both the nominative (l. 27) and the oblique (l. 13) are used to express the vocative.

## Nasalization

According to traditional accounts (e.g. Pope 1952), nasalization in French, involving the assimilation of a vowel to a following nasal consonant, took place over a number of centuries, starting with [a] in the tenth century, followed by [e] then [o] and finishing with [i, y] in the thirteenth century. It is further argued that when these vowels nasalized, they also lowered, perhaps as the mouth opened a little to compensate for the lowering of the velum necessary to allow air to escape out of the nasal passage. Since there is no direct evidence of these changes and it is impossible to rely on orthographical clues, linguists have looked at the patterns of assonance of the early verse texts to help them date these processes. Thus, for example, the fact that words derived from Latin *-ente(m)* and *-ante(m)* assonate in the *Chanson de Roland* has been taken as evidence that [ẽ] had already lowered to [ã] by the early twelfth century. At this stage, the nasal vowels were allophonic, but when later the nasal consonant fell – a change probably not completed until the sixteenth century – they became phonemic in French. Where, however, the nasal consonant was intervocalic it did not fall, and instead the nasal vowel denasalized, probably commencing with [ĩ] and [ẽ] in the fifteenth century and finishing with [õ] in the seventeenth century.

More recent accounts (e.g. Rochet 1976, Matte 1984) have questioned this traditional view of nasalization in a number of important ways. First, they have disputed the evidence that nasalization in French took place in several waves according to the degree of opening of the vowel, and have argued instead that all vowels nasalized (allophonically) at the same time, regardless of vowel height, and probably in the Gallo-Roman period (i.e. before the ninth century). The fact that the pairs *a* followed by a nasal consonant (*N*) and *a* followed by a non-nasal consonant (*C*) and *eN/eC* are not allowed to assonate in poems dating from the ninth to the eleventh centuries, whereas *iN/iC* and *uN/uC* are kept apart, is not regarded as evidence that [a] and [e] had nasalized by this time but [i] and [y] had not. Rather, it is argued that in the case of the first two pairs the quality of the vowels was also different. Matte, for instance, suggests that the vowel of *aC* was [æ], but that the vowel of *aN* was [ɛ̃]; since, on the other hand, *aiN* was probably pronounced as [ɛ̃ĩ] or even [ẽĩ] this could assonate with *aN* as in the first *laisse* of our extract. Conversely, it is maintained that since the pairs *iN/iC* and *uN/uC* differed *only* in (allophonic) nasality, these vowels were considered similar enough to assonate together, since assonance was only approximate. The evidence is, however, complicated by the fact that, while *aN/aC* do not assonate in the earliest texts, they do occasionally assonate in twelfth-century *chansons de geste* as we can see exemplified here in the first *laisse* (ll. 1–4). While traditionally such 'false' assonances were considered to be scribal errors, others have maintained that their occurrence is too frequent not to be considered significant. This leads Rochet (1976: 71) to conclude that if the separation of *aN* and *aC* reveals a variation of timbre for *a* before a nasal, the presence of some cases of mixing, as in our text, indicates that such variation must have been slight.

The case of *oN/oC* is rather more complex. It is likely that both *oN* and *oC* were in a state of flux during Old French. *oC* was being raised in some words (e.g. *jorn* > *jour*), and fronted in others (*seignors* > *seigneur*), while *oN* may well have had a range of variants, of which possibly [ũ] was the dominant one. These vowels were then perhaps allowed to assonate only when they were similar enough in vowel quality. The reversal of the change õ > ũ became generalized later (in the seventeenth century) and may have been associated with the *ouïste* debate (see pp. 279–80).

A second point of dispute between traditional and more recent accounts of nasalization in French has been whether nasalization necessarily entails lowering of the vowel. Linguists have maintained that this is not supported by cross-language comparison. Instead, the lowering of nasals is to be seen as a later change in French (occurring perhaps between the fifteenth and seventeenth centuries), and to be explained with reference to factors specific to French. For instance, it has been hypothesized that the change may be associated with the re-emergence of a mid-nasal vowel [ɛ̃], when the nasal diphthongs *aiN, eiN, oiN, ieN* simplified; the nasals [ĩ] and [ɛ̃] then merged, and the other nasals also lowered to keep an equipollent relationship between the nasal vowels. Alternatively, the pressure for lowering may be attributable to non-phonetic causes: Rochet (1976), for instance, maintains that a possible trigger was the generalization of *-ant* as the marker of the present participle at the expense of *-ent*. In short, it is clear that there is still much uncertainty about the nasalization of French vowels, and that the interpretation of textual evidence is far from being straightforward.

## Morphology

### Verb morphology

The first person singular present indicative does not yet have an analogical *-e* in the first conjugation, so here *quit* (l. 7); the addition of final *-e* to the first person on the analogy of such verb forms as *j'entre, je semble* where the *-e* was used to support the consonant cluster, is first attested in the twelfth century, but does not really become established before the Middle French period. Similarly there is no analogical *-s* on the first person singular of *dei* (l. 25), *vei* (l. 22); this *-s*, added on the analogy of the first person singular forms which historically had *-s* (or *-z*) and of the second person singular forms, was even slower to spread, and it is quite common to find forms without the final *-s* in the fourteenth and fifteenth centuries. (The Old French forms of the present indicative are discussed in greater detail below, pp. 91–92.)

### Adverbs

Four different types of Old French adverb formations are illustrated in this extract. First, there are those derived from Latin forms (*oi*, l. 21 < *hodie*). Second, there are new compound forms comprised of Latin elements such as *mare* (l. 19) < *mala hora*. Third, there are those formed by adding *-ment* (from *-mente* meaning 'with (this) mind') to a feminine adjective (*lungement*, l. 17). Lastly, final *-s* also served as an adverbial marker (*unches*, l. 9).

### Demonstrative pronouns

Both simple and compound forms continue to be available; here then we find *icel* (l. 4) but *cels de France* (l. 11); both *cist, ceste* < *ecce iste* etc. and *cil, cele* < *ecce ille* etc. could be used in Old French as either adjectives or pronouns without distinction of form.

**Syntax**

*Use of tenses*

The mixing of present with past tenses, especially the past historic, but also the perfect, occurs throughout the narrative in *Roland*, although not in the dialogue. The present tense, as in *Alexis*, greatly outnumbers the past historic. This freedom of tense usage allows the action to be viewed from different angles, and permits the author to vary the pace and give dramatic perspective. Fleischman in a series of publications (1985, 1986, 1990b) has convincingly demonstrated how, in an oral text which favours parataxis and therefore cannot use distinctions of clause type to mark grounding, this tense switching constituted an alternative means of delineating the textual foreground and background, creating cohesion, and organizing narrative discourse; moreover such strategies have analogues in the 'natural' narratives of everyday conversations.

*Use of moods*

The most striking feature in this passage is the typical Old French use of the subjunctive in main clauses to indicate a wish (it could also be used for commands): *Aït vos Deus ki unkes ne mentit* (l. 24, cf. ll. 13–15). The major difference between Old and Modern French in this construction is that in Old French there is no need for an introductory *que*. Remnants of this highly productive Old French construction are found in Modern French set expressions like *Vive la France!*, *A Dieu ne plaise!*. There are also two examples of subjunctives in subordinate clauses dependent on negative main clauses (ll. 4, 7).

*Use of subject pronouns*

There is some increase in the use of subject pronouns (ll. 5, 23, 25), and they feature, for instance, in the main clause expressions of volition (ll. 14, 15). However, subject pronouns could also still not be expressed, especially in impersonal constructions (e.g. *i ad*, l. 4), and even if there was a new subject introduced in the clause (*ne quit*, l. 7, *m'avez servit*, l. 17).

*Parataxis*

Parataxis, the simple juxtaposition of clauses rather than the explicit marking of the relationship between clauses by co-ordination and subordination, was frequent in Old French epics, especially in the narrative passages, although less so in the dialogue. This, as we have noted, is another feature associated with the oral performance of the text, and a characteristic shared by the modern spoken language. Here then we find *N'i ad icel ne demeint irance* (l. 4) without the subordinating relative *qui*.

## Word order: adjective position

The same latitude as regards word order we saw in *Alexis* is in evidence in this text, with an initial adverb, for instance, triggering inversion as in lines 1–2. The position of the adjective was very free throughout the Old French period and very few adjectives appear to have had fixed positions: note here *sa blanche barbe* (l. 2).

## Vocabulary

The most intriguing problem is what the significance of AOI (l. 9) is which occurs throughout the poem at the beginning or at the end of *laisses* (or so close as to suggest the scribe has simply slipped a line). It appears to suggest to the *jongleur* that a particularly tense moment is at hand and that a pause for audience reaction is called for. What the letters precisely stand for is even more dubious. One theory is that it is a contraction for Alleluia with *o* for *u*; while such contractions are found in musical manuscripts, it is a less likely explanation in an epic text. Another suggestion is that the letters stand for Alpha Omega Iesus. An alternative hypothesis is that the form derives from the Old French verb *aoire* < *adāugere*, meaning 'to increase', in which case AOI perhaps signifies crescendo or forte.

A number of words of Germanic origin have been assimilated into French, including *brunie* (l. 2), *guarantir* (l. 23), *reguardet* (l. 10). French is, however, also showing ingenuity and flexibility in the creation of derivatives, such as *referir* (l. 27) – *re-* being a very productive prefix in Old French – and *irur* (l. 1), *irance* (l. 4) where two different forms using different suffixes co-exist happily without pressure yet for standardization.

The feudal context and the importance of placing people in the social hierarchy is evident from the choice of vocabulary, with an abundant use of terms like *sire*, *li empereres*, *chevaler*, *reis* and *cataigne*.

## 6 *Le Chevalier de la charrette* (c. 1177–81)

A short extract from this text is included for contrast since here we have
a different sort of literary text, an example of Old French romance. Where
in the epic we saw parataxis, repetition and formulaic expressions, here
the syntax is more complicated and sophisticated with a preference for
hypotaxis, subordination, greater variety of construction and lexis and the
skilful use of, for example, different word orders for stylistic effects, as
well as *enjambement*. In other words, different genres make different use
of Old French resources. The extract here is of lines 4473–86 which marks
the reuniting and reconciliation of Lancelot with Guinevere.

> Qant Lanceloz l'ot correcier,
> De la pes feire et adrecier
> Au plus qu'il onques puet se painne
> Tant qu'il l'a feite; lors l'en mainne
> Li rois la reïne veoir.                                                5
> Lors ne lessa mie cheoir
> La reïne ses ialz vers terre;
> Einz l'ala lieemant requerre,
> Si l'enora de son pooir,
> Et sel fist lez li aseoir.                                             10
> Puis parlerent a grant leisir
> De quanque lor vint a pleisir;
> Ne matiere ne lor failloit,
> Qu'Amors assez lor an bailloit.

> (From *Chrétien de Troyes, Le Chevalier de la charrette (Lancelot)*.
> Texte établi, annoté et présenté avec variantes par
> A. Foulet et K.D. Uitti (Paris, Bordas, 1989, p. 252.)

[When Lancelot hears him growing angry, he strives as best he can to
make and restore the peace until he succeeded. Then the king takes him
to see the queen. [6] This time the queen did not lower her eyes to the
ground, but went happily to meet him and honoured him to the best of
her ability and had him sit beside her. [11] Then they talked at great
leisure about whatever they felt like. And they were not short of subjects,
with which Love supplied them in abundance.]

## COMMENTARY

### Author and scribe

Little is known of the life of Chrétien de Troyes, the author of, amongst
other works, five Arthurian verse romances. Chrétien, a native of
Champagne, who probably died between 1185 and 1190, wrote *Lancelot,
ou, le chevalier de la charrette* at the request of the countess, Marie de

Champagne, who also suggested the theme to him. *Le chevalier de la charrette* was written at the same time as another of his romances, *Yvain, ou, le chevalier au lion*, between 1177 and 1181; it was not completed by Chrétien himself, but by a clerk, Godefroi de Leigni. Of the six surviving manuscripts the best is manuscript C (Bibliothèque nationale 794), copied by the scribe Guiot in a very clear hand in the early thirteenth century.

## Verse form

We have here the usual metre for Old French romances, rhyming octosyllabic couplets with the accent on the eighth syllable in feminine lines.

## Regional features

The language of the author is that of Troyes, or southern Champenois. Champagne was at a crossroads from a trading, cultural and political point of view, and its language was correspondingly variable. While Champenois is essentially a central dialect which therefore has much in common with Francien, it also shares features with its neighbouring dialects to the northeast (Walloon), east (Lorrain) and south-east (Burgundian). The court of Champagne was for a time an important literary centre, reaching its apogee with the romances of Chrétien de Troyes, but towards the end of the thirteenth century the dynasty of the Counts of Champagne died out and Champagne came under direct rule from Paris. The following features are worthy of note:

(a) As in the whole of the eastern region [o] does not diphthongize to [ou] before *r*, but either remains as [o] or is occasionally raised to [u]; here we find *lor* (l. 12), *Amors* (l. 14).
(b) *e* is frequently lowered to *a* when followed by *l* and a consonant: *e* + *l* > *au*; this happens also when *e* + *l* is preceded by *i* or *u*: *ialz* (*ueils*) (l. 7); note the retention of the preconsonantal *l* in the orthography, although it has almost certainly vocalized.
(c) Pretonic *ei* is not differentiated to *oi*, and thus remains, for example, in *leisir* (l. 11).
(d) The reflex of *ē* tonic free between a labial and a nasal consonant is here shown as *ai*: *painne* (l. 3), *mainne* (l. 4).
(e) The former diphthong *ai* is written as *e* before a final consonant or group of consonants, but as *ei* before a simple intervocalic consonant, the orthography therefore showing two stages of evolution of [ai] > [ɛi] > [ɛ]: *feire* (l. 2), *pleisir* (l. 12), *pes* (l. 2).
(f) [ẽn] > [ãn] in Champagne in the eleventh or twelfth century just as it did in the Île-de-France; Guiot shows this new pronunciation in his

orthography (*an, am*, for Francien *en, em*): *lieemant* (l. 8), *an* (l. 14). *en* is, however, often kept in initial syllable before *n* as in *enora* (l. 9).

Note, of course, that in this central dialect there is evidence, as we would expect, of the second wave of palatalization ([k] + [a] > [ʃ]) in *cheoir* (l. 6) < *cadere*.

## Orthography

As the discussion above suggests, the scribe, Guiot, has a carefully worked out and consistent spelling system, which is often held up by scholars as an excellent example of the quasi-phonetic spelling favoured by twelfth-century scribes. Gaston Paris's comment is typical in this respect:

> Dans les manuscrits qui remontent à la seconde moitié du XIIᵉ siècle ou au commencement du XIIIᵉ, on trouve vraiment une orthographe excellente: j'entends surtout les manuscrits d'œuvres poétiques, par exemple ceux de Chrestien de Troyes. Ces textes satisfont sous tous les rapports: ils n'emploient pas un nombre excessif de caractères, ils ont, quand ils viennent de scribes habiles et soigneux, une grande conséquence dans les procédés de notation; ils n'ont pas de préoccupations étymologiques exagérées, et cependant ils conservent quelques traditions utiles: ce sont *des modèles* ...

(Burney 1967: 10–11)

We have already seen, for instance, how *an* is used to suggest the lowering of the nasal vowel, and there is consistency in marking the same sound in different positions, even if this results in the non-differentiation of homonyms. Note, however, that *m, n, r, s* are frequently doubled in his system as in *painne, mainne*.

## Morphosyntax

### Use of the case system

The case system for nouns is well maintained in this text, in sharp contrast to what we observed in *Alexis* and the *Chanson de Roland*; this is due to the different regional provenance of this text and the careful, probably artificial, maintenance of it by a better educated scribe. Here then we find the expected distinctive masculine nominative forms *Lanceloz* (l. 1), *li rois* (l. 5), *Amors* (l. 14).

*Hypotaxis*

The first four lines of our extract illustrate well the more sophisticated use of construction and especially subordination in Chrétien de Troyes in comparison to the *chansons de geste*. A variety of word order patterns are skilfully employed for stylistic effect, and the syntactic units are not confined to a single line (see ll. 4–5, 6–7).

*Negation*

Alongside the use of *ne* alone to mark negation, a number of reinforcing post-verbal particles were employed in Old French, of which the three most important were *pas*, *mie* and *point*. In the twelfth century the principal difference between *mie* (l. 6) and *pas* appears to have been one of region, with *mie* (< *mica*, 'a crumb') particularly favoured in the north and east, and *pas* (< *passum*, 'a step') in central and western areas. *Mie*, of course, proved useful in affording a different rhyme or assonance in verse texts, and is therefore attested outside northern and eastern texts. However, as central dialects increased in importance and formed the basis of standard French, the central particle *pas* increasingly predominated and *mie* occurs only rarely after the middle of the fifteenth century.

*Use of* si

In Old French *si* was used in a number of ways to structure or articulate the discourse. It could, for example, be used at the beginning of clauses to link them with a temporal sense ('then', 'next') – as here in lines 9 and 10 – or with a consecutive or adversative meaning, or simply as an equivalent of 'et' (see text 7, l. 18). A detailed study of these usages is provided by Marchello-Nizia (1985).

**Vocabulary**

We have an example here of a typical Old French usage, and one especially favoured by Chrétien, namely the use of an infinitive as a noun: *pooir* (l. 9). *Einz* (< *antius*) was a common and very useful Old French word meaning 'but, on the contrary' after a negative clause (cf. German *sondern*); it fell out of favour in the seventeenth century when it was criticized by normative grammarians.

# 7 *Le Jeu de saint Nicolas* (*c.* 1200)

PINCEDÉS
**Verse, Cliquet, si me fai boire;**
**Pour poi li levre ne me fent.**

CLIKÉS
**Be! boi assés! Qui te deffent?**
**Boi, de par Dieu, bon preu te fache!**                    4

PINCEDÉS
**Dieus! quel vin! Plus est frois que glache.**
**Boi, Cliquet! Chi a bon couvent;**
**Li ostes ne set que il vent,**
**A seize fust il hors anchois.**                           8

CLIKÉS
**Santissiés pour le marc dou cois**
**Et pour sen geugon qui l'aseme!**

PINCEDÉS
**Voire, et qui maint bignon li teme,**
**Quant il trait le bai sans le marc.**                     12

CAIGNET
**Cliquet, foi que tu dois saint Marc,**
**Taisiés vous ent, n'en parlés mais!**

CLIKÉS
**Mais bevons en bien et en pais;**
**Nous avons encor vin el pot**                             16
**De no premerain demi lot,**
**S'avons de le candaille ardant.**

(© Droz. From Jehan Bodel, *Le Jeu de saint Nicolas*,
édité par Albert Henry (Geneva, Droz, 1981),
vv. 693–710 (pp. 96–97).)

[P: Pour up, Cliquet, and give me a drink;
My lips are nearly cracking.
CL: Hey! Drink up! Who's stopping you?
Drink, for God's sake, and may it do you much good!        4
P: God! what wine! It is colder than ice.
Drink, Cliquet! It's a good deal;
The landlord doesn't know what he's selling,
It would be selling for 16 (deniers) elsewhere.            8
CL: Button up, for the boss of this pub,
And for his inn boy who is duping him!

P: Indeed, and who fingers many of his barrels,
When he draws the red wine without payment.[a]    12
CA: Cliquet, in the name of the faith you owe Saint Mark,
Shut up, stop going on!
CL: Let's rather drink in comfort and peace;
We've still got wine in the pot    16
Of our first half measure,
And a burning candle.]

## BRIEF COMMENTARY

This extract, a scene in an inn taken from the first known French miracle play and probably written around 1200 by the *jongleur*, Jehan Bodel, has been included to try to represent certain more colloquial features of Old French usage; but it equally illustrates the difficulty of such a venture, since we are dealing with a literary artefact which is, moreover, in verse (this section being in octosyllabic rhyming couplets). Note too that the text is based on the sole surviving manuscript (Bibliothèque nationale, fr. 25566), which dates from the late thirteenth or early fourteenth century and shows a mixture of Francien forms with Picard phonological and morphological traits – note, for example, the reduction of $z$ [ts] > $s$, reflected consistently in the spellings of the second person plural forms *taisiés vous, parlés* (l. 14), the Picard ending *-che* for present subjunctive forms (*fache*, l. 4), and the unstressed possessive forms, *sen* (l. 10) and *no* (l. 17). Henry (1981: 33) described the play in the following terms: 'Tout au long de la pièce, se côtoient ou se mêlent le sacré et le profane, le sublime et le comique, le merveilleux des songes et des interventions divines et le réalisme de gens préoccupés d'argent, de nourriture, de vin et de jeu'. There are certainly realistic elements in this scene which apparently employs colloquial expressions and *argot* forms such as *santissiés, marc, cois* (l. 9), *geugon, aseme* (l. 10), *bignon, teme* (l. 11), *bai, marc* (l. 12). The style is animated and lively using exclamations (*Be! Dieus!*) and comic names for the characters. Yet as regards morphosyntax, for example in the regular adherence to the two-case system (note the regular masculine nominative singular forms *li ostes* l. 7, *Dieus* l. 5 (vs. *Dieu*, l. 4) and nominative plural forms (*li levre*, l. 2)), the text appears very conservative and careful. The colloquial flavour might then be considered to be rather superficial in being primarily lexical.

---

a    These four lines are difficult to translate, not least because of the author's use of a number of *argot* terms. I have broadly followed Henry (1962) (see especially pp. 34, 107, 209–10), who summarizes earlier scholars' views and adds his own interpretation. Henry claims that there is a play on *marc* (l. 9), meaning 'boss (of the tavern)' and *marc* (l. 12), a slang word for 'money, payment'. It is further suggested that *asemer* means 'to wear down', and thus perhaps figuratively 'to dupe' and that *teme* derives from *\*tamer*, the literal sense of the line being 'pierces many of his barrels'.

## 8 The Old French Bible (first half of the thirteenth century)

While some parts of the Bible were already translated into the vernacular in the twelfth century, this version, known as *La Bible française du XIII^e siècle*, represents the first complete translation of both Testaments into French (for further details see Sneddon 1993). It is thought to be not the work of one man, but a collective enterprise by a number of different translators; this explains the uneven quality of the translation of the Vulgate and the fact that some parts are glossed, as in our extract, while others are not. Indeed in the case of Genesis, the commentaries take up more space than the text; they represent the adaptation of Latin commentaries, the most important of which is the *glossa ordinaria*, a standard compilation of exegetical texts which from the second half of the twelfth century often accompanied manuscript versions of the Vulgate. While many of the twelfth-century verse translations were intended for oral performance by *jongleurs*, this prose version was probably designed for personal and silent devotion by the faithful. The translation was a great success if the number of manuscripts of it and the annotations on these are anything to judge by. Here is an extract from Genesis, Chapter 1, verses 3–5.

> **[3] Dieux dist: 'Lumiere soit faite.' Et lumiere est faite. [4] Dieux vit que la lumiere fu bonne, et departi la lumiere de teniebres, [5] et il apela la lumiere jor et les teniebres nuit.**

> **(La lumiere qui fu faite le premier jor, ce est la foi qui est**     4
> **coumancement de toutes les vertuz. Ce que la lumiere devise les teniebres, ce est a dire qu'il a grant devise entre les feeulx qui sunt fuiz Dieu et les pecheeurs qui sunt hors de la foi. Et de cele devise trouvons nos en l'Esvangile que Sainz Abraham dist au**     8
> **riche home qui estoit en enfer, qui li avoit requis qu'il envoiast le povre mesel por metre li une goute d'eve sus sa langue por estaindre la chaleur: 'Souviengne toi, dist Abraham, que tu eus ou monde les biens et il ot les max; ore est il confortez et tu es**    12
> **tormentez, et entre nos et vos a si grant confusion et si grant devise que cil qui sunt la ne pueent venir ça, ne cil qui sunt ça ne pueent aler la.' Nequedant nos ne disons pas que cil qui sunt hors de la foi ne puissent venir a la foi et estre saus, mes tant**    16
> **come il en sunt hors, nul bien que il facent ne les puet faire saus.)**

> (© Droz. From Michel Quereuil, *La Bible française du XIII^e siècle.*
> *Édition critique de la Genèse* (Geneva, Droz, 1988), p. 93.)

[[**v. 3**] God said: 'Let there be light.' And there was light. [**v. 4**] God saw that the light was good, and he separated the light from the darkness, [**v. 5**] and he called the light day and the darkness night.

([4] The light which was made on the first day, this is the (Christian) faith which is the fount of all virtues. That the light separates the darkness, this means that there is a great difference between the faithful who are the sons of God and sinners who are outside the faith. [7] And on this difference, we find in the Gospel that Saint Abraham said to the rich man who was in hell, who had asked him to send the poor leper to put a drop of water on his tongue to quench the heat: 'Remember, said Abraham, that you had all good things on earth and he had all that is bad; now he is comforted and you are tormented, and between you and us there is such great confusion and such a great difference that those who are there cannot come here, and those who are here cannot go there.' [15] Nevertheless we do not say that those who are outside the faith cannot come to the faith and be saved, but that as long as they are outside the faith, no good that they may do can save them.)]

## COMMENTARY

### Date and place of composition and base manuscript

Little is known about the translators of this version of the Bible, although it has been suggested that they were probably associated with either the University of Paris or possibly the Dominicans. The translation was possibly executed between 1226 and 1239, and certainly between 1220 and 1260. The base manuscript used here, Bibliothèque de l'Arsenal 5056 (A), dates from the late thirteenth century, and displays occasional features characteristic of eastern and north-eastern dialects, such as the form *fuiz* (l. 7) (for Francien *fiz*) showing the vocalization of *l* in the sequence *il* and then inversion of these sounds.

### Phonology

It is, of course, more difficult to interpret the spelling and comment on the phonology of prose texts where we do not have metre, rhyme or assonance to help us. Note, however, the use in this extract of the form *teniebres* (l. 2), showing the diphthongization of tonic free [ɛ]; this was found side by side with the learned form *tenebres* which eventually triumphed.

**Orthography**

This text illustrates some features typical of Old French spelling:

(a) -*x* was used in final position to represent -*us*, thus *max* (l. 12); but it
was also employed as a simple alternative for -*s* (*Dieux* (l. 1), *feeulx*
(l. 6)). In the case of this last example *eu* represents the coalescence
of [e] and the result of the vocalization of [l] > [u]; however, scribes
frequently continued to show or reinstated the original *l*, so that *eul*
was a common graphy.

(b) A final consonant was frequently omitted before a final flexional *s*:
here the adjective *sauf* + *s* is realized as *saus* (l. 17).

(c) Old French spelling was not, of course, standardized to the same
degree as Modern French orthography; thus, for example, the palatal
nasal consonant could be represented in a number of ways (*gn*, *ng*,
*ngn*, *ign*, *ingn*): note here *souviengne* (l. 11). Similarly, both *an* and *en*
were employed to transcribe the outcome of the nasalization of either
[e] or [a] followed by a nasal consonant: *coumancement* (l. 5).

**Morphology**

*Noun morphology*

Although the majority of the subject nouns in this extract are feminines
for which there were, of course, no distinctive nominative forms, there is
evidence that the two-case system was being maintained in the use of
*sainz* (l. 8) and *Dieux* (l. 1) which contrasts with *fuiz Dieu* (l. 7) in which
the oblique continues to be used in a possessive function.

*Adjective morphology*

There is no evidence here of the assimilation of third-declension adjectives
to the main adjectival class: *si grant confusion et si grant devise* (ll. 13–14).
This latter class is declined regularly: *confortez, tormentez* (ll. 12–13).

*Demonstrative pronouns*

In Old French *cest* < *ecce iste* was used for 'this' and *cel* < *ecce ille* for
'that'. Their forms were as follows (the forms in brackets are relatively
infrequent):

*ecce ille*

|  | singular | | plural | |
|---|---|---|---|---|
|  | masculine | feminine | masculine | feminine |
| nominative | *cil* | *cele* | *cil* | *celes* |
| oblique | *cel, celui* | *cele, (celi)* | *cels, ceus* | |

*ecce iste*

|  | singular | | plural | |
|---|---|---|---|---|
|  | masculine | feminine | masculine | feminine |
| nominative | *cist* | *ceste* | *cist* |  |
|  |  |  |  | *cestes, cez* |
| oblique | *cest, cestui* | *ceste, (cesti)* | *cez* |  |

There were also rare neuters, *cest* and *cel*, which disappeared during the course of the twelfth century. What is distinctive about these Old French forms is the fact that both paradigms could be used as either adjectives or pronouns. Two important changes occurred at the end of the twelfth century: both *cez* and *cels* > *ces*; as a result, from the beginning of the thirteenth century, *ce* began to appear as the masculine singular oblique form when followed by a word beginning with a consonant. This gave the system:

|  | singular | | plural | |
|---|---|---|---|---|
|  | masculine | feminine | masculine | feminine |
| nominative | *cil, cist* | | *cil, cist* | |
|  |  | *cele, ceste* |  | *celes, cestes, ces* |
| oblique | *cel, cest* + V | | *ces* | |
|  | *ce* + C | *(celi, cesti)* |  |  |
|  | *celui, cestui* |  |  |  |

While the pronoun forms were generally not found with the particles *-ci*, *-là* in Old French, in the thirteenth century the form *ceus-ci* is first attested. We shall see that, as in many areas of French morphology, the pronoun system was subjected to considerable analogical re-working during the Middle French period. But in this text the distinctive masculine nominative plural form is typically used: *cil qui* (l. 14).

## Verb morphology

As a broad generalization we may say that Old French showed greater morphological variation in its verb system than its modern counterpart and that this variation was regularized through the working of analogy during the Middle French period. This evolution is perhaps particularly well illustrated by the development of the past historic forms, which we can see represented in this extract by the third person singular forms *dist* (l. 1), *vit* (l. 2), *fu* (l. 2), *departi* (l. 2), *apela* (l. 3), *fu* (l. 4), *ot* (l. 12), and the second person singular form *eus* (l. 11).

The past historic derived from the Latin perfect; the variable stress patterns of this tense resulted in morphological variation in Old French as vowels changed differently according to whether they were stressed or not. Latin perfects which ended in *-avi* or *-ivi* (perfects in *-evi* did not survive into Old French) were stressed throughout the paradigm on the ending and were known as weak perfects (*cantávi, cantavísti, cantávit, cantávĭmus, cantavístis, cantávĕrunt; dormívi, dormivísti, dormívit, dormívĭmus, dormivístis, dormívĕrunt*). During the Vulgar Latin period these forms contracted to *cantái, cantásti, cantát*, etc., producing the following classes of weak perfects in Old French:

| | |
|---|---|
| chantai | dormi |
| chantas | dormis |
| chanta(t) | dormi |
| chantames | dormimes |
| chantastes | dormistes |
| chanterent | dormirent |

The second person singular forms would regularly have had a final *-t* (e.g. *\*chantast*), but these are not attested in French, probably since *-t* was considered to be a third person not a second person singular ending. The first and second person plural endings are similarly not the simple phonetic outcome of their Latin etyma, but the exact history of these forms is obscure. There was also a third class of weak perfects in Old French ending in *-u* which were probably influenced by the pattern of *être* (*fu(i), fus, fu, fumes, fustes, furent*), even though this itself was a strong paradigm in Classical Latin (*fúi, fuísti, fúit, fúimus, fuístis, fúerunt*):

| | |
|---|---|
| paru(i) | parumes |
| parus | parustes |
| paru | parurent |

Alongside these weak classes there were also strong paradigms in which the stress fell on the stem in forms 1, 3 and 6 (first and third persons singular and the third person plural), but on the ending in 2, 4 and 5. In many cases this resulted in a vocalic alternation in the stem according to whether the stem was stressed or not:

| | | |
|---|---|---|
| véni > vin | díxi > dis | sápui > soi |
| venísti > venis | dixísti > desis | sapuísti > sëus |
| vénit > vint | díxit > dist | sápuit > so(u)t |
| venímus > venimes | dixímus > desimes | sapuímus > sëumes |
| venístis > venistes | dixístis > desistes | sapuístis > sëustes |
| vénerunt > vindrent | díxerunt > distrent | sápuerunt > so(u)rent |

Other common verbs in Old French equally showed this vocalic alternation, destined to be ironed out in Middle French: these include the verbs *veoir* (*vi, veis, vit, veimes, veistes, virent*), and *avoir* (*oi, eüs, ot, eümes, eüstes, orent*).

There is probable Latin influence in the use of the form *sunt* (l. 17).

**Syntax**

There are a number of features of the construction and word order of this text which give it a more 'modern' feel than our previous extracts. While this is, of course, partly due to its later date, we must also bear in mind that we have here an attempt to provide simple, easily readable prose for the devout. The author is not constrained by the demands of metre or verse form, nor, as is possible in the case of the Oaths, does he appear to be influenced by his Latin original. Thus it may well be that the variety of word order patterns we saw in *Alexis* or *Roland* are not typical of Old French usage in general, as has sometimes been suggested, but rather characteristic of particular Old French genres and styles. The high incidence of SVC in this passage, not only in main but also in subordinate clauses, is striking. Where this pattern is not employed, the verb is typically found in second position (CVS) with, for example, a clause initial adverb triggering inversion (*ore est il confortez*, l. 12); but already we find *nequedant* (l. 15) being followed by SVC. Allied to this is the increased use throughout of personal subject pronouns which reinforces the tendency of the verb to appear in second position in the clause. The text is, however, somewhat atypical of its age in the position of the object of an infinitive, which usually at this time was placed before the infinitive but is here in its modern position (*por estaindre la chaleur*, ll. 10–11); indeed this position is even employed for a pronominal indirect object (*por metre li une goute*, l. 10).

Other aspects of the syntax are, however, typical of Old French and familiar to us from other texts; these include the use of the article broadly according to semantic considerations, the negative constructions, and the use of a main clause subjunctive to express a command without an introductory *que* (l. 1). One other Old French structure is worth mentioning: *com(m)e* rather than *que* was usual in comparative constructions (*tant come*, ll. 16–17) right up to the seventeenth century when it was criticized by normative grammarians.

**Vocabulary**

The lexeme *mesel* (l. 10) 'leper' is derived from the Latin diminutive form *misellum* from *miser* meaning 'unhappy, wretched'; it has therefore undergone specialization of its meaning. The form of *hors*, used in Old French both as an adverb and as a preposition, is an alternative for *fors* < *foris*, but the source of the initial *h* is uncertain.

## 9 Geoffroy de Villehardouin, *The Conquest of Constantinople* (early thirteenth century)

This extract and brief commentary have been included to illustrate the early use of French in prose histories and chronicles. Just as in the case of the translation of the Bible, verse versions for oral performance were replaced with prose translations, so in the case of history, the verse Arthurian epics of the mid-twelfth century, such as Wace's *Roman de Brut*, were followed in the early thirteenth century by the chronicles of Robert de Clari and Geoffroy de Villehardouin, who are often considered to be the first French historians. If Latin was still thought to be the language of erudition, French was beginning to be deemed suitable for a range of functions, including the more objective presentation of factual material. This is not to say that this is a completely disinterested account: the author, born at Villehardouin, near Troyes around 1150, liegeman of the Count of Champagne, soldier and diplomat, himself played an important and active role in the Fourth Crusade. While it is clear that the account was not written on a daily basis during the Crusade, it is evident that he must have taken notes or kept a journal throughout as a basis for his chronicle. Nevertheless, the account is clear and ordered and written in a plain, unadorned style. The information is presented without much elaboration, emotion or colourful detail in a clear chronological sequence. Clauses, for example, are often simply linked by the co-ordinating conjunction *et*. So, as in the case of the previous text, the constructions and word order patterns seem more familiar to modern readers.

We have already seen how, with medieval texts, there are several layers to consider in the transmission of the text, including the intervention of the modern editor, notably in modernizing the typography, capitalization and punctuation of the text. I have taken the opportunity here to give a more accurate representation of these aspects of a medieval manuscript by adopting the conventions of the printed edition I have chosen to follow.[a] Where abbreviations have been resolved this is marked by the use of italics. Essentially three types of punctuation are used in the base manuscript (Bibliothèque nationale, fonds français, 2137) which dates from the end of the thirteenth century: . followed by a red initial which represents a strong punctuation; . without a red initial which represents medium punctuation; and a red initial not preceded by a . suggesting weak punctuation. Given the different punctuation conventions for Old French texts, some linguists have commented on the difficulty of determining what constitutes a sentence in Old French. This, of course, has important implications for the discussion of other structural features of the medieval language, and especially of preferred word order patterns.

---

a   I have, however, restored the original use of 'u' and 'v' and, in addition, used underlining to indicate a red initial letter and larger type for a larger initial.

The chronicle spans the period from the preaching of the Crusade in 1198 to the death of Boniface in 1207. The extract here describes the departure of the Crusade in 1202 and the first defections (§§47–49)[b]:

**Aprés la pasque entour la penthecoste conmencierent a movoir li pelerin de leur pais. Sachiez que mai*n*te lerme y fu ploree de pitié au partir de leur pais de leur genz *et* de leur amis. Einsint** *ainsi* | –7
**chevauchierent par mi bergoigne. *et* parmi les monz de mongieu. Et par moncenis. *et* par lombardie. Et ainsint conmencierent a** 5
**asamble*r* en uenice. *et* se logiere*n*t en vne isle qui est apelee l'isle saint-nicholas enz ou port.**

**En ce termine mut vns estoires de fla*n*dres par mer ou il avoit mo*u*lt grant plenté d'esvesques *et* de bones ge*n*z armees. De cele estoire fu chevetain. Jehan de neelles chastelain de bruges. *et*** 10
**thierri qui fu filz le conte phelippe de flandres *et* nichole de mailli. Et cil promirent au conte bauduyn de flandres *et* jurerent sus sainz lealment que il iroient par les destroiz de marroth. *et* asambleroie*n*t a l'ost de uenice *et* a lui en quel conques leu q*u*e il orroient dire qu'il retorneroient. Et pour ce en envoierent li quens** 15
***et* henri son frere leur nés chargiees de dras *et* de viandes *et* d'autres choses.**

**Mo*u*lt fu bele cele estoire *et* riche. *et* mo*u*lt y avoit grant fiance li quens de flandres *et* li pelerin. pource que la plus grant plenté de leur serjanz s'en aloient en cele estoire. Mes mauvesement tindrent** 20
**leur seigneurs *et* a touz les autres couvent. pource que cist et maint autre douterent le grant peril que cil de venice avoient empris.**

(From Jofroi de Vileharduyn, *La Conqueste de Costentinoble* d'après le manuscrit n° 2137 de la B.N. par la section de traitement automatique des textes d'ancien français du C.R.A.L., Laboratoire associé au C.N.R.S. (Nancy, Université de Nancy II, 1978), pp. 10–11.)

[After Easter around Pentecost the pilgrims began to leave their country. And know that many a tear was shed there out of pity when they left their country, their family and their friends. They rode through Burgundy, and over the mountains of Montjeu (= Mont Saint Bernard) and Mont Cenis and through Lombardy and thus they began to gather in Venice and camp on an island which is called San Niccolo di Lido.
[8] At this time a fleet sailed from Flanders in which there were a very large number of bishops and good armed men. The leaders of this fleet were Jean de Nesles, Chatelain of Bruges, and Thierry, who was the son of Count Philip of Flanders, and Nicolas de Mailly. [12] And these men promised Count Baudouin of Flanders and swore loyally on the Holy Gospels that they would go through the Straits of Morocco (= Straits of

b  The paragraph numbers are taken from Faral's edition (*Villehardouin, La Conquête de Constantinople*, éditée et traduite par Edmond Faral, 2 vols, Paris, Les Belles Lettres, 1938–39).

Gibraltar) and join with the Venetian army and himself in whatever place they heard he had gone to. And for this reason the Count and Henry his brother sent with them their ships laden with clothes, food and other supplies.

[18] The fleet was very fine and rich and the Count of Flanders and the pilgrims had great confidence in it because the majority of their soldiers were in this fleet. But they broke their word to their lords and to all the others because these and many others feared the very dangerous exploit which the men of Venice had embarked upon.]

## BRIEF COMMENTARY

*origin*

The forms and spellings of the manuscript are typical of its central provenance (note, for example, the clear indication of the second wave of palatalization in *chevetain* < *capitaneum*). The text is also unexceptional in many features of its morphology and syntax: the nominal case system is maintained (*li quens* (l. 19), *vns estoires* (l. 8), etc.), personal subject pronouns are frequently omitted, and the second position is favoured for the verb, although here the order CVS is more common than in our last text. Note the flexibility in the position of co-ordinated adjectives at this period (*moult fu bele cele estoire et riche*) and in the possibility of separating grammatically related elements (*tindrent . . . couvent*, ll. 20–21). Further evidence of the freedom of Old French from the constraints of normative grammar is afforded by the fact that agreement with collective nouns could either be in the singular, since these nouns are grammatically singular or, as here, in the plural *ad sensum* (*la plus grant plenté de leur serjanz s'en aloient*, ll. 19–20). The text illustrates well how Old French tense usage was dependent on the text type and genre. Whereas in the *Chanson de Roland* present, perfect and past historic forms were intermingled to create dramatic perspectives, here, in an historical account, chronological considerations are more important. The past historic is thus used consistently, with the pluperfect used to mark anteriority (*avoient empris*); this use of tenses is accompanied by precise indications of real-world time (*aprés la pasque entour la penthecoste*, l. 1). Thus we should not simply characterize the tense usage of Old French as being free; it was flexible in certain genres to create certain specific effects. Finally, *estoire* (l. 20, 'fleet, army') illustrates the integration of Greek terms into French (< *stolon*); it should not be confused with its Old French homonym *estoire* < *historia*, meaning 'story, history, race'.

# 10 The *Lettre d'Hippocrate* (mid-thirteenth century)

The first extant example of the use of French in a 'scientific' or technical text, the *Comput* of Philippe de Thaon, an early ecclesiastical calendar written in hexasyllabic rhyming couplets, dates from the second decade of the twelfth century. All the surviving manuscripts of this text are Anglo-Norman, as indeed are the majority of early texts of this type, which also include lapidaries and bestiaries in verse. According to Hunt (1990), who along with Rothwell has done much to open up the field of Anglo-Norman non-literary texts to a wider audience, the first Anglo-Norman receipts and charms began to appear around the middle of the twelfth century. The text here, an example of popular medicine, is taken from the *Lettre d'Hippocrate*, the most influential collection of vernacular medical prescriptions before 1300. The tendency we saw towards a simple, unadorned style in the previous text is here accentuated: the objective conveying of the necessary information in a clear, unambiguous form takes precedence over stylistic considerations and there is little attempt to add variety to the rather unsophisticated prose style. On the one hand, it is remarkable that French already possessed the basic technical terms to enable discussion of medical matters (see below); on the other hand, as is clear from this extract on urology, the description appears impressionistic and imprecise to us, and the texts are often very corrupt, suggesting a lack of concern for scientific accuracy. Here, for example, it is difficult to explain the agreements in line 3, *Urine enfievrés al setime jur terminee.*

## DE URINIS

*Si hume est sein* sa urine est devant manger ruge, aprés manger blanche. Urine crasse e truble cum urine de asne signefie dolur del chef proceinement a venir. Urine enfievrés al setime jur[a] terminee, si al quart jur est blanche et al secund jur ruge, signefie garisun. Urine que est crasse[b] e mult blanche si cum cele que est    5
de mutes humurs signefie a venir fevere quarteine. Urine que est sanglentee signefie la vessie estre blescee de aucune purreture que ait dedenz lui. Urine carcive e blanche cum fust velue signefie le mal des reins. Urine que semble pudrus signefie la vessie blescee. Urine que chet par gutettes e si noue desure cum ampulles lunge    10
enfermeté signefie. Urine que noue sure une crasse reelee ague [e] lunge enfermeté signefie. Urine a femme pure e clere, si al urinal lust cum argent e cele femme suvent vomist e si n'ad nul talent de manger, signefie la femme estre enceinte. Urine a femme blanche e pesante e puante signefie dolur des reins e le mariz    15
plein de mal e de enfermeté de freit. Si urine a femme eit escume

a   Other manuscripts have *al secunt jur*.
b   Hunt suggests this is an error and should probably read 'charnuse'.

**de sanc desure e est clere cum ewe, signefie dolur del chef e talent
de dormir e de manger aver perdu pur le enfleure de l'estomac.
Urine de femme que est del peis e de la colur de plum signefie
la femme enceinte e signefie le mariz purri. Urine de femme que       20
est enflé e que ad la tusse e la menisun, si el est de colur de lin,
signefie que la femme ne puet pas estre seine. Si devez cunustre
par les urines les maus a jofne cors e quant vus les avez cunu, si
purrez ver medscines encuntre. E pur ceo que hummes sunt de
divers qualitez, encuntre chescun mal i ad plusurs medscines e ore    25
cumencerunt, primes al chief e pus as aultres membres.**

(From Tony Hunt, *Popular Medicine in Thirteenth-Century England.
Introduction and Texts* (Cambridge, D.S. Brewer, 1990), p. 109.)

[*Of Urines*. If a man is healthy, his urine is red before eating and white after
eating. Fatty and clouded urine like that of a donkey indicates an imminent
malady of the head. If the urine of a man suffering from a seven-day
fever is white on the fourth day and red on the second day, this indicates
a recovery. [5] Urine which is fatty and very white like that of many
humours indicates that a quartan fever is coming. Urine which is bloody
indicates the bladder is damaged by some internal infection. Urine which
is corrosive (fleshy) and white as if furry indicates kidney problems. [9]
Urine which seems dusty indicates a damaged bladder. Urine which falls in
droplets and then floats on top like bubbles indicates a long illness. Urine
which floats on a layer of mottled fat indicates an acute and long illness. A
woman's urine which is pure and clear so it shines in the chamber pot like
silver – and if this woman vomits often and has no desire to eat – indicates
that the woman is pregnant. A woman's urine which is white and heavy and
smelly indicates kidney problems and that the womb is suffering the effects
of a chill. [16] If a woman's urine has a scum of blood on it and is clear like
water, this indicates malady of the head and loss of desire to sleep or eat
because of swelling of the stomach. A woman's urine which is of the colour
of pitch and lead indicates that the women is pregnant and that the womb
is diseased. [20] The urine of a woman who is swollen and has a cough and
diarrhoea, and if it is the colour of flax, indicates that the woman cannot
be restored to health. So you should be able to recognize from the different urines the diseases of young bodies and when you have identified them,
then you can give medicines for them. And since men are of different types,
there are several medicines for each illness, and they will begin now, first
for the head, then for other parts of the body.]

## COMMENTARY

### Base manuscript: Harley 978

Very little is known about the genesis of this text. However, the base
manuscript used here, British Library, Harley 978, illustrates some inter-

esting aspects of medieval manuscripts. First, not all of the manuscript dates from the same period: while the first 34 folios, which includes the medical recipes, were probably written *c.* 1240–50, the rest of the manuscript dates from the second half of the thirteenth century. Second, the manuscript is typical in containing a mixture of text types and works both in French and in Latin; this manuscript includes, amongst other things, a calendar with prognostications, verses in French and Latin, a number of Latin prescriptions and part of an Anglo-Norman verse treatise on falconry, as well as vernacular literary works such as the *Lais* of Marie de France. As we have already noted, the manuscript is Anglo-Norman, as are many of the extant manuscripts of this period; it has been suggested that the manuscript was executed at Reading Abbey, but, whatever its precise provenance, it clearly displays Anglo-Norman colouring.

**Anglo-Norman features**

*Phonology and orthography*

The spelling has a number of features which should now be familiar as characteristic of Anglo-Norman manuscripts; these include:

(a) Close [o] > [u] from the eleventh century on; we thus find *u* for central *o* in the spelling as in *humurs* (l. 6), *dolur* (l. 17), *colur* (l. 21); this is also true before a nasal consonant (*garisun* (l. 5), *lunge* (l. 10), *cunustre* (l. 22), etc.).

(b) Earlier reduction of diphthongs: *ie > e* (here we find both *chef* (l. 3) and *chief* (l. 26); *fevere* (l. 6) and *enfievrés* (l. 3)); *ui > u, i* (*cunustre*, l. 22; *pus*, l. 26; *menisun*, l. 21); *ei > e* (*aver*, l. 18).

(c) Non-differentiation of the diphthong *ei > oi: peis* (l. 19), *freit* (l. 16).

(d) Under the influence of English speech habits, the main stress was intensified and this in turn had an effect on syllables that were less stressed; thus [ə] became unstable in all positions in Anglo-Norman even before the middle of the thirteenth century. Final [ə], for instance, in hiatus with a preceding tonic vowel fell in the course of the late twelfth or early thirteenth century, as is witnessed here by the feminine adjective *enflé* (l. 21; but cf. *blescee*, l. 7). Final post-consonantal [ə] equally began to be unstable during the course of the thirteenth century; this may then explain what at first sight looks like the non-agreement of the adjective *pudrus* (l. 9).

(e) Longer retention of [w] (< *kw*) as in *ewe* (l. 17).

(f) Later retention of final unsupported *-t* and *-d*: this tendency is witnessed in *ad* (l. 21), the third person singular present indicative form of *avoir*; pre-consonantal [ð] also appears to have survived longer than on the continent and is often represented by *d* in Anglo-Norman manuscripts (*medscines*, l. 24).

(g) The spelling of *carcive* (1. 8) does not show the second wave of palatalization; this may be a learned borrowing since *chet* (1. 10) also occurs, or may be a simple error (see note b).

### Morphosyntax

This text illustrates two key features of Anglo-Norman morphology: first, there is no evidence here of the nominal case system in contrast to what we have seen in the two previous texts; and adjectives derived from the Latin third declension occur with an analogical final *-e* in the feminine (*pesante*, 1. 15, *puante*, 1. 15).

## Orthography

In many respects the scribe appears to be attempting to reflect the vernacular pronunciation of his text and the spelling is not overburdened with non-pronounced etymological letters as happened particularly during the Middle French period; witness the spellings *setime* (1. 3), *peis* (1. 19), *plum* (1. 19). On the other hand the *l* in *aultres* (1. 26) was certainly no longer pronounced, and the scribe does not show elision of the vowel in his spelling of *que est* (1. 6) or *sa urine* (1. 1).

## Morphology

Many aspects of the morphology of this text are now familiar to us as typical of Old French: these include the contracted forms of the articles after the prepositions *à* (*al*, *as*), *de* (*del*), *en*, and the adverbial forms ending in *-ment* (*proceinement*, 1. 3) or *-s* (*primes*, 1. 26). The neuter demonstrative, which appears variously as *ce*, *ceo*, *çou*, *ço* and *ceu* in Old French (*pur ceo*, 1. 24), is stressed.

## Syntax

### Use of pronouns

In Old French, and particularly in Anglo-Norman, *que* is often found where in Modern French *qui* would be required, for example, *urine que chet par gutettes* (1. 10). Impersonal subject pronouns are very rare, so that the usual presentative form is *i ad* (1. 25).

### Use of the infinitive

There are two interesting examples of usage of the infinitive in this text. In line 7, the structure *signefie la vessie estre blescee* seems to be modelled on the Latin accusative and infinitive construction, that is, instead of using a subordinating *que* followed by a subject and a finite verb (as in *signefie que la femme ne puet pas estre seine*, l. 22), there is no formal marking of subordination and the main clause is simply followed by the noun (which in Latin would have been in the accusative case) and the infinitival form of the verb. The same construction is used in *signefie la femme estre enceinte* (l. 14).

### Word order

There is little variation of word order pattern as we would expect in a text where stylistic considerations have limited place and the main purpose of the text is the simple conveying of facts: essentially then SVO structures are favoured. As is usual at this period, the direct object precedes the infinitive on which it is dependent: *lunge enfermeté signefie* (ll. 10–11), and co-ordinated adjectives can be separated from the noun they modify: *urine a femme blanche e pesante e puante* (ll. 14–15).

### Vocabulary

It is striking that by this period Anglo-Norman already possesses the basic vocabulary and technical terms necessary for discussion of medical matters. We find here, for instance, *mariz* (l. 15) from Latin *matrix*, itself formed on *mater* (> *mere*) on the analogy of *nutrix* (> *nourrice*) and *genitrix* (> *génitrice*), and *menisun* (l. 21) derived from the verb *menuisier* < *\*minutiare*.

Note that *aucun(e)* (l. 7) at this period has a positive not a negative meaning; this persists into Early Modern French and remains in the literary construction *d'aucuns* 'some (people)'.

## 11 *Donation testamentaire* (1239)

Whereas there are Occitan acts and deeds dating from the early twelfth century, in the North, French only began to replace Latin in legal and administrative documents from the beginning of the thirteenth century. Up to this time, all surviving official acts from the Royal Chancellery except oaths are in Latin and use of the vernacular remained rare in this domain until *c.* 1260. Thereafter the situation changed rapidly, and by the end of the century the number of extant charters and deeds in the vernacular is very great. It is unfortunate for the philologist that the first extant ones are relatively late – there is no Parisian charter before the second half of the thirteenth century – since charters have the advantage over most other text types in having a precise location and dating. For this reason they have been used, notably by Dees (1980), as the most faithful source of establishing a geography of Old French dialects. We should, however, be aware that in the early part of the twelfth century, not all scribes write consistently in one dialect; after about 1280, however, the more pronounced regional features disappear and the use of language in these documents becomes more standardized. The secularization of this domain – as of many others – makes important progress in the thirteenth century: an ordinance of 1281, for example, allowed individuals to obtain deeds without needing the jurisdiction of the Church.

Certain linguistic features are characteristic of legal and administrative texts. As today, they tend to adopt a formulaic and repetitive pattern. The use of the vernacular side by side with Latin, moreover, probably affected the evolution of each; as a result the use of French is often somewhat conservative in legal documents (cf. Strasbourg Oaths), although this does not appear to be particularly the case for this extract.

This is an example of a will dating from 1239 (New Style, i.e. by the Gregorian Calendar) from the Archives départementales de la Haute-Marne (8 H 23, fonds de l'abbaye de Morimond); the year in the text is that of the Julian Calendar (Old Style). It is an original document and not a copy. Although the number of documents in the vernacular varies from region to region, this region is typical in witnessing the marked increase of acts during the century: for the period 1232–44 such texts are rather rare, with only one or two extant per year, and for some years, none at all. This contrasts with the period 1254–70, for which there are between eight and 22 each year and no year without any texts.

**Je, Renart, sires de Chosuel, devise en mon testament et vuel et comant que li segnors li moinnes de Moiremont, ou je et Aliz, ma feme, gerrons, ayent atoz jors mais, parmanablement, lestalage et le eminage dou marchié de Chosuel, por larme de moi et por larme Aliz, ma feme, et por faire nostres aniversaires atoz jors mais, chascun ant, por nos proprement; et se, par aventure,**   5

il avenoit que li marchié de Chosuel, qui est auvenredi, se remuoit,
et quil fust aColumbé, je vuel et comant que cil de Moiremont
aient et prengnent lestalage et le eminage au marchié de Columbé
ausi com en celui de Chosuel. Cest dom, je et Aliz, ma feme,     10
dame de Chosuel, avons doné et outroié a toz jors mais, come
lestalage et le eminage, aus segnors au moines de Moiremont, por
faire mon aniversaire parmanablement, et por faire laniversaire
Aliz, ma feme, atoz jors mais, aMoiremont, chascun ant aprés
samort; enaprés, je vuel et comant que li moinnes et li convers     15
et toz li covenz de deffors et dedanz de Moiremont aient pitance
le jor que il feront nostres aniversaires por ceste rente, chascun
ant, por nos, en lant et au termine que chascun de nos trespassera
de cest siegle. Ce fu fait en lant de lEncarnation Nostre Segnor
mil et douz cenz et .XXXVIII. anz, on mois de fevrier.     20

(From *Documents linguistiques de la France (série française)*, publiés par
Jacques Monfrin avec le concours de Lucie Fossier, Vol. 1: *Chartes en
langue française antérieures à 1271 conservées dans le département de la
Haute-Marne*, Volume préparé par Jean-Gabriel Gigot (Paris, Éditions
du Centre National de la Recherche Scientifique, 1974), p. 9.[a])

[I, Renart, lord of Choiseul, establish in my will and wish and command
that the lord monks of Morimond, where I and Aalis, my wife, will lie,
have for evermore henceforth, permanently, the right to have a stall and
the grain tax of the market of Choiseul, for the sake of my soul and that
of my wife Aalis, and in order to celebrate our anniversaries for evermore, each year, especially for us; [6] and if, by chance, it happened that
the market in Choiseul, which takes place on Friday, should move, and
that it were in Colombey, I wish and command that those of Morimond
have and take the right to a stall and the grain tax in the market of
Colombey just as in that of Choiseul. [10] This gift, I and Aalis my wife,
lady of Choiseul, have given and granted for evermore, both the right to
a stall and the grain tax to the lord monks of Morimond, to celebrate my
anniversary permanently, and to celebrate the anniversary of Aalis my
wife for evermore in Morimond, each year after her death; [15] furthermore I wish and command that the monks and lay brothers and all the
monasteries both outside and within Morimond receive alms on the day
they will celebrate our anniversaries for this revenue, each year, for us in
the year and on the date that each of us shall pass from this earth. This
was executed in the year of the Incarnation of our Lord one thousand
two hundred and thirty-eight, in the month of February.]

a  This is essentially the version of the text given by the editor, Gigot, who has introduced
modern punctuation, distinguished the use of *u* and *v*, *i* and *j*, etc. I have, however,
removed the editorial hyphens used to separate modern words so that the Old French
different pattern of word divisions can be seen.

## COMMENTARY

### Regional features

Champenois texts, as we have seen in the commentary on text 6, essentially display usages common to Francien and other central dialects (such as the clear representation of the second wave of palatalization in *marchié*, l. 4, *chascun*, l. 14), but also share linguistic features with the dialects of the surrounding regions. There are here, for example, certain usages which are characteristic of eastern or northern texts, but not of the Île-de-France; these include the absence of a glide consonant facilitating the pronunciation of certain consonant clusters (*venredi*, l. 7); the early lowering of *e* to *a* before *r* (*parmanablement*, l. 13) and the absence of any indication of diphthongization in the spelling of *segnors* (l. 2).

### Orthography

Despite the co-existence of French with Latin in legal and administrative usage at this period, the spelling here is not, as yet, the heavily latinate orthography which is favoured in Middle French legal documents. This is not to say, however, that we still have the broadly phonemic spelling which we saw in the commentary on Chrétien de Troyes where the oral nature of the text dictated that phonological considerations should take precedence over semantic concerns; there is, for instance, some redundant doubling of consonants as in *deffors* (l. 16), *moinnes* (l. 2). [s] in pre-consonantal position disappeared during late Old French, and first of all before consonants other than [p, t, k]; here, however it is still indicated in the spelling (*estalage*, l. 3, *chascun*, l. 14). Finally, some spellings are difficult to explain and seem due to the individual habits of the scribe (e.g. *ant* (l. 6) < *annus*; *arme* (l. 4) < *animus*).

### Morphology

#### Noun morphology

The noun morphology is typical of thirteenth-century prose texts. Adherence to the two-case system is only spasmodic and there is considerable evidence of uncertainty and confusion over the forms (*li moinnes* (< \*monachus, -i*, l. 15), *li segnors* (l. 2), *toz li covenz* (l. 16)). Note also the form *sires* (l. 1); the imparisyllabic noun has been given a final *-s* on the analogy of the main masculine class (*murs*). Also typical is the non-integration of proper names into the declension system (*Renart*, l. 1).

*Indefinite pronouns and adjectives*

Old French created a range of indefinites which did not exist in Classical Latin. In Old French *chascun* from popular Latin *cascunum*, created from a crossing of *quisque* (*unus*) with *cat(a)* *unum*, could function as either an adjective (*chascun ant*, l. 14) or as a pronoun (*chascun de nos*, l. 18). The adjectival use of *chascun* was criticized by Vaugelas in the seventeenth century and replaced by *chaque* which, while already attested in Chrétien de Troyes, did not become common until the sixteenth century.

*Possessives*

The form of the possessive in *nostres aniversaires* (l. 17) is not the expected one (*noz*); it may be an analogical extension based on the singular *nostre* or the use of the stressed form in unstressed position.

*Verb morphology*

There were two main classes of present indicative forms in Old French. The first derived from Latin present indicatives of the *-are* type and had the following endings -, *-es*, *-e(t)*, *-ons* (or *-omes*, *-oms*, *-om*, *-on*), *-ez*, *-ent*. Note that the final *t* of the third person singular fell early; *-ons* is not the regular development of *-amus* which would have been *\*-ains*, but is probably influenced by *sumus* > *sons* (cf. Price 1971: 178); *-z* > *-s* in the thirteenth century, but *-ez* remains the usual graphy. In the case of the first person singular, where the stem ended in a consonant cluster such as *-bl-*, *-fl-*, *-tr-*, *-vr-* or [dʒ], final *e* [ə] was used as a supporting vowel. During the thirteenth century this began to spread slowly to all first person singular forms and became generalized during Middle French. Here then we have *devise* (l. 1) but *comant* (l. 2). The other Latin conjugations nearly all fell together in the present tense as the distinctive vowel quality of *monet, regit* and *audit* was lost: this gave the following pattern:

| | | | | | |
|---|---|---|---|---|---|
| *vendo* > *vent* | (-) | *dormio* > *dor(m)* |
| *vendis* > *venz* | (*s*) | *dormis* > *dors* |
| *vendit* > *vent* | (*t*) | *dormit* > *dort* |
| *vendimus* > *vendons* | (*ons*) | *dormimus* > *dormons* |
| *venditis* > *vendez* | (*ez*) | *dormitis* > *dormez* |
| *vendunt* > *vendent* | (*ent*) | *dormiunt* > *dorment* |

Note that *-ons* again suggests the possible influence of *sumus*; regularly *-etis*, *-itis* would give *-eiz* > *-oiz* and *-iz* respectively, and *-ez* suggests the early generalization of the second person plural ending of the first class; final *-s*, added to the first person singular on the analogy of the second person, remained optional for a long time and only became established during the course of Middle French. A second sub-class was formed on the basis of inchoative forms with the infix -*sc*-; while these were rare in Classical Latin, they extended to a number of verbs such as *finio* which became *\*finisco*, *\*finiscis*, *\*finiscit*, etc. From these the following Old French type was created:

| | |
|---|---|
| *fenis* | *fenissons* |
| *fenis* | *fenissez* |
| *feni(s)t* | *fenissent* |

In both classes variation could occur in the stem because of the regular working of sound change; the first and second person plurals were stressed on the endings (weak forms) and the other persons on the stem. Some verbs had an additional stem in the first person singular created as a result of palatalization; the conjugation of *vouloir* was originally *vueil* (< *volio*), *vueus, vueut, volons, volez, vuelent*; here the form *vuel* (l. 1) presages the analogical reworking of paradigms which took place on a large scale during Middle French.

The verb *gésir* is defective in Modern French, that is it is really only used in certain tenses (the present and imperfect indicative, also in the present participle and occasionally in the infinitive) and is rare except in the set phrases *ci-gît* 'here lies' and *ci-gisent* 'here lie' (on tombstones). In Old French it was a fully productive verb and is used here in the future (*gerrons*, l. 3).

*Prepositions*

In addition to inheriting many prepositions from Latin, French also created its own complex formations, particularly on the basis of *de, en, à* and *par*. The examples here, *de deffors et dedanz de* (l. 16), illustrate the use of adverbs in the creation of these new prepositions, categories which anyway were not always clearly separated functionally in Old French.

**Syntax**

*Use of personal subject pronouns*

In Old French the personal subject pronouns either could be used in the preverbal atonic position, as in Modern French, or they could have greater autonomy and be separated from their verb: *Je, Renart, sires de Chosuel, devise* (l. 1); such a construction is now impossible except in certain legal formulae and phrases such as *je soussigné*. This greater independence of the subject pronouns in Old French meant they could also be co-ordinated with a nominal subject as is illustrated here: *ou je et Aliz, ma feme, gerrons* (ll. 2–3); *je et Aliz ... avons doné* (ll. 10–11). The stressed and unstressed forms of the first and second persons plural could appear either as *nous, vous*, or, as in this text, *nos, vos* (*por nos proprement*, l. 6). There is an example of the use of an impersonal subject pronoun, generally rare in Old French, because semantically redundant: *il avenoit que* (l. 7).

## Function words

Seventeenth-century grammarians were critical of the Old French tendency not to repeat function words in co-ordinated structures. The structure *por larme de moi et por larme Aliz, ma feme* (ll. 4–5), repeats the *por* before the second noun, but not *de* before the proper name.

## Conditional clauses

The archetypal Old French conditional structure was to have an imperfect subjunctive in both the if-clause (protasis) and the consequent (apodosis). This construction was already rivalled, however, in Old French by the modern structure which has the imperfect indicative in the if-clause and the conditional in the consequent, a construction which made rapid progress during Middle French. Here we have an example of the use of *si* followed by the imperfect indicative, but the second, co-ordinated condition is in the imperfect subjunctive (ll. 6–8).

## Word order

Typically in Old French if the first word of a clause was not the subject, the subject and verb would be inverted. Here there is an early example of what appears to be the left dislocation of the direct object for topicalization, and there is no inversion after this initial object: *Cest dom, je et Aliz, ma feme, dame de Chosuel, avons doné* (ll. 10–11).

## Vocabulary

There are a number of indications in this text of the productivity and creativity of the Old French lexicon. French exploited the processes of suffixation (*estalage* (l. 3), *eminage* (l. 4), *pitance* (l. 16)) and prefixation (*trespassera* (l. 18)) to enrich its stock. We find here in the legal formulae a stylistic device which is very much a feature of Middle French texts, namely the use of doublets or binomial pairs: witness *vuel et comant* (ll. 1–2); *aient et prengnent* (l. 9); *doné et outroié* (l. 11); *parmanablement . . . atoz jors mais* (ll. 13–14).

An interesting example of semantic change is afforded by the verb *deviser* (l. 1), which in Modern French has the meaning 'chat, gossip', but here has the sense 'establish, define' and regularly occurs in medieval French wills. It derives from *\*devisare* for *dividere* meaning 'to divide, distinguish', from which it acquires a range of meanings including 'to choose or outline a plan' (perhaps by extension of the meaning of distinguishing between one option and another), 'to order', 'describe', or 'relate'. The adverb *mais*, derived from *magis*, frequently had a temporal sense in Old French ('henceforth').

## 12 *Lettre de Jean Sarrasin à Nicolas Arrode* (23 June 1249)

This letter is among the earliest extant ones in French (the oldest one dating from 1238). Before that, the surviving private correspondence is in Latin and indeed there are relatively few letters in French before about 1260, which, as we have seen, is roughly the same time as French became commonly employed in administrative documents and charters. The relative lateness of these first extant letters in French is difficult to explain and may simply be due to the fact that personal letters were not considered worth keeping. This suggestion might also explain why, on the contrary, this letter did survive, for its tone appears not to be entirely personal, and it may have had the additional purpose of trying to convey to the influential bourgeois of Paris what was happening on the Crusade. Nevertheless, the style is less formal and more subjective than that of Villehardouin's chronicle (text 9). Given the date of the base manuscript (see below), the language appears rather conservative, or, to use Foulet's terms, 'fort satisfaisant par son respect de la déclinaison et une graphie assez régulière' (Foulet 1924: x).

Here is the opening of the letter:

A seigneur Nicolas Arrode Jehans Sarrazins, chambrelens le roy de France, salus et bonne amour.

Je vous fais a savoir que li roys et la royne, et li quens d'Artois, et li quens d'Anjou et sa femme, et je, sommes haitié dedens la cité de Damiete que Dieus, par son miracle, par sa misericorde  5 et par sa pitié, rendi a la crestienté le dimenche de la quinsainne de Pentecouste.

Aprés ce, je vous fais a savoir en quele maniere ce fu. Il avint, quant li roys et li os de la crestienté furent entré es nez a Aiguemorte, que nous feismes voile le jour de feste saint Augustin  10 qui est en la fin d'aoust; et arrivames en l'isle de Cipre quinze jours devant la feste saint Remi, c'est a savoir le jour de la feste saint Lambert. Li quens d'Angiers descendi a la cité de Lymeçon, et li roys et nous, qui avec lui estions en sa nef, que on apeloit la Monjoie, descendismes l'andemain bien main, et quens d'Artois  15 entor tierce a ce port meismes. Nous fusmes en cele isle a mout pou de gent, et sejournasmes iluec jusques a l'Ascension pour atendre l'estoire qui n'estoit mie venue.

(From Jean Sarrasin, *Lettre à Nicolas Arrode (1249)*
éditée par Alfred L. Foulet (Paris, Champion, 1924), pp. 1–2.)

[To my lord Nicolas Arrode greetings and fond regards from Jean Sarrasin, Chamberlain of the King of France.

[3] I am writing to tell you that the King and the Queen and the Count of Artois and the Count of Anjou and his wife and I hastened

into the city of Damietta which God, through his miraculous ways, mercy and pity surrendered to the Christian people on the fifteenth day of Pentecost.

[8]   Next I want to tell you how this occurred. It happened, when the King and the Christian army had boarded the ships at Aigues-Mortes, that we set sail on the Feast of Saint Augustine, which is at the end of August; and we arrived on the island of Cyprus fifteen days before the Feast of Saint Remi, namely on the Feast of Saint Lambert. [13] The Count of Angers went down to the city of Limisso [Limassol], and the King and we who were with him in his ship which was called 'Monjoie', went down very early the next day, and the Count of Artois around nine in the morning to the port itself. We were on this island with very few men and we stayed there until Ascension to wait for the fleet which had not arrived.]

## BRIEF COMMENTARY

### Date and place of composition and base manuscript

The author of this letter, Jean Sarrasin, a member of the Parisian upper middle class, participated in the Seventh Crusade under St Louis of France. In this letter he recounts to his friend Nicolas Arrode what happened on the Crusade, starting from the departure from Aigues-Mortes in August 1248. The letter is always inserted in a manuscript of one of the Continuations (known as the Continuation Rothelin after the eighteenth-century abbot who had a manuscript of it) of the *Roman d'Eracles*, which is the French translation of William of Tyre's *Historia rerum in partibus transmarinis gestarum* ('History of things done in foreign parts'), a history of the Latin kings of Jerusalem up to 1184. The base manuscript used here (Bibliothèque nationale, fonds français 9083) dates from the beginning of the fourteenth century and shows few regional peculiarities. The editor, Foulet, has made the occasional small 'correction' to the text, emending *Monnoie* to *Monjoie* (l. 15) and inserting *l'andemain* (l. 15) on the basis of the text of other manuscripts.

### Morphosyntax

Given the date of the manuscript it is surprising to find such careful adherence to the two-case system. The forms of the past historic are well represented in this extract (see text 8): for the third person singular we may note *rendi* (l. 6), *fu* (l. 8), *descendi* (l. 13). Note that in the first person plural forms there is hesitation between the endings *-(V)mes* and *-(V)smes* in which an *s* was introduced, perhaps on the analogy of the second person plural forms: *feismes* (l. 10); *arrivames* (l. 11); *descendismes* (l. 15); *fusmes* (l. 16); *sejournasmes* (l. 17).

The use of tenses in this letter is similar to that in Villehardouin. Alongside adverbs indicating the precise temporal situation of events there is a more chronologically determined use of tenses. Whereas the imperfect was relatively rare in descriptions in early Old French texts, and especially in verse, with the expansion of prose to new domains came an increase in the thirteenth century in the use of this tense to describe persons or things (*estions* (l. 14), *apeloit* (l. 14)). There was also a parallel increase in the use of the pluperfect (*estoit venue*, l. 18) alongside the past anterior (l. 9).

This text also illustrates the greater autonomy of personal subject pronouns discussed in the commentary on the last text. We have an example of the co-ordination of a pronominal subject with nominal subjects (ll. 3–4), and of the separation of a nominal subject from its verb by an interpolated adverbial phrase: *que Dieus, par son miracle, par sa misericorde et par sa pitié, rendi . . .* (ll. 5–6). Once again there is an example of the use of an impersonal subject pronoun *il* (l. 8).

As in the other prose texts we have discussed, the word order shows a preference for the ordering destined to become the norm for Modern French usage (SVC) in main clauses and even in subordinate clauses (*que on apeloit la Monjoie*, ll. 14–15). Note, however, the position of the prepositional phrases in *qui avec lui estions en sa nef* (l. 14).

The verbal periphrasis *faire a savoir* (l. 3; meaning 'to make known') was common in Old French; it illustrates the greater variation in verb government tolerated at this period before Modern French norms were established in the Classical period.

**Vocabulary**

*Main* (l. 15) derived from Latin *mane* was a commonly used adverb in Old French with the meaning 'in the morning'. *L'andemain* (l. 15) is still used in its original Old French form; gradually confusion over the use of the article led to the agglutination of the *l'* to the noun (*landemain* is attested from the last decade of the thirteenth century on) and the addition of a new article, giving the Modern French form, *le lendemain*.

# III Middle French

## French in the fourteenth and fifteenth centuries

Until relatively recently the study of Middle French has been somewhat neglected. Viewed as an era of linguistic instability paralleling the political upheavals of the age and as a period of transition between the heyday of Old French and the stability and fixity of Modern French, there has been, moreover, considerable uncertainty and debate as to its temporal limits. Using a number of different external or internal linguistic criteria for its dating, commentators have suggested as its *terminus a quo* a range of dates between the middle of the thirteenth century and the end of the fourteenth century, and as its *terminus ad quem* dates ranging from the last quarter of the fifteenth century right up to the first third of the seventeenth century. Here we have chosen to take the beginning of the fourteenth century as our starting point since we witness in the texts from then on a number of features which, taken together, differentiate them from those of the previous era: phonologically, we may note, for example, the reduction of diphthongs and the loss of hiatus or the dropping of [ə] in certain contexts; as regards morphosyntax, the final elimination of the two-case system, analogical reworkings in the verb system, important changes in the personal pronoun and demonstrative systems and the increased use of SV word order; and lexically, a (re)latinization of the vocabulary. This is a period marked by wars, epidemics and social and political upheavals. We have also considered that, while the sixteenth century has much in common with the usage of the previous two centuries, it is sufficiently different to merit separate treatment, not least since French spreads rapidly to new domains during the Renaissance.

The Middle French period witnessed the continued rise of prose. If the literature of Middle French rarely reaches the heights of the great Old French epics and verse romances, there is nevertheless much of merit and value. Here we have included two contrasting examples of literary prose (texts 13, 14) and two verse pieces (texts 15, 16) which can render some clues as to the phonology of the period, otherwise almost entirely masked by the orthographical habits of the age which paid much less attention to representing the phonological reality and placed far greater emphasis on semantic and visual considerations. During this period we also see French continuing to make progress against its two rivals, the dialects and Latin. While, of course, the local dialects continued to be *spoken*, the written language progressively is less marked by dialectal features, the rate of their elimination varying naturally from region to region, and from text type to text type. The situation in relation to Latin is more complex. The humanist revival of Latin, bringing with it a renewed interest in the Classics and the translation into French of classical texts, highlighted, on the one hand, the gulf between Latin and the vernacular and the unsuitability of the former to fulfil some everyday functions. On the other hand, some authors, striving to give French the weight and dignity of its classical fore-bear, modelled their use of French on Latin syntactic and lexical usages (see, for example, text 14).

The syntax of Middle French is often characterized as complex, rambling and unstructured. While this is no doubt true to some extent, clear and simple structures could also be employed (see the contrasting passages from *Le Menagier de Paris*, text 17); once again it is important to take the type of text and its function into consideration before making sweeping generalizations about the period. If the syntax of legal texts is heavily influenced by Latin, and has long periods containing a string of loosely co-ordinated subordinate clauses (text 18), the usage in texts which employ French for scientific or technical purposes (text 19), or try to mirror more closely the modalities of speech (text 20), shows greater similarities with modern constructions.

## 13 *Cent nouvelles nouvelles* (mid-fifteenth century)

This is an extract from the *Cent nouvelles nouvelles*, an example of a new genre of anecdotal fiction which pretended to draw its material from everyday events. Thirty-six different narrators tell stories which are then compiled by 'l'acteur'. Here is the eighty-fourth story, said to be told by Monseigneur le Marquis de Rothelin:

**Tandiz que quelqu'ung s'avancera de dire quelque bon compte, j'en feray ung petit qui ne vous tiendra gueres; mais il est veritable et de nouvel advenu. J'avoie ung mareschal qui bien et longuement m'avoit servy de son mestier; il luy print volunté de soy marier; si le fut, et a la plus devoiée femme qui fust, comme on disoit en tout le   5 païs. Et quand il cogneut que par beau ne par lait il ne la povoit oster de sa mauvaistié, il l'abandonna, et ne se tint plus avec elle, mais la fuyoit comme tempeste; car, s'il l'eust sceue en une place, jamais n'y eust tiré, mais tousjours au contraire. Quand elle vit qu'il la fuyoit ainsi, et qu'elle n'avoit a qui tencer ne monstrer sa devoiée maniere,   10 elle se mist en la queste de luy et partout le suyvoit, Dieu scet disant quelx motz; et l'aultre se taisoit et picquoit son chemin. Et elle tant plus montoit sur son chevalet, et disoit de maulx et de male- dictions a son pouvre mary, plus que ung deable ne saroit faire a une ame damnée. Un jour entre les aultres, voyant que son mary ne   15 respondoit mot a chose qu'elle proposast, le suyvant par la rue, devant tout le monde cryoit tant qu'elle povoit: 'Vien ça, traistre! parle a moy. Je suis a toy, je suis a toy!' Et mon mareschal, qui estoit devant, disoit a chacun mot qu'elle disoit: 'J'en donne ma part au deable, j'en donne ma part au deable!' Et ainsi la mena tout du long   20 de la ville de Lille toujours cryant: 'Je suis a toy'; et l'autre respon- doit: 'J'en donne ma part au deable!' Tantost après, comme Dieu voulut, ceste bonne femme mourut, et l'on demandoit a mon mareschal s'il estoit fort courroucé de la mort de sa femme; et il disoit que jamais si grand eur ne luy advint, et que si Dieu luy eust   25 donné un souhait a choisir, il eust demandé la mort de sa femme, 'laquelle, disoit il, estoit tant male et obstinée en malice que, si je la savoye en paradis, je n'y vouldroye jamais aller tant qu'elle y fust, car impossible seroit que paix fust en nulle assemblée ou elle fust. Mais je suis seur qu'elle est en enfer, car oncques chose creé   30 n'approucha plus a faire la maniere des deables qu'elle faisoit.' Et puis on luy disoit: 'Et vrayement il vous fault remarier et en querre une bonne, paisible et preude femme. – Maryer! disoit il; j'aymeroye mieulx me aller pendre au gibet que jamais me rebouter ou dangier de trouver enfer, que j'ay, la Dieu mercy, a ceste heure   35 passé.' Ainsi demoura et est encores. Ne sçay je qu'il fera.**

(From *Conteurs français du XVIe siècle*. Textes présentés et annotés par Pierre Jourda (Paris, Gallimard, 1965), pp. 303–4.)

[While (we are waiting for) someone else to come forward to tell some good story, I shall compose a short one, which will take hardly any time at all; but it is true and happened recently. I had a marshal who had served me well and for a long time in his job; and he decided to get married; and he did so, and to the most dissolute woman – so it was said – in the whole country. [6] And when he realized that neither by good or ill could he persuade her from her evil ways, he abandoned her, and no longer lived with her, but fled her like a storm; for if he had known her to be in one place, he would never have gone there, but rather in the opposite direction. When she saw that he fled her in this way, and that she had no one to scold or to show her dissolute ways, she set out to look for him and followed him everywhere, saying God only knows what; and he kept quiet and went on his way. [12] And she continued all the more to ride her little horse and to say evil things and to curse her husband more than any devil could do to a damned soul. One day, seeing that her husband didn't respond to anything she said, following him down the road she shouted out in front of everyone as loud as she could: [17] 'Come here traitor!, speak to me. I'm yours, I'm yours!'. And my marshal, who was in front, said in reply: 'I give my share to the devil, I give my share to the devil!'. And he fled from her in this way all through the town of Lille, one always calling out: 'I'm yours'; and the other replied, 'I give my share to the devil!'. [22] Soon after, as it pleased God, this good woman died, and the marshal was asked whether he was very upset by the death of his wife; and he said that he had never had such good fortune and that if God had granted him the choice of one wish, he would have asked for the death of his wife, 'who, he said, was so evil and fixed in her malice that, if I knew she were in paradise, I would never want to go there as long as she were there, for it would be impossible for there to be peace in any gathering where she was. [30] But I'm certain she's in hell, for never has any created thing acted more like devils than she did'. And then people said to him: 'and indeed you ought to remarry and find yourself a good, peaceful and honourable wife'. [33] 'Marry!, he said, I would rather hang myself from the gallows than ever put myself again in the danger of finding hell which, thank God, I have escaped at this time.' Thus he remained and is still. And I do not know what he will do.]

## COMMENTARY

### Who is the author?

There is much dispute about the identity of 'l'acteur', the anonymous editor of the tales; various suggestions have been made about his identity, including the names of some of the contributors such as Antoine de la Sale, 'M. de la Roche' or Philippe Pot, and Philippe de Laon. Whatever the case, it seems that the tales were composed between 1456 and 1462 for Philip the Good, Duke of Burgundy, by men of his court and that the work was equally intended for a court audience. There is only one extant manuscript which dates from 1480–90 and is now located in Glasgow University Library (Hunter 252).[a]

## Orthography

If one allows for the inadequacies of the Latin alphabet for transcribing the vernacular, the spelling of twelfth- and thirteenth-century texts had represented pronunciation relatively well. However, from about the late thirteenth century on, the control of spelling fell into the hands of the *praticiens* or legal clerks, men of restricted learning employed to copy the increasing number of texts not only in Latin but also in French. A number of factors helped to widen the gap between spelling and pronunciation. First, the *praticiens* peppered their French forms with non-pronounced etymological letters, perhaps influenced by their Latin writing habits; here, for example, we find *advenu* (l. 3), *compte* (l. 1, see below), *oncques* (l. 30). Second, the angular gothic script employed, which used a series of up and down strokes, made it often difficult to read (see Figure 6). Thus, for instance, a *g* was added to *un* to differentiate it from other possible readings (*nu*, *vu*, *vii*, etc.), just as *y* was preferred to *i* particularly in final position (*feray* (l. 2), *luy* (l. 4)). In the case of *sceue* (l. 8) a *c* was added to the past participle of *savoir* to differentiate it from *sen* or *s'en* and from there extended to other parts of the verb. Unfortunately, the scribes failed to realize that *savoir* derived not from *scire* but from *sapere*. A third reason for the widening gap is simply that the pronunciation of French was continuing to change without the spelling reflecting these changes; here then we find *dangier* (l. 35), although it is likely that by this time the *i* had been absorbed into the preceding [ʒ], and *proposast* (l. 16) still showing the preconsonantal *s*. In short, visual and semantic considerations began to dominate over phonological considerations, with families of words being brought closer together and homonyms distinguished. In this respect this text is less encumbered by non-pronounced letters than our next one, which is heavily latinate and shows the tendencies we have noted above pushed to the extreme. Here then we still find *lait* (l. 6) for 'ugly', as yet undifferentiated from its homonym *lait* 'milk'.

a   Jourda (1965: xlvii) mistakenly gives the location as Edinburgh. This edition seems to follow that of Champion (1928) more closely than Sweetser's (1966) which introduces a number of errors.

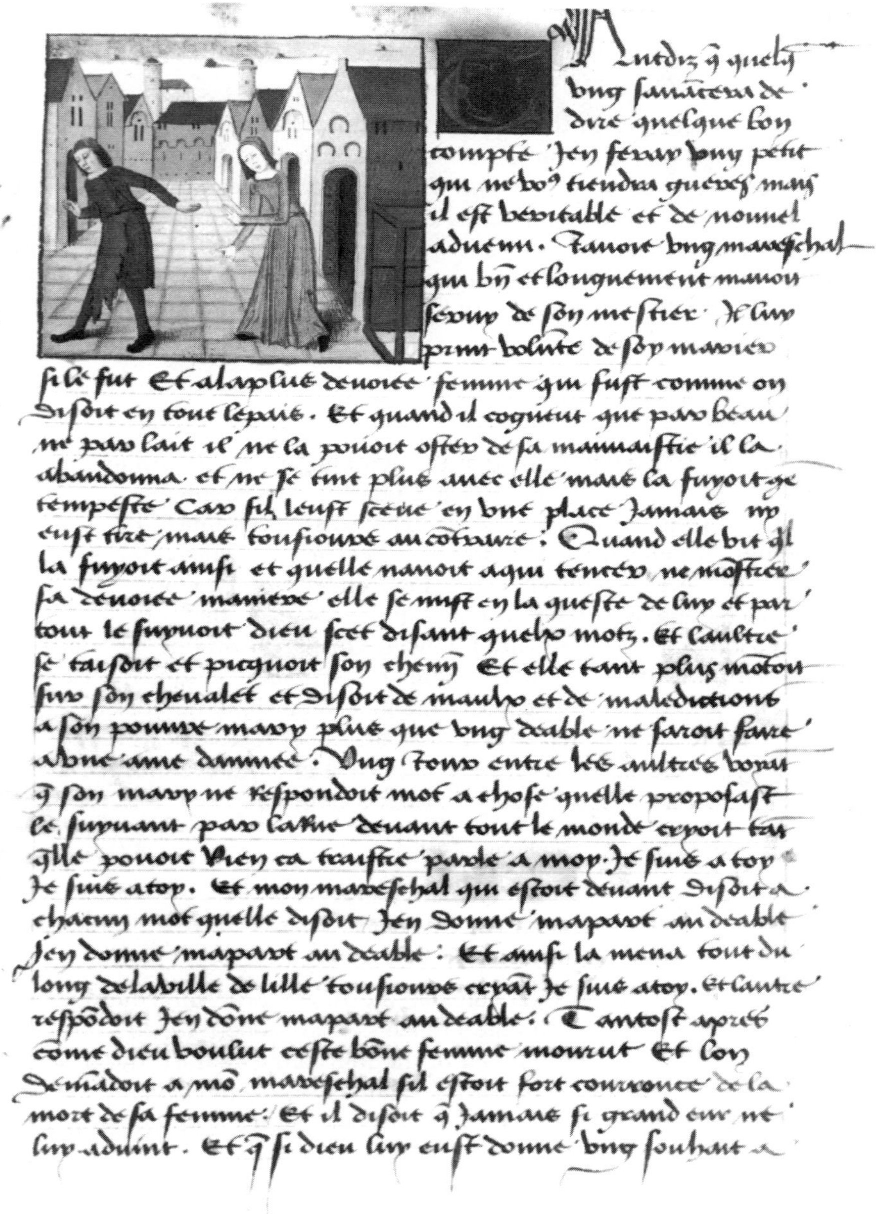

*Figure 6* Manuscript of the 84th Story of the *Cent nouvelles nouvelles*

*Source:* Glasgow University Library, Hunter 252, fol. 175ʳ. Reproduced by permission of Glasgow University Library, Department of Special Collections.

**Morphology**

*Personal pronouns*

A number of changes in the pronoun system occurred in Middle French. During this period the form *je* became established at the expense of the Old French alternatives *gié* or *jou*. The indirect object form of the third person singular in both genders had been *li* throughout Old French; from the fourteenth century on, however, we begin to find *lui*, the tonic form, replacing *li*, first for the masculine and then in the feminine, until by the second half of the fifteenth century the modern usage predominates. Here then we have: *il luy print* (l. 4).

*Verb morphology*

There was a great deal of analogical reworking of forms throughout the Middle French period, ironing out irregularities in paradigms created by the 'blind' working of sound change. This was, for instance, true of first person present indicative forms where *-e* became generalized for *-er* verbs (e.g. *donne*, l. 19), except when the stem ended with a vowel, and *-s* in the other conjugations, with *-s* appearing early on in the verb *être* (*suis*, l. 18), and other verbs gradually following. In the second person imperative, the form without a final *-s* remained common in the fourteenth century, but in the following century the final *-s* began to be present, especially when the stem ended in a consonant; this process, however, is not evident here (*vien*, l. 17). As for the imperfect endings, we find the availability of both the Old French endings and newer forms:

|   | singular | plural |
|---|----------|--------|
| 1 | *-oie, -oies, -ois* | *-iiens, -iens, -ions* |
| 2 | *-oies* | *-iiez, -iez* |
| 3 | *-oit* | *-oient* |

In the case of the first person singular the older form *-oie* continued to be normal throughout the Middle French period, as here (*avoie*, l. 3); *-ois* began to appear in texts at the end of the fourteenth century and in some fifteenth century texts, but remained relatively rare. In the third person singular, on the other hand, the Old French ending *-oie* was replaced systematically by *-oit* (*povoit* (l. 6), *fuyoit* (l. 8), *suyvoit* (l. 11), etc.). In the case of the conditional endings there was likewise considerable variation in the first person endings with the following possibilities attested, *-oie* (*aymeroye*, l. 34), *-aie, -oyes, -oys*. The workings of analogy were perhaps nowhere more obvious than in the past historic paradigms, both as regards the endings and the stems. Here, for instance, we find examples of the reworking of stems in *voulut* (Old French *volt*, *vout* or *voust*), a form based on the past participle and first attested in the fourteenth century and which eliminated the older forms in the fifteenth century (l. 23); and *print*, competing from the thirteenth century on with Old French *prist*, and probably created on the analogy of the past historics of *tenir* and *venir* (l. 4).

## Syntax

### *Loss of the case system*

A notable feature of Middle French texts is the fact that from the early fourteenth century on we no longer find any systematic use of the two-case system. In the majority of cases the oblique came to replace the nominative for two main reasons: first, the forms of the masculine oblique, using *s* as a plural marker, were analogous to those of the main class of feminines; second, the oblique forms were more used in any Old French text than the nominatives since they had to fulfil a wide range of functions. In a few rare cases the nominative survived (e.g. *sœur*, *traître*) or, in the case of imparisyllabics, both the nominative and the oblique remained but were differentiated semantically (e.g. *sire* (also *sieur*) and *seigneur*; *gars* and *garçon*; and the special case of *homme* and *on*). This text then is typical of the period in showing no traces of distinctive nominative forms, although the phrase *la Dieu mercy* (l. 35), with the absence of a preposition and the preposing of the possessive, is a fixed relic of an earlier productive construction.

### *Use of articles*

The articles similarly lost all markers of declension and simply remained as markers of gender and number. Some enclitic forms, however, continued to be common including *ou* for *en le* (l. 35), and *es* for *en les*, which now survives only in certain fixed expressions (e.g. *docteur ès lettres*). This text illustrates well the trend in Middle French away from using the article according to semantic considerations towards using it before all nouns as a general nominal marker showing gender and number. The definite article has lost its demonstrative force, but still retains some of its particularizing force. Articles then were still optional, as in Old French, before nouns used in an abstract or general sense (e.g. *paix*, l. 29), but there are equally examples of articles appearing in these contexts (e.g. *ung deable*, l. 14). Likewise, there is a tendency for articles not to be used after prepositions (*en malice*, l. 27, *en paradis*, l. 28), but they do appear where the head noun is modified, perhaps because of the heightened specificity this implies (*en la queste de luy*, l. 11).

*Use of pronouns*

This extract illustrates well the increased use of subject personal pronouns during Middle French; while we are not yet at the stage of having a subject pronoun with every verb, as was required by seventeenth-century grammarians, they appear much more regularly than in Old French texts, and feature, for instance, in inverted structures (*ne sçay je*, l. 36). Note that at this time it was usual to find the tonic forms (*moi, toi, soi*) before infinitives and participles (*de soy marier*, l. 4). Two comments need to be made about the use of relative pronouns. First, the relatives *lequel, laquelle, lesquels, lesquelles* were greatly favoured, perhaps because they are more explicit in marking gender and number than *qui* (l. 27). Second, the use of relatives was rather loose and *qui* and *que*, *qui* and *ce qui*, etc. were not clearly differentiated; note here: *ne sçay je qu'il fera* (l. 36).

*Negation*

Alongside the use of *ne* on its own, which still sufficed in Middle French to mark negation (*ne sçay je*, l. 36), there was a range of negative particles available, such as *ne . . . mot* (ll. 15–16).

*Word order*

If in some Middle French texts the word order appears complex and latinate (see text 14) and variation is exploited for stylistic purposes, the loss of the case system and of the flexibility afforded by this also meant that in general there was less variation than in Old French. The use of SVC, one of the most common structures in Old French, greatly increased in Middle French prose, as indeed is the case here; in this order the subject, which is typically also the topic of the sentence, occurs in initial position. Marchello-Nizia (1979: 351) notes that whereas in Old French texts the proportion of main clauses with SV never exceeded 50 per cent, by Middle French this rises to between 52 and 75 per cent depending on the text type (see the commentary on text 14 for examples of inversion). Moreover, SV was almost the only word order used in subordinate clauses. This is not to say, of course, that the word order of Middle French texts appears completely modern: there are considerable differences in the positioning of the other parts of speech in relation to the principal constituents. We may note here, for example, the placing of the clitic pronoun before the finite verb rather than the infinitive, a construction which continues to outnumber the modern ordering during the period (*me aller pendre*, l. 34), or the flexibility in the positioning of adverbs (*qui bien et longuement m'avoit servy*, ll. 3–4).

**Vocabulary**

The noun *eur* (l. 25) from *\*agūrium* (for *augurium*) remained in use until the seventeenth century, when it fell into disuse; it survives, however, in a number of derivations (*bonheur, malheur, heureux*). The changing meanings of *mareschal* (l. 3) illustrate well the processes of semantic change. Derived from the Frankish form *\*marhskalk* it literally meant 'horse servant'. Its meaning subsequently evolved along two different paths, the first giving the sense *maréchal-ferrant*, 'blacksmith', where the name is specialized to refer to perhaps the principal 'horse servant'; the second privileging the idea of 'officer' and particularly 'army officer' and thence extending to an officer of high rank. Finally, note that the spelling *compte* is simply an orthographical variant (based on the Latin *computus*) for *conte*; only gradually did the two spellings come to be associated each with a different meaning.

# 14 Alain Chartier, *Le Quadrilogue invectif* (1422)

This literary text contrasts with the previous one in adopting a much more eloquent, rhetorical style which is heavily influenced by Latin usage. Set against a background of war, with the Dauphin forced into difficulty by Henry V of England, Chartier, a supporter of the Dauphin, tries to analyse the causes of France's troubles. He orchestrates a discussion between France and the three Estates of the Realm (the People, Nobility and Clergy), which is full of recriminations and complaints. The tone is therefore polemical, as in the following extract in which the Clergy argues for a return to past ideals of chivalry and loyalty to the rightful king:

> **Reste maintenant le tiers point ou nous avons a declairer quelle obeissance doit estre gardee vers le prince guerroiant pour sa chevalerie et pour ses subgiez. Si fais ma premisse jouxte la tres-griefve sentence de Valere: que discipline de chevalerie estroitement retenue et rigoureusement gardee maintient les   5 seigneuries acquises, et si acquiert celles qui sont a l'encontre defendues.**
>
> **Et qu'est discipline de chevalerie si non loy ordonnee et gardee en l'exercice des armes et des batailles soubz le commandement du chief et pour l'utilité publique?   10**
>
> **Ceste ont gardee si curieusement tous ceulx qui oncques acquirent hault honneur et victoire par proesce d'armes que nulle chose ne se faisoit contre droit de chevalerie ou contre le commandement du chief dont la punicion ne feust capitale ou mortelle. Bien y apparut au fait memorable de Manlius Torquatus, lequel,   15 ou temps qu'il conduisoit les legions rommaines, fist trenchier la teste a son propre filz pour ce qu'il s'estoit combatu aux ennemis contre son commandement, jaçoit ce que il eust la victoire obtenue; et en ce cas la victoire que fist le vaillant jouvencel comme vainqueur ne peut effacier la desobeissance qu'il fist   20 comme transgresseur, pour quoy la rigueur de la discipline chevalereuse vainqui la pitié naturelle du pere, car cellui que Nature admonneste d'estre pere misericors pour le devoir de sang acquiter se monstra juge rigoureux pour la loy d'armes aigrement observer.   25**

> (From *A Medieval French Reader*, edited by C.W. Aspland (Oxford, Clarendon Press, 1979), p. 273, by permission of Oxford University Press.)

[There now remains the third point where we must explain what sort of obedience should be observed towards the prince fighting for his knights and for his subjects. And I make my proposal following the very solemn opinion of Valerius: that knightly discipline which is strictly kept and rigorously maintained keeps those domains which have been acquired and acquires those which are defended against it.

[8] And what is knightly discipline if not the law established and observed in the practice of arms and in battles under the command of the leader and for the common good?

[11] All those who ever acquired high honour and victory through the prowess of arms have always kept this so carefully that nothing was done against the knights' code or against the command of the leader which did not receive capital or mortal punishment. [15] This was clearly seen in the memorable action of Manlius Torquatus who, at the time that he was leading the Roman legions, had his son's head cut off because his son had fought against the enemy against his orders, even though he won the victory; and in this case the victory which the brave young man won as victor could not efface the disobedience he displayed as transgressor, as a result of which the rigour of knightly discipline outweighed the natural pity of the father, for he whom Nature admonishes to be a merciful father to respect the duty of family ties proved himself to be a rigorous judge in order to observe strictly the law of arms.]

## COMMENTARY

### Author and base manuscript

The author, Alain Chartier, was born in Normandy, *c.* 1385, but studied at the University of Paris and spent most of his life in the capital; his usage therefore shows very few, if any, regionalisms. Chartier acted as *notaire et secrétaire royal* to both Charles VI and the Dauphin, later Charles VII, with whom he travelled to Bourges in 1418. The *Quadrilogue invectif* was written between April and August 1422, and the base manuscript (Bibliothèque nationale, fonds français 126) also dates from the first half of the fifteenth century.

### Orthography

The influence of Latin permeates all structural levels of this text, and not least the orthography which is heavily laden with non-pronounced etymological letters, as in *subgiez* (l. 3), *soubz* (l. 9), *oncques* (l. 11) and *griefve* (l. 4). If we compare *ceulx* with its usual Old French spelling *cels*, we can see that the vocalization of the *l* > *u* is shown by the *u* and the *x* (= *us*) and that, in addition, the *l* has been restored. Double letters, which are not especially typical of Old French, are now frequent, either for etymological reasons or, as here, as an indication of nasalization (and later denasalization): *admonneste* (l. 23), *rommaines* (l. 16).

**Morphology**

*Adjective morphology*

During Middle French, great progress was made with the assimilation of adjectives derived from Latin third declension ones to the main class, through the addition of an analogical *-e* in the feminine. Less common adjectives tended to be assimilated first (note here *griefve* < *gravis*), with perhaps the most common adjective of this type – *grant* – showing variation over a long period. Adjectives ending in *-al* and *-el* were also often late to adopt a distinctive feminine form, but here, in an early fifteenth-century text, we have *capitale* (< *capitalis*) and *mortelle* (< *mortalis*).

*Demonstrative adjectives and pronouns*

There was considerable reworking of the system of demonstratives during Middle French. In line with the loss of the case system for nouns, adjectives and articles, the distinctive Old French masculine nominative singular and plural form, *cil*, fell, leaving the oblique forms to fill the subject function. The demonstrative pronoun system from about the middle of the fourteenth century until the sixteenth century was as follows:

|          | masculine        | feminine         |
|----------|------------------|------------------|
| singular | *cestui, celui*  | *ceste, cele*    |
| plural   | *ceus-ci, ceus-la* | *cestes, celes* |

Thus we find here, *tous ceulx qui* (l. 11) and *cellui que* (l. 22). The adjectival forms for the same period were:

|          | masculine                        | feminine                    |
|----------|----------------------------------|-----------------------------|
| singular | *cest* + V, *cel* + V            | *ceste, cele*               |
|          | *ce* + C                         |                             |
| plural   | *ces*                            | *ces* (*cestes* now very rare) |

As is illustrated in *Ceste ont gardee ... tous ceulx ...* (l. 11), both these paradigms continued to be used in either pronominal or adjectival functions.

*Verb morphology*

Two past historic forms merit attention. *Vainqui* (l. 22) does not yet show the analogical *-t* (see text 13), which only became frequent in the second half of the fifteenth century. *Peut* (l. 20), on the other hand, modelled on *fut*, has replaced earlier *pot*.

**Syntax**

During Middle French, and especially in the sixteenth century, the style of many authors was influenced by Latin syntactic patterns. This influence might take the form of direct imitation of Latin constructions such as the use of the so-called *relatif de liaison* (see texts 17 and 18), or of the accusative and infinitive structure after verbs of thinking or saying, or copying the Latin ablative absolute construction. Alternatively the influence may be less tangible, as here the phrasing appears to try to emulate Latin classical style.

*Use of articles*

As in our previous text, we find that the article is still not obligatory with nouns used in a general or abstract sense (*discipline de chevalerie*, l. 4), when nouns are modified by some other part of speech such as an adjective (*hault honneur et victoire*, l. 12), when they refer to an individual or a personified thing (*Nature*, l. 23) and after prepositions (*par proesce d'armes*, l. 12). All these cases of non-usage perpetuate Old French patterns, but the high incidence of them in our extract may also be partly attributable to a desire to imitate Latin which did not, of course, use articles.

*Use of subject pronouns*

The impersonal subject pronoun *il* continues to be optional in Middle French. In line 3 *si* is used in a way common in Old French to fill the sentence-initial slot when the subject pronoun is absent; it is not really possible to translate it in this situation (cf. Marchello-Nizia 1985).

*Use of tenses and moods*

The tenses of Middle French now have a modern look. The subjunctive is used in this extract after a negative antecedent (l. 14) and after the conjunction *jaçoit ce que* meaning 'although'.

*Agreement*

Rules for the agreement of the past participle were not established at this period and there was considerable variation in usage both between authors and within the same text. There are two examples in this extract of agreement being made with a preceding direct object, as is now the rule: *ceste ont gardee . . .* (l. 11) and *jaçoit ce que il eust la victoire obtenue* (ll. 18–19); note in this latter example the possibility in Middle French of inserting the object between the auxiliary and past participle, which Modern French no longer tolerates.

*Word order*

We noted in the previous commentary the increase in SV structures during the Middle French period. However, it is also typical of Middle French usage to find inversion of subject and verb when a complement of some kind – whether a nominal or pronominal direct object or an adverb – was placed in initial position because this complement had a clear relationship to what had gone previously. This so-called progressive word order – progressing from the known to the unknown – might then be triggered by an initial adjective like *tel, semblable, pareil* or an adverb like *tant* or *autant*. Such an explanation certainly seems to account for the inversion in:

> *Ceste ont gardee . . . tous ceulx qui . . .*
> [O     V        S           ]

in which the initial object clearly refers back to the content of the previous sentence. In relative clauses the likelihood of finding SV was much higher, although occasionally the verb was still placed in final position or, as in Modern French, was postponed if the verb was semantically weak and the subject modified (*la victoire que fist le vaillant jouvencel comme vainqueur*, ll. 19–20).

Middle French was much less strict about keeping elements which are grammatically related in close proximity in the clause; for example there is no difficulty about separating *discipline de chevalerie* from *maintient* by a long adjectival phrase (ll. 4–5). Equally, there was greater flexibility than in Modern French in the positioning of adjectives. As for questions, the Old French construction which simply inverted a nominal subject and its verb whether in total interrogation (*est morte m'amie?*) or in partial interrogation (*quant fust avenus chis afaires?*) persisted in Middle French, although there are also some instances of the modern construction with *reprise* during this period (cf. Foulet 1970: 232–35). Here there is an example of simple inversion in line 8: *Et qu'est discipline de chevalerie . . .?*.

**Vocabulary**

There was a great deal of lexical creation in Middle French, which was especially necessary with the spread of French to new domains and the need to find French equivalents for Latin terms in translations. These creations were very often calqued on Latin – and more rarely on Greek – but the influence of Latin did not stop there for it also led to the remodelling of Old French forms to bring them closer to their Latin etymon, and the attributing of a Latin meaning to a cognate French term. All these processes are represented here: for instance, *tres-griefve* (l. 4) is an attempt to mirror the Latin superlative; *capitale*, already borrowed from Latin in the twelfth century, comes from the same root as *chief* (l. 10) which shows the sound changes; and *transgresseur* is a thirteenth-century borrowing from ecclesiastical Latin. The form of *jouxte* (l. 3) has been remodelled on the basis of Latin *juxta* (Old French *jo(u)ste*) and *sentence* (l. 4) has the meaning 'opinion' of its Latin etyma rather than its usual Old French sense of 'judgement'. Note that *curieusement* (l. 11) means 'carefully' and did not acquire its modern sense of 'curiously' until the sixteenth century.

A final point to note is the use of a number of co-ordinated pairs of synonyms or near-synonyms, which was a frequent Middle French stylistic device: *estroitement retenue et rigoureusement gardee* (l. 5); *capitale ou mortelle* (l. 14). Once again the importance of translation in this period may have a role to play in the frequency of these binomials; some authors may have believed that a single French word could not suffice to render a single Latin term.

## 15 *Le Testament Villon* (mid-fifteenth century)

In view of the widening gap between spelling and pronunciation we are very dependent on verse texts of the period to give us some indication of the important phonological changes occurring during Middle French. This is an extract (ll. 273–312) from the *Testament* by François Villon, pseudonym of François de Montcourbier or François des Loges, who was probably born to a humble family in Paris in 1431; aside from his poetic output, he is perhaps best known for his life of crime, resulting in his spending much of his life in prison or banishment from Paris. The poem takes the form of a mock will:

Povre je suis de ma jeunesse,
De povre et de peticte extrasse;
Mon pere n'eust oncq grant richesse,
Ne son ayeul nommé Orrace;                            4
Povreté tous nous suit et trace.
Sur les tumbeaux de mes ancestres,
Les ames desquelz Dieu embrasse,
On n'y voit couronnes ne ceptres.                     8

De povreté me grementant,
Souventeffoiz me dit le cueur:
'Homme, ne te doulouse tant
Et ne demaine tel douleur!                            12
Se tu n'as tant qu'eust Jaques Cueur,
Mieulx vault vivre soubz groz bureau
Pouvre, qu'avoir esté seigneur
Et pourrir soubz riche tumbeau.'                      16

Qu'avoir esté seigneur ... Que dis?
Seigneur, lasse! ne l'est il mais?
Selon les davitiques diz
Son lieu ne congnoistra jamaiz.                       20
Quant du seurplus, je m'en desmez:
Il n'appartient a moy, pecheur;
Aux theologiens le remectz,
Car c'est office de prescheur.                        24

Sy ne suis, bien le considere,
Filz d'ange portant diadame
D'estoille ne d'autre sidoire:
Mon pere est mort, Dieu en ait l'ame!                 28
Quant est du corps, il gist soubz lame;
J'entens que ma mere mourra
– El le scet bien, la povre femme! –
Et le filz pas ne demourra.                           32

**Je congnois que pouvres et riches,**
**Sagez et folz, prestres et laiz,**
**Nobles, villains, larges et chiches,**
**Petiz et grans, et beaulx et laitz,** 36
**Dames a rebrassés colletz,**
**De quelconque condicïon,**
**Portans atours et bourreletz,**
**Mort saisit sans excepcïon.** 40

(From *Le Testament Villon*, édité par Jean Rychner et
Albert Henry (Geneva, Droz, 1974), pp. 40–42.)

[I've been poor since my childhood,
Of poor and lowly origins;
My father never had great wealth,
Nor his grandfather called Horace; 4
Poverty follows and hounds us all,
On the tombs of my ancestors
– May God keep their souls –
No crowns or sceptres are seen. 8

When I complain about my poverty,
Often my heart says to me:
'Man, don't be so distraught
and don't show such grief! 12
If you don't have as much as Jaques Cœur had,
It's better to live under coarse cloth,
A poor man, than to have been a lord
And rot under a rich tomb.' 16

Than to have been a lord ... What are you saying?
Alas! Isn't he a lord any more?
According to the Psalms of David
'His place shall not know him again'. 20
As for the rest, I wash my hands of it:
It doesn't belong to me, sinner that I am;
I hand it back to the theologians,
For it's the business of a preacher. 24

And indeed, you may well know, I am not
The son of an angel wearing a crown
Decorated with a star or other heavenly body:
My father is dead – May God keep his soul! 28
As for his body, it's lying under a tombstone;
I know that my mother will die
– She knows it full well, poor woman! –
And the son will not tarry. 32

I know that poor and rich,
Wise and foolish, priests and laity,
Nobles, common folk, generous and mean,
Small and great, and handsome and ugly,                               36
Ladies with turned back (low-cut) collars,
Of whatever rank,
Wearing elegant hairstyles and tiaras,[a]
Death takes them all without exception.]                              40

## COMMENTARY

### Author and scribe

The *Testament* was probably composed in 1461–62. The base manuscript
used by the editors is Bibliothèque nationale, fonds français 20041, the
dating of which is uncertain. The editors comment that there are three
different hands in the manuscript and that the scribe of our section was
rather careless, making slips for example, in copying *n* and *u*, and probably not very well educated; in short, 'un professionnel, sans doute, qui
copiait pour copier' (Rychner and Henry 1974: 17).

### Verse form

The verse form employed is huitains (eight-lined verses) of octosyllabic
lines which rhyme in the following scheme: ababbcbc. The syllable count
of lines together with rhyme patterns help to give clues about contemporary pronunciation. Note that at this time the rhyming of homophones
was permitted provided they had different meanings and were of different
word classes: *dis* (V) : *diz* (N); *laiz* (N) : *laitz* (adj).

### Phonology

It is during the Middle French period that the majority of the Old French
diphthongs were levelled to monophthongs. For example, it is clear
that the diphthongs [ue] derived from tonic free [ɔ] and [eu] derived from
tonic free [o] have both reduced to either [œ] or [ø] – depending on
the type of syllable[b] – since *cueur* (l. 13) rhymes with *douleur* (l. 12)
and *seigneur* (l. 15). Similarly [ai] must have levelled since *mais* (l. 18) and

a  Literally, 'pad, wad' and perhaps employed here to refer to something used as a base
   for an elaborate hairstyle.
b  Aside from the minimal pairs *jeûne* [ʒøn] and *jeune* [ʒœn] and *veule* [vøl] and *veulent*
   [vœl], these vowels are in complementary distribution in Modern French, with [ø] always
   occurring in final open syllables, [œ] in the majority of final closed syllables, except before
   [z], and the choice of vowel in non-final syllables largely dependent on what vowel would
   appear in the simple term in final position (thus [ø] in *deuxième* because of *deux* and
   [œ] in *jeunesse* because of *jeune*).

*jamaiz* (l. 20) rhyme with *desmez* (l. 21) and *remectz* (l. 23). The fate of the diphthong derived from tonic free [e] was more complex: in Old French [ei] became [oi] and then [wɛ]; as early as the thirteenth century there is evidence of a popular tendency, which occurred especially in Paris and Normandy, to reduce [wɛ] to [ɛ], but equally there was resistance to this change, as later metalinguistic texts testify. Here in this fifteenth-century text we find *sidoire* (l. 27) rhyming with *considere* (l. 25).

Another major change which occurred in Middle French was the loss of vowels in hiatus. It is evident from the syllable count that *theologiens* (l. 23) must have been pronounced as if it were *thologiens*. As regards vowels before a nasal consonant these have nasalized and lowered; there is continuing evidence in this verse of a + N rhyming with e + N, pronounced [ãmə]. What is interesting is that *diadame* (l. 26), a word (ultimately of Greek origin) borrowed into French in the fourteenth century, has also been assimilated to this process.

Two other phonological points are worth noting. The rhyming of words ending in *-estre* with those ending in *-etre* (*ancestres*, l. 6 : *ceptres*, l. 8) confirms that [s] was no longer pronounced in this preconsonantal position. Finally, there was a tendency during Middle French for [ɔ] in both tonic and pretonic position to be pronounced as [u] (spelling *ou* for *o*), giving, for instance, *chouse* for *chose*; this is perhaps suggested by the spelling of *doulouse* (l. 11), although the spelling is typical of the age in not being a good reflection of pronunciation habits (e.g. *soubz*, l. 16; *beaulx*, l. 36).

## Morphology

*El* (l. 31) is a northern variant of the third person singular feminine subject pronoun. Note that whereas the first person present indicative forms of non *-er* verbs all end in *s* or *z*, testifying to the workings of analogy, the second person imperatives do not have a final *-s* (*doulouse*, l. 11; *considere*, l. 25), and the future forms of verbs with a stem ending in *-r* still have a reduced form with loss of schwa [ə]: *demourra* (l. 32).

## Syntax

### Use of the subjunctive

The main-clause use of the subjunctive without an introductory *que* to express a wish continues to be productive during Middle French. There are two examples of it here, in lines 7 and 28.

### Word order

The word order CSV had been rare in Old French but became characteristic of Middle French usage notably when the subject was a pronoun.

In this poem it is used very effectively for expressive purposes, for example in *Povre je suis* (l. 1), which places the key word at the beginning of the line – as it also is in lines 5 and 15 – or in the last of our stanzas. In Old and Middle French it was equally possible for *pas* to precede negative *ne* (l. 32).

## Vocabulary

The verb *grementer* (l. 9) (also found as *gaimenter, gramenter*) is thought to be a hybrid formed from the Germanic exclamation *\*wai!* 'alas!' and the Latin-based *lamenter. Lasse!* (l. 18) was a common exclamation in Old and Middle French; the masculine form of the adjective now survives in the exclamation *hélas!*. *Trace* (l. 5) derived from *\*tractiare* has the meaning 'pursue, dog'; its modern meaning, 'lay out, map out, trace' did not appear before the sixteenth century. *Bureau* (l. 14) is an excellent example of how semantic change can be caused by metonymy, that is when there is real-world contact between the old meaning and the new. *Bure* or its derivative *bureau* originally referred, as here, to a type of coarse cloth. Since this cloth was frequently used on the top of writing desks, the meaning extended to refer to not just the part, but the whole object and from there further extended to refer to the room in which the table was typically situated and thence to a committee meeting in such a room. Lastly, we may note the enumeration of the last stanza, which is not uncommon for the period; here we find pairs of antonyms.

# 16 *La Farce de Maître Pathelin* (mid-fifteenth century)

This text is comparable to text 7, the extract from *Le Jeu de saint Nicolas*, since it is also a farce which, if aimed at a cultivated public, nevertheless seems to represent more informal, casual speech. The usage is therefore in sharp contrast to the careful, eloquent prose of Chartier (text 14). As ever, great care must be taken about making suppositions about spoken usage on the basis of literary texts, especially since the drama is in rhyming verse. In this brief extract (ll. 1007–34) the draper realizes that he has been tricked by the lawyer Pathelin:

LE DRAPPIER

Quoy? Dea, chascun me paist de lobes,
chascun m'enporte mon avoir
et prent ce qu'il en peult avoir.
Or suis je le roy des meschans:                                   4
mes[me]ment les bergiers des champs
me cabusent. Ores le mien,
a qui j'ay tousjours fait du bien,
il ne m'a pas pour bien gabbé:                                    8
il en viendra au pié l'abbé,
par la benoiste couronnee!

THIBAULT AIGNELET, BERGIER

Dieu vous doint benoiste journee
et bon vespre, mon seigneur doulx!                                12

LE DRAPPIER

Ha! es tu la, truant merdoulx
Quel bon varlet! Mais a quoy faire?

LE BERGIER

Mais qu'il ne vous vueille desplaire,
ne sçay quel vestu de roié,                                       16
mon bon seigneur, tout deroié,
qui tenoit ung fouet sans corde,
m'a dit ... mais je ne me recorde
point bien au vray que ce peult estre.                           20
Il m'a parlé de vous, mon maistre,
je ne sçay quelle adjournerie ...
Quant a moy, par saincte Marie,
je n'y entens ne gros ne gresle.                                 24
Il m'a broullé de pelle mesle
de brebis a ... de relevee,
et m'a fait une grant levee
de vous, mon maistre, de boucler.                                28

(From *La Farce de Maître Pierre Pathelin*. Texte établi et
traduit, introduction, notes, bibliographie et chronologie
par Jean Dufournet (Paris, Flammarion, 1986), pp. 138, 140.)

[THE DRAPER
What? My word! everyone is feeding me deceits,
everyone is stealing my wealth from me
and takes what he can get of it.
Now I am king of the unfortunate:                                    4
even the shepherds in the fields
deceive me. Now my man,
whom I have always treated well,
will not get away with mocking me:                                   8
he will be made to repent at the feet of the abbot,
by the blessed Virgin Mary!

THIBAULT AIGNELET, SHEPHERD
May God grant you a good day
and a pleasant evening, my lord!                                     12

THE DRAPER
Ah! Are you there, you filthy traitor?
A good servant you are! But good for what?

THE SHEPHERD
Not wanting to offend you,
Some man or other dressed in striped cloth,                          16
my good lord, and completely dishevelled,
who was holding a whip without a rope,[a]
said to me . . . but I don't remember
correctly what it could be about.                                    20
He spoke to me about you, my master,
about some writ or other to be served . . .
As for me, by holy Mary,
I understand not a jot about it.                                     24
He got me all jumbled up
(talking) about sheep at . . . in the afternoon
he reproached me greatly,
my master, on your behalf.]                                          28

## BRIEF COMMENTARY

### The advent of printing

So far the text of our extracts has been based on extant manuscripts.
However, from 1470 on printing presses were established in Paris and by
the end of the fifteenth century there were probably about a hundred
presses in Paris and Lyons. Initially the majority of printed works were

a   This refers to an usher or bailiff with his wand.

in Latin, but gradually more and more texts were in French. This had important consequences for the standardization of the vernacular since printers tended to prefer forms which were not strongly localized and had to address the problem of different authors' orthographic practices.

The *Farce de Maître Pathelin* was written and first performed some time between 1456 and 1469. The version here is based on the first printed edition by Guillaume Le Roy which appeared in Lyons in either 1485 or 1486, some twenty years later.[b]

### Verse form and phonology

As in the previous extract, the verse form is helpful to the philologist in disclosing something about the phonological system of the period. This text is written in octosyllabic rhyming couplets. We have a number of indications of the reduction of diphthongs to simple vowels including the rhyme of *estre* and *maistre* (ll. 20–21), and the syllable count of the lines containing the words *paist* (l. 1), *peult* (l. 3), etc. We have clear evidence too that the etymological letters which have been restored to the spelling are not pronounced: thus *champs* (l. 5) rhymes with *meschans* (l. 4). The *l* of *peult* (< *potet*, l. 3) has perhaps been inserted on the analogy of a verb like *vouloir* where the *l* is etymological. Finally, there are occasional forms which suggest that while the text is broadly written in the language of the Île-de-France, there are still, even in the fifteenth century, traces of regional usage. In our extract *merdoulx* (l. 13; for *merdeux*) rhymes with *doulx* (l. 12): the non-differentiation of [ou] to [eu] was a feature typical of the Picard and Norman dialects.

### Morphology

Two verb forms are worthy of note. *Doint* (l. 11) is the usual Old French present subjunctive of *donner*, not yet replaced by the analogical formation *donne*. On the other hand, the future of *venir* is *viendra* (l. 9), which has been remodelled on the basis of the stressed present indicative stem, perhaps encouraged by the homophony of the earlier form *vendra* with the future of *vendre*.

### Vocabulary

A number of exclamations (*Dea*, l. 1; *Ha!*, l. 13), expressions such as *ne gros ne gresle* (l. 24) or *pelle mesle* (l. 25), and rather coarse terms such as *merdoulx* (l. 13) help to characterize the informal usage of lower-class

---

b   A facsimile of this edition can be found in Émile Picot (ed.), *Maistre Pierre Pathelin. Reproduction en fac-similé de l'édition imprimée vers 1485 par Guillaume Le Roy à Lyon* (Paris, Société nouvelle de librairie et d'édition Cornély et Cie, 1907).

speakers. The prefix *ca-* in *cabusent* (l. 6) may be an instance of the pejorative prefix of Picard origin (Guiraud 1986: 32) which is found in a number of words including *cabosse* and *caboche*. *Vespre* is still employed here with its etymological meaning of 'evening' (l. 12); today *vêpres* is reserved for the specialized meaning of 'vespers, evening prayer'.

# 17 *Le Menagier de Paris* (end of the fourteenth century)

We now turn to some examples of French prose in non-literary texts. Here we have two contrasting extracts from a book on housekeeping written around 1394 by an anonymous, but clearly well educated and prosperous, bourgeois for his much younger wife; it covers a wide range of matters including gardening, the keeping of horses, hawking, and cookery. The style and use of French within this text vary greatly according to the subject matter. In the first passage, the opening of the prologue, the tone is formal and, in the words of the editors, 'characteristic of fourteenth-century prose at its most unreadable, where a long succession of sub-ordinate clauses keeps the reader waiting in vain for a main verb, and where the author's probable professional association with the law leads him to introduce a series of pleonastic doublets in the legal style' (Brereton and Ferrier 1981: lviii). Elsewhere, as in the passage detailing how to cook sturgeon, the style is clear and concise, the instructions are simply conveyed, and the tone is much more informal. Once again we have a clear illustration, and here within the same text of one author, that variation was just as much a feature of the usage of earlier periods as it is today.

Here is the beginning of the *Prologue*:

> Chiere seur, pour ce que vous estans en l'eage de quinze ans et
> la sepmaine que vous et moy feusmes espousez, me priastes que
> je espargnasse a vostre jeunesse et a vostre petit et ygnorant
> service jusques a ce que vous eussiez plus veu et apris; a laquelle
> appreseure vous me promectiez d'entendre songneusement et      5
> mettre toute vostre cure et diligence pour ma paix et amour garder
> (si comme vous disiez bien saigement par plus sage conseil, ce
> croy je bien, que le vostre) en moy priant humblement en nostre
> lit, comme en suis recors, que pour l'amour de Dieu je ne vous
> voulsisse mie laidement corrigier devant la gent estrange ne devant   10
> nostre gent aussi, mais vous corrigasse chascune nuit, ou de jour
> en jour, en nostre chambre et vous ramenteusses les desconte-
> nances ou simplesses de la journee ou journees passees et vous
> chastiasse s'il me plaisoit; et lors vous ne fauldriez point a vous
> amender selon ma doctrine et correption et feriez tout vostre   15
> pouoir selon ma voulenté, si comme vous disiez. Si ay tenu a grant
> bien et vous loe et scay bon gré de ce que vous m'en avez dit, et
> m'en est depuis souventesfoiz souvenu.

This is from the section on cooking fish:

> Esturgon. Eschaudez, ostez le limon, couppez la teste et la fendez
> en deux. Et premierement le fendez au long par le ventre, comme   20
> l'en fait ung pourcel; puis soit wydié, tronçonné, et mis cuire en

vin et en eaue; et que le vin passe, et que a la mesure qu'il se
esboudra que l'en y mecte tousjours vin. Et congnoist l'en qu'il
est cuit quant la couanne se lieve de legier. Et ce que l'en mengue
chault, l'en y met du l'eaue du bouly et espices, comme ce feust     25
venoison. Et ce que l'en veult garder doit estre mis reffroidier, et
mengier au percil et au vinaigre.

(From <i>Le Menagier de Paris</i>, edited by Georgine E. Brereton and
Janet M. Ferrier, with a foreword by Beryl Smalley
(Oxford, Clarendon Press, 1981), pp. 1, 239.)

[Dear sister, because you are aged fifteen and the week in which we were
married you asked me to be indulgent of your youth and of your small
and ignorant service until you had seen and learnt more; [4] you promised
me to listen carefully to this instruction and to give all your care and
attention to keeping my peace and love (as you said most wisely following
wiser advice, I do believe, than your own), asking me humbly in our bed,
as I am mindful, that for the love of God I should not insultingly correct
you in front of strangers, or indeed in front of our servants, but that I
should correct you each night, or from day to day, in our chamber and
remind you of the misdeeds or foolish acts of the day or past days and
chastise you as it pleased me; [14] and then you would not fail to rectify
your behaviour according to my advice and correction and you would do
all you could according to my will, as you said. I considered this very
highly and praise and thank you for what you said to me, and I have
recalled it frequently since.

[19] Sturgeon. Take the scales off, remove the gut, cut off the head and
split it in two. And first split it lengthwise along the stomach, as one does
a piglet; then it must be gutted, cut into pieces, and put to cook in wine
and water; and if the wine goes and if in time it evaporates, then keep
adding wine to it. [23] And you know it's cooked when the skin lifts up
gently. And if you want to eat it hot, put it in boiling water with spices
as if it were venison. And what you want to keep must be left to get cold,
and eaten with parsley and vinegar.]

## Base manuscript

There are three surviving manuscripts of this text. The base one used here
(Bibliothèque nationale, fonds français 12477) dates from the fifteenth
century and was probably copied in either the north of France or in
Hainaut judging by the style of its decoration and the presence of certain
northern forms (note, for instance, *wydié*, l. 21).

**Phonology and orthography**

Many of the features which we have seen to be characteristic of Middle French orthography are represented. We find the visual devices to aid legibility (*ygnorant*, l. 3, *ung*, l. 21), the accumulation of non-pronounced etymological letters (*sepmaine*, l. 2 < *septimāna*) and the doubling of consonant symbols (*couppez*, l. 19, *reffroidier*, l. 26). It is also evident, from comparison of this text with Middle French verse texts, that the spelling is conservative and does not reflect the sound changes of the age. The spelling then does not show the absorption of [i] after a [ʃ] or [ʒ] (*chiere*, l. 1, *corrigier*, l. 10, *mengier*, l. 27), nor the loss of vowels in hiatus (*eage*, l. 1, *veu*, l. 4), and allows both *saigement* (l. 7) and *sage* (l. 7). Note, however, that there is a possible hint at use of [u] for [ɔ] in the spelling of *voulenté* (l. 16).

**Morphology**

*Adjective morphology*

Present participle forms, which follow the pattern of Latin third declension adjectives, rarely have an *-e* in the feminine in Middle French texts. An example of this is provided in line 1 where *estans* refers to the wife.

*Verb morphology*

Once again the main interest as regards the morphology of the text concerns verbs. Gradually during the course of Middle French there was some unifying of the stem of verbs where sound change had created two different stems. However, in the case of the verb *lever*, derived from *levare*, the two present tense stems remained, tonic *liev-* resulting from the diphthongization of tonic free [ɛ] and *lev-*, the weak stem. Where the present tense stem ended in a vowel, the first person present indicative forms continued characteristically not to have a final *-s* (*croy*, l. 8, *scay*, l. 17). The forms of the verb *vouloir* are unusual in that during Middle French authors generally used *voult*, *voudrent* for the past historic, but preferred the forms with *s* in the stem for the imperfect subjunctive *voulsisse* (l. 10; see Marchello-Nizia 1979: 226).

**Syntax**

*Use of pronouns*

Various features of Middle French use of personal pronouns are illustrated in these passages. First, while much more common, the use of subject pronouns is by no means obligatory, and a verb may still be introduced by *si* as in Old French: *si ay tenu* (l. 16). Second, it is usual to have the stressed forms preceding infinitives and participles as in *en moy priant* (l. 8). Third, the stressed forms come to replace the unstressed forms in co-ordinated constructions in Middle French; Old French *vous et je* here has become *vous et moy* (l. 2). Finally, note that the husband addresses his wife as *vous*; the choice of pronoun may be a mark of respect.

### Use of the subjunctive

All persons of the imperfect subjunctive continue to be in common use in Middle French, and here we have a series of first person forms dependent on the verb *prier* (ll. 8ff). The third person present subjunctive is used in the recipe for the instructions alongside the second person plural imperative forms.

### Negation

There is an example of a rather late instance of the negative construction *ne . . . mie* (ll. 9–10), which was not much used after the beginning of the fifteenth century.

### Co-ordination

In co-ordinated constructions it was possible, but not essential, to repeat function markers, even where, for example, co-ordinated nouns were of a different number or gender and the 'understood' function marker was therefore of a different form from the one expressed. There are examples of this in *les descontenances ou simplesses de la journee ou journees passees* (ll. 12–13) and in *pour ma paix et amour garder* (l. 6).

### Other constructions

There is evidence of the author trying to imitate a Latin construction in *a laquelle appreseure . . .* (ll. 4–5). In this structure, known as the *relatif de liaison*, a clause begins with a relative pronoun or a relative adjective followed by a noun, but the sense is rather that of a demonstrative, that is 'you promised me to listen carefully to *this* instruction'. Note also the participial construction in line 1, which is typically inserted between a subject pronoun and its verb, and delays the appearance of the main verb. Another common feature of Middle French prose was the extensive use of *que* as a means of linking parts of a sentence in a rather loose way without any explicit indication of the relationship between the clauses; such usages are exemplified in the cooking instructions (ll. 22–23).

*Word order*

As we have already seen, direct objects dependent on infinitives or participles typically preceded them: *pour ma paix et amour garder* (l. 6). Note that the object pronoun of an imperative could either precede or follow it, but that in the second of a pair of co-ordinated imperatives it was usual for the pronoun to be first (*couppez la teste et la fendez*, l. 19), a construction which continued to be used right into the seventeenth century as is exemplified by Boileau's famous line, *polissez-le sans cesse et le repolissez*. Indeed, there are literary examples, albeit archaisms, dating from the nineteenth and sometimes even from the twentieth century; witness, for example, the opening of Musset's poem *La Nuit de mai*, first published in 1835: 'Poète, prends ton luth et me donne un baiser' (cf. Price 1971: 151).

**Vocabulary**

Once again we observe a number of examples of the typical Middle French stylistic device of having co-ordinated pairs of synonyms or near-synonyms: *cure et diligence* (l. 6), *loe et scay bon gré* (l. 17). *Vinaigre* (l. 27) is an example of a compound noun which from the thirteenth century on gradually replaced the earlier term *aisil*.

# 18 Land sale, 23 May 1380

From the middle of the thirteenth century on there was rapid centraliza-
tion of the legal system; with this came a marked increase in the number
of legal documents produced in French and a decrease in the number of
regional features used in them. The following text concerns the sale of
land by Pierre des Hayes to King Charles V for the sum of 200 gold
francs; the land was for the estate of the Château de Vincennes, which,
after Paris, was the King's favourite residence and on which he decided
in 1379 to build the Sainte-Chapelle.

The language used is characteristic of legal documents of the period.
Sentences are long and complex, subordinate clauses are loosely
strung together and many of the structures are latinate. The set formulae,
enumerations and repetitions to reinforce and clarify the sense all combine
to typify legal style.

A tous ceuls qui ces lettres verront, Hugues Aubriot, chevalier,
garde de la prévosté de Paris, salut. Savoir faisons que par
devant Jehan Hurtaut et Gieffroy de Dampmart, clercs notaires
jurez du Roy, notre Sire, establis de par lui en son Chastellet
de Paris, fu personnelment establi noble homme monseigneur        5
Pierre des Hayes, chevalier, demourant à Beautheil, en la
chastellenie de Coulommiers-en-Brie, sicomme il disoit. Lequel,
de son bon gré et certaine science, recongnut et confessa parde-
vant les dis notaires avoir vendu, transporté, quictié et déleissié
desorendroit à tousjours, perpétuellement et promis garantir    10
de tous empeschemens au Roi, notre très redoubté et souverain
Seigneur, pour lui et ses aians cause, l'héritage et tout le droit
quexconques que ledit chevalier avoit et povoit avoir, demander
et réclamer en l'ostel des Hayes, séant en la paroisse dudit
Beautheil, et en toutes les terres, prez, bois, aunoiz, estans,    15
cens, rentes, revenues et autres possessions quiexconques
appartenans et appendans audit hostel, quelles qu'elles soient,
du quel hostel et appartenances la propriété appartenoit et
appartient au Roy, notre dit Seigneur, par la confiscacion de
feu Guillaume d'Andrezel, escuier, au quel le dit chevalier avoit   20
piéçà transporté et délaissié à tousjours ycelle propriété par
certain traictié fait entre eulx. Ceste vente faite pour et parmi
le pris et la somme de deux cens francs d'or du coing de France,
que le dit vendeur en confessa avoir eu et receu du Roy, notre
dit Seigneur, et s'en tint pour bien paié et l'en quicta à tousjours   25
et tous autres à qui quictance en povoit et peut apartenir,
laquele vente et tout le contenu en ces lettres le dit vendeur
promist ... En tesmoing de ce, nous, à la relacion des dis
notaires jurés, avons mis à ces lettres le scel de la dite prévosté.

**Ce fu fait l'an mil CCC quatre-vins le mercredi vingt-trois jours    30
de mai.**

### G. de DAMMART,
### HURTAUT.

(From *Chartes et documents de la Sainte-Chapelle de Vincennes (XIVᵉ et XVᵉ
siècles)* par Claudine Billot avec le concours de Josiane di Crescenzo (Paris,
Éditions du Centre National de la Recherche Scientifique, 1984), p. 377.)

[To all those who will see these letters, Hugues Aubriot, knight and guard
of the domain of the provost of Paris, sends greetings. We hereby declare
that my lord Pierre des Hayes, knight, residing at Beautheil (in the castel-
lany of Coulommiers-en-Brie) was personally confirmed as a nobleman,
as he said (he was), in the presence of Jean Hurtaut and Geoffroi de
Dammart, notary clerks sworn to the service of our lord the king and
established by him at the Châtelet in Paris. [7] This man, through his good
will and certain knowledge, recognized and confessed in front of the said
lawyers that he had sold, transferred, left and abandoned henceforth, for
evermore and promised to guarantee free of all impediments to the King,
our most feared and sovereign lord, for the sake of himself and his descen-
dants, the inheritance and all rights whatsoever which the said knight had
and could have, demand and claim in the domain des Hayes which is situated in the parish of the said Beautheil, and in all the lands, fields, woods,
groves, ponds, quit-rents, rents, revenues and other possessions whatsoever belonging and attached to the said house, whatever they are, the
ownership of the which house and belongings belonged and belongs to
the King, our lord, through the confiscation of the late Guillaume
d'Andrezel, squire, to whom the said knight had long ago transferred and
abandoned for ever this property by a fixed treaty made between them.
[22] This sale completed for and through the price and the sum of 200
gold francs of the coinage of France, which the said vendor confessed to
have obtained and received from the king, our lord, and considered himself
well paid and free from claiming a debt for evermore along with all others
to whom some claim could or may belong, and this sale and all the contents
of these letters the said vendor promised . . . [28] In witness of this, we,
in the capacity of the said sworn lawyers have put the seal of the said
provostry on these letters. This was done in the year 1380, on Wednesday
23 May.]

## COMMENTARY

### Orthography

In a text in which there appears to be considerable influence from comparable documents in Latin, it is not surprising that the spelling shows a
number of unpronounced etymological letters, as in *redoubté* (l. 11) or

*traictié* (l. 22). The endings of *confiscacion* (l. 19) and *relacion* (l. 28) have not yet, however, been restored to *-ation*. Of course, in a legal document of this kind what was important was not to represent pronunciation, but to convey unambiguously the meaning. For Middle French scribes, taught to read and write in Latin, the addition of etymological letters was not a hindrance to comprehension (as it may seem to us today), but a natural bridge between their copying of Latin and vernacular texts. Nor is it surprising that at this period their grasp of the processes of sound change was weak; it was quite natural for an *l* to be restored in a word like *eulx* (l. 22) alongside the *x* and the *u*.

## Morphology

### Adverb morphology

As we have seen, adjectives derived from the Latin third declension were, at different rates, assimilated to the main class of adjectives; here *appartenans et appendans* (l. 17) exemplifies the fact that present participles were rather slow to change. This analogical reworking also had an effect on the form of adverbs since *-ment* was added to the feminine adjective; thus here *personnelment* is an adverb regularly formed on the basis of an adjective in *-el* which has not yet acquired an *-e* in the feminine.

A number of temporal adverbs are employed including the compound formation *desorendroit* ('henceforth', l. 10) and *piéçà* ('long ago', l. 21) which was criticized in the seventeenth century and gradually fell out of use.

### Determiners

The forms *ledit*, *ladite*, etc. were frequently used in Middle French; especially common in legal texts (*les dis notaires*, l. 9), they came also to be favoured by certain authors. They could also combine with the prepositions *à* and *de* as here in *audit hostel* (l. 17) and *dudit Beautheil* (ll. 14–15); and *dit* could be used together with a possessive adjective (*notre dit Seigneur*, l. 19).

### Demonstratives

The series of demonstratives prefixed by *i-* (or *y-*) continued alongside those without *i-* in Middle French (*ycelle propriété*, l. 21). It has been pointed out that the frequency of occurrence of the terms with *i-* seems to depend on the text type (Marchello-Nizia 1979: 132–33): while they appear to be rare in drama, they are very common in legal texts, particularly the adjectival forms, as in our extract. Where they occur in literary texts they are often preceded by a preposition, and notably *de*, suggesting that their usage may be guided by syntactic and rhythmic considerations outside the legal domain.

## Syntax

The influence of Latin on the syntactic structure is felt not only in general terms, for example in the long and complex sentences, the accumulation of clauses, both finite and non-finite, and the separation of grammatically related elements (notably subject and verb) by an interpolated clause (see especially ll. 7–22); there are also constructions which are direct calques of Latin ones. For instance, the clause *ceste vente faite* ... (l. 22) seems to be an attempt to replicate the Latin ablative absolute construction (albeit imperfectly since no case distinctions for nouns remain). The *relatif de liaison*, severely criticized in the seventeenth century, is also highly characteristic of legal texts; the new sentence in line 7 begins with the relative pronoun *lequel* which has the value of a demonstrative. By modern standards the co-ordination of elements is lax: words of different gender may be co-ordinated without the function marker being repeated in its correct form before the second term (*de son bon gré et certaine science*, l. 8).

## Vocabulary

The tendency to use co-ordinated pairs of synonyms or near-synonyms is carried to its extreme in Middle French legal texts in which there may even be three or more related terms together. Note, for instance, *avoir vendu, transporté, quictié et déleissié desorendroit à tousjours, perpétuellement* (ll. 9–10) or the accumulation of terms in *terres, prez, bois, aunoiz, estans, cens, rentes, revenues* ... (ll. 15–16).

# 19 Nicolas Chuquet, *Le Triparty en la science des nombres* (late fifteenth century)

We turn now to our example of Middle French usage in a technical or scientific context. This is an extract from the first treatise on algebra written in French by Nicolas Chuquet. In the fourteenth century Nicole Oresme had written five mathematical works in Latin; the pressure to write in French may have come from the commercial world (Flegg, Hay, Moss 1985: 12) since Chuquet's work contains commercial arithmetic and practical geometry alongside the more advanced material. The first part of his *Triparty* is concerned with arithmetic and covers, for the most part, similar ground to that in many of the early printed arithmetical treatises (27). It is written in a clear and concise way, giving the text a much more 'modern' feel than was true of our previous legal text; it is worth recalling here, however, that the differences have been partly masked by the intervention of the editor who has added modern punctuation, apostrophes and accents. As in twentieth-century technical texts the style is made more objective through the widespread use of impersonal, infinitival, participial and passive structures. Here is the opening which introduces the Hindu–Arabic numerals:

> **Nombrer si est le nombre en l'entendement conceu par figures communes artificielement representer ou de paroles perceptiblement exprimer. Pour savoir nombrer et user de ceste science, il convient savoir qu'ilz sont dix figures en cest art, par lesquelles on peult escripre et figurer tout nombre, qui sont telles:** 5
> **0.9.8.7.6.5.4.3.2.1. Dont la premiere devers la partie dextre vault ou signifie ung, la seconde d'aprés en tyrant a senestre vault deux, la tierce troys, l'aultre quatre, et ainsi continuant jusques a la dixieme, qui de soy ne vault ou signifie rien. Mais elle occupant ung ordre fait valoir celles qui sont aprés elle, et pour ce est** 10
> **appellee chiffre ou nulle ou figure de nulle valeur. Et *nota* que en cest art les figures qui sont a la part dextre sont dictes et pevent estre convenablement appellees primes, et les aultres prochaines en tyrant a senestre sont dictes secondes, et les aultres prochaines ensuivans sont tierces et les aultres quartes et ainsi continuant** 15
> **sans fin. *Item*, plus est de savoir que une chascune de ces dix figures estant prime, c'est assavoir estant ou premier ordre, vault une foiz sa valeur; et elle estant seconde vault dix foiz sa valeur; et si elle est tierce elle represente cent foiz sa valeur; et si quarte, mille foiz; si quinte, dix mille foiz; et si sixte, cent mille foiz; et** 20
> **ainsi en augmentant tousjours par proporcion decuple ...**

(From *Chrestomathie de la langue française au quinzième siècle*, par Peter Rickard (Cambridge, Cambridge University Press, 1976), pp. 237–38.)

[To count is to represent symbolically by common figures or to express aloud in words the number conceived in one's understanding. In order to know how to count and to use this science, it is necessary to know that there are ten figures in this art by means of which one can write and express any number, and these are 0, 9, 8, 7, 6, 5, 4, 3, 2, 1. [6] Of these the first on the right-hand side is worth or represents one, the second, moving leftwards, is worth two, the third three, the next four and so on up to the tenth which, on its own, has no value or signifies nothing. But when it is put in a sequence, it gives value to those numbers that come after it, and for this reason it is called cipher or null or figure of no value. [11] And note that in this art the figures which are in the right-hand place are said to be and can conveniently be called first, and the next going left are called second and the next following third and the next fourth and so on without end. [16] Moreover, a further thing to know is that each one of these figures being first, that is first in order, is worth once its value; and if it is (in) second (position) it is worth ten times its value; and if it is third it represents a hundred times its value, and if fourth, a thousand times its value; and if fifth, ten thousand times, and if sixth, a hundred thousand times, and so on always increasing by tenfold proportion . . .]

## COMMENTARY

### Author and manuscript

Chuquet was probably born in the early 1440s. It is thought he set up business in Lyons around 1480, copying, translating and drawing up commercial and legal documents (Flegg, Hay, Moss 1985: 15). Increasingly in demand for his mathematical skills, he completed his mathematical treatise in 1484. The base manuscript, written in Chuquet's own hand, is now located in the Bibliothèque nationale in Paris (fonds français 1346). The work did not, however, appear in print until 1880.

### Morphology

Many of the features new to Middle French, such as the gradual analogical reworking of adjectival forms (compare *telles*, l. 5, with *ensuivans*, l. 15), have been discussed elsewhere and will not be repeated here. There are, however, two important changes to the personal pronoun system that occurred in Middle French and are represented in this text, which merit attention. From the fourteenth century on the third person masculine plural form, *il*, acquired a final *-s* (or the orthographic variant *-z*) on the analogy of other plural forms (*ilz*, l. 4). As regards the stressed feminine singular form, Old French *li* was superseded by *elle* (*aprés elle*, l. 10).

**Syntax**

Middle French syntax was not yet constrained by the often harsh demands for regularity and standardization which so characterized the work of seventeenth-century normative grammarians. In the first sentence of our extract *conceu* is followed by *par* but *exprimer* by *de*; the parallel free variation of *par* and *de* in passive structures in Middle French did not suit later tastes which introduced a semantic nuance between *par* and *de*, with *de* being favoured when the agent's role is rather inactive, notably with verbs of emotion (*il est aimé de*), and when a state rather than an action is expressed (e.g. *il est entouré de*). We also find here confusion between an impersonal and a personal construction in the use of *ilz sont* (l. 4) which has been made to agree with *dix figures* which follows.

*Use of* si

In Old and Middle French the adverb *si* was sometimes placed between a subject noun and its finite verb to emphasize the relationship between the subject and the quality attributed to it, particularly, as here, in definitions: *Nombrer si est le nombre . . .* (l. 1; see Marchello-Nizia 1979: 257–58); in this example an infinitive is filling the subject slot. As with other uses of *si* which are broadly used to structure the discourse, the particle in this case is untranslatable.

*Word order*

Note that in Middle French, modifiers of infinitives may be placed before the infinitive (ll. 2–3). While the structures of this text are mostly clear and unambiguous, there are nevertheless typical instances of the separation of a subject from its finite verb by an interpolated participial clause (*Mais elle occupant ung ordre fait valoir celles . . .* , ll. 9–10; *et elle estant seconde . . .* , l. 18).

**Vocabulary**

As the use of French spread to new domains, it was, of course, essential to find the necessary, often specialized, vocabulary relevant to the subject. In fifteenth- and sixteenth-century texts *chiffre*, of Arabic origin, was used to denote zero, and was only later extended in meaning to refer to any numeral; for this latter sense Middle French rather used *figure*. The ordinals are referred by the series *prim(e), second(e), tiers/(ce), quart(e), quint(e),* etc. *Prin* or *prim* was occasionally used as an alternative to *premier* during Old and Middle French, but was mostly restricted to certain set expressions such as *de prime face*. *Tiers*, rivalled by *troisi(e)me* from the second half of the fourteenth century on, was not used as an ordinal much beyond the sixteenth century and now only features in set expressions (*une tierce personne, le tiers état*); and *quart* and *quint* had likewise largely given way to *quatrième* and *cinquième* by the end of the Middle French period.

*Senestre* (ll. 7, 14) and *dextre* (l. 6) were the usual words for 'left' and 'right' in Middle French. *Gauche*, first attested in the second half of the fifteenth century, gradually replaced in the sixteenth century *senestre*, which may have been weakened by superstitions about the left hand. *Dextre*, the reworked form of Old French *destre*, likewise gave way to *droit* in the sixteenth century, and *senestre* and *dextre* are now reserved for use in the specialized realm of heraldry. Finally, note that the insertion of pure Latin borrowings such as *nota* and especially *item* into French texts was not uncommon at this time.

## 20 *La Manière de langage* (end of the fourteenth century)

This extract has been included for a number of reasons. First, it is an example of an early French metalinguistic text. In the period before the sixteenth century, when the activity of writing grammars really took off in France, various kinds of metalinguistic texts were produced, and principally in England for the benefit of foreigners. These were: *nominalia* or thematic glossaries which are known from the twelfth century on, and the most famous of which is Walter of Bibbesworth's *Traité*, a verse vocabulary dating from the second half of the thirteenth century; spelling treatises, which also touched upon questions of morphology and syntax; grammars following in the tradition of the Latin grammarian Donatus and bearing the name *Donait*, the most interesting of which is the *Donait françois* dating from the first decade of the fifteenth century and commissioned by John Barton; *cartaria* or *artes dictaminis*, collections of model letters; and finally, what we have here, collections of conversations for travellers and merchants. Second, in providing model conversations for those who needed a practical knowledge of French and a supply of useful expressions and phrases, these texts are a good source of information about informal and conversational usages. Third, this text, like the majority of its kind, was produced in England; it provides valuable information about the status and form of French in England during the Middle French period and about the influence of continental usage on insular speech.

During most of the Old French period, from the Norman Conquest in 1066 up to the middle of the thirteenth century, French had been the native tongue of the English nobility and indeed of some of the middle class. Anglo-Norman was a living, autonomous dialect with, as we have seen, a flourishing literary tradition. Starting with the annexation of Normandy by Philippe Auguste in 1204, however, England was increasingly cut off from the continent; the number of native speakers of French declined and French became for many a foreign language which needed to be learned, especially by the nobility at court and by merchants who retained links with France.

This is a short extract from the longest and most important section of the work which furnishes model conversations for travellers:

**Et quant il venra au matinee, il soi levera sus bien matin, et**
**appellera tantost son chambrer par nom ainsi:**
**'Janyn, dors tu?**
**– Non il, mon signeur.**
**– Que fais tu doncques?**
**– Mon signeur, s'il vous plaist, je sounge.**
**– Reveille toi, de par le deable et de par sa mere ou tout. Quey**
**ne m'as tu reveillié bien matin, comme je te commandoi hier soir?**

5

– Mon signeur, par mon serement, si fesoi je.

– He! tu mens fausement parmy la gorge. Quelle heure est il main-  10
tenant?

– Mon signeur, il n'est que bien matin encore.

– Adoncques ne peut chaloir. *Vel sic:* Adoncques je ne fais compt.
*Vel sic:* Doncques je ne fais force. *Vel sic:* Il ne m'en chaut
doncques.                                                    15

    Ore, leve toy. *Vel sic:* Ore, levez sus tost. *Vel sic:* Ore, sourdez
vous le cul tost, et appareillez à diner'.

(From La Manière de langage qui enseigne bien parler et écrire le<br>
français. Modèles de conversations composés en Angleterre à la fin du<br>
XIV<sup>e</sup> siècle. Nouvelle édition – avec Introduction et Glossaire – publiée par<br>
Jean Gessler (Brussels, Édition universelle; Paris, Droz, 1934), pp. 67–68.)

[And when morning comes, he will get up very early and will imme-
diately call his page by his name in this way:
'Janin, are you asleep?
– No, my lord.
– What are you doing then?                                   [5]
– My lord, if it pleases you, I am thinking.
– Get up for the sake of the devil, or his mother or the whole lot.
Why did you not wake me up early, as I told you to do last night?
– My lord, I swear I did.
– Oh! You're lying through your teeth. What time is it now?   [10]
– My lord, it's still early in the morning.
– Then it doesn't matter. *Or thus:* Then I don't mind. *Or thus:* Then
I don't care. *Or thus:* Then I'm not bothered.

    Then get up. *Or thus:* Now get up quickly. *Or thus:* Get off your [16]
backside and prepare for breakfast'.]


## COMMENTARY

### Author and base manuscript

The text, which is anonymous, was composed in 1396. The presence of a
number of anglicisms in the conversations, the inclusion of unusual forms
(e.g. *commandoi*, l. 8, *fesoi*, l. 9), and slips such as the incorrect use of
gender (*au matinee*, l. 1) and the use of *quey* (l. 7) for 'why?', nevertheless make it quite clear he was not a native speaker of French himself
and emphasize the decline in the knowledge of French in England at this
time. References in the text to Orléans perhaps suggest that this is where
he was a student. The base manuscript, British Library Harley 3988, shows
Anglo-Norman traits.

**Anglo-Norman features**

In an interesting study Kristol (1989) analysed Anglo-Norman metalinguistic texts with a view to determining the degree of influence in them
of continental French, and particularly that of the Île-de-France, from the
early thirteenth century to the beginning of the fifteenth century. He used
as his yardstick for measuring the 'Anglonormanicity' of each text four
phonological characteristics of Anglo-Norman: the use of [u] (spelt *u*, *ou*)
for standard [ø] (spelt *eu*); the velarization of [ãn], written *aun* in Anglo-
Norman; the outcome of the diphthongization of tonic free [e] which
became [ɛ] in Anglo-Norman (spelt *e* or *ei*) but [wɛ] (spelt *oi*) on the
continent; and the result either of the diphthongization of tonic free [ɛ]
or of [a] plus palatal which became [je] (spelt *ie*) in 'standard French' but
[e] (spelt *e*) in Anglo-Norman. Of course, as he himself admits, he can
only measure these in terms of the orthography, and it is likely that 'standard' spellings mask insular pronunciations.[a] This is particularly true of
the spelling *an* which always occurs rather than *aun* in our text, but which
from the evidence of other texts most likely had still the velar pronunciation. As regards the first feature, Kristol argues that this text marks the
turning point when the number of regional spellings drops significantly
(to *c*. 35 per cent); the imposition of continental forms was therefore
rather late in England. In short, although the author declares that he
intends to teach 'à droit parler et escrire doulz françois selon l'usage et
la coustume de France' (Gessler 1934: 43), the text still has a light Anglo-
Norman colouring in the spelling (e.g. *chambrer* for *chambrier*, l. 2).[b] What
is perhaps more surprising is the fact that we find forms which appear to
be Picardisms. A notable example here is the future form of *venir* without
a glide *d* (*venra*, l. 1), which is not characteristic of either Francien or
Anglo-Norman. Thus it seems that it was not until the fourteenth century
in England that continental spelling habits really imposed themselves and
that these were not necessarily pure Francien norms, but included possible
Picard traits.

**Syntax**

*Use of pronouns*

The stressed forms of the pronouns *moi*, *toi*, *soi* which were commonly
used before non-finite forms of the verb in Middle French were also occasionally employed before finite forms, but only when they fell in absolute

a   Another indication of the failure of the spelling to reflect pronunciation is furnished by
    *serement* (l. 9) in which the internal [ə] would certainly not have been pronounced at
    this time.
b   In a number of peripheral regions, including Anglo-Norman, [o] raised to [u] before
    nasalization took place. The *ou* of *sounge* (l. 6) therefore probably indicates the vowel
    [ū] rather than central [ō] > [ɔ̃] (*songe*) (cf. Zink 1986: 221).

initial position in a sentence (*moy merveil* ... ), were in an elliptical (*je doy plus amer, et vous moy*) or co-ordinated structure (*Dieu et toy, sire, regracie*), or followed an imperative (*estudie toy* ... ) (Marchello-Nizia 1979: 188–89). The example here *il soi levera* (l. 1) appears, therefore, to be idiosyncratic. Note that there is variation as to whether to introduce an impersonal construction with *il* or not (*il venra*, l. 1; but *adoncques ne peut chaloir*, l. 13).

## Contradiction and denial

We have already seen a number of ways in which *si* could be used during Old and Middle French. Another one is illustrated here by *si fesoi je* (l. 9) in which the introductory *si* has an adversative sense, contradicting the previous assertion. In Old and Middle French *non* was rarely used on its own to express 'no' as opposed to 'yes', although it frequently occurred with a verb (e.g. *non feras*). In response to a positive question the normal negative response was to use a compound form based on stressed *non* and a personal pronoun, either *nenil, non il* (l. 4), or, more rarely, *naje, naie* (*ne je*).

## Vocabulary

The register of the conversation appears to be colloquial and includes a number of low-register or familiar phrases such as *mentir parmy la gorge* (l. 10), together with expressions which are even rather coarse (*sourdez vous le cul*, ll. 16–17). Alternatives are offered for expressing the same idea in different ways and in the case of the last two lines (ll. 16–17) the variants given seem to get progressively more informal, even though there is a shift from *tu* to *vous*.

The meaning of the noun *le dîner* (l. 17) has shifted radically through its history reflecting changing social customs and habits. According to Ullmann, this meal took place at 9 a.m. in the Middle Ages, at 10 a.m. under Charles V, moved back to 11 a.m. by the time of Henri IV and noon during the reign of Louis XIV. The meal then gradually came to be taken later and later in the day until in the nineteenth century it came to denote the evening meal (Ullmann 1965: 247). This, in turn, has affected the meaning of other related terms, including that of its etymological doublet *déjeuner*.

# IV Renaissance French
## French in the sixteenth century

If, as regards the internal evolution of the language, the sixteenth century continues many of the developments of the previous period, a number of external factors, whether political, social, cultural or religious, combine to make it a key period in the history of French, a time when the vernacular comes to be increasingly viewed as a possible rival and indeed as a successor to Latin, and concerted efforts are made not only to codify but also to 'enrich' the language, in particular by attempting to give it the lexical resources necessary to compete with its classical forebear. We have already noted the impact of the advent of printing from the late fifteenth century on which meant much wider diffusion for the written vernacular, and the effect of humanist attempts to bring Latin closer to its classical purity, rendering it less able to express all that was necessary for modern life. To this we must add the effect of the Renaissance, resulting in France not only in the desire to translate the great classical works into French but also in the import of Italian culture, and the Reformation with its demands for the laity to have direct access to the Bible.

French then steadily consolidated and strengthened its position as it was increasingly used in new domains; even strongholds of Latin such as dialectics and scientific disciplines, such as astrology and the natural and physical sciences, opened their doors to the vernacular. This expansion of French is represented here by two religious texts (the Protestant theological treatise of Calvin (23) and Olivétan's version of the Bible for Protestants (24)), an extract from the important medical texts of the surgeon Ambroise Paré (text 25), the geographical account of André Thevet based on his own voyages (text 26), and finally the use of French in a metalinguistic text (text 27).

However, with the spread of French to new disciplines came an enhanced awareness of the language's inadequacy and calls to improve and enrich it, such as Tory's *Champ fleury* (1529) or Du Bellay's *Deffence et illustration de la langue françoyse* (1549). The doctrine of *richesse*, crystallized in Ronsard's assertion 'plus nous aurons de mots en nostre langue, plus elle sera parfaitte' (Brunot 1966–79: II, 168), meant that new lexical resources were added to French, whether 'learned' words, borrowings from other languages, dialects or registers, archaisms or neologisms. This lexical creativity is perhaps nowhere more evident than in the prose of Rabelais (text 21), but was also necessary in technical texts such as those by Paré (text 25).

If the sixteenth century was undoubtedly preoccupied with expansion, Renaissance scholars also called for regulation of the language, and we find the first serious attempts to analyse and codify it. A constant theme of sixteenth-century writers on French is the assertion that the language is changing too rapidly and needs to be fixed and regulated if it is to have the stability and dignity of Latin. Throughout the century the relationship of French to Latin comes under scrutiny. If, particularly in the first half of the century and in the work of translators, there are conscious efforts to calque Latin terms and imitate Latin constructions, there are also signs of attempts to assert the independence of French, illustrated here, for example, by Meigret's (albeit unsuccessful) attempts to loosen the grip of etymology on French orthography (text 27). This text equally shows that, if the written language of the Renaissance was increasingly standardized, regional pronunciations were still very much alive; even a grammarian of the stature of Louis Meigret records Lyonnais pronunciation traits.

## 21 François Rabelais, *Gargantua* (1534)

For our first example of a sixteenth-century literary work we have chosen
extracts from Rabelais's great comical and satirical work, *Gargantua*, which
was first published in 1534. François Rabelais (1483–1553) was in many
respects a typical Renaissance man of humanist learning, having studied
many subjects in depth including scholastic and biblical theology, medicine and law; but his use of French differs from anything previous in its
exuberant use and display of the *richesses* of the lexicon, its pleasure in
the comic potential of language, and its exploitation of the different
stylistic and syntactic possibilities of the vernacular. If, as in the second
extract, Rabelais's syntax is frequently latinate with a preference for
hypotaxis and imitation of Latin constructions, it can equally be simple
as in the comparison of monks with monkeys of the third extract. In its
creativity and innovation, Rabelais's use of language both characterizes
but also pushes to its limits the variety and stylistic possibilities of
sixteenth-century French, from which other writers could select the register
most suited to their purposes.

From Chapter 14: *Comment Gargantua fut mys soubz aultres pedaguoges.*

**A tant son pere aperceut que vrayment il estudioyt tresbien et y
mettoyt tout son temps, toutesfoys qu'en rien ne prouffitoyt, et
que pys est, qu'il en devenoyt fou, niays, tout reveux et rassoté.**

**Dequoy se complaignant à Don Philippe des Marays, Viceroy
de Papelygosse, entendit que mieulx luy vauldroit rien n'aprendre    5
que telz livres soubz telz precepteurs aprendre. Car leur sçavoir
n'estoyt que besterye et leur sapience n'estoyt que moufles, abas-
tardisant les bons et nobles esperitz et corrumpent<sup>a</sup> toute fleur de
jeunesse.**

**'Et qu'ainsy soyt, prenez (dist il) quelq'un de ces jeunes gens    10
du temps present, qui ayt seulement estudié deux ans. On cas<sup>b</sup>
qu'il ne ayt meilleur jugement, meilleurs parolles, meilleur propos
que vostre filz, et meilleur entretien et honnesteté entre le monde,
reputez moy à jamais un taillebacon de la Brene.' Ce que à
Grantgosier pleut tresbien, et commenda qu'ainsi feust faict.    15**

**Au soir, en soupant, ledict des Marays introduict un sien jeune
paige de Villegongys, nommé Eudemon, tant bien testonné, tant
bien tyré, tant bien espousseté, tant honneste en son maintien,
que mieulx resembloyt quelque petit angelot q'un homme.**

---

a   While this is the form that appears in early editions, the sense makes it clear that another
    participle, *corrumpant*, is required here.
b   The editorial notes offer the variant *En cas* which is a more usual expression.

From Chapter 28: *Comment Ulrich Gallet fut envoyé devers Picrochole.*

**Les letres dictées et signées, Grandgouzier ordonna que Ulrich**   20
**Gallet, maistre de ses requestes, homme saige et discret, duquel**
**en divers et contencieux affaires il avoyt esprouvé la vertus et bon**
**advys, allast devers Picrochole pour luy remonstrer ce que par**
**eulx avoit esté decreté.**

**En celle heure partit le bon homme Gallet, et, passé le gué,**   25
**demanda au meusnier de l'estat de Picrochole, lequel luy feist**
**responce que ses gens ne luy avoient laissé ny coq ny geline, et**
**qu'ilz s'estoient enserrez en La Roche Clermaud, et qu'il ne luy**
**conseilloyt poinct de proceder oultre, de peur du guet, car leur**
**fureur estoyt enorme. Ce que facilement il creut, et pour celle**   30
**nuict hebergea avecques le meusnier.**

**Au lendemain matin se transporta avecques la trompette à la**
**porte du chasteau, et requist es guardes qu'ilz le feissent parler**
**au roy pour son profit.**

**Les parolles annoncées au roy, ne consentit aulcunement qu'on**   35
**luy ouvrist la porte, mays se transporta sus le boulevard, et dist**
**à l'embassadeur: 'Qu'i a il de nouveau? Que voulez vous dyre?'**

From Chapter 38: *Pourquoy les Moynes sont refuyz du monde, et pourquoy*
*les uns ont le nez plus grand que les aultres.*

**'Il n'y a rien si vray que le froc et la cagoule tire à soy les oppro-**
**bres, injures et maledictions du monde, tout ainsi comme le vent**
**dict Cecias attire les nues. La raison peremptoyre est par ce qu'ilz**   40
**mangent la merde du monde, c'est à dire les pechez, et comme**
**mache-merdes l'on les rejecte en leurs retraictz, ce sont leurs**
**conventz et abbayes, separez de conversation politicque comme**
**sont les retraictz d'une maison. Mays, si entendez pourquoy un**
**cinge en une famille est tousjours mocqué et herselé, vous enten-**   45
**drez pourquoy les moynes sont de tous refuys, et des vieulx et**
**des jeunes. Le cinge ne guarde poinct la maison, comme un chien;**
**il ne tire pas l'aroy, comme le beuf; il ne produict ny laict ny laine,**
**comme la brebis; il ne porte pas le faiz, comme le cheval. Ce qu'il**
**faict est tout conchier et degaster, qui est la cause pourquoy de**   50
**tous repceoyt mocqueries et bastonnades. Semblablement, un**
**moyne (j'entends de ces ocieux moynes) ne laboure comme le**
**paisant, ne garde le pays comme l'homme de guerre, ne guerit les**
**malades comme le medicin, ne presche ny endoctrine le monde**
**comme le bon docteur evangelicque et pedagoge, ne porte les**   55
**commoditez et choses necessaires à la republicque comme le**
**marchant. Ce est la cause pourquoy de tous sont huez et abhorrys.'**

[Then his father realized that in truth he (sc. Gargantua) was studying very well and applying all his time to it, that nevertheless he was in no way profiting from it and, what is worse, as a result he was becoming stupid, idiotic, completely foolish and feeble-minded.

[4] Complaining about this to Don Philippe des Marays, Viceroy of Papeligosse, he recognized that it would be better for him to learn nothing than to study such books and under such teachers. For their knowledge was but stupidity and their wisdom but twaddle, corrupting good and noble minds and tainting all the flower of youth.

[10] 'And to prove it, take', he said, 'one of these young people of the present day who has only studied for two years. If he doesn't have better judgement, speech and discourse than your son, and better bearing and civility in company, consider me for ever a bacon slicer from Brenne'. This pleased Grantgousier greatly and he ordered this to be done.

[16] In the evening at dinner the said Des Marays introduced one of his pages from Villegongys called Eudemon, who was so neat, so spruce, so well presented and who had his hair so beautifully combed that he looked more like a little angel than a man.

[20] When the letter had been dictated and signed, Grandgousier ordered that Ulrich Gallet, Master of Requests, a wise and discreet man, whose virtue and wise counsel he had experienced in various contentious matters, should go to Picrochole to tell him what had been decreed by them.

[25] The good man left at once and, having passed the ford, he asked the miller in what condition Picrochole was; he replied that Picrochole's men had left him neither cock nor hen and that they had occupied La Roche-Clermault, and that he did not advise him to go any further for fear of the scouts whose fury was enormous. And he readily believed this and stayed that night with the miller.

[32] The next morning he went out with a trumpeter to the gate of the castle and asked the guards to let him speak to the king about a matter to his advantage.

[35] When the king had been told this, he in no way agreed to open the gate, but got up on the bulwark and said to the ambassador: 'What is new? What do you want to say?'

[38] 'It is indeed true that the frock and cowl attract opprobrium, insults and the curses of the world, just as the wind called Caecias attracts the clouds. The certain reason for this is that they eat the world's excrements, that is to say sins, and as turd-chewers they are sent back to their privies, which are their convents and monasteries, cut off from political conversation as latrines are from a house. [44] But if you understand why a monkey in a family is always mocked and teased then you will understand why monks are shunned by all, both old and young alike. A monkey doesn't guard the house like a dog; it doesn't pull the plough like the ox; it doesn't produce milk or wool like the ewe; it doesn't carry loads like

the horse. All it does is defecate on and spoil everything, which is the reason why it is mocked and beaten by all. [51] In the same way a monk (I mean those idle monks) doesn't work like the peasant, doesn't protect the land like the soldier, doesn't cure the sick like the doctor, doesn't preach or teach like the good preacher and teacher, doesn't bring goods and commodities essential to the nation like the merchant. This is the reason why they are hated and abhorred by everyone.']

## COMMENTARY

### Orthography

Written before the great *querelle de l'orthographe* of the middle of the century (see below, text 27), Rabelais's spelling perpetuates many of the features we have described in relation to Middle French (see especially, pp. 102, 125) such as the use of non-pronounced etymological letters (*mieulx*, l. 5; *faict*, l. 15; *poinct*, l. 29; *repceoyt*, l. 51, etc.), and the widespread use of *y* rather than *i* not only in final position (*luy*, l. 5; *aroy*, l. 48) but also internally (*dyre*, l. 37). Note that sixteenth-century spelling does not show the so-called euphonic *t* in inverted questions such as *Qu'i a il de nouveau?* (l. 37) inserted to remove the hiatus on the analogy of those verbs where the third person singular ended in a -*t* (e.g. *vient-il?*); the comments of grammarians and spelling reformers however make it clear that this was already pronounced by this time.

### Morphology

Morphologically, the usage here is not markedly different from Modern French. The following points are, however, worthy of note. The gender of some nouns in the sixteenth century was different from modern usage and there was hesitation particularly about the gender of nouns beginning with a vowel such as *amour*, *espace*, *orage* or *ouvrage*. Here we find *trompette* being used in the feminine to refer to the person playing the trumpet (l. 32). The stressed possessives *mien*, *tien*, *sien*, etc. can still be used with an article and placed before the noun as in the example *un sien jeune paige* (ll. 16–17). The more explicit relative pronouns, *lequel*, *laquelle*, etc., are highly favoured at this time; they have the advantage over *qui* and *que* of marking gender and number even if they appear to us somewhat more cumbersome. Similarly *duquel* is often preferred to *dont* (l. 21). Note that *que* may be used where in Modern French we would require the subject form *qui* (*que mieulx resembloyt*, l. 19), particularly when the antecedent is *ce*, as in *ce que à Grantgosier pleut tresbien* (ll. 14–15). In the example *et que pys est* (ll. 2–3) the *ce* is in addition not employed. Finally, as regards demonstratives, Rabelais's usage seems to be somewhat archaic in that he persists in using *celle* in its adjectival function, although generally *cette* was preferred by this time (*en celle heure*, l. 25, *celle nuict*, ll. 30–31). The uses of *ce* are more extensive than today; here *ce* is placed in an emphatic initial position and preferred to its rivals *ceci* and *cela: Ce est la cause* ... (l. 57).

## Syntax

### Latinate constructions

Imitating the Latin ablative absolute construction, Renaissance writers favoured unattached participial clauses of the type *les letres dictées et signées* (l. 20) or *les parolles annoncées au roy* (l. 35) which often occurred, as here, at the beginning of sentences or indeed at the beginning of paragraphs, thereby providing a link with the previous idea. Rabelais's tendency to omit personal subject pronouns more frequently than many of his contemporaries may also be viewed as a latinism or archaism. Note especially the absence of a subject pronoun here before *entendit* (l. 5), *ne consentit* (l. 35) where the main clause is preceded by a participial clause.

If the Old French poets favoured paratactic structures, Renaissance prose writers preferred hypotaxis. Sentences frequently begin with a relative adjective or pronoun providing a link with the previous sentence as in *Dequoy se complaignant* ... (l. 4) or *Ce que facilement il creut* ... (l. 30); again we may suspect possible Latin influence here.

### Use of prepositions

There are instances where sixteenth-century French used a preposition where it would no longer be required today. Thus, like many of his contemporaries, Rabelais uses a preposition in the temporal adverbial phrases *au soir* (l. 16) and *au lendemain matin* (l. 32) (cf. Huguet 1894: 288). In passive structures the uses of *de* and *par* are not yet differentiated and *de* is common: *de tous sont huez et abhorrys* (l. 57).

### Agreement

In the Renaissance as in Middle French there was greater freedom in agreement patterns with co-ordinated nouns than there is today. Co-ordinated subject nouns could either be followed by a plural verb as today or the verb could be made to agree with the closest noun as in the example *le froc et la cagoule tire* (l. 38).

### Negation

*Ne* on its own continued to suffice to mark negation in the sixteenth century and it was not until the next century that grammarians prescribed that all negatives should have two parts; there are a number of examples of *ne* alone marking negation in lines 52–57. Likewise *ni* may be used without *ne* as in *ne presche ny endoctrine* (l. 54).

## Word order

If, from the fourteenth century on, SV structures had come to predominate, the sixteenth century retained more freedom to vary word order patterns, often to good stylistic effect, than was tolerated in the following period. No longer did an initial adverb almost automatically trigger inversion, as had been the case during Old French, but this possibility was still frequently exploited, as in *En celle heure partit le bon homme Gallet* (l. 25). There was also greater freedom to separate elements which are grammatically or morphologically related, as in *au meusnier de l'estat de Picrochole, lequel* (l. 26), in which *lequel* refers not to the word immediately preceding it, but to *meusnier*; such sixteenth-century usages were severely criticized by later normative grammarians. Prepositional structures commonly appeared before the verb they modify: *par eulx avoit esté decreté* (ll. 23–24), *sont de tous refuys* (l. 46).

## Vocabulary

These extracts are perhaps most interesting lexically in that they show Rabelais exploiting the full range of lexical possibilities available. Even in the first extract, described by one commentator as 'volontairement monotone' (Marzys 1993: 177), Rabelais displays the richness of the lexicon in the accumulation of the adjectives *fou, niays, reveux* and *rassoté* (l. 3). He contributes to the expansion of French literary vocabulary by including terms from a wide range of sources. First, there are a number of latinisms or 'learned' words, which may be relatively long established in the language such as *peremptoyre* (l. 40) dating from the thirteenth century, or *malediction* (l. 39) or *medicin* (l. 54, replacing Old French *mire*) from the fourteenth, or may be recent calques such as *ocieux* (l. 52). *Republicque* (l. 56), adapted from Latin *res publica* at the beginning of the fifteenth century, extended its meaning from *chose publique* – and this expression was itself employed as a loan translation – to referring to the state in the sixteenth century. The influence of Latin, however, went beyond the simple calquing of words from Latin: *conventz* (l. 43) is a latinized form of Old French *couvent*, *letres* (l. 20) is used in a plural form but with a singular meaning in imitation of Latin *litteras*, and *vertus* (l. 22) is latinate both in having a final *s* and in the revival of its Latin meaning.

A second source of richness for the literary language exploited by sixteenth-century authors was the dialects. *Cagoule* (l. 38) for Old French *cogole* is a Midi form, which is attested for the first time in Rabelais, while *aroy* (l. 48) may simply be a graphic variant of the Gascon form *aray* or may hail from Berry. An important number of words entered French from Italian during the sixteenth century including some very common verbs such as *briller* and *réussir* and words relating to the military and artistic domains; it is likely that *bastonnades* (l. 51) is an Italianism. Later in the century Henri Estienne wrote a number of satirical works criticizing what he perceived to be the over-use of Italianisms particularly in the language of the Court. Such interventions coupled with the growing dislike by the French of Italians particularly after the Massacre of St Bartholomew (1572) for which Catherine de Médicis was generally perceived to be responsible, and the enhanced cultural strengths of French following its own later Renaissance meant that the peak for borrowings from Italian was the period 1540–60.

A fourth source of enrichment was lexical creation using native resources and exploiting the processes of prefixation, suffixation and composition. We may note here, for instance, *testonné* (l. 17) created in the second decade of the century by suffixation or the parasynthetic formation (that is, formed by adding a prefix and a suffix) *espousseté* (l. 18) created at the end of the fifteenth century using *poussière* as its base. Rabelais creates a number of comical words peculiar to himself through composition, such as *taillebacon* (l. 14) or *mache-merdes* (l. 42), and indeed composition, not greatly exploited during Old French, is also favoured by sixteenth-century poets who formed such compound adjectives as *sonne-pieds*, perhaps through imitation of Greek (Rickard 1968: 296).

As regards meaning, *refuys* (l. 46) is given the new sense 'avoided', and *moufles* (l. 7) is commonly used with a figurative meaning during this period to refer to something worthless. Rabelais exploits the semantic potential of the lexicon in puns such as his use here of *retraictz* (ll. 42, 44) in its dual sense of 'latrines' and 'place to which one retreats'.

Finally note that there are a number of terms used which have now either disappeared from usage or have become archaic or literary. *Besterye* (l. 7) has given way to *bêtise* which uses a different suffix, just as *reveux* (l. 3) has ceded to *rêveur*. *Angelot* (l. 19) containing the diminutive suffix *-ot* is now little used except in the specialized field of art history – while the diminutive suffixes were favoured in Old French, the modern language often prefers to use an adjective instead – and the synthetic superlative form *pys* (l. 3) is now largely restricted to such phrases as *tant pis*.

# 22 Michel de Montaigne, *Essais* (1588)

This famous work by Michel de Montaigne (1533–92) was published some fifty years after *Gargantua*. Having studied law and pursued a career in the *parlement* or high judicial court in Bordeaux, Montaigne sold his seat in 1570 and spent the rest of his life reading and writing in the Château de Montaigne. The first two books of the *Essais* were published in 1580, but the third book, from which our text is taken, did not appear until the edition of 1588. With the *Essais* Montaigne created a new form of short prose compositions, recording his thoughts and treating the themes in a somewhat informal and personal way. We may here already see signs of the greater sobriety to come in the following century as the intellectual optimism of the beginning of the century gives way to scepticism. But French by the end of the century is also less dependent on its classical forebear, particularly as regards construction and word order. However, as with Rabelais, there is still much of interest with respect to the lexicon, and we may note Montaigne's preference for concrete vocabulary.

This is an extract from the last essay, *On Experience*, thought to have been written in 1587:

Pourquoy est-ce que nostre langage commun, si aisé à tout autre usage, devient obscur et non intelligible en contract et testament, et que celuy qui s'exprime si clairement, quoy qu'il die et escrive, ne trouve en cela aucune maniere de se declarer qui ne tombe en doubte et contradiction? Si ce n'est que les princes de cet art,   5
s'appliquans d'une peculiere attention à trier des mots solemnes et former des clauses artistes, ont tant poisé chaque sillabe, espluché si primement chaque espece de cousture, que les voilà enfrasquez et embrouillez en l'infinité des figures et si menuës partitions, qu'elles ne peuvent plus tomber soubs aucun reiglement et pre-   10
scription ny aucune certaine intelligence. *'Confusum est quidquid usque in pulverem sectum est.'* Qui a veu des enfans essayans de renger à certain nombre une masse d'argent vif? Plus ils le pressent et pestrissent et s'estudient à la contraindre à leur loy, plus ils irritent la liberté de ce genereux metal: il fuit à leur art et se va   15
menuisant et esparpillant au delà de tout compte. C'est de mesme, car, en subdivisant ces subtilitez, on apprend aux hommes d'accroistre les doubtes; on nous met en trein d'estendre et diversifier les difficultez, on les alonge, on les disperse. En semant les questions et les retaillant, on faict fructifier et foisonner le monde   20
en incertitude et en querelles, comme la terre se rend fertile plus elle est esmiée et profondément remuée. *'Difficultatem facit doctrina.'* Nous doubtions sur Ulpian, redoutons encore sur Bartolus et Baldus. Il falloit effacer la trace de cette diversité innumerable d'opinions, non poinct s'en parer et en entester la posterité.   25

**Je ne sçay qu'en dire, mais il se sent par experience que tant d'interprétations dissipent la verité et la rompent. Aristote a escrit pour estre entendu; s'il ne l'a peu, moins le fera un moins habile et un tiers que celuy qui traite sa propre imagination. Nous ouvrons la matiere et l'espandons en la destrempant; d'un subject   30 nous en faisons mille, et retombons, en multipliant et subdivisant, à l'infinité des atomes d'Epicurus. Jamais deux hommes ne jugerent pareillement de mesme chose, et est impossible de voir deux opinions semblables exactement, non seulement en divers hommes, mais en mesme homme à diverses heures. Ordinairement   35 je trouve à doubter en ce que le commentaire n'a daigné toucher. Je bronche plus volontiers en pays plat, comme certains chevaux que je connois, qui chopent plus souvent en chemin uny.**

(From *Les Essais de Michel de Montaigne*. Édition conforme au texte de l'exemplaire de Bordeaux ... par Pierre Villey rééditée sous la direction et avec une préface de V.-L. Saulnier, 3rd edition (Paris, Presses Universitaires de France, 1978), pp. 1066–67.)

[Why is it that our ordinary language, so simple for all other purposes, becomes obscure and unintelligible in contracts and wills, and that a man who can express himself so clearly in whatever he says or writes cannot find any way in such documents to declare his meaning which does not sink into doubt and contradiction? [5] Unless it is that the 'princes' of that art, applying themselves with a particular attention to choosing solemn words and forming clauses arranged with art, have so weighed up each syllable and so precisely dissected each type of clause connector that they end up tangled up and bogged down in an infinite number of figures and such minute divisions that they can no longer be made subject to any rule or prescription or to any certain interpretation. '*Whatever is cut into tiny pieces becomes confused.*' Who has seen children trying to arrange a mass of quicksilver into a certain number of piles? [13] The more they press and knead it and strive to bring it under control, the more they irritate the liberty of that noble metal: it eludes their art and divides and scatters itself into innumerable bits. It's just the same here, for in subdividing these subtleties men are taught to increase their doubts; and by extending and diversifying our difficulties they are amplified and dispersed. [19] In sowing doubts and then pruning them, the world is made to produce abundant crops of uncertainties and disputes, just as the earth becomes more fertile the more it is broken up and deeply dug over. '*Learning creates difficulty.*' We had many doubts on reading (the glossator) Ulpian, doubt still more with Bartolo and Baldus. The traces of this diversity of innumerable opinions should be effaced; they should not be used to adorn ourselves or fill the heads of posterity.
[26] I do not know what to say about it except that it can be seen by experience that so many different interpretations dissipate and destroy

the truth. Aristotle wrote to be understood; if he failed, much less will a
less able man succeed or a third party rather than a man discussing his
own ideas. By diluting our material we saturate it and increase its volume;
out of one subject we make a thousand and by multiplying and subdividing
we fall into the infinity of atoms of Epicurus. [32] Never did two men
judge the same thing in the same way and it is impossible to find two
absolutely identical opinions, not only in different men but in the same
man at different times. I commonly find some matter for doubt in passages
that the commentator has not deigned to touch. I stumble more readily
on flat ground like certain horses I know that trip more often on an even
path.]

## COMMENTARY

### Morphology

The introduction of analogical verb forms, ironing out irregularities in
paradigms created by the blind operation of sound change, continues
during the course of the sixteenth century; there is, however, considerable
variation in the speed of the analogical reworking, both as regards different
verb forms and in terms of different writers. On the one hand, we may
observe that the Old French present indicative singular forms of *trouver*
(*truis*, *trueves*, *trueve*) have been replaced by forms modelled on the
unstressed stem (found in the first and second persons plural), and here
represented by *trouve* (l. 4). On the other hand, the present subjunctive
forms of *dire* are still *die*, *dient* (l. 3) and have not yet been replaced by
the forms fashioned on the stem of *disant*, that is *dise*, *disent*. The past
participle *poisé* (l. 7) is a strong form based on the tonic stem.

The other verb form of interest in this extract occurs in *se va menuisant
et esparpillant* (ll. 15–16). In Modern French the form *chante* expresses not
only 'I sing' but also the durative or imperfective sense 'I am singing'. In
Old French a verbal periphrasis comprised of the auxiliary verb *aller* or
*être* together with the form ending in -*ant*, e.g. *va chantant, est chantant*,
was frequently used to express the latter meaning. While the use of the
auxiliary *être* was already rare in this context in the sixteenth century, the
construction with *aller* remained common. In the seventeenth century
grammarians such as Vaugelas suggested that the construction should be
reserved for verbs which themselves express some idea of motion, e.g. *la
rivière va serpentant*. Today this verbal periphrasis is rather rare and
considered literary (Grevisse 1993: 1194); the -*ant* form may also be
preceded by *en*, in which case *aller* seems to have less of an auxiliary function and to retain more of its semantic content.

**Syntax**

Montaigne's syntax appears much more modern to us than Rabelais's and there is little or no evidence in this passage of influence or imitation of Latin. We may note, for instance, the use of *est-ce que* in partial interrogation (l. 1) which is attested from the medieval period; the use of *est-ce que* in total interrogation was not, however, attested until the middle of the sixteenth century when it was relatively rare and may well have had a rather emphatic meaning. There is a tendency too for function words to be repeated somewhat more often in co-ordinated structures (e.g. *en incertitude et en querelles*, l. 21), although this is far from being regular. An interesting case of non-repetition is afforded by *se va menuisant et esparpillant* (ll. 15–16) in which, as was quite usual at this period, one *se* suffices for both verbs.

**Vocabulary**

There are some signs of the sixteenth-century penchant for lexical creativity in this extract, although not to the same degree as at the beginning of the century.[a] The example here of *enfrasquez* (l. 8) is the only one given in Huguet (1925–67) and the term is not included by Cotgrave in 1611. The use of *artiste* (l. 7) to mean 'fait avec art' also seems to have occurred for the first time in the middle of the century, perhaps in the work of Thevet. *Primement* (l. 8) is used by Montaigne to mean 'exactly' and his are the only examples with this sense in Huguet; our author also appears to have been innovative in using *cousture* (l. 8) 'seam' to refer to clausal connectors in language.

We may once again note a number of terms which are no longer in everyday usage and would today be considered obsolete, archaic or literary. These include *innumerable* (l. 24) now replaced by *innombrable*, the use of which is first attested in 1584 but only as an isolated example before it reappears at the very end of the eighteenth century; *esmiée* (l. 22) which has been overtaken by *émietter*; and *entester* (l. 25) which is now archaic. *Solemne* (l. 6) was the usual form of this adjective throughout the Middle French and Renaissance periods, but has been replaced by *solennel*, probably formed on the analogy of other adjectives in the religious domain such as *éternel*, *spirituel*. *Argent vif* (l. 13) derived from *argentum vivum* has given way to *vif-argent*. Finally, *peculier(e)* (l. 6) was commonly used in the sixteenth century to mean 'particular'.

---

a   Two excellent sources of information about sixteenth-century lexical usage are Huguet's *Dictionnaire de la langue française du XVIᵉ siècle* (1925–67) and Cotgrave's *Dictionarie of the French and English Tongues* (1611).

# 23 Jean Calvin, *Institution de la religion chrestienne* (1541)

By the beginning of the sixteenth century there were already calls for the laity to have direct access to the Bible in the vernacular. Olivétan's translation of the Bible for Protestants (see text 24) and his cousin Jean Calvin's *Institution de la religion chrestienne* mark important stages in this process, with Calvin's work viewed very much as a statement of belief of the reformed Protestantism which centred on Geneva. Calvin's text represents a number of important features contributing to the development of French in the sixteenth century. It is significant that the work was not originally written in French but in Latin. The translation of classical Greek and Latin texts by such men as Jacques Amyot contributed to the expansion of the lexicon as translators had to seek French means of expressing Latin concepts. Calvin's work was first published in 1536 as *Institutio christianae religionis*; the Latin text was then greatly expanded in the second Latin version of 1539. It is this version which Calvin himself translated in 1541, symbolizing the desire to make religious texts more accessible to a greater range of people, but the French text is in no way a slavish translation of the original. It is true that the style is at times latinate, but Calvin's pedagogical concerns mean that there is also a desire for clarity and simplicity of expression. With its clearer sentence patterns and simpler constructions, Calvin's prose differs markedly from Rabelais's usage and has led commentators to call him 'l'un des principaux artisans du français moderne' (Benoît 1957: 7), paving the way for the strict demands for unambiguous syntactic structures which typifies the work of many seventeenth-century grammarians.

> **Il nous fault maintenant examiner la volunté, en laquelle gist la liberté, si aucune y en a en l'homme. Car nous avons veu que l'eslection appartient à icelle plus qu'à l'entendement. Pour le premier, à fin qu'il ne semble que ce qui a esté dict des Philosophes, et receu communément, serve pour approuver**   5
> **quelque droicture estre en la volunté humaine, c'est que toutes choses appètent naturellement le bien, il nous fault notter que la vertu du franc Arbitre ne doibt pas estre considerée en un tel appétit, qui procède plustost d'inclination de nature que de certaine deliberation. Car les théologiens Scolasticques mesmes**   10
> **confessent qu'il n'y a nulle action du franc Arbitre, sinon là où la raison regarde d'une part et d'autre. Par laquelle sentence ilz entendent l'object de l'appétit debvoir estre tel qu'il soit soubzmis à eslection, et la deliberation debvoir precéder, pour donner lieu à l'eslection. Et de faict si nous reputons quel est ce desir**   15
> **naturel de bien en l'homme, nous trouverons qu'il luy est commun avec les bestes brutes. Car elles desirent toutes leur proffit, et**

**quand il y a quelque apparence de bien qui touche leur sens, elles
le suyvent. Or l'homme en cest appétit naturel ne discerne point
par raison selon l'excellence de sa nature immortelle ce qu'il doibt     20
chercher, et ne le considère pas en vraye prudence; mais sans
raison et sans conseil il suyt le mouvement de sa nature comme
une beste. Cela n'appartient donc de rien au franc Arbitre, à
sçavoir si l'homme est incité d'un sentiment naturel à appéter le
bien, mais il fauldroit qu'il le discernast par droicte raison, l'ayant     25
congneu qu'il l'esleust, et l'ayant esleu qu'il le poursuyvyst.**

(From Jean Calvin, *Institution de la religion chrestienne.*
Texte établi et présenté par Jacques Pannier, vol. 1
(Paris, Les Belles Lettres, 1936), pp. 130–31.)

[We must now examine the will in which liberty resides, if man possesses
any. For we have seen that the power of choice belongs to this rather than
to the intellect. First of all, so that it does not seem that what was said
by the Philosophers and generally received serves as proof that there is
any rectitude in the human will, that is that all things naturally desire
what is good, we must note that the power of free will should not be
considered in any of these desires which proceed more from natural
instinct than from a deliberate decision. [10] For even the scholastic theologians admit that there is no act of free will except where reason looks
this way and that. By this they mean that the thing desired must be such
that it is the object of choice and that deliberation must precede so that
it can be followed by choice. [15] And in fact if we consider what is this
natural desire for good in man we will find that he has it in common with
wild animals. For they all desire what is to their advantage and when there
is some semblance of good which arouses their senses, they follow it. Now
man in this natural desire does not, according to the excellence of his
immortal nature, rationally choose what he should seek and does not
consider it in a truly wise fashion; but without reason and without counsel
he follows his natural instinct like the lower animals. [23] This then has
nothing to do with free will, that is when man is led by natural impulse
to look for good; rather he should discern what is good through sound
reasoning, choose what he has thus recognized and, having chosen it,
pursue it.]

## COMMENTARY

### Morphology

By the sixteenth century the demonstratives with an initial *i-* (*icelle*, l. 3)
were becoming rarer in literary texts, but were not yet restricted to legal
texts. Note that the sixteenth century does not always make a clear distinction between the pronominal forms with and without *-ci* or *-là*, although

there was a growing tendency towards the modern situation. In general adjectives derived from the Latin third declension have been assimilated to the predominant pattern, so that *immortelle* (l. 20) now has a distinctive feminine form.

## Syntax

Once again sixteenth-century preferences for hypotactic structures are very much in evidence in this extract. Calvin's freedom from a slavish copying of Latin is evidenced, for example, in the regular use of subject pronouns, even with impersonal verbs (*il nous fault*, l. 1, *il ne semble*, l. 4, etc.), or in his use of articles even with abstract nouns such as *la volunté* (l. 1), *la liberté* (ll. 1–2) or *l'entendement* (l. 3) or when the noun is already modified, for instance by *tel* (*un tel appétit*, ll. 8–9). Even where Calvin uses a latinate construction such as the *relatif de liaison* in line 12 (*Par laquelle sentence ilz entendent ...*) this is not necessarily a direct imitation of the original Latin (which is *Quo intelligunt*), although the participial structures of the last two lines do seem to be a direct rendering of his original text. Once again we may note the increased tendency to repeat function markers in co-ordinated structures (*sans raison et sans conseil*, ll. 21–22). As regards word order, there is a clear preference for SV structures and, unlike the usage of the majority of his contemporaries, Calvin does not automatically invert subject and verb after an initial *or* (l. 19).

Probably in imitation of the Latin accusative and infinitive construction, sixteenth-century writers favoured infinitival subordinate clauses alongside those introduced by *que* and containing a finite verb. Such clauses appeared typically after verbs of saying (e.g. *dire, avouer*), thinking (*penser, cuidier*, etc.), knowing (*savoir, apprendre*) and desiring (*vouloir, commander*, etc.). There are two examples of such structures in our text, one following *approuver* (*serve pour approuver quelque droicture estre en la volunté humaine*, ll. 5–6), the other after *entendre* (*ilz entendent l'object de l'appétit debvoir estre tel*, ll. 12–13), matching an infinitival structure in the Latin original. It should be noted, however, that Calvin uses a subordinate clause introduced by *que* after *confessent* (l. 11).

## Vocabulary

Here too the desire for ease of comprehension and the motive of making his text accessible to ordinary people seems to dictate that Calvin avoids too many neologisms or the expansive use of vocabulary of a Rabelais. This is not to say that Calvin avoids learned words, indeed many of his key terms are simply the French correlate of the Latin form (*volunté*, l. 1, *liberté*, l. 2, *eslection*, l. 3, *appètent*, l. 7), but these were already well established in French by the sixteenth century. The range of adjectives employed is also rather restricted – note the repeated use of *naturel*. *Sentence* (l. 12) is used with its Latin meaning, but this was common to a number of sixteenth-century authors. Once again we can see that generalizations about the usage of a period (here that there is great creativity and a desire to display the *richesse* of the French lexicon in the sixteenth century), while valid to some extent, may break down when we take into account the function of the text and the author's purpose.

# 24 Robert Olivétan's translation of the Bible (1535)

Olivétan's version of the Bible for Protestants was the first in French not to translate the Latin Vulgate, but to return to the original Hebrew Old Testament and the Greek New Testament. Olivétan, born in the first decade of the century, and sharing the new learning of the Renaissance, was evidently competent in these languages, and his version, written in simple plain prose, opened the way for others to produce new versions which, with the advent of printing, could reach a wider audience. His translation was not, however, a commercial success, probably for a number of reasons, not least of them being practical considerations: it was produced in Gothic type which was not popular (see Figure 7), and in folio format, making it too large to carry around comfortably.

This is Olivétan's version of Genesis, Chapter 1, verses 3–8. The punctuation of the original has been retained to illustrate how this differs from modern usage; note especially the use of oblique slashes or *virgulae* which, through the modification of first their appearance – they came to resemble a right-hand bracket – and then their position in relation to the surrounding letters, became the commas of today.

**Et Dieu dist: Que la lumiere soit faicte/ et la lumiere fut faicte.**
**Et Dieu veit que la lumiere estoit bonne: & Dieu separa la lumiere**
**des tenebres/ & appella la lumiere/ iour: et les tenebres/ nuict.**
**Lors fut faict du soir & du matin/ le premier iour.**

**De rechef Dieu dist: Que le firmament soit faict entre les eaues:** 5
**et quil separe les eaues/ des eaues. Dieu donc feit le firmament/**
**et diuisa les eaues qui estoient soubz le firmament dauec celles**
**qui estoient sus le firmament. Et fut ainsi faict. Et Dieu appella**
**le firmament/ ciel. Lors fut faict du soir et du matin/ le second**
**iour.** 10

(From *La Bible. Qui est toute la Saincte escripture. En laquelle
sont contenus/ le Vieil Testament & le Nouueau/ translatez
en Francoys* (Neuchâtel, P. de Wingle, 1535).[a])

[And God said, 'Let there be light', and there was light. And God saw that the light was good; and God separated the light from the darkness and called the light day, and the darkness night. Then was created from the evening and the morning the first day.

[5] Again God said, 'Let there be a firmament between the waters to separate water from water'. God then made the firmament and separated the waters under the firmament from the waters above the firmament. And thus it was done. And God called the firmament heaven. Then was created from the evening and the morning the second day.]

a  This extract has been transcribed from the copy of Olivétan's Bible held in Cambridge University Library (Syn.2.53.3).

*Figure 7*   Olivétan's translation of the Bible (1535), Genesis, Chapter 1

*Source:*   R. Olivétan, *La Bible. Qui est toute la Saincte escripture. En laquelle sont contenus/ le Vieil Testament & le Nouueau/ translatez en Francoys* (Neuchâtel, P. de Wingle, 1535). Reproduced by permission of the Syndics of Cambridge University Library.

**BRIEF COMMENTARY**

Direct comparison of this text with the thirteenth-century translation of the Bible (text 8) provides a clear illustration and summary of some of the changes which have occurred in French over a period of some three hundred years. The orthography has acquired a number of unpronounced letters, including those which indicate the etymology of words (*faicte*, l. 1) and double consonants (*appella*, l. 3), although *Dieu* (l. 1) no longer has the final -*x* of the thirteenth-century version; forms have also been reworked to bring them closer to the Latin etyma (*tenebres*, l. 3). Morphologically, we can see the now familiar analogical reworking of Old French forms, so that *fu* has become *fut* (l. 8) with a characteristic third person singular ending. However, the conservative nature of the spelling means that *dist* is still written with a preconsonantal *s* (l. 1), and the form *veit* (l. 2) seems to have been remodelled on the second person singular form *veïs* in which the *e* probably would not have been pronounced beyond the fourteenth century, although it normally remained in sixteenth-century spelling. Syntactically, we may observe the regularization of the use of the article, no longer conditioned as in Old French by semantic considerations (*et la lumiere fut faicte*, l. 1), and the use of an introductory *que* in a main clause command which in Old French was marked by the presence of the subjunctive verb alone.

## 25 Ambroise Paré, *La Methode de traicter les playes faictes par hacquebutes et aultres bastons à feu* (1545)

While popular medical texts had already appeared, notably in England, during the Old French period (cf. text 10), it was not until the sixteenth century that serious, professional medical texts came to be written in French rather than Latin. A number of writers published important medical treatises in this period, including Jean Canappe, Julien le Paulmier, Jacques Dalechamps and Laurent Joubert, but perhaps the most important contribution was made by Ambroise Paré (1510–90), considered by many to be the <u>father of modern surgery.</u> Ambroise, a renowned army surgeon and later surgeon to four French kings, was probably encouraged to use the vernacular by his desire to pass on his experience to young barbers and surgeons, for his work is addressed 'aux jeunes chirurgiens de bon vouloir'. Interestingly, Paré was mocked for choosing to write in French, suggesting that French did not conquer new domains without some resistance.

The printed text as published in 1545 has been transcribed precisely with the exception that long f has been replaced by *s*. Sixteenth-century typographical habits will be discussed in the commentary.

### La methode curatiue des fractures faictes par fleches ou bastons à feu

Consyderé que souuent aduiẽt, tant pour la grande violẽce des boulletz et ballottes des hacq̃butes, que des traictz, principalement des gros garots d'arbaleste, que les os sont rompus & fracturés: ie n'ay voulu obmettre en traicter, selõ ce que i'en ay veu par experiẽce. Et pource q̃ lesd. fractures aduiẽnẽt souuẽt de       5
long, aulcunesfoys de trauers, q̃lq̃foys obliques, les vnes incõpletes, les aultres completes: les vnes auec pties esgales, les aultres dẽtelées, inesguales, & esquilleuses: Il fault, cõme i'ay prescript, cõsyderer la partie, en laquelle est la fracture, pource que aulcunesfoys aduient à la teste, quelquefoys aux costes, ou à l'os       10
de l'adiutoire, ou à l'os femoris: aussi à l'un, ou à deux fociles: pareillemẽt es ioinctures: parquoy selon icelles differences & indicatiõs prinses des parties, fault diuersifier la cure.

*Signes de fracture.*

Les signes des fractures sont plusieurs, entre lesquelz le premier & plus euident est, quãd en traictant des mains la partie bleßée,       15
lon y treuue les parties de l'os diuisées, en y sentant trepidation, & attrition des parties fracturées. Semblablement, par l'impotence & figure du membre variée & chãgée: principalemẽt, si la fracture est en l'os adiutoire, ou au grãd focile, & nõ au petit: pource

q̃ ce n'est celuy qui soutient le faiz. Außi fault entendre, que les 20
fractures en telles parties, comme l'os adiutoire, ou femoris, sont
plus difficiles à curer, q̃ celles qui sont en l'un des fociles: car elles
sont plus difficiles à tenir vnies, qu'en l'ũ desdicts fociles.

### La cure des fractures n'est tousiours semblable.

Oultreplus fault consyderer l'aage, car les fractures faictes es
ieunes, sont trop plus faciles à curer, qu'elles ne sont es vieux: 25
pource qu'il n'y a tant d'humidité substantificque aux vieux qu'aux
ieunes: combien qu'on peult arguer, que les vieux ont plus
d'humidité: à quoy i'ay satisfaict, disant l'humidité substantifique,
& naturelle, à la difference de celle des vieux, laquelle n'est telle,
mais superflue & excrementeuse. Parquoy est moins apte & propre 30
pour faire la generatiõ du callus.

### La maniere de guerir les fractures.

Le commancement de la cure doibt estre cõme i'ay dict: ostãt
premieremẽt sans violẽce les esquilles totalemẽt separées des deux
parties fracturées: (car s'elles adheroiẽt auec vne d'icelles,
n'auroiẽt besoing d'estre ostées, & se pourroiẽt agglutiner par la 35
vertu nutritiue de l'os. Puis fault esgualer et reduire l'os en sa
situation, le tenant en bonne figure auec bendes & compresses,
esclacs, astelles faictes de boys, plomb, fer blanc, cuir conroyé,
gros papyer de chartes, ou escorce d'arbres: & selon la diuersité
des fractures & membres, fault diuersifier les bendes, compresses, 40
astelles, & aultres remedes, lesquelz seront escriptz cy apres.

(From *La Methode de traicter les playes faictes par hacquebutes
et aultres bastons à feu* ... composée par Ambroyse Paré maistre
Barbier, Chirurgien à Paris (Paris, V. Gaulterot, 1545), fols 36ʳ–37ᵛ.[a])

[*The way to cure fractures made by arrows or firearms.*
Seeing that it often happens, as much on account of the great force of
bullets and harquebus shots as on account of arrows, especially the great
bolts of crossbows, that bones are broken and fractured, I did not want
to omit their treatment, according to my own personal experience of this.
[5] And because the said fractures often occur lengthwise, sometimes
across, sometimes slanting, some incomplete breaks, others complete, some
in equal parts, others jagged, unequal and splintered, it is necessary, as I
have said, to consider in what part of the body the fracture is, because
sometimes it happens to the head, sometimes to the ribs or to the humerus
or the femur or one of the bones of the forearm or lower leg;[b] similarly
to the joints. Therefore it is necessary to vary the cure according to these
differences and the symptoms noted in the different parts.

a  The transcription was made from the copy held in Emmanuel College Library, Cambridge
   (S2.4.45).
b  *Focile* refers either to the radius and ulna or the tibia and fibula.

*Signs of a fracture.*

[14] There are many signs of a fracture among which the first and most obvious is when one is handling the injured part one finds there the broken parts of the bone, noting there to be trembling and abrasion of the fractured parts. Similarly, through weakness and change or alteration to the shape of the limb especially if the fracture is to the humerus or the radius or tibia and not to the ulna or fibula, because these are not weight-bearing. [20] It must also be understood that fractures to parts such as the humerus or femur are more difficult to cure than those to one of the bones of the forearm or lower leg; for they are more difficult to hold together than those of the forearm or lower leg.

*The cure of fractures is not always the same.*

[24] It is moreover necessary to consider the age (of the patient), for fractures in young people are easier to cure than those in the elderly, because there is not so much 'substantial' moisture in the old as in the young. One might argue that the old have more moisture, but I have satisfied this objection by saying 'substantial' or natural moisture which is different from that of the old, which is not such but rather superfluous and to be excreted. For this reason it is less apt and suitable for the growth of calluses.

*The way to cure fractures.*

[32] The beginning of the cure should be as I have said: first removing without force the splinters which have completely separated from the two fractured parts (for if they were joined to one of them there would be no need for them to be removed and they might join together again by the nourishing force of the bone). [36] Then it is necessary to straighten and put the bone back in its place, holding it in good shape with bandages and compresses, splinters,[c] splints made of wood, lead, tinplate, dressed leather, thick document paper or tree bark; and, according to the different types of fractures and limbs, you should vary the bandages, compresses, splints and other remedies which will be described below.]

## COMMENTARY

### Typography

Early printed texts continued medieval manuscript habits in including a number of abbreviations. A tilde placed above a vowel was used in place of a following *m* or *n*, whether the vowel was nasalized or not, thus *dētelées* (l. 8) for *dentelées*, *adheroiēt* (l. 34) for *adheroient*. The same sign placed over a *q* (l. 20) was an abbreviation for *que* (so *q̄lq̄foys*, l. 6, for *quelque-*

---

c   The meaning of this is unclear. *Eclast* referred to a scrap or shred of something and
    could either refer to a small piece of wood (used as a splint) or a piece of cloth (used
    as a bandage).

*foys*), while a straight horizontal line through the downstroke of a *p* represented *par* (l. 7) and *lesd.* (l. 5) was short for *lesdi(c)tes*. *ß* was occasionally used in place of *ss* (*außi*, l. 20). Printers generally failed to make the modern distinction between *u* for a vowel and consonantal *v*; instead they were frequently employed as positional variants with *v* favoured in initial position and *u* elsewhere (note here, however, *un*, l. 11). As for *j*, this was rarely used throughout the period and *i* was used for both the vocalic and the consonantal value (e.g. *ioinctures* (l. 12) for Modern French *jointures*).

From the 1530s on, the acute accent in word-final position, the cedilla and the apostrophe were gradually introduced. A grave accent was occasionally used on *à* (l. 10) to differentiate the preposition from the verb *avoir*, but its usage did not generalize until the following century (see also text 27).

## Orthography

The text is typical of sixteenth-century usage in containing a large number of silent letters, frequently added on the basis of the word's etymology (*ioinctures*, l. 12, *doibt*, l. 32, *escriptz*, l. 41, etc.). Characteristic too is the doubling of consonants in *boulletz*, *ballottes* (l. 2) and the use of *y* where today *i* is found (*consyderé*, l. 1, *i'ay*, l. 8). *Bendes* (l. 37) may be a regional variant of *bandes*, or simply an alternative spelling, since *an* and *en* had long ceased to be pronounced differently.

## Morphology

### Adjective and adverb morphology

Throughout this text adjectives and derived adverbs from Latin third declension forms regularly have an *e* in the feminine, even common ones like *grand* or *tel* (*la grande violẽce*, l. 1, *en telles parties*, l. 21, *principalemẽt*, l. 18). *Trop* was often used at this time to modify a comparative construction as in *trop plus faciles* (l. 25).

### Contracted forms and elision

*Es* (ll. 12, 24) continued in usage as a contracted form of *en les*. The fact that the form *se* was usual in Old French for 'if' probably explains the elision of the vowel before feminine *elle(s)* (l. 34).

*Demonstrative adjectives and pronouns*

By the beginning of the sixteenth century the adjectival demonstrative system was beginning to look completely modern:

|          | masculine         | feminine |
|----------|-------------------|----------|
| singular | *ce* + C, *cet* + V | *cette*  |
| plural   | *ces*             | *ces*    |

As regards the pronominal forms, the semantic distinction between *cestui* and *celui* was gradually disappearing and the use of *-ci* and *-là* with them became much more common; usage was therefore moving towards the following system:

|          | masculine                   | feminine                            |
|----------|-----------------------------|-------------------------------------|
| singular | *cestui-ci*                 | *ceste-ci*                          |
|          | *cestui-la/celui-la*        | *ceste-la/celle-la*                 |
| plural   | *ceus-ci*                   | *cestes-ci/* less likely *celles-ci* |
|          | *ceus-la*                   | *celles-la/* less likely *cestes-la* |

The forms continued to be used without the *-ci* or *-là*, as in Modern French, when the meaning was not 'this one, that one' but 'the one(s)' and they were followed by a relative clause (l. 20) or a prepositional phrase, usually beginning with *de* (l. 29). In addition the forms beginning with *i-* were still employed, particularly by more conservative authors, as in this text (*icelles differences*, l. 12; *vne d'icelles*, l. 34).

*Verb morphology*

The stem of *treuue* (l. 16) has not yet been remodelled on the weak stem by Paré. *Prinses* (l. 13), rather than the more usual *prises*, is used as the past participle of *prendre*; its formation appears to have been encouraged by the fact that *je prins* etc. (on the analogy of *tin* etc. of *tenir*) appeared alongside *pris* as the past historic of the verb.

## Syntax

*Government*

Gougenheim (1974: 163–64) notes that in Old French a number of verbs were constructed with *à* where in Modern French *de* is used. These include *craindre*, *essayer*, *choisir* and *omettre*. In the case of this last verb the usual sixteenth-century construction was with a simple infinitive, perhaps in imitation of Latin; this is the usage favoured by Paré: *ie n'ay voulu obmettre en traicter* (l. 4).

*Co-ordination*

Whereas Calvin tended towards the modern preference for repeating function markers in co-ordinated constructions, Paré, as in a number of other respects (note, for instance, the greater frequency of omission of subject pronouns), tends to be conservative and favours non-repetition: *icelles differences & indicatiōs* (ll. 12–13), *l'impotence & figure* (ll. 17–18).

*Choice of mood*

The conjunction *combien que* (l. 27) meaning 'although' is used by Paré with the indicative mood. When the conjunction first appeared in the fourteenth century it was followed by the subjunctive but in the next two centuries it is found with either the indicative or subjunctive without any differentiation of meaning. It was still employed by authors such as Malherbe and Balzac at the beginning of the seventeenth century, but had largely died out by the end of the century.

*Sentence connectors*

A number of adverbs were favoured by Middle French and sixteenth-century authors to establish a logical connection between different sentences; these include *partant, pourtant,*[d] *dont* and the adverb used here *parquoy* (l. 30). A similar function is fulfilled by *oultreplus* (l. 24) which helps to give a sense of heightened cohesion to the text.

*Word order*

Paré's usage perpetuates many of the features of word order that we have seen to be characteristic of Middle French texts and is therefore somewhat different from Calvin's which points the way forward to the seventeenth-century preference for the regular use of SV. For instance, Paré has no qualms about not placing morphologically or grammatically related elements next to each other; note then the following placements of the adjective: *les parties de l'os diuisées*, l. 16, *l'impotence & figure du membre variée & chāgée*, ll. 17–18. The clitic pronoun continues to appear before the finite verb rather than the infinitive, as in *se pourroiēt agglutiner* (l. 35).

A typical feature of sixteenth-century prose – again perhaps encouraged by Latin influence – was the delaying of the main clause as illustrated, for example, by the first two sentences of our extract. These sentences

d  The meaning of this adverb gradually evolved during the course of the sixteenth century. While Calvin, for instance, still employed it as a translation of Latin terms meaning 'therefore', later in the century it was used for 'however', a sense which arose from its use in negative contexts.

each begin with a complex subordinate clause which contains a number of adverbial phrases and postpones the appearance of the main verbs, which are respectively *ie n'ay voulu* (l. 4) and *Il fault* (l. 8).

## Vocabulary

It was not only in literary texts that the need was felt to create neologisms. Innovation was also necessary in scientific texts if the vernacular was to be able to discuss the more technical aspects of the discipline in a precise and unambiguous fashion. Paré is himself generally thought to be responsible for the creation of *fracturé* (l. 4) derived from *fracture*, a thirteenth-century latinism, and *callus* (l. 31), a direct calque from Latin. He is also credited with being the first to use *agglutiner* (l. 35) in a medical context as opposed to the more general sense of 'join' which had been current since the fourteenth century. Other recent additions to the French lexicon used here by Paré include *esquilleuses* (l. 8), *l'os femoris* (l. 11), *substantifique* (l. 28), *excrementeux/-se* (l. 30) and *compresses* (l. 37), a back-formation from the verb *compresser*. Not surprisingly, much of the technical vocabulary is of Latin origin, whether of recent importation or longer established in the language (e.g. *curatif/-ive* was borrowed in at the beginning of the fourteenth century). *Conroyé* (l. 38) is the expected form from the Latin verb *\*conredare*; in Modern French *corroyer*, the *n* has been assimilated to the following *r*. The term *focile* (l. 11) is no longer current today perhaps because the ambiguity of its meaning rendered it unsuitable for technical discussion. Finally, note that in this type of text, there is of course no pressure on the author to vary his terms for stylistic reasons (here, for example, *parties* is used repeatedly); what is important is the clear and unambiguous conveying of the information.

## 26 André Thevet, *Les Singularitez de la France Antarctique* (1557/8ᵃ)

This text serves both as an example of sixteenth-century usage in a factual account, here of a voyage of discovery, and of the spread of French to the new domain of geography – or *cosmographie* as it was called at the time. The author, André Thevet (1516/17–92), a Franciscan monk who enjoyed the protection of noble families linked to the monarchy, had already made several journeys in the 1540s to Italy, Switzerland, Naples and Africa, and a trip to the Middle East which was related in his *Cosmographie de Levant* (1554). In 1555 he became *aumônier* or chaplain to the expedition led by Villegagnon to Brazil which landed there in November 1555. However, Thevet fell ill and had to leave Brazil at the end of January 1556, as is recounted in our extract; the return journey apparently took him past Haiti, Cuba and Florida and close to Canada. All this is recounted in his *Singularitez de la France Antarctique*, a work which was highly popular in his day and earned him the role of Royal Cosmographer to four French kings (Henri II, François II, Charles IX and Henri III).

The style is appropriately plain and unadorned for a factual account. Thevet of course was faced with the problem of giving French names to the places he encountered: the designation *France Antarctique* for Brazil is obviously motivated by chauvinism.

### De nostre departement de la France Antarctique, ou Amerique. CHAP. 60.

Or auons nous cy dessus recueilli & parlé amplement de ces
nations, desquelles les meurs & particularitez, n'ont esté par les
Historiographes anciens descrites ou celebrées, pour n'en auoir
eu la cõgnoissance. Apres donc auoir seiourné quelque espace de
temps en ce païs, autant que la chose, pour lors le requeroit, &    5
qu'il estoit necessaire pour le contentement de l'esprit, tant du
lieu, que des choses y contenuës: il ne fut question que de regarder
l'opportunité, & moyen de nostre retour, puis qu'autrement
n'auions deliberé y faire plus longue demeure. Donques soubs la
conduite de monsieur de Bois-le conte, Capitaine des nauires du   10
Roy, en la France Antarctique, homme magnanime, & autant bien
appris au fait de la marine, outre plusieurs autres vertus, comme
si toute sa vie en auoit fait exercice. Primes donc nostre chemin
tout au contraire de celuy par lequel estions venus, à cause des
vents qui sont propres pour le retour: & ne faut aucunement   15
douter, que le retour ne soit plus long que l'allée de plus de quatre
ou cinq cens lieuës, & plus difficile. Ainsi le dernier iour de Ianuier

---

a  The text was published in 1557 but bearing the date 1558.

**à quatre heures du matin, embarquez auec ceux qui ramenoyent
les nauires par deça, feimes voile, saillans de ceste riuiere de
Ianaïre, en la grande mer sus l'autre costé, tirant vers le Ponent,    20
laissée à dextre la coste d'Ethiopie, laquelle nous auions tenuë en
allant.**

(From André Thevet, *Les Singularitez de la France Antarctique,
autrement nommée Amerique: & de plusieurs Terres et Isles
decouuertes de nostre temps* (Paris, Héritiers de Maurice de la Porte,
1558), fol. 118[r-v].[b])

*[About our department of Antarctic or American France [=Brazil]*
Now we have recorded and spoken amply above about these nations whose
customs and peculiarities were not described or celebrated by the ancient
historiographers because they did not know about them. Having then
stayed for some time in this country, as long as the matter at that time
required and it was necessary to satisfy the mind, both about the place
and the things contained there, it was merely a question of looking for
the opportunity and the means for our return since in any case we had
not thought to make a longer stay there. [9] Then, under the leadership
of Monsieur de Bois le Conte, Captain of the King's ships in Antarctic
France, a generous man and, besides several other virtues, even better
versed in naval matters as if he had practised them all his life, we therefore set our path in the exact opposite path from the one by which we
had come because of the winds which were suitable for our return; and
it should in no way be doubted that the return journey was longer than
the voyage there by more than four or five hundred leagues, and more
difficult. [17] So on the last day of January at four o'clock in the morning,
having embarked with those who brought the ships back here, we set sail,
going out from this river called Janeiro into the open sea on the other
side, heading westwards, and leaving to our right the coast of Ethiopia
[= Black Africa as far as the Gulf of Guinea], which we had followed on
our way there.]

## COMMENTARY

### Typography

The printer here does not employ the abbreviations favoured by Paré's
printer; the only exception is the tilde on *cōgnoissance* (l. 4) to indicate
the omission of a following *n*. For most of the sixteenth century the acute
accent was restricted, as in this text, to use in word-final position, but use
of the trema (*lieuës*, l. 17), cedilla (*deça*, l. 19), apostrophe (*l'esprit*, l. 6)

---

b    British Library, London, C.107.d.1. Also available in facsimile reprint, Paris, Le Temps,
1982.

and grave accent on the preposition *à* (l. 21) gradually became more and more established as the century progressed.

Compared with Olivétan's text (24), the use of punctuation is more modern, with the comma replacing the oblique slash. Note, nevertheless, that the use of the full stop does not necessarily mark the end of what we would consider to be a sentence and the sense runs on, for example, between *exercice* and *Primes* (l. 13) which is the main verb.

## Orthography

While there are still a considerable number of unpronounced letters in Thevet's spelling (e.g. *esté*, l. 2, *nostre*, l. 8, *soubs*, l. 9), his orthography is much less heavily etymological than that of many of the other sixteenth-century texts we have analysed. Here then we find *autrement*, l. 8, *aucunement*, l. 15, *douter*, l. 16. While the importance of semantic considerations continued to predominate over phonetic representation throughout the century, by the end of the period the apogee of the zeal for etymological spellings was already passing.

## Morphology

As regards the morphology, this text differs little from Modern French usage; we may note, for instance, the regular formation of feminine adjectives or the forms of the demonstratives. The Old French past historic form of *prendre* was *presimes* which was remodelled to *preïmes* in the thirteenth century; the subsequent loss of vowels in hiatus during Middle French reduced this form further and this pronunciation is reflected in the spelling of *primes* (l. 13).

## Syntax

If the morphology of our extract differs little from usage today, this is not true of the syntax. Thevet frequently omits the subject pronoun, even where there is a change of subject as in the following example: *il ne fut question que de regarder l'opportunité, & moyen de nostre retour, puis qu'autrement n'auions deliberé y faire plus longue demeure* (ll. 7–9). His usage is also rather elliptical by later standards, as the following construction suggests: *& ne faut aucunement douter, que le retour ne soit plus long que l'allée de plus de quatre ou cinq cens lieuës, & plus difficile* (ll. 15–17). Allied to this is the tendency not to repeat the determiner in co-ordinated noun phrases (*les meurs & particularitez*, l. 2). In relative clauses Thevet favours the more explicit relative pronouns *lequel, laquelle*, etc. (l. 21) and employs *desquelles* (l. 2) in preference to *dont*.

Once again we may detect the influence of Latin in the use of the un-attached participial clause: *laissée à dextre la coste d'Ethiopie* (l. 21) – note that the participle is placed in front of the nominal subject. However, Thevet equally employs the *après avoir* construction (l. 4) which is preferred today for the marking of anteriority. Note that the adjectival and verbal functions of the present participle were not yet differentiated so that the participle agreed with the subject in either function (here *saillans*, l. 19); usually, however, this agreement was only in number and not gender, with forms in *-antes* functioning verbally only very rarely. As regards the agreement of a past participle conjugated with *avoir* and with a preceding direct object, the trend, as here, was towards making the agreement, although this was not yet obligatory: *la coste d'Ethiopie, laquelle nous auions tenuë en allant* (ll. 21–22).

The word order of our extract displays many features which we have seen to be typical of Middle French usage, including the inversion of subject and verb after an initial *or* (l. 1), the placing of the agent of the passive between the auxiliary and the past participle (*n'ont esté par les Historiographes anciens descrites ou celebrées*, ll. 2–3), and the postponement of the main clause verb by a number of circumstantial complements, as is the case in the last sentence of the passage.

**Vocabulary**

On the whole, Thevet uses common, well-established lexical items. There are, however, some innovations, including the use of *marine* (l. 12) to refer not to the sea but to 'art de navigation'; he also prefers the learned *embarquer* to the more 'popular' *s'enbarchier*, attested in fifteenth-century texts. Note that Thevet favours the use of co-ordinated pairs of near-synonyms or semantically related terms, which we have already observed in a number of Middle French texts (*recueilli & parlé*, l. 1, *meurs & particularitez*, l. 2, *descrites ou celebrées*, l. 3).

# 27 Louis Meigret, *Le Trẹtté de la grammẹre françọẹze* (1550)

We have already noted the increasing difficulties in trying to discuss the pronunciation of Middle French because of the widening gap between supposed pronunciation and the orthography of the day; so far we have had to rely on clues gleaned from assonance and rhyme patterns and the syllable count of lines of verse texts to make suppositions about phonological change. In the sixteenth century a new source of information about contemporary pronunciation can be identified in metalinguistic texts, and particularly in those works which argued that French spelling should be reformed to bring it closer to pronunciation habits. In the forefront of those arguing for the urgent reform of French orthography was Louis Meigret, born in the first decade of the sixteenth century in Lyons, and the author of a number of translations of Greek and Latin classics.

Our extract comes from Meigret's *Trẹtté de la grammẹre françọẹze* (1550), which is of interest to us in a number of respects. Not only is it a valuable source of information about sixteenth-century pronunciation, being the longest example we have of a text published entirely in reformed spelling (see Figure 8), and of the sorts of arguments put forward by the reformers for change, it was also the first grammar of French written in French by a Frenchman, which has led many to consider Meigret to be the first true French grammarian. Furthermore, from the criticisms of some of his contemporaries we learn that Meigret represented some features of Lyonnais pronunciation in his spelling, giving us a clear indication that regional variations in pronunciation were still very much alive. We shall see in our commentary that, while much valuable information is available to us from such texts, their interpretation is also, as we have come to expect, problematic.

This is an extract from the beginning of the second chapter, which discusses the vocalic system of French:

### Dẹ' voyẹlles. Çhap. II.

**Or qant ao' voyẹlles je treuue qe la lange Frãçọẹz' ẹn a juqes ao nombre de sẹt, si diuẹrses ẹntr' ẹlles, qe l'une ne peut étre prononçée pour l'aotre, sans manifẹst' offẹnse de l'orẹlle:: qoẹ qe lẹs aocunes ayet ẹntr' ẹlles vne grand' affinité. Nous auons donc, a, ẹ, ouuert, e clós, i, ou, clós (aotremẹnt ne l'oze je noter) o ouuẹrt, u. Ẹ combien (affin qe je comẹnç' ao' premieres) q'a, eyt grãd' affinité auẹq l'ẹ ouuert, qe jestime tẹl, qe nou' le prononçons ẹn mẹs, tẹs, sẹs, vẹrt, pẹrs, sẹrf, ẹ pour leqel vous ecriuez qelqefoẹs ai, ou ẹs, a l'imitaçíon de l'ançíen abus de l'ecritture: com' ẹn maistre, mais, paix, estre, teste, beste: il ẹt toutefoẹs çẹrtein, qe nou' ne lẹs ozerions prononçer ẹn a. Combien aosi qe çet ẹ ouuẹrt, eyt grand' affinité auẹq l'e clós, tẹl qe vou' le prononçez ẹn merite,** 5 10

## GRĀM. FRANÇOEZE.

nou' prononçons ęn notre lange dę' vocables
qe le Latin,ne leGręc ne fauroęt ecrire par leurs
charaȼtęres:d'aotant q'il' ne lęs ont jamęs u ęn
vzaje:come fōt l,ñ,f,molles.Car il n'ęt pas vrey
fęmblable q'il' lęs vffet lęffé inçęrteines, ę fans
qelqe charaȼtęre,ou propre marqe,attédu leur
grāde dilijęnç'ęn toutes aotres chozes louables.
Ao regard de noz ançętres,il' lę' nous ont noté
d'aofi pouur'inuęnçíō,q'a eté leur cōfideraçíon
a garder la proprieté,ę puiffançe dę' lęttres.

### Dę' voyęlles.　Çhap.　II.

R qant ao' voyęlles je treuue qe la
lange Frāçoęz'ęn a juqes ao nombre-
de fęt, fi diuęrfes ęntr' ęlles , qe l'une
ne peut ętre prononçée pour l'aotre,
fans manifęft' offęnfe de l'oręlle:: qoę qe lęs aocunes ayet ęntr' ęlles vne grand'affinité.Nous
auons donc,a,ę,ouuert,e clós, i, ou,clós( aotre-
męnt ne l'oze je noter) o ouuęrt, u . Ę combien
(affin qe je comęnç' ao' premieres) q'a,eyt grā-
d' affinité auęq l'ę ouuert, qe jeftime tęl, qe
nou' le prononçons ęn męs , tęs, fęs, vęrt,pęrs,
fęrf,ę pour leqel vous ecriuez qelqefoęs ai , ou
ęs, a l'imitaçíon de l'ançíen abus de l'ecritture:
com' ęn maiftre,mais, paix,eftre,tefte,befte:il ęt
toutefoęs çęrtein,qe nou' ne lęs ozerions prononçer ęn a . Combien aofi qe çet ę ouuęrt,eyt
grand' affinité auęq l'e clós, tęl qe vou' le pro-

non-

*Figure 8*　Meigret's *Tretté de la grammęre françoęze* (1550), fol. 6ᵛ

*Source:*　L. Meigret, *Le Tretté de la grammęre françoęze* (Paris, C. Wechel, 1550), fol. 6ᵛ.
Reproduced by permission of The British Library, London (C.175.b.28).

**benitre, perir, mere, pere: il ne se trouuera toutefoȩs vocabl' ȩn**
**toꞟte la lange Françoȩze, aoꝗel le Courtizant seuffre la**
**pronõȭíaȭíon de l'un pour l'aotre: ȩ mȩmemȩnt l'ȩ ouuȩrt pour** 15
**l'e, clós. Ie vou' lȩss' a pȩnser qȩlle graȭ' aora l'e clós, ȩn sȩ' vo-**
**cables mȩs, tȩs, sȩs, si nou' l'y pronõȭons, come nou' fezons ȩn**
**pere, mere: ȩ come font je ne sey ꝗels effeminez miñons auȩꝗ vn**
**prȩꝗe clós resȩrremȩnt de bouche: creñans a mon auís ꝗe la voȩs**
**virille de l'home ne soȩt point tant harmonieuze, ny aggreabl' ao'** 20
**dames, q'une lache, foȩbl' ȩ femenine.**

(From *Le Trȩtté de la grammȩre françoȩze, fȩt par Louís*
*Meigrȩt Líonoȩs* (Paris, C. Wechel, 1550; fols 6ᵛ–7ʳ·ᵃ)

[Now as for the vowels, I find that the French language has them to
the number of seven, so different from each other, that one cannot be
pronounced for another without obvious offence to the ear, even though
some of them have a great affinity to each other. [4] We have then *a*,
open *ȩ*, close *e*, *i*, close *ou* (which I dare not note in any other way),
open *o*, *u*. And although (to begin with the first ones) *a* has a great affinity
with open *ȩ*, which I consider to be the sound we pronounce in *mȩs*
'my', *tȩs* 'your', *sȩs* 'his', *vȩrt* 'green', *pȩrs* 'blue-green', *sȩrf* 'servant', and
for which you sometimes write *ai* or *ȩs*, following the old abusive way
of writing as in *maistre* 'master', *mais* 'but', *paix* 'peace', *estre* 'to be',
*teste* 'head', *beste* 'beast', it is nevertheless certain that we would not dare
to pronounce them with *a*. [11] Similarly, although this open *ȩ* has a
great affinity with close *e*, as you pronounce it in *merite* 'merit', *benitre*
'to bless', *perir* 'to perish', *mere* 'mother', *pere* 'father'; nevertheless
no word will be found in the entire French language in which the courtier
would tolerate the pronunciation of one for the other, and especially
open *ȩ* for close *e*. [16] I leave you to consider what (ill) grace close *ȩ*
would have in these words, *mȩs*, *tȩs*, *sȩs*, if we pronounced them as we
do *mere* and *pere* and as some effeminate little dears do with their mouths
nearly closed, fearing, in my opinion, that the virile voice of a man will
not be as harmonious or pleasing to the ladies as one which is feeble,
weak and feminine.]

## COMMENTARY

### The sixteenth-century debate about spelling reform

Meigret's first work preaching the need for spelling reform was his *Traité
touchant le commun usage de l'escriture françoise* (1542); in this only the
examples are in reformed spelling, not the text, and Meigret clearly had
experienced difficulties in trying to find a printer willing to publish his

---

a   British Library, London, C.175.b.28. Also available in facsimile reprint, Menston, Scolar,
1969.

project. In 1547 he persuaded the printer to use 'ę' in his translation of Cicero's *De officiis*, and in the following year the whole of his translation of Lucian's *Le Menteur* appeared in reformed spelling. However, his grammar of 1550 is the most extensive phonetic text of the sixteenth century.

Already in the 1530s the printer Geoffroy Tory had introduced the acute accent and the cedilla into French spelling, but it was really only with the work of Meigret that the latter became fully established in usage. The foundation of his system was the observation of the principle that there should be one symbol for each sound and only one sound represented by each symbol; it is perhaps surprising therefore that he did not differentiate the uses of *u* and *v*. Meigret identified three fundamental problems with traditional spelling: *diminution*, or the use of one letter for two sounds, *superfluité*, or the inclusion of unpronounced letters in a word (e.g. the *b* of *debuoir*), and *usurpation*, or the incorrect use of one letter for another.

Meigret's reforms met with considerable opposition. The most important of his critics was Jacques Peletier du Mans, a fellow reformer, who disagreed with, for example, the details of Meigret's vowel system. But there were many others such as Guillaume des Autelz who ridiculed the whole project and its goals.

Meigret's reforms had little impact on sixteenth-century spelling for a number of reasons, not least the fact that they were set against the background of the publication of Robert Estienne's highly influential *Dictionaire francoislatin* (1539/40) which had used and promoted traditional, etymological spelling. Moreover, reformers were unable to agree amongst themselves, and so failed to offer united resistance to well-established orthographical habits. More influential in the long term were Ronsard's more moderate proposals which will be discussed later (p. 195). Ronsard admired Meigret's system, but shied away from using such a radical system himself for fear of alienating his readers.

## Pronunciation

We shall see that in some respects Meigret's pronunciation was rather archaic and affected by the speech habits of his native Lyons. In other cases he failed to show sufficient sensitivity to pronunciation differences. His description of the vowels of French nevertheless provides interesting insights into contemporary pronunciations.

### Vowels

According to Meigret, French has seven vowels (compared with Peletier who lists nine oral and four nasal vowels); later we learn that each of these can be long or short with an acute accent used to mark length in his system. Meigret was the first to note a distinction between open and close *e* ([ɛ], noted by Meigret as ę, and [e] written *e*), and his transcription of the front unrounded vowels ([i, e, ɛ, a]) is unproblematic.

Nasal vowels

Note that Meigret makes no mention of nasal vowels in listing the vowels of French, and does not mark them systematically in any special way, although occasionally a tilde is used, as in traditional spelling, in place of a following *m* or *n*. Since Meigret elsewhere criticizes ill-bred Parisians for their excessive nasalization, we may surmise that in his Lyonnais pronunciation the nasal vowels were only lightly nasalized as in many southern French dialects today. This might explain why the first vowel of *sęns* is transcribed in the same way as *męs*. What is more surprising is the fact that Meigret still uses different symbols for *ęn* and *an* which had longed ceased to be pronounced differently in standard French.

Back rounded vowels

Meigret, in common with the majority of sixteenth-century reformers, only includes two symbols for the back rounded vowels which he calls *ou clos* and *o ouuert*; these are perhaps equivalent to modern [u] and [ɔ]. It is possible that in the sixteenth century [o] was a much closer vowel than today, so that it was possible for a provincial writer to confuse it with [u]. We know from other sources that [u] was sometimes pronounced for [o] especially in court circles (the so-called *ouïstes*), giving *chouse* for *chose*, *ouse* for *ose*, and that this also occurred in some regions of France including Lyons; this seems to confirm the closeness of these vowels. That said, the transcription of these back vowels is often confusing and inconsistent.

*e muet* or schwa

While Meigret made an important contribution in distinguishing open and close *e*, he failed to note the third *e* [ə] found, for example, in *lequel* (*leqel*, l. 8), and he is criticized by other reformers for this omission. For Meigret the difference between [e] and [ə] seems to be one of length only and he fails to notice the difference in quality.

Front rounded vowels

Meigret only lists one front rounded vowel [y] written in his system as *u*. While other reformers indicate that they pronounced *eu* as in *eureus* with a simple vowel ([Ö]), it is possible that in Meigret's Lyonnais speech *eu* still retained a diphthongal pronunciation.

Diphthongs and triphthongs

In our extract Meigret notes two diphthongs, *oę* and *ao*. The spelling *oę* seems to represent the pronunciation [wɛ] *(qelqefoęs*, l. 8, *foębl'*, l. 21), but *ao* (*aotre*, l. 3, *aosi*, l. 11) is more problematic. On the analogy of *oę* we may surmise that *o* transcribes [w], and it is possible that for Meigret this was still a diphthong, although other reformers criticize his spelling. Once again Meigret's pronunciation is seen to be either regional or somewhat archaic; elsewhere in the *Grammęre* he lists no fewer than sixteen diphthongs and four triphthongs for French.

*Mère* and *père*

From Meigret's transcription it appears that these words were pronounced by him as [merə] and [perə] and not as today [mɛr] and [pɛr].

*Consonants*

Once again Meigret introduces new symbols to notate the different consonants including *ç* for [s], *çh* for [ʃ], and *ꞑ* for [ɲ]. The letter *g* is consistently given the value [g], so *lange* (l. 1) (= *langue*), and *j* is used for [ʒ]. Meigret does not consistently eliminate all double consonants (e.g. *affinité*, l. 7). The spelling *pręqe* (l. 19) indicates that the *s* was not pronounced by Meigret. It is more difficult to account for the final *t* of *Courtizant* (l. 14), a word borrowed from Italian; a possible explanation is that there was confusion between the noun and the present participle of *courtiser*, perhaps encouraged by the fact that the suffix *-an* was not very common in French.

**Morphology**

For Meigret the marking of pronunciation took precedence over the marking of grammatical function. He argued that if the function of words was clear in speech then it ought equally to be so in writing without the need of unpronounced function markers such as the different verb endings for the different persons of the verb. Thus he does not consider it necessary to put a final *e* on a feminine adjective before a noun beginning with a vowel, since the final consonant will already be sounded in this context: *sans manifęst' offęnse* (l. 3), *grãd' affinité* (l. 7).

The stems of the verbs *trouver* and *souffrir* have not yet levelled in Meigret's usage, thus *je treuue* (l. 1, cf. *trouuera*, l. 13), *le Courtizant seuffre* (l. 14). In the case of many *-er* verbs this variation had already disappeared, but it tended to linger in the verbs *demeurer*, *éprouver*, *pleurer*, *trouver*. It was also found in certain verbs in other conjugations such as *souffrir*, *secourir*, *couvrir*, *courir*, and of course still subsists in a number of verbs today: *vouloir, mouvoir, mourir, pouvoir*. Finally, note the infinitive *benitre* (l. 13, normally spelt *benistre* or *beneistre* at this time) which co-existed with the alternative *benire*; this is now firmly established as an *-ir* verb, *bénir*.

## Vocabulary

Sixteenth-century grammarians required the necessary metalinguistic vocabulary to be able to describe and analyse French. The term *vocable* (l. 16), created at the end of the fourteenth century, was commonly used in metalinguistic texts of the sixteenth and seventeenth centuries, but was rarely used in the eighteenth century. *Voyel* was introduced in the fifteenth century, originally with the masculine gender, in place of Old French *voieul*; the form *voyęlle* (l. 1), with feminine gender, appeared later in the century, probably on the analogy of *consonne*. Lastly, *pronõçíaçíon* (l. 15, *prononciation*) was first used in the linguistic sense in the sixteenth century: earlier its usage had been confined to legal contexts where it had the sense 'proclamation, decree'.

# V Classical and Neo-Classical French

## French in the seventeenth and eighteenth centuries up to the Revolution

In broad terms the seventeenth century may be characterized as a period of restrictive codification and control of French, in contrast to the richness, expansion and relative freedom of usage of the previous century. We have seen that already by the last two decades of the sixteenth century the peak of the expansion of French to new domains and the concomitant creation of neologisms had passed and the influence of Latin and Italian on French lessened. The work of the grammarians of the second half of the sixteenth century had also stemmed from a desire to give French greater fixity and dignity. It was these new trends which found their focus and were crystallized in the work of François de Malherbe who, in criticizing the usage of the sixteenth century poet Desportes, emphasized the need for purity and clarity of expression, and the importance of eliminating any potential ambiguity. Malherbe himself never produced a formal grammar (see Brunot 1891), but the spirit of his work permeated the efforts of the normative grammarians of the seventeenth century, which led to the establishment of the basic rules of written French grammar, fundamentally unchanged to this day. The key stages in the increasing control of French are well known and include the foundation of the French Academy in 1635, and the publication of Vaugelas's *Remarques sur la langue françoise* in 1647 (text 28). Believing French had reached a state of perfection, grammarians aimed to eradicate uncertainties of usage of pronunciation, spelling and morphology. The rambling and loosely connected sentences of sixteenth-century authors were censured; syntactic clarity and the marking in unambiguous fashion of grammatical relations came to be considered of paramount importance. The lexicon of the *honnête homme* was restricted by the elimination of words deemed too new, archaic, *bas*, or overly technical; in addition, words which in the previous century had been used as broad synonyms were semantically differentiated. The effects of the efforts of the normative grammarians can be clearly seen by comparing the early seventeenth-century usage of François de Sales (text 29) with the pellucid 'classical' prose of Voltaire (text 30), which is strikingly modern. For Voltaire, the French language had reached a state of perfection in the seventeenth century and its usage therefore should not change; indeed, if anything, even greater emphasis was placed on clarity of expression and syntactic structure and on fixity of word order in the eighteenth century. In matters of lexicon, however, the eighteenth century showed greater latitude; indeed even at the end of the seventeenth century La Bruyère expressed regret at the loss of what he considered to be useful words (see Rickard 1992: 272–73).

While this account undoubtedly characterizes the predominant spirit of the Classical and Neo-Classical age, it provides only a partial account of the diversity of linguistic usage and variation found during the seventeenth and eighteenth centuries. Indeed, through their characterization of which usages were acceptable, seventeenth-century normative grammarians themselves conceded that not all writers and speakers were adhering to the recommended norms. Alongside the *style noble*, here represented by an extract from Racine (text 32), there existed in the seventeenth century the *style burlesque* of a Scarron, or the representation of speech of peasants or of *Précieuses* by Molière; more informal style is illustrated by the extract from Laclos's *Les Liaisons dangereuses* (text 31), written in the form of letters. An example of factual, non-literary prose is afforded by a column from a monthly newspaper (text 33). While seventeenth-century grammarians banned technical terms from good usage, they of necessity tolerated them in their own specialized spheres (as in, for example, the musicological texts of Marin Mersenne in which musical terminology is employed); in the eighteenth century, with the evolution of scientific and technical fields such as chemistry, came the renewed expansion of vocabulary and, through such popularizing works as the *Encyclopédie*, exposure of such neologisms to a wider audience. An example of the formulation of vocabulary appropriate to a new domain is provided from the field of economics (text 34).

Of the various parameters of variation, two others are illustrated here: medium and geography. The extract from Héroard's journal (text 35) indicates that many features associated with spoken usage today were common at least as far back as the seventeenth century; since Héroard is recording the usage of a young child, we may also glean from it some ideas about variation according to age.

Second, aside from the continued regional variation within France itself, the seventeenth century was also the first period of French colonial expansion, and witnessed, for example, the settlement of Canada, Martinique and Guadeloupe and the establishment of trading posts in Senegal and Madagascar. Through contact between French-speaking masters and African slaves, pidgins and creoles were created; here we have an early attestation of Haitian creole (text 36).

## 28 Claude Favre de Vaugelas, *Remarques sur la langue françoise* (1647)

*[handwritten: art influence on development of language]*

Since grammarians played an important role in the development of the French language during the classical period, we will start the section with a metalinguistic text. Claude Favre de Vaugelas (1585–1650), although himself from Savoy, was one of the key figures in the standardization and control of French in the seventeenth century. For Vaugelas, codification served various ends: not least it contributed to the fixing of the language in what was considered to be its present state of perfection and helped ensure others gained pleasure from one's linguistic usage since it was believed hearers liked to hear ideas expressed in the way they themselves would have formulated them. Vaugelas elaborated the idea of good usage as that of an elite: he defined it as the linguistic behaviour of the *plus saine partie* of the court and of the best authors of the day. In his highly influential *Remarques*, which ran to more than twenty editions in the period up to 1738, Vaugelas gives a series of randomly ordered observations on points of doubtful usage, and, if possible, aims to resolve uncertainty and recommend *le bon usage*. Writing for a predominantly court audience, Vaugelas prefers to reduce the use of technical terms to a minimum; in these extracts Vaugelas restricts himself to *terminaison* (l. 15), *periode* (l. 36), *conjonction* (l. 26) and *conjonctiue* (l. 37), *pluriel* and *singulier* (ll. 65–66) and *diphthongue* (l. 4) which, like the majority of his contemporaries, he uses indiscriminately to refer to diphthongs and digraphs. He also employs the case labels *nominatif*, *accusatif* (ll. 25–26), showing a continued dependence on Latin grammar, despite his avowed desire to describe French in its own right.

Here are four observations dealing with questions of pronunciation, verb morphology, syntactic structure and lexical purity:

*Portrait, pourtraict.*

*[handwritten: diphthong disappearing]*

**Il faut dire *portrait*, & non pas *pourtrait* auec vn *u*, comme la plus part ont accoustumé de le prononcer, & de l'escrire. Il est vray qu'on a fort long-temps prononcé en France l'*o* simple comme s'il y eust eu vn *u* apres, & que c'eust esté la diphthongue *ou*, comme *chouse*, pour *chose*, *fouβé*, pour *fossé*, *arrouser*, pour**       5
**arroser*, & ainsi plusieurs autres. Mais depuis dix ou douze ans, ceux qui parlent bien disent *arroser*, *fossé*, *chose*, sans *u*, & ces deux particulierement, *fouβé*, & *chouse*, sont deuenus insupportables aux oreilles delicates. Les Poëtes sont bien aises que l'on ne prononce plus *chouse*, parce qu'encore que la rime consiste**       10
**principalement en la prononciation, si est-ce qu'ils n'ont jamais fait rimer *chouse*, par exemple auec *jalouse*, mais tousjours auec les mots terminez en *ose*, comme *rose*, tellement que toutes les fois que *chose* finissoit le vers & faisoit la rime, s'il estoit employé**

le premier, & que *rose*, ou quelque autre mot de cette terminaison 15
s'ensuiuist, le Lecteur ne manquoit jamais de prononcer *chouse*,
qui ne rimoit pas apres auec *rose*, & cela estoit egalement
importun au Lecteur & au Poëte.

*Print, prindrent, prinrent.*
Tous trois ne valent rien, ils ont esté bons autrefois, & M. de
Malherbe en vse tousjours, *Et d'elle prindrent le flambeau, dont* 20
*ils desolerent leur terre, &c.* Mais aujourd'huy l'on dit seulement,
*prit*, & *prirent*, qui sont bien plus doux.

*Netteté de construction.*
Lors qu'en deux membres d'vne periode qui sont joints par la
conjonction *et*, le premier membre finit par vn nom, qui est à
l'accusatif, & l'autre membre commence par vn autre nom, qui 25
est au nominatif, on croit d'abord que le nom qui suit la conjonction, est au mesme cas que celuy qui le precede, parce que le
nominatif & l'accusatif sont tousjours semblables, & ainsi l'on est
trompé, & on l'entend tout autrement que ne le veut dire celuy
qui l'escrit. Vn exemple le va faire voir clairement. *Germanicus* 30
(en parlant d'Alexandre) *a egalé sa vertu, & son bonheur n'a*
*jamais eu de pareil.* Ie dis que ce n'est pas escrire nettement, que
d'escrire comme cela, *a egalé sa vertu, & son bonheur, &c.* parce
que *sa vertu* est accusatif, regi par le verbe *a egalé*, & *son bonheur*
est nominatif, & le commencement d'vne autre construction, & 35
de l'autre membre de la periode. Neantmoins il semble qu'estant
joints par la conjonctiue, *et*, ils aillent ensemble, ce qui n'est pas,
comme il se voit en acheuant de lire la periode entiere. On appelle
cela *vne construction lousche*, parce qu'elle semble regarder d'vn
costé, & elle regarde de l'autre. Plusieurs excellens Escriuains ne 40
sont pas exents de cette faute. Il ne me souuient point de l'auoir
jamais remarquee en M. Coeffeteau; je sçay bien qu'il y aura assez
de gens, qui nommeront cecy vn scrupule, & non pas vne faute,
parce que la lecture de toute la periode fait entendre le sens, &
ne permet pas d'en douter. Mais tousjours ils ne peuuent pas nier, 45
que le lecteur & l'auditeur n'y soient trompez d'abord, & quoy
qu'ils ne le soient pas long temps, il est certain qu'ils ne sont pas
bien aises de l'auoir esté, & que naturellement on n'aime pas à
se mesprendre. Enfin c'est vne imperfection qu'il faut euiter, pour
petite qu'elle soit, s'il est vray qu'il faille tousjours faire les choses 50
de la façon la plus parfaite qu'il se peut, sur tout lors qu'en matiere
de langage il s'agit de la clarté de l'expression.

*Du barbarisme, premier vice contre la pureté.*

**Pour les mots, on peut commettre vn barbarisme en plusieurs façons, ou en disant vn mot qui n'est point François, comme** *pache,* **pour** *pacte,* **ou** *paction,* **ou vn mot qui est François en vn sens &**   55
**non pas en l'autre, comme** *lent* **pour** *humide, sortir* **pour** *partir,* **ou qui a esté en vsage autrefois, mais qui ne l'est plus, comme** *ains, comme ainsi soit,* **& vne infinité d'autres, ou enfin vn mot, qui est encore si nouueau, & si peu estably par l'Vsage, qu'il passe pour barbarisme, à moins que d'estre adoucy par vn,** *s'il faut*   60
*ainsi parler, si i'ose vser de ce mot,* **ou quelque autre terme semblable, comme nous auons dit ailleurs; Ou bien en se seruant d'vn aduerbe pour vne preposition, comme de dire** *dessus la table,* **pour** *sur la table, dessous le lit,* **pour** *sous le lit, dedans le lit,* **pour** *dans le lit***; ou en disant au pluriel vn nom, qui ne se dit**   65
**bien qu'au singulier, comme** *bonheurs,* **ou au contraire, comme** *delice,* **pour** *delices . . .*

(Claude Favre de Vaugelas, *Remarques sur la langue françoise vtiles à ceux qui veulent bien parler et bien escrire* (Paris, Veuve Jean Camusat et Pierre le Petit, 1647), pp. 340–41, 98, 112–14, 568.[a])

[*Portrait, pourtraict.*

One should say *portrait* 'portrait' and not *pourtrait* with a *u* as the majority are used to pronouncing and writing it. It is true that for a very long time simple *o* has been pronounced in France as if there were a *u* following and it were the diphthong *ou*, for example, *chouse* for *chose* 'thing', *foussé* for *fossé* 'ditch', *arrouser* for *arroser* 'to water', and many others similarly. But for ten or twelve years those who speak well have said *arroser, fossé* and *chose* without a *u*, and these two in particular, *foussé* and *chouse*, have become intolerable to sensitive ears. [9] Poets are very content that people no longer pronounce *chouse*, because although rhyme depends principally on pronunciation, nevertheless they never rhyme *chouse* for example with *jalouse*, but always with words ending in *-ose*, like *rose*, so that whenever *chose* ended the line and came at the rhyme, if it were employed first and *rose* or some other word with this ending followed, the reader never failed to pronounce *chouse* which subsequently did not rhyme with *rose*, and this was equally irritating for the reader and the poet.

*Print, prindrent, prinrent.*
[19] All these are worthless. They used to be fine and M. de Malherbe always uses them for example, *Et d'elle prindrent le flambeau, dont ils desolerent leur terre, &c.* ('and took from her the flaming torch with which they devastated their land'), but today one simply says *prit* 'he took' and *prirent* 'they took' which are much more sweet-sounding.

a   Cambridge University Library, Bb*.2.25 (D). Also available in facsimile reprint, Geneva, Slatkine, 1970.

*Clarity of construction.*

[23] When in two clauses of a sentence which are joined by the conjunction *et*, the first clause ends with a noun in the accusative and the second begins with another noun which is in the nominative, one first of all thinks that the noun following the conjunction is in the same case as the one preceding it, since the nominative and accusative forms are always the same, and thus one is mistaken and understands it quite differently from what the writer intends. [30] An example will make this clear: *Germanicus* (en parlant d'Alexandre) *a egalé sa vertu, & son bonheur n'a jamais eu de pareil* 'Germanicus (speaking of Alexander) matched his virtue, and his happiness was never equalled'. I maintain that to write like this, *a egalé sa vertu, & son bonheur, etc.*, is not to write clearly, since *sa vertu* is an accusative governed by the verb *a egalé*, and *son bonheur* is in the nominative, and the beginning of a new construction and of the second clause of the sentence. Nevertheless it seems that as they are joined by the conjunction *et*, they go together, which is not the case, as is clear from reading to the end of the whole sentence. [38] This is called a *construction lousche* 'cross-eyed construction', because it seems to look one way and it looks another. Many excellent writers are not free from this fault. I do not remember ever having noticed it in the work of M. Coëffeteau. I know full well that there will be plenty of people who will call this a nicety and not a fault, because the reading of the whole sentence makes the meaning clear and does not permit any doubt about it. But nevertheless they cannot deny that the reader and listener have been misled about it first of all, and although this is not for long, it is clear that they are not very pleased to have been so, and that naturally one does not like to be mistaken. [49] In short, it is an imperfection to be avoided, however small it is, if it is true that one must always do things in the most perfect way possible, especially in matters of language where the clarity of expression is concerned.

*Concerning barbarisms, the first vice against purity.*

[53] As regards words, one may commit a barbarism in several ways, either by saying a word which is not French such as *pache* for *pacte* or *paction* 'pact', or a word which is French in one meaning and not in another, such as *lent* for *humide* 'damp', *sortir* for *partir* 'to leave', or which used to be in usage, but no longer is, like *ains* 'but, on the contrary', *comme ainsi soit* 'seeing that, since', and an infinite number of others, or finally a word which is still so new and so little established by usage that it counts as a barbarism unless it is mitigated by an 'if I may be permitted to speak thus' or 'if I may venture to use this word', or some other similar term, as we have said elsewhere; [62] or else by using an adverb for a preposition, for example in saying *dessus la table* for *sur la table* 'on the table', *dessous le lit* for *sous le lit* 'under the bed', *dedans le lit* for *dans le lit* 'in the bed'; or in saying a noun in the plural which is only acceptable in the

singular, such as *bonheurs* 'happiness(es)' or vice versa, such as *delice* for *delices* 'delights'.]

## COMMENTARY

We will first discuss the content of Vaugelas's pronouncements and prescriptions and then consider his own linguistic usage in the text.

### Vaugelas's comments on aspects of good usage

#### Pronunciation

The *Remarques* afford a number of insights into contemporary usage, and include discussion of the popular tendency to pronounce [ar] for [ɛr], the pronunciation of *oi* as [wɛ] or [ɛ], and the pronunciation of so-called *h aspiré*, etc. In the observation entitled *Portrait, pourtraict* (ll. 1–18) Vaugelas provides evidence of, and helps settle, the dispute between the *ouïstes* (favouring [u]) and the *non-ouïstes* (preferring [o]). Vaugelas proves to be a *non-ouïste*, arguing that in the last ten to twelve years those who speak well have favoured *arroser*, *chose*, *fossé* and *portrait*, that is the pronunciation with [o] rather than [u]. The recent nature of the change is underlined by the fact that in the *fautes d'impreßion* of the work *rabouteuse* is corrected to *raboteuse*.

#### Vaugelas's comments on verb morphology

We have seen how during the course of Middle French there was considerable reworking of the verb system through analogical pressures. Where variation or hesitation remained, this was largely removed from good usage in the seventeenth century by the pronouncements of grammarians. This fixing of one usage as correct is illustrated by Vaugelas's comments on *print*, *prindrent*, *prinrent* (ll. 19–22), which are eliminated in favour of *prit*, *prirent*. In other observations Vaugelas still allows some flexibility, for instance in the choice of *vesquit* or *vescut* (1647: 109) as the past simple of *vivre*, or *die* or *dise* as the present subjunctive of *dire* (349), but subsequent grammarians eliminate this choice and establish modern usage.

#### Vaugelas's comments on syntax

The demand for *netteté* 'clarity' in matters of syntax is paramount in the seventeenth century and grammarians criticize the loosely connected constructions of their sixteenth-century forebears. Vaugelas was at the vanguard of a movement advocating a sentence type in which all grammatical relationships are unequivocally marked. The comment here (ll. 23–52) illustrates how strict were the conditions placed on the avoidance of ambiguity in co-ordination. Although he himself admits that reading to the end of the sentence makes the meaning of his example perfectly clear – and indeed the presence of the comma would seem to exclude the reading of *et* as co-ordinating the two noun phrases – he argues that, since the reader may first misread the sentence, this is sufficient for it to be unacceptable. Given such stringent requirements on the avoidance of any potential ambiguity and the demand that all elements should be immediately comprehensible as they are read in linear succession, it is difficult to see how Vaugelas could use *et* as a clausal co-ordinator at all. Thus the Academy, commenting on Vaugelas's observation, permits this usage since the finite verb immediately follows the subject of the second clause. Nevertheless the spirit of the observation, that syntactic usage must in all cases be clear and unambiguous and that perfection should always be sought, pervades much of the usage of seventeenth- and eighteenth-century authors.

## Vaugelas's comments on vocabulary

If *netteté* is the key term as regards syntactic usage, the desire for *pureté* 'purity' dominates the discussion of lexical matters. In his discussion of *barbarismes* (ll. 53–67), Vaugelas details some of the ways in which speakers and authors contravene the demands of purity of usage: by using an incorrect form, a form with an unacceptable meaning, an archaism, a neologism (although Vaugelas is not as strict in condemning these as some of his seventeenth-century successors such as Bouhours), or a word in an incorrect function. This then reacts against the expansive tendency of the sixteenth century: rather than seeking to enrich the lexical resources of French, writers on French generally considered that the quality and correct employment of terms should take precedence. This restrictive attitude towards the lexicon joins with the literary ideal of finding the *mot juste*[b] to place high demands on the speaker or writer.

## Vaugelas's own usage

### Orthography

Vaugelas's own orthography seems to be guided by two at times contradictory principles. First, his own comments suggest he favours a spelling which reflects pronunciation; for instance, he says that the *d* should be removed from words such as *adjourner*, *adjouster*, *adjuger*, 'car à quel propos laisser vn *d*, qui n'est là que comme vne pierre d'achoppement

---

b  See, for example, La Bruyère (1965: 85): 'Entre toutes les différentes expressions qui peuvent rendre une seule de nos pensées, il n'y en a qu'une qui soit la bonne'.

pour faire broncher le Lecteur?' (1647: 439). Thus we find here spellings such as *exents* (l. 41). On the other hand, Vaugelas's respect of usage is perhaps responsible for more conservative spellings such as *sçay* (l. 43) or *mesprendre* (l. 49). As for accents, final [e] is generally marked by an acute accent (*prononcé*, l. 3, *trompé*, l. 29), but in the masculine plural *ez* is preferred (*terminez*, l. 13) and the acute accent is rare in other positions (*estably*, l. 60, *egalement*, l. 17); the grave accent is largely reserved for *à* (l. 24). The cedilla and diaeresis are used, but the circumflex hardly occurs (*eust*, l. 4, *estre*, l. 61).

## Morphology

Allowing for orthographic differences, and notably the continued use of *-oit*, etc. in imperfect endings, the morphology is in very large measure that of Modern French. An exception is *sçay* (l. 42), despite the fact that Vaugelas elsewhere recommends the forms *ie crois*, *fais*, *dis*, *crains*, etc. rather than *croy*, *fay*, *dy*, *crain*, etc. (1647: 131). Such contraventions of his own recommendations perhaps suggest that Vaugelas did not simply record usage, as he himself claimed, but also aimed to guide usage towards greater regularity.

## Syntax

Since Vaugelas favours a clear and unambiguous syntax in which all grammatical relationships are explicitly marked, it is not surprising to find, for example, the repetition of function markers as in *de le prononcer, & de l'escrire* (l. 2). A number of other features of his syntactic usage merit attention:

### Agreement

Various agreement issues discussed in the seventeenth century are illustrated in our extract. For instance, there was considerable debate as to the correct agreement with collective nouns and Vaugelas was largely responsible for the present ruling that *la plupart* takes a plural verb (ll. 1–2; 1647: 41–42). There was also much uncertainty about whether present participles should agree or remain invariable; Vaugelas is still somewhat hesitant (426–33), but favours a move towards the modern position of invariability, as indeed his usage here suggests (*estant joints*, ll. 36–37). Furthermore, Vaugelas was responsible for fixing the 'neuter' value of the personal attributive pronoun (27–29), although examples from seventeenth-century authors suggest that this usage took some time to become established. Vaugelas argues that a woman referring back to the adjective *malade* in a phrase such as *quand ie le suis* should use *le* and not *la*; a plural pronoun would be equally unacceptable when more than one person was referred to. This is exemplified here by & *quoy qu'ils ne le soient pas long temps* (ll. 46–47).

## Hypothetical clauses

Vaugelas follows his own recommendation (1647: 395–96) in using *que* followed by the subjunctive in a second co-ordinated hypothetical clause: *s'il estoit employé* ... & *que* rose, *ou quelque autre mot de cette terminaison s'ensuiuist* (ll. 14–16). The use of an imperfect or pluperfect subjunctive after *si* is still very common at this period (l. 4).

## Pronominal verbs

Pronominal usages with a passive meaning are attested at least as far back as the thirteenth century (*or se cante* 'now it is sung'); by the fifteenth century such usages had become fairly frequent, and indeed could have an agent expressed with them or have an animate subject, neither of which is allowed today. Meigret in the sixteenth century expressed reservations about such usages, but Vaugelas employs them without comment (*comme il se voit*, l. 38; *qui ne se dit bien qu'au singulier*, ll. 65–66). He also makes use of the impersonal form *il s'agit* (l. 52) in its modern sense, which is a seventeenth-century calque from Latin.

## Negation

Vaugelas was influential in establishing the rule that all negatives should have two parts, and he carefully follows this recommendation. He himself is uncertain about the difference between *pas* and *point* (1647: 409), which he uses fairly interchangeably in the extract.

## Word order

Vaugelas's promotion of clarity means that he favours a word order in which the elements are immediately comprehensible in their linear succession. It is therefore not surprising that he largely avoids inversion and favours SVO. As regards the position of the clitic pronoun in a sentence like *je ne le veux pas faire* or *je ne veux pas le faire*, Vaugelas, writing in a period of transition (Galet 1971), is uncertain which usage to support, but prefers the older one (*je le veux faire*) on the grounds that it is more used (1647: 376–77). Galet's statistics for the usage of seventeenth-century authors suggest that his judgement was correct for his day, and that the modern position of the pronoun only predominated in the second half of the century with variation remaining for some time. In his own usage Vaugelas likewise favours the order with clitic climbing: *vn exemple le va faire voir clairement*, l. 30.

## 29 François de Sales, *Introduction à la vie dévote* (early seventeenth century)

François de Sales (1567–1622), Roman Catholic bishop of Geneva from 1602, was a leader of the Counter-Reformation, active in the struggle against Calvinism. His *Introduction à la vie dévote*, first published in 1609, and in its definitive edition in 1619, was the first major Roman Catholic theological work designed to be a guide for the laity seeking spiritual perfection in their daily lives and its author became the first writer in French to be named doctor of the Church in 1877.

As well as its interest as a Roman Catholic work written in French, it provides a good example of early seventeenth-century prose. Vaugelas admired the clarity of François de Sales's style, yet in a number of respects his usage is typical of the first decades of the seventeenth century and differs therefore from the recommendations of Vaugelas.

The work is addressed to *Philothée*, 'lover of God'. Here are two short extracts, the first discussing the dangers of the pleasures of the world, and the second reflecting on the nature of meditation.

*Premiere partie. Chap. XXIII. Qu'il se faut purger de l'affection aux choses inutiles & dangereuses.*

Les ieux, les bals, les festins, les pompes, les commedies en leur substance ne sont nullement choses mauuaises, ains indifferentes, pouuans estre bien & mal exercees, tousiours neantmoins ces choses-là sont dangereuses: & de s'y affectionner, cela est encore plus dangereux. Ie dis doncques, Philothée qu'encor qu'il soit   5 loisible de ioüer, dancer, se parer, iouyr[a] des honnestes comedies, banquetter; si est-ce que d'auoir de l'affection à cela, c'est chose contraire à la deuotion, & extremement nuisible & perilleuse. Ce n'est pas mal de le faire, mais ouy bien de s'y affectionner. C'est dommage de semer en la terre de nostre cœur des affections si   10 vaines & sottes: cela occupe le lieu des bonnes impressions, & empesche que le suc de nostre ame ne soit employé és bonnes inclinations.

*Seconde partie. Chap. V. Des considerations, seconde partie de la meditation.*

Apres l'action de l'imagination, s'ensuit l'action de l'entendement, que nous appellons meditation, qui n'est autre chose, qu'vne ou   15 plusieurs considerations faites, à fin d'esmouuoir nos affections en Dieu, & aux choses diuines: en quoy la meditation est differente de l'estude & des autres pensees, & considerations, lesquelles ne se font pas pour acquerir la vertu, ou l'amour de

a   Other editions have the verb *ouïr* 'to hear', instead.

Dieu, mais pour quelques autres fins & intentions, comme pour   20
deuenir sçauant, pour en escrire, ou disputer. Ayant doncques
enfermé vostre esprit, comme i'ay dit, dans l'enclos du suject que
vous voulez mediter, ou par l'imagination, si le subiect est sensible,
ou par sa simple proposition, s'il est insensible; vous commencerez
à faire sur iceluy des considerations, dont vous verrez des exem-   25
ples tous formez és meditations que ie vous ay donnees. Que si
vostre esprit trouue assez de goust, de lumiere & de fruict sur
l'vne des consideratiõs, vous vous y arresterez sans passer plus
outre; faisant comme les abeilles, qui ne quittent point la fleur
tandis qu'elles y trouuent du miel à recueillir. Mais si vous ne   30
rencontrez pas selon vostre souhait en l'vne des considerations,
apres auoir vn peu marchandé, & essayé, vous passerez à vne
autre: mais allez tout bellement & simplement en ceste besongne
sans vous y empresser.

> (From *Introduction à la vie deuote; Du bien-heureux François
> de Sales, Euesque de Geneue, Instituteur de l'Ordre de la Visitation
> de saincte Marie*. Derniere edition. Reueüe, corrigée, & augmentée par
> l'Autheur, auant son decez ... (Lyon, Chez la vefue de Claude Rigaud &
> Claude Obert, 1630), pp. 97–98, 121–22.[b])

*[Part I, Chapter 23. That we ought to purge ourselves of the affection for
things which are useless and dangerous.*
Games, balls, feasts, ceremonies, and plays are not inherently bad things,
but rather neutral, for they can be performed in a good or bad fashion;
nevertheless these things are dangerous, and it is even more dangerous
to have a fondness for them. [5] Therefore I say, Philothea, that although
it is permissible to play, dance, dress up, enjoy honest plays and have
banquets, nevertheless to have an affection for these things is contrary to
devotion and extremely harmful and dangerous. It is not a bad thing
to do these things, but it is indeed bad to have an affection for them.
It is a pity to sow in the earth of our hearts such vain and stupid affections; it occupies the place of good impressions and prevents the sweetness
of our soul from being employed in good inclinations.

*Part II, Chapter 5. Of the reflections, which constitute the second part of
meditation.*
[14] After the work of the imagination comes the work of the understanding which we call meditation; this is nothing but one or two reflections
which are conceived in order to arouse our affection for God and for
heavenly things. Hence meditation is different from study and other types
of thoughts and reflections which are not for the sake of acquiring virtue
or the love of God, but for other purposes and ends, such as to become
learned or in order to write or dispute about them. [21] Having thus, as

b   Cambridge University Library, Q*.13.14.

I have already said, confined your mind within the bounds of the subject upon which you wish to meditate, either by the imagination, if the subject is perceptible, or by the simple proposition of it, if it is imperceptible, you will begin to have reflections upon it, of which you will find ready-made examples in the meditations which I have given to you. [26] But if your mind finds enough of relish, light and fruit in one of these reflections, stop there without going any further; acting like the bees who do not leave the flower as long as they find honey to collect there. But if you do not find what you wish in one of these reflections, having worked it over and tried it a little, go on to another one; but proceed quite gently and simply in this task without rushing.]

## COMMENTARY

### Orthography

While certainly free of the worst excesses of the heavily etymological spelling of the fifteenth and sixteenth centuries, this extract perpetuates many features typical of the previous century, such as the gemination of consonants (*commedies*, 1. 1, *banquetter*, 1. 7) and the retention of unpronounced letters (*sçauant*, 1. 21, *doncques*, 1. 21, *subiect*, 1. 23). In this last example, we may observe a lack of standardization since the spelling *suject* (1. 22) also occurs. As we would expect at this period, the use of accents is restricted largely to the acute in final position (but note the mono-syllable *és*, 1. 12), the cedilla, already firmly established by this time, the diaeresis, and the grave accent on *à* (1. 16). For much of the century *j* remained rare and *i* was used for both [i] and [ʒ]; *u* and *v* were broadly positional variants, with *v* favoured in initial position and *u* elsewhere. The tilde is occasionally used still at the beginning of the century replacing a following *m* or *n* (*consideratiõs*, 1. 28).

### Morphology

#### Articles

We find late examples of the contraction *és* (ll. 12, 26), which did not survive beyond the seventeenth century except in a few set expressions.

#### Adverbs

In Old French a common adverbial marker alongside -*ment* was a final -*s*. Some relics of this survive into the seventeenth century in words such as *donc*, which could have three different forms; thus *doncques* (1. 5) ending in adverbial *s* occurred alongside *doncque* and *donc* (cf. *encor*,

l. 5 (in the conjunction *encor que*) and *encore*, l. 4).[c] Vaugelas recommends *encore* (1647: 252) but *doncques* (392), and the spelling *auecque* for the preposition, not *auecques* (391), underlining thereby the fact that there was still considerable variation in the middle of the century.

### Demonstratives

By this time the demonstrative forms with an initial *i* such as *iceluy* (l. 25) were already archaic or reserved for familiar contexts. Spillebout (1985: 65) has no example of these forms after 1623 and two of his examples come from François de Sales.

### Relative pronouns

The use of *lequel, laquelle* in the subject function, so favoured in sixteenth-century texts, is also found (l. 19), but becomes less common as the century progresses. For Vaugelas (1647: 115–16), while these forms are useful for disambiguating which of the nouns is referred to where there are two or more antecedents of different number or gender, he recommends that elsewhere they should generally be avoided because they are heavy and cumbersome. On the other hand, François de Sales uses *dont* (l. 25), the modern usage, rather than *desquelles*.

## Syntax

### Use of articles

The desire for absence of ambiguity and for regular and explicit marking of function led in the seventeenth century to the expectation that every noun should be accompanied by a determiner, except in certain fixed contexts such as *c'est dommage* (ll. 9–10). While François de Sales repeats the article in the opening enumeration (l. 1), there is also an example of an omission of the type later censured by Vaugelas in *c'est chose contraire à* (ll. 7–8).

### Agreement

By this period the rule for the agreement of a past participle with a preceding direct object was already fixed (e.g. *donnees*, l. 26), although other usages took much longer to establish (e.g. *nous nous sommes rendus maistres/puissans*, see Vaugelas 1647: 175–81). François de Sales here makes the present participle agree (l. 3) as was still quite normal at the beginning of the century.

c   Note that the -*s* is here restricted to those adverbs ending in a vowel and that the forms *\*doncs*, *\*encors*, etc. are not attested.

## Negation

Negative *ne* is regularly accompanied by a negative particle in this extract; this is principally *pas* or *point*, but in line 2, for instance, *nullement* is used as an emphatic negative meaning 'not at all'.

## Latinisms

There is an instance of a latinate construction of the type more frequently associated with sixteenth- rather than seventeenth-century usage, namely the calquing of *quod si* as *que si* in initial position to mean either 'and if' or 'but if' (l. 26). Many of the latinate constructions favoured by sixteenth-century authors were criticized in the seventeenth century and fell out of usage, notably the *relatif de liaison* and the use of unattached participle clauses imitating the Latin ablative absolute construction.

## Word order

In the main François de Sales takes care over the ordering of the constituents and favours SVO. An example of inversion is found after the adverbial phrase *apres l'action de l'imagination* (l. 14). Not surprisingly, the clitic pronoun is placed before the finite verb rather than the infinitive (*il se faut purger*, title of chapter 23).

## Vocabulary

A number of conjunctions which fell out of usage during the course of the century are still employed by François de Sales. These include three conjunctions expressing opposition: *ains* 'but, on the contrary' (l. 2), used after a negative clause (cf. German *sondern*); *si est-ce que* (l. 7); and *ouy bien* (l. 9). Already in the *Remarques* Vaugelas comments that *ains* has fallen from usage (see text 28, ll. 57–58), while at the end of the century La Bruyère regrets the loss of what he considers to be a useful term (Rickard 1992: 272). It is indeed somewhat ironic that at a time when grammarians were calling for the clear and unambiguous marking of clausal connections a number of conjunctions fell into disuse.

The use of *s'affectionner à* in its pronominal form was a fairly recent formation, probably first attested in Montaigne (1580). On the other hand, the figurative sense of *se purger* is today rather archaic.

# 30 Voltaire, *Candide* (1759)

We now turn to three examples of literary usage and first the classical prose of Voltaire, pseudonym of François-Marie Arouet (1694–1778). In his *Siècle de Louis XIV* Voltaire praised the state of perfection reached by the French language during that age and the achievements of the best classical authors which he aimed to emulate in his own vast output (Voltaire 1966: 45–60).

This is an example from *Candide*, his most famous *conte philosophique*, first published in 1759. One is immediately struck by how closely this text resembles literary prose of today: the morphological and syntactic usage of written Modern French is in its essentials established and the style reflects the classical ideal of clarity of expression. In the tale, Voltaire, using such techniques as wit and irony, understatement and exaggeration, satirizes the optimism of Leibniz and Jean-Jacques Rousseau which appeared hollow in the wake of such events as the Lisbon earthquake of 1755. The extract is from chapter 18 and recounts what Candide and Cacambo saw in the land of Eldorado.

> **Cacambo témoigna à son hôte toute sa curiosité: l'hôte lui dit, Je**
> **suis fort ignorant, & je m'en trouve bien; mais nous avons ici un**
> **Vieillard retiré de la Cour, qui est le plus savant homme du**
> **Royaume, & le plus communicatif. Aussitôt il méne Cacambo chez**
> **le Vieillard. Candide ne jouait plus que le second personnage, &** 5
> **accompagnait son valet. Ils entrèrent dans une maison fort simple,**
> **car la porte n'était que d'argent, & les lambris des apartements**
> **n'étaient que d'or, mais travaillés avec tant de goût, que les plus**
> **riches lambris ne l'effaçaient pas. L'antichambre n'était à la vérité**
> **incrustée que de rubis & d'émeraudes, mais l'ordre dans lequel** 10
> **tout était arrangé réparait bien cette extrême simplicité.**
>
> **Le Vieillard reçut les deux étrangers sur un sopha matelassé de**
> **plumes de colibri, & leur fit présenter des liqueurs dans des vases**
> **de diaments; après quoi il satisfit à leur curiosité en ces termes.**
>
> **Je suis âgé de cent soixante & douze ans; & j'ai apris de feu** 15
> **mon père, Ecuyer du Roi, les étonnantes révolutions du Pérou**
> **dont il avait été témoin. Le Royaume où nous sommes est l'an-**
> **cienne patrie des Incas qui en sortirent très imprudemment pour**
> **aller subjuguer une partie du Monde, & qui furent enfin détruits**
> **par les Espagnols.** 20
>
> **Les Princes de leur famille qui restèrent dans leur pays natal**
> **furent plus sages; ils ordonnèrent du consentement de la nation,**
> **qu'aucun habitant ne sortirait jamais de nôtre petit Royaume; &**
> **c'est ce qui nous a conservé nôtre innocence & nôtre félicité. Les**
> **Espagnols ont eu une connaissance confuse de ce pays, ils l'ont** 25

**appelle**[a] *El Dorado*; **& un Anglais nommé le Chevalier** *Raleig,*
**en a même aproché il y a environ cent années; mais comme nous**
**sommes entourés de rochers inabordables & de précipices, nous**
**avons toujours été jusqu'à présent à l'abri de la rapidité des**
**nations de l'Europe, qui ont une fureur inconcevable pour les cail-** 30
**loux & pour la fange de nôtre terre, & qui pour en avoir nous**
**tueraient tous jusqu'au dernier.**

(From *Candide, ou l'Optimisme, traduit de l'allemand de*
*Mr. le Docteur Ralph* ([n.p.], [n.pub.], 1759), pp. 147–50.[b])

Cacambo indicated to the landlord how curious he was to know more.
The landlord said to him, 'I am very ignorant, and I like it that way; but
we have an old man here who has retired from the court and who is the
most knowledgeable man in the kingdom, as well as the most communicative.' He straight way took Cacambo to the old man's house. It was
Candide who was playing second fiddle now and accompanying his servant.
[6] They entered a very modest house, for the door was made only of
silver, and the panelling of the rooms was of nothing but gold, but worked
in such good taste that the finest panelling would not outshine it. In truth
the antechamber was studded only with rubies and emeralds, but the
pattern in which they had been arranged more than made up for this
extreme simplicity.
[12] The old man received the two strangers on a sofa stuffed with
hummingbird feathers, and offered them various liquors in diamond-
studded goblets. After this he satisfied their curiosity in the following
terms:
[15] 'I am 172 years old, and I learnt from my late father, who was equerry
to the King, of the extraordinary upheavals which he had witnessed in
Peru. The kingdom we are in was formerly the native land of the Incas
who most unwisely left it to go and conquer another part of the world
and were finally wiped out by the Spaniards.
[21] The princes of their house who stayed in their native land were wiser;
they decreed, with the consent of the nation, that no inhabitant should
ever leave our small kingdom, and this is what has preserved our inno-
cence and happiness. [24] The Spaniards had a vague knowledge of this
country, and an English knight called Raleigh even came fairly close to
it about 100 years ago; but since we are surrounded by unscalable rocks
and cliffs, we have always been until now sheltered from the rapacity of
the European nations, who have an unaccountable passion for the pebbles
and the mud of our earth, and who, in order to get hold of some, would
kill us to the very last man.']

---

a   This is a typographical error for *appellé*.
b   Cambridge University Library, Syn.7.75.8.

**COMMENTARY**

**Orthography**

Alongside the radical spelling reforms proposed in the sixteenth century for instance by Meigret (text 27), the poet Ronsard had proposed more moderate reforms for use in verse: these included the use of ¢ to denote an elided [ə], the removal of many double consonants and unpronounced etymological letters, the regular use of -*s* in place of final -*x* or -*z*, the substitution of *f* for *ph* in words derived from Greek, and the use of internal accents. While Ronsard himself soon abandoned his reformed spelling, it was used by a number of poets, but lost support by the end of the century. It did not, however, sink without trace. A number of Dutch printers had adopted the reforms, and when their editions flooded the French market in the seventeenth century, many of Ronsard's reforms were slowly re-introduced, so that by the second half of the century a simplified spelling system began to prevail. While the first edition of the Academy dictionary (1694) tended to be conservative in its spellings, by the third edition (1740) it had become clear that the spelling had to be revised since there was a huge gap between the Academy's recommendations and the practice of publishers. Thanks largely to the efforts of the Abbé d'Olivet, the spelling of some 5,000 words out of a total of about 18,000 was reformed: a large number of double consonants were simplified (although double *n* remained and geminate *t* and *l* to mark the open quality of the preceding vowel), silent letters, and notably *s*, were removed (the notable exception being *est* of the verb *être*), internal accents were added, *y* was replaced by *i* in words like *soy* etc. (but not in words derived from Greek), and *t* was removed from the plural forms of nouns and adjectives ending in -*ant* or -*ent*. It is this spelling which is reflected in our extract from Voltaire which differs quite markedly from Vaugelas's orthography of only a century earlier. With the exception of *méne* (l. 4) and *nôtre* (l. 23), the use of accents is what we would expect today (a number of circumflexes were eliminated from the fourth edition of the Academy dictionary of 1762, which otherwise only contained relatively minor revisions); the spellings likewise appear modern, save *sopha* (l. 12) with *ph* rather than *f*, and *apris* (l. 15) with a single *p*. Note also the establishment of the consonantal and vocalic values respectively for *j* and *i* and *v* and *u*.

Perhaps the most interesting feature of Voltaire's spelling is the use of -*ait* etc. in the imperfect and conditional endings (e.g. *jouait*, l. 5, *tueraient*, l. 32). Sixteenth-century grammarians had discussed the pronunciation of *oi* and generally advocated the pronunciation [wɛ]; nevertheless [ɛ] was common in the sixteenth and seventeenth centuries and came to be accepted in a number of words including these verb endings. Despite this, the spelling -*oit* remained throughout the seventeenth century and was espoused by most eighteenth-century authors. It is largely thanks to the influence of Voltaire that the Academy finally adopted the spelling *-ait* etc. in the 1835 edition of its dictionary, rather than *è* favoured by many reformers.

## Morphology and syntax

Voltaire's use of morphology and syntax appears almost entirely modern. We may note, for instance, the clear distinction made between the comparative and superlative form of adjectives (*plus sage*, l. 22, *le plus savant*, l. 3); in the middle of the previous century Vaugelas (1647: 75) had still felt it necessary to specify that the article had to be used in the superlative (for seventeenth-century examples of the non-use of the article in the superlative see Spillebout 1985: 38). Grammatical relationships are clearly and explicitly marked and SVO prevails. There is a tendency, however, for adjectives to appear in the prenominal position (*cette extrême simplicité*, l. 11, *les étonnantes révolutions*, l. 16). Note too the separation of the co-ordinated superlative adjectives by the noun, so typical of Middle French usage, in *le plus savant homme du Royaume*, & *le plus communicatif* (ll. 3–4). After this usage had been condemned by Vaugelas (1647: 156–57), classical authors increasingly tended to avoid it.

## Vocabulary

In spite of the reluctance of seventeenth-century normative grammarians to accept neologisms, some new terms continued to be created during that century and gradually became established in general usage. Evidence of this process is afforded by *colibri* (l. 13), first attested *c.* 1640 and of uncertain origin; *inabordable* (l. 28), which first appears in Cotgrave's dictionary of 1611 and then acquired figurative uses later in the century; *matelasser* (l. 12), formed from *matelas* in the second half of the century; and *sopha* (l. 12), which was introduced into French from Arabic in the sixteenth century with the meaning 'estrade élevée couverte de coussins', but only acquired its modern meaning towards the end of the seventeenth century.

While the comments of grammarians succeeded in exiling a number of words and expressions from good usage which in turn led to their eventual demise, this was not always the case: despite Vaugelas's condemnation of *à présent* (1647: 224), it continued to be used (see l. 29) and has remained in common usage.

Similarly, despite the debate about the acceptability of *car* in the early part of the seventeenth century, it survived (l. 7). Finally, note that Voltaire uses the older way of expressing numerals above twenty joining the elements with *et: soixante & douze* (l. 15). While this was usual in the sixteenth century, the modern forms without *et* already occurred, and during the seventeenth century Oudin formulated the modern rule which was increasingly observed as the century progressed, and generally adopted in the eighteenth century. Thus in its dictionary of 1718 the Academy favours *trente et un*, but considers *vingt et deux* a Gasconism (Seguin 1972: 79).

# 31 Pierre-Ambroise-François Choderlos de Laclos, *Les Liaisons dangereuses* (1782)

Pierre-Ambroise-François Choderlos de Laclos (1741–1803) pursued an army career. His only novel, *Les Liaisons dangereuses*, may have been considered scandalous when it first appeared in 1782, but this did not prevent it from achieving great popularity with a large number of pirated editions of it appearing from 1782 on. The novel is composed of a series of letters written by the various characters, and Laclos varies the style and tone of his writing to reflect their different personalities. This is an example of the spontaneous, affective usage of Cécile Volanges; it provides a good illustration of the literary representation of 'style familier' or informal, relaxed usage which contains elements of spoken usage. The letter is addressed to a close female friend whom Cécile addresses as *tu*.

### Lettre XXIX
**Cécile Volanges à Sophie Carnay**

Je te le disois bien, Sophie, qu'il y avoit des cas où on pouvoit écrire; et je t'assure que je me reproche bien d'avoir suivi ton avis, qui nous a tant fait de peine, au chevalier Danceny & à moi. La preuve que j'avois raison, c'est que madame de Merteuil, qui est une femme qui sûrement le sait bien, a fini par penser comme moi. 5
Je lui ai tout avoué. Elle m'a bien dit d'abord comme toi: mais quand je lui ai eu tout expliqué, elle est convenue que c'étoit bien différent; elle exige seulement que je lui fasse voir toutes mes lettres & toutes celles du chevalier Danceny, afin d'être sûre que je ne dirai que ce qu'il faudra; ainsi, à présent, me voilà tranquille. 10
Mon Dieu, que je l'aime madame de Merteuil! elle est si bonne! & c'est une femme bien respectable. Ainsi il n'y a rien à dire.

Comme je m'en vais écrire à M. Danceny, & comme il va être content! il le[a] sera encore plus qu'il ne croit: car jusqu'ici je ne lui parlois que de mon amitié, & lui vouloit toujours que je dise mon 15
amour. Je crois que c'étoit bien la même chose; mais enfin je n'osois pas, & il tenoit à cela. Je l'ai dit à Mde de Merteuil; elle m'a dit que j'avois eu raison, & qu'il ne falloit convenir d'avoir de l'amour, que quand on ne pouvoit plus s'en empêcher: or je suis bien sûre que je ne pourrai pas m'en empêcher plus long-temps; après tout 20
c'est la même chose, & cela lui plaira davantage.

Mde de Merteuil m'a dit aussi qu'elle me prêteroit des livres qui parloient de tout cela, et qui m'apprendroient bien à me conduire, & aussi à mieux écrire que je ne fais: car, vois-tu, elle me dit tous mes défauts, ce qui est une preuve qu'elle m'aime bien; elle 25

---

a The text has *se*.

m'a recommandé seulement de ne rien dire à maman de ces
livres-là, parce que ça auroit l'air de trouver qu'elle a trop négligé
mon éducation, et ça pourroit la fâcher. Oh! je ne lui en dirai
rien.

C'est pourtant bien extraordinaire qu'une femme qui ne m'est    30
presque pas parente, prenne plus de soin de moi que ma mère! c'est
bien heureux pour moi de l'avoir connue!

Elle a demandé aussi à maman de me mener après demain à
l'opéra, dans sa loge; elle m'a dit que nous y serions toutes seules,
& nous causerons tout le temps, sans craindre qu'on nous entende:    35
j'aime bien mieux cela que l'opéra. Nous causerons aussi de mon
mariage: car elle m'a dit que c'étoit bien vrai que j'allois me marier;
mais nous n'avons pas pu en dire davantage. Par exemple, n'est-ce
pas encore bien étonnant, que maman ne m'en dise rien du tout?

Adieu, ma Sophie, je m'en vas écrire au chevalier Danceny. Oh!    40
je suis bien contente.

De ... ce 24 Août 17**.

(From *Les Liaisons dangereuses, ou lettres recueillies dans une Société,
& publiées pour l'instruction de quelques autres. Par M.C. . . . .
de L. . .*, vol. 1 (Amsterdam, Paris, Durand, 1782), pp. 144–47.[b])

[Cécile Volanges to Sophie Carnay

I told you, Sophie, that there are circumstances in which you can write;
and I assure you that I greatly regret having followed your advice which
has caused the Chevalier Danceny and myself so much pain. The proof
that I was right is that Mme de Merteuil, who certainly knows about such
things, ended up thinking like me. [6] I told her everything. First of all
she said the same to me as you, but when I had explained everything to
her, she agreed that things were indeed different; she merely insists that
I show her all my letters and all those of the Chevalier Danceny so that
she can be sure that I only say what is proper; and so, for the moment,
my mind is at rest. Heavens, how fond I am of Mme de Merteuil! She is
so good! And such a respectable woman. So nothing can be said.
[13] What letters I'm going to write to M. Danceny and how pleased he
is going to be! He will be even more pleased than he thinks, for up till
now I spoke to him only of my friendship and he always wanted me to
speak of my love. [16] I think it much the same thing, but I didn't dare,
although he very much wanted it. I told Mme de Merteuil and she told
me I was right and that you should never admit to love unless you could
no longer help it. Well I'm quite sure that I will not be able to help it for
much longer; after all it amounts to the same thing and it will give him
greater pleasure.
[22] Mme de Merteuil also told me that she would lend me some books
about all this which will teach me to behave properly and also to write

b  Cambridge University Library, 7735.d.956

better than I do: for, you see, she tells me all my faults, which proves how much she loves me; she merely advised me not to saying anything to Mama about these books, because it might appear as if she had neglected my education, and that might anger her. Oh! I shall say nothing to her about them.

[30] Nevertheless it's quite extraordinary that a woman who is hardly related to me should take more care of me than my mother! How lucky I am to have met her!

[33] She has also asked Mama to allow her to take me the day after tomorrow to her box at the opera; she told me that we shall be quite alone there, and that we'll talk the whole time without fear of being over-heard: I much prefer that to the opera. We shall talk about my marriage too, for she told me that it is indeed true that I am to be married; but we have not been able to discuss it any further. Really, isn't it quite amazing that Mama has said nothing to me about it at all?

[40] Goodbye, my dear Sophie, I'm going to write to the Chevalier Danceny. Oh! how happy I am.

From . . . , 24 August 17**.]

## COMMENTARY

### Orthography

With the exception of the imperfect and conditional endings, for which Laclos follows the majority of eighteenth-century authors in retaining the spelling *-oit* etc., the spelling appears almost entirely modern. During this period, variation as to whether compounds should be written as one word, hyphenated, or as separate words was gradually eliminated and one form standardized. Whereas François de Sales wrote *à fin* as two words (text 29, l. 16), Laclos writes it as one (l. 9); on the other hand, *long-temps* (l. 20) is still hyphenated.

### Morphology

Once again we may note how areas of morphology on which seventeenth-century grammarians still felt it necessary to comment have by this time become standardized in their modern form. Laclos, for example, clearly distinguishes the usage of *qui, que* and *ce qui, ce que* (l. 25). The main interest here concerns verb morphology. First, we may note the use of the *passé surcomposé* or double compound form in *je lui ai eu tout expliqué* (l. 7) to express anteriority in a subordinate clause where the main clause verb is in the perfect. This usage may be seen as paralleling the use of the past anterior in a temporal subordinate clause with a past historic in the main clause, and the formation of the double compound forms may well be associated with the demise of the past historic from the spoken language. There are instances of such usages of double compound forms at least as far back as the fifteenth century,[c] and they are noted by grammarians from the sixteenth century on. If we look at examples of where they are used in eighteenth-century texts, it appears that already they were associated with more informal usages (Ayres-Bennett 1994); over the last 150 years they have increasingly been stigmatized by grammarians. This may partly be explained by the fact that they also have a main clause usage, as in *j'ai eu fait des foins à la main* in which choice of the double compound form implies both that this happened in a distant past and that I no longer carry out the action. With changing attitudes towards the dialects, such examples have acquired negative connotations. Another reason for the fact that the double compound forms have always remained on the margins of acceptability may be that anteriority may be marked in a number of other ways, or may not need to be marked explicitly since the context often makes the sense clear. On the other hand, the use of <u>aller + infinitive</u> first to mark a future with some link to the present (e.g. predetermined) and then as a simple alternative to the future, also attested for the first time <u>in the fifteenth century,</u> has continued to grow in popularity and is very widely used today, especially in the spoken language; here there is an example of this construction in reported speech, *c'étoit bien vrai que j'allois me marier* (l. 37).

Note that the form of the present subjunctive of *dire*, which was discussed by Vaugelas, is now fixed as *dise* (l. 15) rather than *die*. Laclos still apparently hesitates whether to use *je m'en vais* (l. 13) or *je m'en vas* (l. 40) (cf. Vaugelas 1647: 27), and the latter is still preferred by a number of eighteenth-century grammarians (Seguin 1972: 82–83).

## Syntax

### Use of pronouns

The emphatic pronoun *lui* is used in the subject function to express a contrast (l. 15) without the need of a following unstressed pronoun *il*. Today such a construction is increasingly considered to be literary.

### Use of the subjunctive

Eighteenth-century grammarians hesitated in their pronouncements on the use of the subjunctive and tended to base their recommendations on semantic considerations rather than formal rules (Seguin 1972: 122–23). We may note a tendency for the subjunctive no longer to be employed after verbs of thinking used affirmatively, unless the affirmation was

---

c   Indeed, there are examples of pluperfect double compound forms in main clauses dating from the thirteenth century; see Carruthers 1993: 5–9.

attenuated, but an increase in the use of the subjunctive after verbs of emotion. Thus here all the verbs and expressions of volition or emotion are followed by a subjunctive in the subordinate clause (*vouloir que*, l. 15, *c'est bien extraordinaire que*, l. 30, *sans craindre que*, l. 35, *n'est-ce pas bien étonnant que*, ll. 38–39). Since Old French, infinitival constructions have increased in usage thereby avoiding the need for a subjunctive as in *c'est bien heureux pour moi de l'avoir connue!*, ll. 31–32.

### Agreement of tout

There had been considerable hesitation as to whether *tout* should agree, as it had in Old French, or remain invariable. In the *Remarques* (1647: 95–97) Vaugelas had asserted that *tout* is adverbial and invariable in the masculine, but that in the feminine *tout* agrees, whether it is followed by a word beginning with a consonant or a vowel, the only exception being *tout autres* in the plural. The present ruling that *tout* is invariable except before a feminine noun beginning with a consonant or *h aspiré* and established by the Academy in 1704 is observed by Laclos in *toutes seules* (l. 34). It reflects the failure of classical grammarians to apply logically and consistently their belief that *tout* is adverbial and therefore invariable.

### Dislocation

The use of a right dislocated structure, *que je l'aime madame de Merteuil!* (l. 11) with the pronoun anticipating the following noun phrase, is an informal feature which is very typical of spoken usage today.

### Word order

There are a number of examples which illustrate the fixing of word order since the middle of the seventeenth century. These include the position of the negative particles before an infinitive as recommended by Vaugelas (1647: 409), *de ne rien dire* (l. 26); the position of the clitic pronoun before the infinitive rather than the finite verb, *j'allois me marier* (l. 37); and the relative ordering of the direct and indirect object pronoun (cf. Vaugelas 1647: 33–34), with the indirect object preceding the direct object (*je te le disois*, l. 1), except when there are two third person pronouns.

### Vocabulary

Several words and expressions are used to characterize an informal style. Most notable is the use of *ça* alongside *cela*; while there are occasional examples of this in lower register usage in the seventeenth century, it did not become common in written language before the nineteenth century. Note also the discourse markers *vois-tu* (l. 24) and *par exemple* (l. 38), and the exclamations *oh!* (l. 28), *Mon Dieu!* (l. 11). It is evident that the writer is not concerned to vary greatly her vocabulary and repeats the same words and constructions.

*Opéra* (l. 34) is an example of a seventeenth-century borrowing from Italian; it probably entered the language when Mazarin introduced Italian opera to Paris around the middle of the century. Although the peak of borrowing from Italian had passed by about 1560, words associated with the fine arts continued to be adopted.

## 32 Jean Racine, *Britannicus* (1669)   *classical tragedian playwright*

*Britannicus* by Jean Racine (1639–99) was first performed in December 1669. Racine was held in the highest esteem by the eighteenth century as the paragon of *le style noble*. For seventeenth-century writers on French it was considered essential that the three principal styles, *le style noble*, *le style médiocre* and *le style bas*, should be kept clearly apart since each had its own appropriate words and expressions. An anecdote recorded by Racine's son Louis, that his father studied Vaugelas's *Remarques* and translation of Quintus Curtius Rufus amongst other works while he was away from Paris in Uzès since he feared he would forget how to use French properly and be corrupted by provincial usage while he was there (Racine 1962: 23), suggests Racine's respect for *le bon usage* and the influence of normative grammar on even the greatest creative geniuses of the age.

This extract from Act V, Scene VI is spoken by Nero's mother Agrippina. It follows the spelling and punctuation of the last edition to appear during Racine's lifetime (Paris, 1697).

> **Poursui, Neron, avec de tels Ministres.**
> **Par des faits glorieux tu te vas signaler.**
> **Poursui. Tu n'as pas fait ce pas pour reculer.**
> **Ta main a commencé par le sang de ton Frere,**
> **Je prevoi que tes coups viendront jusqu'à ta Mère.**                5
> **Dans le fond de ton cœur, je sçay que tu me hais,**
> **Tu voudras t'affranchir du joug de mes bienfaits,**
> **Mais je veux que ma mort te soit mesme inutile:**
> **Ne crois pas qu'en mourant je te laisse tranquille.**
> **Rome, ce Ciel, ce jour que tu receus de moi,**                     10
> **Par tout, à tout moment, m'offriront devant toy.**
> **Tes remords te suivront comme autant de furies.**
> **Tu croiras les calmer par d'autres barbaries.**
> **Ta fureur s'irritant soy-mesme dans son cours,**
> **D'un sang toûjours nouveau marquera tous les jours.**              15
> **Mais j'espere qu'enfin le Ciel las de tes crimes**
> **Ajoûtera ta perte à tant d'autres victimes,**
> **Qu'aprés t'estre couvert de leur sang et du mien,**
> **Tu te verras forcé de répandre le tien;**
> **Et ton nom paroistra, dans la race future**                        20
> **Aux plus cruels Tyrans une cruelle injure.**

> (From *Jean Racine, Théâtre de 1668 à 1670*. Texte établi et présenté par G. Truc (Paris, Les Belles Lettres, 1953), p. 168.)

[Continue, Nero, with such ministers.
You will distinguish yourself with glorious deeds.
Continue. You have not taken this step to retreat.

Your hand has begun with your brother's blood,
I foresee that it will go on to strike your mother.                    5
In the depths of your heart I know that you hate me.
You will want to free yourself of the yoke of my services.
But I want my death to be useless to you:
Do not think that by dying I leave you tranquil.
Rome, this heaven, this light of day, which you received from me,   10
Everywhere, at all times, will remind you of me.
Your remorse will pursue you like the Furies,
You will think to calm it by other atrocities.
Your fury, becoming irritated with itself in its pursuits,
Will mark each day with fresh blood.                                15
But I hope that the heavens, finally tired of your crimes,
Will add your loss to that of so many other victims;
That having covered yourself in their blood and in mine,
You will find yourself forced to shed your own;
And your name will appear in future generations                    20
A cruel insult to the cruellest of tyrants.]


## BRIEF COMMENTARY

The play is written in alexandrines (twelve-syllable lines) grouped in
rhyming couplets. The versification is helpful, for example, in determining
that for Racine the second person singular present indicative of *haïr* had
a monosyllabic pronunciation (l. 6); Vaugelas (1647: 20) notes that there
was considerable hesitation over the conjugation of the present indicative
of this verb, with some people favouring a bisyllabic pronunciation in the
three persons singular, some eliding the pronoun (*i'haïs*), and yet others
conjugating the plural as *hayons, hayez, hayent*, rather than the recommended *haïssons, haïssez, haïssent*. The second person imperative *poursui*
(l. 1), without a final -*s*, and the first person present indicative forms *prevoi*
(l. 5) and *sçay* (l. 6), are late remnants of Old French usage; such examples are rare after the middle of the century. In earlier usage the role of
*soi* as opposed to *lui* had been rather ill-defined; in the seventeenth century
*soi* gradually became restricted to use with indefinite subjects and where
no antecedent is present. Here then we have an example of *soi-même* with
an abstract noun as subject (l. 14). As regards syntax, we may observe the
plural verb following *Rome, ce Ciel, ce jour* (ll. 10–11) despite the fact
that these nouns appear to be in apposition, and Racine's fluctuation as
to whether to place the clitic object pronoun before the finite verb or the
dependent infinitive (*tu te vas signaler*, l. 2, but *tu voudras t'affranchir*,
l. 7, *tu croiras les calmer*, l. 13).

The use of abstract nouns, particularly in the plural, is typical of this
elevated style: *remords* (l. 12), *barbaries* (l. 13). Racine also uses *futur(e)*
(l. 20), which in Vaugelas's eyes was highly acceptable in verse, but not

in prose (1647: 463–64). As we have noted, there was concern to differentiate the meaning of formally related terms; one example is the pair *fureur* and *furie*. It is not clear, however, that Racine's use of *fureur* (l. 14) adheres to Vaugelas's distinction (446) that '*fureur*, denote dauantage, *l'agitation violente du dedans*' whereas *furie* refers rather to '*les actions violentes du dehors*'. Finally, the adjective *glorieux* (l. 2) could be used pejoratively in the seventeenth and eighteenth centuries.

# 33 *Mercure de France* (1732)

As an example of factual prose we have chosen a piece from an eighteenth-century monthly newspaper, the *Mercure de France* which from 1724 on was under the direction of Antoine de la Roque. The journal, addressed to an educated public, aimed to mix the serious and the entertaining; while about 50 per cent of each issue was devoted to literary matters, there were also chronicles from the academies and colleges, news from Versailles and Paris, details of marriages and deaths, and what we have exemplified here, foreign news.

It is often stated that, in comparison to English, French tends to avoid the passive. While this is doubtless to some extent true, we can see that in objective, factual accounts such as this, passives and impersonal constructions abound, just as they do in French journalism today. The desire for clear and explicit marking of the function of the terms is as evident here as in our literary examples. We may observe, for example, the repetition of the preposition *pour* before the second of two co-ordinated infinitives (*pour feliciter . . . et pour l'assurer* (ll. 2–4)).

*Nouvelles étrangeres de Turquie et de Perse*
On a appris que toutes les Provinces de la Perse avoient envoyé
des Députés à Ispahan pour feliciter le Roi de Perse sur la résolution qu'il a prise de ne point éxécuter le dernier Traité conclu
avec le Grand Seigneur, et pour l'assurer qu'elles lui fourniront
tous les secours nécessaires pour reprendre les Villes que la situa-   5
tion de ses affaires l'avoit obligé de ceder; que chaque Province
lui avoit envoyé un état des Troupes qu'elle pouvoit lui fournir,
avec offre de les payer et entretenir pendant deux ans; que le Roi
de Perse avoit actuellement une Armée de 50000. hommes en
Georgie; une autre de 60000. hommes qui s'étoit emparée des   10
passages par lesquelles les Turcs sont entrés dans le Pays pendant
la guerre précédente; et une troisiéme avec laquelle le Roi de
Perse faisoit le Siege d'Erivan. Cette Place n'est point prise
comme le bruit en a couru, mais on ne doute pas qu'elle ne le
soit bien-tôt, les vivres et les munitions de guerre y manquant.   15
    Les Lettres reçûes depuis portent, que les Troupes Persanes qui
avoient leurs quartiers le long de la Mer Caspienne, en étoient
parties pour se rendre en Armenie, que le Roi de Perse avoit déja
repris plusieurs petites Places de la Georgie qui avoient été cedées
au G. S. par le dernier Traité, qu'une autre armée étoit en marche   20
vers Tauris, que la Ville de Bagdat étoit bloquée, et qu'on atten-
doit un renfort de 15000. hommes pour ouvrir la tranchée.
    Les dernieres Lettres de Constantinople portent, que la maladie
contagieuse continuoit de faire de grands ravages, tant dans
la Ville que dans les environs; qu'on recevoit très-souvent de   25

mauvaises nouvelles de Perse; que le peuple paroissoit toujours
disposé à se soulever; que le Divan étoit divisé et ne prenoit
aucune résolution pour prévenir les maux dont l'Empire Ottoman
est menacé; que le Gr. Viz. ayant eu quelque differend avec l'Aga
des Janissaires, avoit obtenu du G. S. sa déposition, dont les         30
Troupes paroissoient mécontentes; qu'on avoit eu des preuves que
le feu avoit été mis par des mal-intentionnés aux maisons qui
furent brûlées il y a quelque tems près de l'Arsenal, et que le
G. V. avoit fait arrêter huit de ces Incendiaires, qui avec plusieurs
autres séditieux avoient formé le dessein de mettre le feu à dix      35
ou douze endroits de la Ville.

(From *Mercure de France, dédié au Roy. Septembre. 1732.*
(Paris, G. Cavelier, La Veuve Pissot, J. de Nully, 1732), pp. 2036–37.[a])

[Foreign news from Turkey and Persia.
We have learnt that all the provinces of Persia had sent Deputies to
Esfahān to congratulate the King of Persia on the resolution he has made
not to execute the last Treaty concluded with the Sultan and to assure
him that they will provide him with all the help necessary to retake the
towns which the state of his affairs had forced him to yield; that each
province had sent him an assessment of the troops with which it could
provide him, with the offer of paying for them and maintaining them for
two years; [8] that the King of Persia now had an army of 50,000 men in
Georgia; another of 60,000 men who had taken possession of the cross-
ings through which the Turks entered the country during the last war; and
a third with which the King of Persia was conducting the siege of Yerevan.
This place has not been taken as rumour has had it, but doubtless it soon
will be, since there is a shortage of the necessary provisions and munitions of war.
[16] The letters which have been received since report that the Persian
troops which had their quarters along the Caspian Sea had left them to
go to Armenia, that the King of Persia had already retaken several small
places in Georgia which had been yielded to the Sultan by the last treaty,
that another army was making towards Tauris, that the town of Baghdad
was blocked and that they were waiting for a reinforcement of 15,000 men
to open the way through.
[23] The last letters received from Constantinople report that the conta-
gious illness was continuing to cause great devastation, both in the town
and in the surroundings; that very often bad news was received from
Persia, that the people appeared always ready to revolt, that the Divan
was divided and was taking no decision to prevent the troubles with which
the Ottoman Empire is threatened; [29] that the Grand Vizier, having had
some quarrel with the Aga of the Janizaries, had obtained his deposition
from the Sultan, about which the troops appeared discontent; that there

a    A facsimile reprint is available, Geneva, Slatkine, 1968.

had been proof that the houses which were burnt some time ago near the Arsenal had been set on fire by some ill-intentioned men, and that the Grand Vizier had had eight of these arsonists arrested, who, with several other rebels, had planned to set fire to ten or twelve places in the town.]

## COMMENTARY

### Orthography

It was not until 1740 that the Academy finally simplified *eu* to *u* (except in *j'eus*, *j'eusse*, etc.), belatedly catching up with the general use of printers (e.g. *assurer*, l. 4). The use of internal accents differentiates eighteenth- from seventeenth-century usage, but there is still variation. *Vîlle* (l. 21) is presumably a typographical error, since the word is elsewhere used without the circumflex, but note that *feliciter* (l. 2), *ceder* (l. 6) and *étrangeres* (title) have not yet been standardized in their modern form. Indeed the grave accent was only introduced systematically in the Academy's dictionary of 1740 and many changes in its usage were made, for example, in 1762 (see Beaulieux 1927: II, 89–91). The use of punctuation appears much more modern than in our sixteenth-century texts, but there was a tendency, as here, for important words to be capitalized.

It was not until the end of the eighteenth century that the spellings *dessin* and *dessein* were differentiated in meaning. *Dessein* (l. 35, from *desseigner*), was usual for both meanings right up to the end of the century rather than *dessin* (from *dessigner*, and influenced by Italian *disegno*) which did not feature in the Academy dictionary until 1798.

### Morphology

A number of uncertainties about the gender of nouns were resolved during the seventeenth century, particularly that of nouns with an initial vowel such as *affaire*, *étude*, *ivoire*, *espace*. In our extract, *passage* (l. 11) is used in the feminine; there is, however, no evidence that this usage was widespread. Note that names of countries (*la Perse*, l. 1) and of seas, rivers, etc. (*la Mer Caspienne*, l. 17) regularly have an article; this was not deemed necessary in Old French since they referred to unique objects and therefore did not require further determination. The only exception remains non-use of the feminine singular article with names of countries and regions after *de*, either when *de* means 'from' or after certain nouns, as in *le Roi de Perse* (l. 2).

**Syntax**

*Use of tenses*

It appears that the choice between the *passé simple* (past historic) and *passé composé* (perfect) tenses was as complex in the eighteenth century as it is today (cf. Seguin 1972: 119–20). Given the fundamental values of these two tenses, that is that the *passé simple* refers to an action situated squarely in the past without reference to its relationship to the present (past punctual), and the *passé composé* is a present perfective, referring to a past action which has present relevance, it is not surprising that the latter should become associated with speech in which the discourse tends to be related to the here and now of the speaker. In the first paragraph of our extract the *passé composé* is employed since it recounts what has been learnt from Turkey and Persia; note that anteriority is marked by the pluperfect (ll. 1, 6, etc.) and not by a *surcomposé*. The principal functions of the imperfect as the marker of duration and repetition are clearly reflected in the third paragraph. Finally, the past historic is favoured (*furent brûlées*, l. 33) for completed actions divorced from the present narration.

*Use of participles*

Present participles used verbally no longer agree (l. 15). Strictly speaking, the subject of a participial clause and of the main clause should be identical according to classical grammarians. This is not the case in the example, *les vivres et les munitions de guerre y manquant* (l. 15) which is perhaps tolerated because the subject of the main clause is the indefinite pronoun *on* and there is therefore not likely to be any ambiguity.

*Government*

Classical grammarians also prescribed whether particular verbs should be followed by a simple infinitive or by an infinitive preceded by *à* or *de*. There was a tendency for *obliger de* to be replaced by *obliger à* in the seventeenth century, but the writer here uses the older construction (l. 6). In this domain some latitude was left for individual preference, so that, for instance, *continuer* may still today be followed by *à* or *de* (l. 24).

*Negation*

The older usage of combining *ne . . . pas* with *rien* or *aucun* was already criticized by Vaugelas (1647: 405–6); here the modern usage of *ne . . . aucun* (ll. 27–28) is exemplified. *Pas* or *point* appear to be used simply as stylistic variants (ll. 13–14).

**Vocabulary**

The extract exemplifies how a large number of words derived from Latin during Middle French have become assimilated into the general lexicon. We observe, for instance, *munitions* (l. 15), *renfort* (l. 22), *ravages* (l. 24), calqued in the fourteenth century, and *feliciter* (l. 2) and the noun *séditieux* (l. 35), dating from the fifteenth. *Armée* (l. 9) also entered French in the fourteenth century, co-existing up to the sixteenth century with the Old French term *ost*, which gradually fell out of usage, probably weakened through being reduced to a single vowel. *Incendiaire* (l. 34) is attested from the thirteenth century, but until the beginning of the seventeenth century the usual words for 'fire' were *embrasement* or *brûlement* not *incendie*; *mal-intentionné* (l. 32) is another seventeenth-century formation which has survived. Finally, note that *actuellement* was originally a philosophical term with the meaning 'actually, in fact'; here it is used in its modern temporal sense (l. 9).

## 34 Victor Riqueti, marquis de Mirabeau and François Quesnay, *Philosophie rurale ou économie générale et politique de l'agriculture* (1763/4)

The need to establish an appropriate vocabulary for new science and technology continued during this period. In contrast to the syntactic fixity of the age, the lexicon constantly changed and expanded in the eighteenth century. As the scope of knowledge broadened, new words and expressions were needed for the discussion of new ideas. In some cases this involved the creation of a completely new term, in others the specialization or definition of an existing word or its usage in a new syntagma with a precise technical meaning.

Since both Brunot (1966–79: VI.1) and Seguin (1972) discuss the elaboration in the eighteenth century of a technical vocabulary for the new field of economics we have included an extract from a work written by two of the founders of the discipline, Mirabeau and Quesnay's *Philosophie rurale* ..., first published in 1763. Both François Quesnay (1694–1774) and Victor Riqueti, marquis de Mirabeau (1715–89) were political economists associated with the Physiocrats, the first systematic school of political economy. They believed in the need for reform of France's inefficient tax system and in the supremacy of agriculture over commerce as a source of wealth. Quesnay was responsible for the articles on *fermier* (1756) and *grain* (1757) for the *Encyclopédie* which helped to introduce economic thought and the language associated with it to a wider audience; the need for clear definitions of the technical terms was therefore vital.

**Le commerce d'exploitation de marchandises de main-d'œuvre, ne raporte rien à la Nation au-delà du prix des matieres premieres, si ce n'est le paiement de la rétribution de l'Ouvrier, de l'Entrepreneur & du Commerçant; & la Nation ne profite de ce commerce mercantile, que par la vente des denrées que ces**   5
**Ouvriers achetent dans le pays, pour leur consommation & pour la fabrication de leurs ouvrages. Ce profit pourrait, à leur défaut, être remplacé par la vente de premiere main des productions du cru, achetées & exportées par tous les Marchands qui font le commerce de ces mêmes productions. Ainsi le commerce**   10
**d'exploitation de marchandise de main-d'œuvre, n'assure pas plus le débit des denrées, & ne profite pas plus à la Nation, que le simple commerce d'exportation des productions naturelles du pays, quand ce commerce y est libre & facile.**

    **Il est vrai que, quand les débouchés sont difficiles, l'exporta-**   15
**tion des marchandises de main-d'œuvre fabriquées dans le pays, peut être préférable par la consommation des subsistances, que les Fabricans y achetent, & par l'emploi de matieres qu'ils réduisent**

à un moindre volume, qui les rend plus faciles à transporter. Ce
commerce réduit alors, dans la vente à l'Etranger, le prix de la    20
rétribution du travail du Fabricant, au prix de la matiere premiere;
mais cette ressource précaire, qui peut être enlevée à chaque
instant à une Nation, par l'industrie ou par les loix somptuaires de
ses voisins, ne doit être considérée que comme un accessoire très-
subordonné à l'avantage d'un prompt & facile débouché, qui    25
procure tout-à-coup un prix avantageux à la vente des productions; & ce seroit une politique aveugle & absurde, que celle qui
tiendroit à bas prix les productions du cru, pour faciliter la subsistance des Fabricans & des Ouvriers.

> (From Victor Riqueti, marquis de Mirabeau, and François Quesnay,
> *Philosophie rurale ou économie générale et politique de l'agriculture, Réduite
> à l'ordre immuable des Loix physiques & morales, qui assurent la prospérité
> des Empires*, vol. 1 (Amsterdam, Les Libraires associés, 1764), pp. 123–24.[a])

[Trade in the production of manufactured goods brings nothing to the
nation above the price of the raw materials, except payment of the wages
of the worker, contractor and merchant, and the nation does not benefit
from this commercial trade except by the sale of the commodities which
the workers buy in the country for their consumption and for the manu-
facture of their goods. [7] This profit could be replaced in their absence
by the sale at first hand of raw products bought and exported by all the
merchants who trade in these same products. Thus the business of
exploiting manufactured goods no more assures the sale of commodities
and no more benefits the nation than the simple business of exporting the
natural products of the country, when trade is free and easy.
[15] It is true that when it is difficult to find outlets, the export of manufactured goods produced in the country may be preferable on account of
the consumption of supplies which the manufacturers buy there and
through the use of materials which they reduce to a lesser volume, which
makes them easier to transport. [19] This trade therefore reduces, in the
sale abroad, the level of the remuneration of the manufacturer's work to
the price of the raw materials, but this precarious resource, which can be
taken from a nation at any moment by the industry or by the sumptuary
laws of its neighbours, should be considered as very inferior and of minor
importance compared to the advantage of a prompt and easy outlet which
immediately provides an advantageous price for the sale of the products;
and it would be a blind and absurd policy to keep the raw products at a
low price in order to help keep manufacturers and workers.]

a   Cambridge University Library, Pryme d.132.

**BRIEF COMMENTARY**

Since the main interest of this text for us concerns the development of the technical vocabulary, we shall limit our comments to an alphabetical glossary of a selection of the economic terms used, with a short discussion of their formation and usage. Note the use of the term *philosophie* in the title which was, of course, one of the key terms of the century, and had the sense of 'libre examen universel' or 'méthode universelle' (Brunot 1966–79: VI.1, 12). From this, other expressions were created including *économie philosophique*, *philosophie économique* and the expression used by Mirabeau and Quesnay *philosophie rurale*.

**GLOSSARY**

*commerçant* Brunot (306) points out that this was a new term, probably used for the first time at the very end of the seventeenth century and adopted by even the purist Voltaire and the Academy dictionary of 1740. *Commerçant* co-existed with *marchand* and *négociant*, and as might be expected of a period from which the first dictionaries of synonyms date, various attempts were made to differentiate their meanings.

*commerce* The term *commerce* on its own tended to be used to refer to the exchange of natural products, with the phrase *commerce de marchandise de main d'œuvre* reserved for the trade of manufactured goods. *Marchandise* had existed since the twelfth century, but when joined to *main d'œuvre* 'manpower, labour' a phrase dating from the beginning of the eighteenth century, it acquired a precise technical usage.

*consommation* The difference between *consumer* and *consommer* had already been outlined by Vaugelas in the middle of the seventeenth century (1647: 300) and was well established by this period.

*débouché* Opposite of *obstruction* (Brunot 1966–79: VI.1, 324–25). The verb *déboucher* was attested in the 1640s, but the noun did not appear until 1723. However, by the middle of the century its usage, replacing *décharge*, had become common, although it was not accepted into the Academy dictionary until 1798.

*denrées* This term, derived from *denier* and referring to 'commodities, foodstuff', contrasted with *matière première*, which denoted the raw materials which needed to be transformed by man's skill.

*entrepreneur* The noun *entrepreneur* had existed in French since the thirteenth century with the very general sense of 'celui qui entreprend'. Adopted by the economists in the eighteenth century, it acquired the modern sense of someone at the head of an *entreprise*.

*exploitation* Once again this is a term which had been in usage since Old French, when it was used as a legal term. It was adopted by the economists in the middle of the century and given the meaning of 'trade, business'.

***exportation*** It is uncertain whether this word was taken directly from Latin or borrowed from English. It appeared in the writings of the first economists and by the 1730s was frequently used.

***mercantile*** The adjective is attested from the early seventeenth century, but was adopted by the economists and used in all kinds of technical expressions including *contract mercantile, détail mercantile* and the example we have here *commerce mercantile*. Brunot (309) observes that the term developed a pejorative force in the eighteenth century probably because of its usage in the phrase *système mercantile*, a highly unpopular system of economics associated with Colbert and economists of the early part of the eighteenth century which consisted in exporting more than was imported in order to make the country wealthy.

***subsistance*** While the term *subsistance* had been employed in French since the end of the fifteenth century, it was not used to refer to a person's upkeep and food before the mid-seventeenth century. Once again it is clear that, where it was necessary, the seventeenth century was not afraid to innovate.

## 35  Jean Héroard's record of the Dauphin's speech (early seventeenth century)

As we have already noted, there are fundamental problems about trying to find out about the spoken word of the past. The recordings and corpora on which analyses of contemporary spoken French depend have to give way to the fundamentally unsatisfactory data of the written word, which can never be more than a partial reflection of direct speech. In the case of French, the problems are compounded by the tradition of standardization which is especially characteristic of the seventeenth century and by the nature of the orthographic system which falls lamentably short of the phonemic ideal of having each sound unambiguously represented by only one symbol. In order to find out about the speech of the *Grand Siècle*, scholars have to piece together clues offered by diverse texts, including the comments of grammarians and lexicographers, and the representation of direct speech in popular literature, texts in patois and comic theatre, satire and burlesque. In addition, comparative data, allowing reconstruction in a way similar to the reconstruction of Vulgar Latin forms, may be of value; comparison may be made for instance between 'standard' French and the French taken overseas by colonizers and settlers in the seventeenth century. If, for example, 'French' creoles that are widely separated geographically share a common feature which is no longer a feature of French spoken in France, one may hypothesize that it was perhaps present in the spoken and popular usages which constitute the source of those creoles.

However, we are particularly fortunate in that for the seventeenth century there is an additional, extremely rare source of information about spoken French in the Journal kept during the period 1601–28 by Jean Héroard, personal physician to the Dauphin, later Louis XIII. The linguistic significance of the text derives from the fact that Héroard attempted to transcribe as accurately as possible the speech of the Dauphin, notably for the period 1605–10, when the Dauphin was aged between 3¼ and 9¼. In the manuscript the Dauphin's speech is transcribed in a quasi-phonetic script written in a larger, more rounded hand.

Here are two short extracts from the Journal when the Dauphin was aged 4 years 11 months and 6 years 7 months respectively. The Dauphin's speech (**D.**) is noted in italic and Héroard's glosses of divergences from the norm in the traditional orthography of the day are included as footnotes. The context of the utterance as furnished by the editor, Ernst, is given in square brackets and the identity of the speaker indicated by his or her initial in large capitals.

**3.8.1606**

... [Il ne se laisse pas peigner.] M<sup>e</sup> de Montglat le menace du fouet, ce fust encore pis *he maman me doné¹ pa le fouet.* M. laissé vous pigner et vous ne l'aurés pas. D. *je vou croi pa, vou me le doneré²* [Sa remueuse veut le peigner.] D. *fi vou senté³ le laict. je veu pa que vou me pignié⁴.* R. M<sup>r</sup> autresfois vous avés   5
bien voulu que je vous aie pigné. D. *je croi bien, vou santé⁵ atheure⁶ la bave de ma petite sœu⁷* la petite Madame qu'elle remuoit ... [Il dit à M<sup>r</sup> de Ventelet d'aller prendre un cerf volant au parc.] Il refuse de y aller. le voila en cholere. M<sup>e</sup> de Montglat le menace du fouet. *he maman ga me donné pa le fouet. dite li⁸*   10
*qu'il y aille.* M. non, vous ne l'aurés pas, pourveu que vous ne soiés pas opiniastre. D. *mai c'e vou qui esté⁹ opinate, vou voulé pa qu'il y aille. quan je sui poin opinate, vou voulé pa qu'il y aille: maman ga, si vou li dite¹⁰ qu'il y aille je paleray¹¹ hau¹² a la meche:* l'on s'en prinst a rire, *a la vilaine elle en ry¹³*   15
...//...

1. -és   2. -és   3. -es   4. -és   5. sentés   6. a ceste heure   7. sœur   8. luy
9. estes   10. ne luy dictes   11. parleray   12. hault   13. rit

**26.5.1608**

...//...dict a M<sup>r</sup> de Viq gouverneur de Calais qui avoit une jambe de bois. *av'ou¹ fai faire une cheville a vote jambe pou la faire plié².* V. non M<sup>r</sup>. D. *jl y fau faire mete³ une petite r[l]\*oue⁴ pou la faire plié, pui une cheville pou l'areté⁵: voulé vou courj conté⁶*   20
*moy dan la galerie je vou donneray cinquante pa⁷* ... en soupant entretient son petit jardinier *peti jadinié quan j'arej⁸ mangé le fraize⁹ qui son¹⁰ en mon jadin j fauda¹¹ en planté d'aute¹²: j fau faire une pote au cabiné¹³ de mon jadin pour y enfemé¹⁴ me chien¹⁵: j'ay un cadena¹⁶ où jl y a cen¹⁷ clé¹⁸ j li fauda mete¹⁹*   25
...

1. avés vous   2. -er   3. mettre   4. rouë   5. l'arrester   6. -tre   7. pas
8. J'auray   9. -es   10. sont   11. il faudra   12. -tres   13. -et   14. enfermer
15. -iens   16. -at   17. cent   18. clefs   19. mettre

\* There appears to be an 'r' with an 'l' written over it in the manuscript. Héroard comments on the fact that the Dauphin had difficulty articulating [r] and that he often used [l] instead.

(From G. Ernst, *Gesprochenes Französisch zu Beginn des 17. Jahrhunderts. Direkte Rede in Jean Héroards 'Histoire particulière de Louis XIII' (1605–1610)* (Tübingen, Max Niemeyer Verlag, 1985), pp. 357, 516.)

[... [He refuses to have his hair combed.] Madame de Montglat threatens him with the whip, but that made it even worse. 'Oh Maman, don't whip me.' *Mme de Montglat:* 'Have your hair combed and you won't be'. *Dauphin:* 'I don't believe you, you will whip me'. [His change-nurse<sup>a</sup> tries

a   An assistant nurse in a noble family, responsible for changing and cleaning the infant.

to comb his hair.] *Dauphin:* 'Pooh! You smell of milk. I don't want you to comb my hair'. *Change-nurse:* 'Monsieur, you used to like me combing your hair'. [6] *Dauphin:* 'That may be true, but at the moment you smell of my little sister's dribble', the little Madame that she was changing . . . [He tells M. de Ventelet to go and get a kite from the park.] He refuses to go. Now he is angry. Mme de Montglat threatens to whip him. *Dauphin:* 'Oh, Maman Ga (her nickname), don't whip me, Tell him to go'. *Mme de Montglat:* 'No, you shan't have it unless you stop being stubborn'. [12] *Dauphin:* 'But it's you that's stubborn, you don't want him to go there. When I'm not stubborn, you don't want him to go there. Maman Ga, if you don't tell him to go there, I'll talk loudly during mass'. They begin to laugh. 'Oh, the horrible woman, she's laughing at it . . .'.

[17] . . . said to M. de Viq, Governor of Calais, who had a wooden leg. 'Have you had a pin made for your leg so that it can bend?' [19] *M. de Viq:* 'No. Monsieur'. *Dauphin:* 'You ought to have a little wheel put in it to make it bend, and a pin to stop it. Do you want to race against me in the gallery, I'll give you a start of 50 feet' . . . While eating he talked to his little gardener: 'Little gardener, when I have eaten the strawberries in my garden you will have to plant some more. You should put a door in the arbour in my garden so my dogs can be shut in there; I've a padlock which has 100 keys, you should put that on it . . .'.]

## COMMENTARY

### Héroard's transcription

Héroard's quasi-phonetic transcription of the Dauphin's speech is striking for its time and there are notable differences, for example, between the transcription used to record the Dauphin's speech (e.g. *li dite*, l. 14, *opinate*, l. 13, *peti jadinié*, l. 22) and the traditional etymological spelling of the glosses or record of the speech of other people (e.g. *dict*, l. 17, *opiniastre*, l. 12, *petit jardinier*, l. 22). In favour of its authenticity we may note that Héroard wrote entries sometimes several times a day and even adds comments on the tone of voice or intonation pattern employed. In addition he includes a number of discourse features typical of speech. Note here the use of interjections (*he*, l. 2, *fi*, l. 4, *a la vilaine*, l. 15), repetition (e.g. *qu'il y aille*, ll. 11–14), *mais* as an introductory discourse marker (*mai c'e vou qui esté opinate*, l. 12), as well as the affectionate nickname *maman ga* to refer to his governess Madame de Montglat. On the other hand, the transcription is not strictly consistent: the letter 'i', for instance, transcribes both [i] and [j] in *jadinié* (l. 22), whilst the sound /i/ is represented by 'i' (*opinate*, l. 12), 'j' (*j fau*, l. 23) and 'y' (*ry*, l. 15). Moreover, standard orthographic forms occasionally intrude, such as *laict* (l. 5). Nevertheless, such an attempt to describe accurately the authentic speech of the day is extremely precious.

## Problems of interpretation

Before we look at some of the features of seventeenth-century speech indicated in the Journal, it is essential to observe that even a text of such rare value poses problems of interpretation. Given the lack of comparable texts, a major difficulty lies in how we should interpret deviations from standard forms – whether they should be considered as 'standard' features of the speech of the day, 'substandard' features employed because of the spontaneity of the discourse, features typical of a child's language (it is regrettable that the speech of the adults around the Dauphin was not transcribed in the same way for comparison), or traits peculiar to his speech. We must obviously be wary of making sweeping generalizations about seventeenth-century spoken French on the basis of this text alone, since we are dealing with the special case of a young child with an Italian mother, whose position as heir to the throne made his socio-cultural situation unique. However, with care and using comparative data from other sources of seventeenth-century spoken usage, and notably the comments afforded by metalinguistic texts, we may gain evidence of and evaluate a whole range of linguistic features characteristic of the Dauphin's speech.

## Phonetics and phonology

*Final consonants*

A number of words which today are always pronounced with a final consonant are shown in the Dauphin's speech not to have a final pronounced consonant; in the extract non-pronunciation of the *r* of *sœur* (*sœu*, l. 7) and of infinitives ending in *-ir* (e.g. *courj*, l. 20) is illustrated. Metalinguistic texts confirm that these were the usual pronunciations in conversation at the time when the following word began with a consonant and that the 'r' was later restored probably as a 'spelling pronunciation'. Most problematic is the interpretation of *fouet* (l. 2) where today the final *t* is silent but in Héroard's transcription it is notated in all 72 instances of the word. There is evidence that Héroard notes the different pronunciation of words according to phonetic context and is aware of liaison; for instance, *pour* is transcribed as *pou* before a word beginning with a consonant (*pou la faire plié*, ll. 18–19), but as *pour* where the following word begins with a vowel (*pour y enfemé*, l. 24). Note the indication too of the pronunciation [i] for [il], which has sometimes been described as an innovation in contemporary spoken French, but evidently has a longer history. The pronoun *il* is transcribed as 'j' in the preconsonantal position (e.g. *j fauda*, l. 23), but as *il/jl* before a vowel (*il y aille*, l. 11, *jl y fau faire mete* l. 19, etc.).

*Loss of [r]*   in rapid speech today

The Dauphin's speech confirms grammarians' comments that [r] following a consonant and in final position was frequently not pronounced in familiar speech at this time. Thus we find *vote* (l. 18 for *votre*), *mete* (l. 19 for *mettre*), *conte* (l. 20 for *contre*), etc. The loss of [r] before a consonant in pretonic position however (*jadinié*, l. 22, *jadin*, l. 23) is more likely to be attributable to the fact that we have a child speaking, since by 1609–10 the [r] is almost always present.

Av'ou

Vaugelas (1647: 89) confirms that *av'ou* (l. 18) was commonly heard in speech for *avez-vous*. The other syncopated form *atheure* (l. 7) for *à cette heure* may equally be attributable to the speed of delivery in conversation or may be a childish variant of the more widely attested reduced form *ast(h)eure*, which the Dauphin also uses, albeit less frequently.

*Other features of the Dauphin's pronunciation*

The substitution of [ʃ] for [s] is occasionally found in the Dauphin's speech as in *meche* for *messe* (l. 15). This is probably an idiolectal trait, that is, a peculiarity of his speech. Sixteenth-century grammarians such as Palsgrave note the pronunciation *pigner* for *peigner* (l. 3) but by 1672 Ménage comments: 'Le petit peuple de Paris dit *pigne* ... Aujourd'huy tous les honnestes gens et de la ville et de la cour prononçent *peigne*' (Thurot 1881–83: I, 350). Finally, the pronunciation *j'arej* (l. 22) for *j'aurai* equally seems to have been on the wane by the time of the Journal; Bèze (1584) comments on its usage with approbation, but there is no further comment by grammarians on its usage after this date (Thurot 1881–83: I, 432–33).

## Morphology and Syntax

Li *for* lui

The Dauphin's speech shows that in seventeenth-century speech *li* (e.g. *dite li*, l. 10) was still commonly used for *lui*, although it is generally stated that *lui* had replaced *li* before the end of the fifteenth century. It is possible that phonetic factors are also at work here and that there is a reduction of [ɥi] to [i].

*Negation*

Notably from the late 1970s on, there has been considerable debate about the 'age' of the contemporary spoken language: whether it is conservative or innovatory, as has been implied since at least 1929 by Frei's coining of the term *français avancé* to refer to all the elements of 'substandard French' – including spoken usages – which he considered were likely to be accepted one day as the norm. Many have questioned whether features identified as typical of speech today are in fact innovations, as has often been stated, and suggest that perhaps the variation is rather stable variation, that is inherently present in the language of all ages. One feature which has been much discussed in this context is the loss of the pre-verbal *ne* of negation – giving, for example, *je sais pas* rather than *je ne sais pas* – which is a common feature of speech now. Héroard's text is interesting in this respect affording numerous examples of the use of *pas*, *point*, etc. without *ne*: *je vou croi pa* (1. 3), *quan je sui poin opinate* (1. 13), *vou voulé pa* (1. 13), and again with the imperative *me doné pa le fouet* (1. 2). It is interesting to note that Héroard does not usually gloss such cases (although he does 'explain' the omission of *ne* in line 14 where no *pas* or *point* is present), which might suggest that he considered the non-use of *ne* to be normal. There is, however, the possibility that this usage may be attributable to the Dauphin's age since in general (although not exclusively) *ne* is present in the speech of the other speakers. Note, for example, the use of *ne* by Madame de Montglat (*non, vous ne l'aurés pas, pourveu que vous ne soiés pas opiniastre*, ll. 11–12). Unfortunately no conclusions can be drawn from such examples given Héroard's lack of interest in notating exactly the speech of the people around the Dauphin. Despite these problems of interpretation, it is highly valuable to have a clear record that the Dauphin at least regularly marked negation by post-verbal *pas* or *point* alone.

*Choice of clause structure and clausal links*

Features typical of the organization of speech today are illustrated in these extracts. We may observe, for instance, the use of a presentative to topicalize or emphasize a certain element (*c'e vou qui esté opinate*, l. 12) and the tendency for parataxis or the simple juxtaposition of clauses (ll. 6, 25).

## 36 French in the world: an early example of Haitian Creole (mid-eighteenth century) *during U.S. slave trade*

The French explored the world later than the Portuguese and Spaniards, and with fewer resources. The Spaniards had settled on the eastern end of the island of Hispaniola from 1492 on, and began the transportation of slaves from Africa to the colony; by the end of the sixteenth century the native Arawak Indians had been wiped out through exhaustion, disease and murder. French pirates based in the Cayman Islands began to establish plantations on the western end of Hispaniola and founded Port-de-Paix, subsequently claimed by the French West India Company; the French continued to introduce black slave labour from Africa to cultivate sugar, tobacco, and cotton. In 1697 the western part of the island was ceded to France and renamed Saint-Dominique.

*trade language*

France lost most of its first Empire during the course of the eighteenth century; there were violent revolutions in Haïti in 1803, following the example of the Revolution in France, which led to the country declaring independence in 1804 under the original Arawak name, Haïti. The influence of French has, however, been much more persistent; in 1987, Haitian creole was finally recognized as an official language side by side with French, which has limited usage for certain higher language functions.

*labor language*

Wherever the French used black labour, the contact between speakers of two very different languages caused the language of the French-speaking masters to change dramatically, leading to the creation of a pidgin. A pidgin is a transactional language for very limited communicative purposes used between adults who do not speak the same language. It has a simple phonology, invariant morphology, basic syntax and very reduced lexicon. A creole is essentially a pidgin which has acquired native speakers; with this comes an expansion of the functions the language can fulfil, an elaboration of the lexicon, and the marking of more complex grammatical functions. There is much dispute about the precise way creoles have been formed, although it is generally agreed that they are created, not by the gradual process of evolution which we have so far illustrated, but by catastrophic change. The racial implications of the formation of creoles have also made their treatment a sensitive subject, and for this reason many avoid calling them 'French creoles', and instead prefer the designation 'French lexicon creoles'.

Apart from a very few short snippets of creole, this is one of the earliest attestations of a creole text,[a] said to be a well-known song. The poem was apparently composed by a native speaker around 1757 ('M. Duvivier de la Mahautière, mort Conseiller au Conseil du Port-au-Prince'), but it was not recorded until some forty years later by Moreau de Saint-Méry, who

a   This may, of course, explain some of the rather unusual features of the text, some of which will be discussed in the commentary.

*Tagalag → Philippine language influenced by Spanish - not a creole* was from Martinique. It is impossible to tell how far his knowledge of Martinique creole influenced his transcription. His attitude towards creole seems to have been ambiguous. On the one hand, he speaks of it as 'un français corrompu, auquel on a mêlé plusieurs mots espagnols francisés, & où les termes marins ont aussi trouvé leur place' (Saint-Méry 1797: 64). But he equally adds, 'Il est mille riens que l'on n'oseroit dire en français, mille images voluptueuses que l'on ne réussirait pas à peindre avec le français, & que le créol exprime ou rend avec une grace infinie' (65). The creole text is accompanied by a free versified translation said to have been done by a creole speaker. Note that Moreau de Saint-Méry himself used the term *créol*, used in French to refer to a type of language since the late seventeenth century.

**Sur l'Air:** *Que ne suis-je la fougère!*

**1**

Lisette quitté la plaine,
Mon perdi bonher à moué;
Gié à moin semblé fontaine,
Dipi mon pas miré toué.
La jour quand mon coupé canne,
Mon songé zamour à moué;
La nuit quand mon dans cabane,
Dans dromi mon quimbé toué.

**1**

Lisette, tu fuis la plaine,
Mon bonheur s'est envolé;
Mes pleurs, en double fontaine,
Sur tous tes pas ont coulé.                   4
Le jour, moissonnant la canne,
Je rêve à tes doux appas;
Un songe dans ma cabane,
La nuit te met dans mes bras.                 8

**2**

Si to allé à la ville,
Ta trouvé geine Candio,
Qui gagné pour tromper fille,
Bouche doux passé sirop.
To va crer yo bin sincère,
Pendant quior yo coquin tro;
C'est Serpent qui contrefaire
Crié Rat, pour tromper yo.

**2**

Tu trouveras à la ville,
Plus d'un jeune freluquet,
Leur bouche avec art distille
Un miel doux mais plein d'apprêt; 12
Tu croiras leur cœur sincère:
Leur cœur ne veut que tromper;
Le serpent sait contrefaire
Le rat qu'il veut dévorer.                    16

**3**

Dipi mon perdi Lisette,
Mon pas souchié *Calinda*.
Mon quitté *Bram-bram sonnette*.
Mon pas batte *Bamboula*.
Quand mon contré laut' négresse,
Mon pas gagné gié pour li;
Mon pas souchié travail pièce:
Tout' qui chose a moin mourri.

**3**

Mes pas, loin de ma Lisette,
S'éloignent du Calinda;
Et ma ceinture à sonnette
Languit sur mon bamboula.                     20
Mon œil de toute autre belle,
N'apperçoit plus le souris;
Le travail en vain m'appelle,
Mes sens sont anéantis.                       24

### 4

| | |
|---|---|
| Mon maigre tant com' gnon souche, | Je péris comme la souche, |
| Jambe à moin tant comme roseau; | Ma jambe n'est qu'un roseau; |
| Mangé na pas doux dans bouche, | Nul mêts ne plait à ma bouche, |
| Tafia même c'est comme dyo. | La liqueur s'y change en eau.   28 |
| Quand mon songé toué, Lisette, | Quand je songe à toi, Lisette, |
| Dyo toujour dans jié moin. | Mes yeux s'inondent de pleurs. |
| Magner moin vini trop bête, | Ma raison lente & distraite, |
| A force chagrin magné moin. | Cède en tout à mes douleurs.   32 |

### 5

| | |
|---|---|
| Liset' mon tandé nouvelle, | Mais est-il bien vrai, ma belle, |
| To compté bintôt tourné: | Dans peu tu dois revenir: |
| Vini donc toujours fidelle. | Ah! reviens toujours fidelle, |
| Miré bon passé tandé. | Croire est moins doux que sentir. 36 |
| N'a pas tardé davantage, | Ne tarde pas d'avantage, |
| To fair moin assez chagrin, | C'est pour moi trop de chagrin; |
| Mon tant com' zozo dans cage, | Viens retirer de sa cage, |
| Quand yo fair li mouri faim. | L'oiseau consumé de faim.   40 |

(From M.L.E. Moreau de Saint-Méry, *Description topographique,
physique, civile, politique et historique de la partie française de l'Isle
Saint-Domingue*, vol. 1 (Philadelphia, Chez l'auteur, 1797), pp. 65–66.)

[Lisette, you've left the plain
I've lost my happiness;
My eyes are like a fountain
Since I no longer see you.                                     4
By day when I cut the cane,
I think of my love;
At night when I am in my cabin,
In my sleep I embrace you.                                    8

If you go to the town
You will find there a young Candio (whipper-snapper),
Who has, to win over the girls,
A mouth sweeter than syrup.                                   12
You will believe them to be most sincere,
But their heart is too treacherous,
It's the serpent who imitates
The call of the rat, to deceive them.                        16

Since I have lost Lisette,
I do not think of Calinda.
I abandon my belt of bells,
I do not beat my bamboo drum.                                 20

When I meet another woman,
I have no eyes for her;
I don't think in the least about work:
Everything that is mine is dying.                                    24

I grow thin like a tree stump,
My leg is like a reed,
No food is sweet in my mouth,
Even taffia tastes like water.                                       28
When I think of you, Lisette,
There are always tears in my eyes.
I'm behaving more and more foolishly
My grief is taking me over by force.[b]                              32

Lisette, I've heard the news
That you are thinking of returning soon.
Come then, still faithful,
It is better to see than to hear.                                    36
Do not delay any longer.
It causes me too much grief;
I am like a bird in a cage
When they make it die of hunger.]                                    40


## COMMENTARY

Given the limitations of space it is, of course, impossible to give a full
account of creole usage, and we simply offer an account of some salient
features exemplified by our extract.


### Problems of interpretation

Perhaps the greatest difficulty concerns the interpretation of the spelling.
Creoles have not been standardized (note *gié*, l. 22, and *jié*, l. 30, for 'eyes'),
and a recommended orthography was not recognized by the Haitian
government until 1961. The attitude of the transcriber towards the creole
may also complicate the interpretation: since the creole has its origins in
spoken and popular seventeenth-century usages, the creole text may, for
instance, have been 'corrected' in attempt to make it more intelligible or
bring it closer to *le bon usage*; we may suspect this, for example, in the
case of *quand* (l. 5) and *qui* (l. 11). Finally, it may have been incorrectly
set by ignorant printers.

---

b   A difficult couplet. We have taken *Magner* in line 31 to be derived from *manière*, and
    thus to mean 'behaviour'. In the case of line 32, *magné* is assumed to come from *manier*,
    and to have the meaning 'handle, deal with' (/manje/ is current in Mauritian with this
    meaning).

*grammatical simplifications*

**Phonology**

Creoles do not have front rounded vowels and these are generally replaced by the corresponding front unrounded series. While this is not shown systematically in our text, it is suggested in spellings such as *bonher* (l. 2), *geine* (l. 10). The spelling of *crer* (l. 13) bears witness to the variation in seventeenth-century French between the pronunciations [wɛ] or [wa] and [ɛ] in a number of lexical items, and *bin* (l. 13) and *bintôt* (l. 34) show the reduction of the nasal diphthong of *bien*, which is typical of popular spoken French today. Another feature of creoles is that *r* tends to weaken or fall, except in syllable initial position; while this is not noted systematically here, we may note *batte* (l. 20), *laut'* (l. 21); there also appears to be an example of metathesis involving *r* (*dromi*, l. 8).

**Morphology**

*Determiners*

In Haitian creole today it is usual for the determiner *-là* to appear after the noun, but it may also be placed, as here, in the prenominal position as *la* or *l* before a vowel. In the case of *la jour* (l. 5) we may suspect contamination from *la nuit*. Nouns are not marked for gender or case, nor is a determiner obligatory (*cabane*, l. 7). The indefinite article, variously pronounced as [ju, jun, un, õ, jõ], etc., is here represented in the spelling as *gnon* (l. 25).

*Personal pronouns*

The personal pronouns mostly derive from the French stressed forms *moi, toi, lui, nous, vous* and *eux*, although in the case of the first person singular, nasalized forms abound in this text. The function of the personal pronouns is determined according to their position, thus *yo* is the subject in *quand yo fair li mouri faim*, 'when they make him die of hunger' (l. 40), the direct object in *tromper yo*, 'deceive them' (l. 16), and the possessive in *quior yo*, 'their heart' (l. 14). In the second person singular, *to* (l. 13) appears in the preposed position, *toué* (l. 4) when the pronoun follows the verb, while in the first person singular we find *mon* before a verb (l. 2), and *moin* (l. 3) or *moué* (l. 6) elsewhere. The third person singular form of the personal pronoun, regardless of gender, is *li* (l. 40). Note that there is also an example of an elided form (*to > t*) before the verbal marker *a* (from *va*, marking futurity) which begins with a vowel (*ta*, l. 10).

*Verbs*

Verb forms in creole are invariable; they are assumed to be derived either from the infinitive or the third person singular present indicative form, or perhaps even from the past participle (e.g. *quitté*, l. 1, *coupé*, l. 5, *perdi*, l. 2). The different verb classes are reduced to one basic paradigm, so that we find alongside *songé* (l. 6) from *songer*, *tandé* (l. 33) from *entendre*. These forms may refer to any time of the action and do not inflect for person or number. A series of preverbal markers is, however, available to mark aspect, such as *fèk* for the completive ('have just'), *apr* or *apé* for the imperfective or durative. These have parallels in verbal periphrases which were common in Middle French, but often criticized by classical grammarians (*il est après à faire, il ne fait que penser*). Here *va* (l. 13) – or the reduced form *a* – is used to mark futurity (l. 10).

## Syntax

*Clause structure*

The clause structure is simple with the function of the terms derived largely from their relative positions. A typical sentence comprises a topic and a comment and does not need the copula, *être*, when referring to the present tense: *quand mon dans cabane* (l. 7) 'when I am in my cabin', *mon maigre* (l. 25) 'I am thin'. As we might expect, parataxis is also frequent (ll. 33–34). The comparative is expressed by the verb *passé* (l. 12) preceded by a simple adjective and followed by the standard.

*Negation*

The negative is expressed either by *pas* alone (ll. 18–20), here used in the preverbal position, or by *na pas* (l. 27). Note the use of *n'a pas* in an imperative (l. 37); this may support the view that *na pas* should be considered an independent negative marker since the structure of the creole imperative cannot be derived directly from the cognate standard construction, *ne tarde pas*; alternatively, it may derive from a reinterpretation of *ne pas tarder*. Finally, in line 23, the negative is reinforced by the intensifier *pièce*.

*Word order*

The word order is overwhelmingly SVO; object pronouns always follow the verb and subject pronouns are never omitted. *Tro* (l. 14), used adverbially, is placed here after the adjective it modifies; this rather unusual position may be due to poetic licence.

**Vocabulary**

A very high proportion of the lexicon is of French origin, which may, however, appear in a reduced or modified form, or with a change of meaning. Thus, for example, we find *gié* (l. 3) or *jié* (l. 30) for 'eyes', and *négresse* (l. 21) used in the general sense of 'woman'. Creoles also contain terms and usages which disappeared from standard French in the seventeenth century; an example of this is furnished by *assez* (l. 38) used before an adjective to mark intensity. Other words and expressions have their origin in popular French; for example, *quimbé* (l. 8) is derived from the popular expression *tiens bien* or *tiens bon*. There are also creole terms for local objects: *tafia* (l. 28), a shortened form of *ratafia*, refers to a kind of alcoholic drink.

A number of nouns appear in restructured form with an agglutinated element. In the case of *zozo* (l. 39) (from *les oiseaux*), and *zamour* (l. 6) from (*les amours*), the liaison consonant from the plural determiner has been agglutinated, while *dyo* (l. 28) derives from the partitive, *de l'eau*.

# VI Modern French

## From the Revolution to the present day

If the Revolutionary ideal of educating all citizens to read and write French had little immediate effect, the Revolution nevertheless influenced the development of the language, and notably the lexicon, as fresh terms and new meanings were required to reflect the rapidly changing political situation. The opening up of the literary language to a wider range of registers, already begun in the eighteenth century, gathered pace in the following century, as expressed in Victor Hugo's celebrated lines from *Réponse à un acte d'accusation*:

> Je fis souffler un vent révolutionnaire.
> Je mis un bonnet rouge au vieux dictionnaire [. . .]
> J'ai dit aux mots: Soyez république! soyez
> La fourmilière immense, et travaillez! croyez,
> Aimez, vivez! . . .

> (Hugo 1973: 43, 46)

Since 1945 especially, this has proceeded further as distinctions between written and spoken usages, standard and popular terms have become increasingly blurred.

But it is not just the lexicon which has changed since the Revolution. Until relatively recently the nineteenth century was somewhat neglected by historians of the language since it was considered to be a period of stability and consequently of little interest. Many of the rules governing contemporary written usage were undoubtedly formulated in the seventeenth century and established by the numerous school grammars of the nineteenth century. The effect of the normative grammarians on the written language can be observed if we compare the following verses from Segond's translation of the Bible – reprinted a number of times during the twentieth century – with Olivétan's version (text 24):

> Dieu dit: Que la lumière soit! Et la lumière fut. Dieu vit que la lumière était bonne; et Dieu sépara la lumière d'avec les ténèbres. Dieu appela

la lumière jour, et il appela les ténèbres nuit. Ainsi, il y eut un soir, et il y eut un matin: ce fut le premier jour.

(Segond 1957)

But while there is much continuity between standard written French of the seventeenth and twentieth centuries, many aspects of French pronunciation, morphology and syntax have also evolved during the modern period, whether we think of the new literary uses of the imperfect tense in *style indirect libre* (text 38), or the narrative imperfect, or developments in the spoken language such as the tendency to replace [œ̃] by [ɛ̃], the preference for regular -*er* verbs (*solutionner* and *émotionner* rather than *résoudre* and *émouvoir*), or use of the conditional form in both clauses of conditional sentences. Lower registers have of course been particularly productive and innovative both lexically and syntactically.

It is this multiplicity and diversity of usages which makes the selection of representative texts for the modern period particularly problematic. As an example of 'standard' modern literary French we have selected a passage from a 1980 Tournier novel (text 37). A poem by Desnos (text 39) provides just one example of how the resources of French may be exploited and the language pushed to its limits, and indeed beyond, but many other kinds of literary creativity could have been illustrated, whether we think of the prose of Proust or Robbe-Grillet, or the sonnets of Mallarmé. Text types represented for earlier periods have been picked up here to allow comparison; this includes the use of French in newspapers (text 40), medical texts (41), and legal and official documents (42). In the case of the first two we may observe ways in which French has created new terms in different fields to respond to new needs; in the case of the legal text, its conservative and formulaic nature warns us of the dangers of assuming that the conservative usage of the Strasbourg Oaths (text 1) is in some way typical of ninth-century French.

We have seen how throughout its history the French lexicon has drawn on other languages to enrich the stock of words of Latin origin, from the early influx of Germanic terms to the Italianisms which entered French particularly at the Renaissance. Since the seventeenth century, French has borrowed from English, but in the twentieth century with the rise of the USA as a world power, improved travel and greater mobility, and an increasing desire for quick and easy international communication, the rate of borrowing has accelerated, with English terms being assimilated to a greater or lesser extent. This influx has been met with considerable resistance in a country where purist ideals are still upheld, at least by the establishment; an example of the attempts to control and regulate the use of French is provided by text 43.

Our last two texts illustrate just some of the parameters of variation to which French is subject. Since the Revolution, dialects have been viewed with growing contempt and many former dialects are now extinct, although

Picard, for example, is still relatively robust. But the dialects have not vanished without trace; as their usage dwindled, regional pronunciations and local lexical items have left their mark on the French of different areas. Text 44, a transcription of spoken Midi French, allows discussion of features of spoken and regional French. Beyond France, French is spoken on every continent, although its hold in the Indian subcontinent is tenuous. Of the many different faces of *la francophonie*, one example is furnished by Maillet's representation of Acadian French as spoken in New Brunswick, Canada (text 45), an extract which also contains many popular features. Indeed, as we shall see, it is often difficult to separate clearly the different parameters of variation which go to make up the richness and diversity of modern French usages.

## 37 Michel Tournier, *Gaspard, Melchior & Balthazar* (1980)

This is an example of standardized literary prose usage; the sentences are clear and carefully balanced, and the rules as laid down in normative grammars are adhered to. This applies both to the narration of the story and the conversation in which, for example, the preverbal negative particle *ne* is preserved (l. 24).

The novel *Gaspard, Melchior & Balthazar* by Michel Tournier (born in Paris in 1924) was first published in 1980. This is the opening of the novel which tells the story of Gaspard.

Je suis noir, mais je suis roi. Peut-être ferai-je un jour inscrire sur le tympan de mon palais cette paraphrase du chant de la Sulamite *Nigra sum, sed formosa.* En effet, y a-t-il plus grande beauté pour un homme que la couronne royale? C'était une certitude si établie pour moi que je n'y pensais 5 même pas. Jusqu'au jour où la blondeur a fait irruption dans ma vie ...

Tout a commencé lors de la dernière lune d'hiver par un avertissement assez embrouillé de mon principal astrologue, Barka Maï. C'est un homme honnête et scrupuleux dont la 10 science m'inspire confiance dans la mesure où lui-même s'en méfie.

Je rêvais sur la terrasse du palais devant le ciel nocturne tout scintillant d'étoiles où passaient les premiers souffles tièdes de l'année. Après un vent de sable qui avait sévi huit 15 longs jours, c'était la rémission, et je gonflais mes poumons avec le sentiment de respirer le désert.

Un léger bruit m'avertit qu'un homme se trouvait derrière moi. Je l'avais reconnu à la discrétion de son approche: ce ne pouvait être que Barka Maï. 20

– La paix sur toi, Barka. Que viens-tu m'apprendre? lui demandai-je.

– Je ne sais presque rien, Seigneur, me répondit-il avec sa prudence habituelle, mais ce rien, je ne dois pas te le cacher. Un voyageur venu des sources du Nil nous annonce une 25 comète.

– Une comète? Explique-moi, veux-tu, ce qu'est une comète, et ce que l'apparition d'une comète signifie.

– Je répondrai plus facilement à ta première question qu'à la seconde. Le mot nous vient des Grecs: ἀστὴρ κομήτηςᵃ 30 ce qui veut dire *astre chevelu.* C'est une étoile errante qui

a  The Greek has been slightly amended.

apparaît et disparaît de façon imprévisible dans le ciel, et qui se compose pour l'essentiel d'une tête traînant derrière elle la masse flottante d'une chevelure.

– Une tête coupée volant dans les airs, en somme. Continue.    35

– Hélas, Seigneur, l'apparition des comètes est rarement de bon augure, encore que les malheurs qu'elle annonce soient presque toujours gros de promesses consolantes. Quand elle précède la mort d'un roi, par exemple, comment savoir si elle ne célèbre pas déjà l'avènement de son jeune successeur? Et les vaches maigres    40 ne préparent-elles pas régulièrement des années de vaches grasses?

Je le priai d'aller droit au fait sans plus de détours.

– En somme, cette comète que ton voyageur nous promet, qu'a-t-elle de remarquable?    45

– D'abord elle vient du sud et se dirige vers le nord, mais avec des arrêts, des sautes capricieuses, des crochets, de telle sorte qu'il n'est nullement certain qu'elle passe dans notre ciel. Ce serait un grand soulagement pour ton peuple!

– On prête souvent aux astres errants des formes extra-    50 ordinaires, glaive, couronne, poing serré d'où sourd le sang, que sais-je encore!

– Non, celle-là est très ordinaire: une tête, te dis-je, avec un flot de cheveux. Mais il y a toutefois à propos de ces cheveux une observation bien étrange qui m'a été rapportée.    55

– Laquelle?

– Eh bien, à ce qu'on dit, ils seraient d'or. Oui, une comète à cheveux dorés.

– Voilà qui ne me paraît guère menaçant!

– Sans doute, sans doute, mais crois-moi, Seigneur, répéta-t-il    60 à mi-voix, ce serait un grand soulagement pour ton peuple si elle se détournait de Méroé!

(From Michel Tournier, *Gaspard, Melchior & Balthazar*
(Paris, Gallimard, 1980), pp. 9–11.)

[I am black, but I am king. One day, perhaps, I shall have engraved on the tympanum of my palace this paraphrase of the Shulamite's song: *I am black, but beautiful.* For is there any greater beauty for a man than a royal crown? This was so certainly established for me that I gave it no thought at all. Until the day when blondness burst into my life . . .
[8] It all began at the time of the last moon of winter with a rather muddled warning from my chief astrologer, Barka Maï. He is an honest, scrupulous man whose science I trust as much as he himself distrusts it.
[13] I was dreaming on the palace terrace before a night sky sparkling with stars and where the first warm breezes of the year passed. Following a sandstorm which had raged for eight long days came a lull, and with

the feeling that I was breathing in the desert, I filled my lungs.

[18] A faint sound told me that there was a man behind me. I had recognized him from the discreet way he approached: it could only be Barka Maï.

'Peace be with you, Barka. What have you come to tell me?' I asked him.

[23] 'I know virtually nothing, my lord', he replied with his usual prudence, 'but this nothing must not be concealed from you. A traveller come from the sources of the Nile has announced a comet to us.'

'A comet? Explain, if you will, what a comet is and what the appearance of a comet means.'

[29] 'I shall answer your first question more easily than the second. The word comes to us from the Greek ἀστὴρ κομήτης, which means *long-haired star*. It's a wandering star which appears and disappears in the sky in unpredictable fashion, and which consists essentially of a head dragging behind it a mass of flowing hair.'

[35] 'A severed head flying through the air, in short. Go on.'

'Alas, my lord, the appearance of a comet is rarely a good omen, even though the misfortunes they announce are almost always ripe with comforting promises. When, for example, one precedes the death of a king, how can you tell whether it is not already celebrating the arrival of his young heir? And do not lean cows regularly prepare the way for years of cows which are fat?'

[43] I asked him to come straight to the point and not to digress any further.

'In short, what is remarkable about this comet which your traveller promises us?'

'First of all, it comes from the south and is heading north, but with halts, capricious and sudden changes of course, detours, so that it is by no means certain that it will cross our sky. That would be a great relief for your people!'

[50] 'Wandering stars are often said to have extraordinary shapes, to look like a sword, crown, or clenched fist with blood gushing from it, and goodness knows what else!'

'No, this one is quite ordinary: as I've told you, it's a head with flowing hair. There is, however, a very strange observation about the hair, which has been reported to me.'

[56] 'What is it?'

'Well, reports say that it is golden. Yes, a comet with golden hair!'

'That doesn't seem very menacing to me!'

'Perhaps not, perhaps not, but believe me, my lord', he repeated under his breath, 'it would be a great relief for your people if it turned away from Meroë.']

**COMMENTARY**

**Orthography**

The recognized standard orthography for French has not changed fundamentally since the Revolution. Since the sixth edition of the Academy dictionary of 1835, when the *oi*, pronounced [ɛ], of imperfect and conditional verb endings and of various lexical items such as *monnoie* and *foible* finally ceded to *ai*, modifications have been minor and largely confined to individual terms. Since the beginning of the twentieth century there has been a whole series of proposals for reforming French orthography, not least since its complexity makes it difficult for French schoolchildren to master. While some of these have been radical in nature, the majority have been of a moderate kind addressing the most glaring problems such as the spelling of words of Greek origin (*photographe* or *fotografe*) and unpronounced double or etymological letters. The most recent proposals, the *Rectifications de l'orthographe* from the Conseil supérieur de la langue française (1990), have been greeted with a luke-warm response; they suggest amongst other things, that the circumflex accent should no longer be obligatory on *i* and *u* except in verb endings and on certain words where it would serve to differentiate them from other words (e.g. *mûr* 'ripe', *mur* 'wall'). The obstacles to the adoption of a reformed spelling are not only practical; there are also ideological and sentimental objections to changing the appearance of written French.

French spelling, while broadly phonemic in theory, falls lamentably short of the ideal one-to-one relationship between sound and symbol. Thus in our extract the sound [s] is represented in five different ways in *scrupuleux* (l. 10), *science* (l. 11), *terrasse* (l. 13), *ciel* (l. 13), *façon* (l. 32); conversely the letter *s* represents [s] in *sur* (l. 2), [z] in *mesure* (l. 11) and has no phonetic realization in the ending of *rêvais* (l. 13). In the case of this last example we can observe how much of written French morphology relies on orthography. The accents, introduced late into French when other means of indicating vocalic quality were already in use – giving anomalies like *nez* and *dé*, *je jette* but *j'achète* – and in an unsystematic fashion, are particularly problematic; here [ɛ], for instance, is represented by a grave accent in *derrière* (l. 18) but by a circumflex in *honnête* (l. 10).

**Syntax**

Tournier follows the prescriptions of modern French written grammar. Whereas in Old French the use of certain categories such as the article was largely guided by semantic criteria, syntactic rules now hold sway. Thus, the article has become a nominal marker which generally appears before all nouns, except in certain specified contexts, for instance enumerations (l. 51). This is equally true for the use of the subjunctive, although there are a few contexts where a meaningful choice can still be made between indicative and subjunctive forms, including after the conjunction *de sorte que* which introduces a result clause when followed by the indicative (l. 48), but a purpose clause when followed by the subjunctive. In very general terms we may say that if the spoken language tends towards simplicity and rapidity of communication, the written language favours explicit and regular marking of grammatical function and meaning. Accordingly, while the spoken language tends to avoid use of the past historic, past anterior and imperfect and pluperfect subjunctive forms, literary prose makes use of a greater range of past tenses to mark explicitly temporal and aspectual notions: the imperfect for the past imperfective (ll. 13–15); the simple past for the past punctual (l. 23); and the compound past for the present perfective (l. 6). Again, the written language maintains a distinction between *j'y pense* (l. 5) – where *y* is used as an equivalent of the preposition *à* followed by a noun when the noun refers to an animal, thing, place or abstract concept (whether singular or plural) – and *je pense à lui* where the reference is to a human; this, however, is frequently not observed in lower register speech.

Written French is essentially an SVO language, but inversion survives in a number of rule-governed situations. These include interrogation (ll. 3, 21, 44–45) – where the spoken language may simply use the affirmative word order with the appropriate intonation pattern to mark the question – and *incise* (e.g. *lui demandai-je*, ll. 21–22). In the case of *que sais-je encore!* (ll. 51–52), the interrogative structure has an exclamatory value. Whereas in Old French an initial adverb almost invariably triggered inversion of subject and verb, this now only survives in a small subset of adverbs as a relic, including *peut-être* (l. 1); in more informal usage inversion may be avoided here by the insertion of a *que*. In other contexts inversion is not rule-governed, but is preferred for the sake of clarity, rhythm or balance: a typical occurrence of this is in a subordinate clause when the verb is short and the nominal subject is complex (*où passaient les premiers souffles tièdes de l'année*, ll. 14–15) or when the author wishes to avoid ending a clause with a semantically weak verb (*Explique-moi, veux-tu, ce qu'est une comète*, ll. 27–28). As regards adjectival position, when two adjectives are co-ordinated by *et* they can no longer be placed one before and one after the noun, as was favoured in Middle French (*un homme honnête et scrupuleux*, l. 10, and not *\*un honnête homme et scrupuleux*).

## Vocabulary

In Old French *une rien* referred to 'a thing', from Latin *rem*. By the sixteenth century this had been largely eliminated by *le rien* (l. 24) (note the change of gender), which had acquired a negative meaning through appearing so frequently with *ne* in negative sentences. *Augure* (l. 37), the learned form from *augurium*, attested from the twelfth century on, has survived into Modern French whereas, as we have seen, its popular counterpart *(h)eur* disappeared as an independent noun in the seventeenth century, remaining only in the derivatives *bonheur, malheur, heureux*, etc. The literary language has constantly looked to Latin for new words, which often have more phonetic body than terms which have undergone phonetic reduction through the history of French; thus *imprévisible* (1. 32) dates from the first half of the nineteenth century.

**Style**

Modern French is sometimes described as an abstract language. One reason for this is that writers seem to favour the use of abstract nouns as is exemplified here, for instance, in phrases such as *à la discrétion de son approche* (1. 19), *un flot de cheveux* (ll. 53–54). We will see that in certain fields such as science and technology and in journalism, this preference is carried further and that a great deal of information is conveyed through nominal constructions where in English a verbal construction would be more normal.

## 38 Gustave Flaubert, *Madame Bovary* (1856/7)

Gustave Flaubert (1821–80) began writing *Madame Bovary* in 1851; the
novel originally appeared in six fortnightly instalments in the *Revue de
Paris* between 1 October and 15 December 1856. Having been declared
an outrage to public and religious morality, the work was tried and
acquitted in early 1857 and was published in book form with great success
in the same year. Its influence may be measured by the fact that *bovaryste*,
first used by Flaubert himself in his correspondence, entered the language
and spawned the related noun, *bovarysme*.

For Flaubert, style was more important than plot, and the text therefore provides us with one of the greatest examples of carefully crafted
nineteenth-century literary prose which, as here, is able to combine irony
with lyricism. Through the use of such techniques as *style indirect libre*
(see below), Flaubert furnishes shifting perspectives and perceptions of
the events. This extract is taken from Part 3, Chapter 6 when Emma has
left her lover Léon early one day.

Un jour qu'ils s'étaient quittés de bonne heure, et qu'elle s'en
revenait seule par le boulevard, elle aperçut les murs de son
couvent; alors elle s'assit sur un banc, à l'ombre des ormes.
Quel calme dans ce temps-là! comme elle enviait les ineffables
sentiments d'amour qu'elle tâchait, d'après des livres, de se          5
figurer!

Les premiers mois de son mariage, ses promenades à cheval
dans la forêt, le Vicomte qui valsait, et Lagardy chantant, tout
repassa devant ses yeux ... Et Léon lui parut soudain dans le
même éloignement que les autres.                                       10

– Je l'aime pourtant! se disait-elle.

N'importe! elle n'était pas heureuse, ne l'avait jamais été. D'où
venait donc cette insuffisance de la vie, cette pourriture instantanée des choses où elle s'appuyait? ... Mais, s'il y avait quelque
part un être fort et beau, une nature valeureuse, pleine à la fois     15
d'exaltation et de raffinements, un cœur de poète sous une forme
d'ange, lyre aux cordes d'airain, sonnant vers le ciel des épitha-
lames élégiaques, pourquoi, par hasard, ne le trouverait-elle pas?
Oh! quelle impossibilité! Rien, d'ailleurs, ne valait la peine d'une
recherche; tout mentait! Chaque sourire cachait un bâillement         20
d'ennui, chaque joie une malédiction, tout plaisir son dégoût, et
les meilleurs baisers ne vous laissaient sur la lèvre qu'une irréalisable envie d'une volupté plus haute.

Un râle métallique se traîna dans les airs et quatre coups se
firent entendre à la cloche du couvent. Quatre heures! et il lui       25
semblait qu'elle était là, sur ce banc, depuis l'éternité. Mais un
infini de passions peut tenir dans une minute, comme une foule

**dans un petit espace.**
**Emma vivait tout occupée des siennes, et ne s'inquiétait pas**
**plus de l'argent qu'une archiduchesse.** 30

> (From G. Flaubert, *Madame Bovary*. Sommaire biographique,
> introduction, note bibliographique, relevé des variantes et notes
> par Claudine Gothot-Mersch (Paris, Garnier, 1971), pp. 289–90.[a])

[One day, when they had parted early, and she was walking back alone along the boulevard, she saw the walls of her convent. She sat down on a bench under the shade of the elm trees. What peace there had been in those days! How she longed for the ineffable feelings of love which she had tried to imagine from the books she read!

[7] The early months of her marriage, the rides through the forest, the Viscount waltzing and Lagardy singing, all these came once more before her eyes . . . And Léon suddenly appeared to her as far away as the others.

'But I do love him!' she said to herself.

[12] No matter! She was not happy, never had been. Why did her life seem such a failure? Why did everything she relied on immediately turn sour? . . . But if somewhere there was a strong, handsome being, with a valiant nature, both passionate and refined, a poet's heart in the form of an angel, a lyre with strings of bronze raising elegiac epithalamia to the heavens, why should she not find him by chance? [19] No, it was impossible! Besides, nothing was worth looking for; everything was a lie! Every smile concealed a yawn of boredom, every joy a curse, every pleasure its own disgust, and the sweetest kisses only left on your lips a hopeless desire for a higher ecstasy.

[24] A metallic grating hovered in the air and four strokes sounded from the convent bell. Four o'clock! It seemed to her that she had been there on this bench for all eternity. But an infinity of passions can be contained in a minute, like a crowd in a small space.

[29] Emma lived completely immersed in her passions, and was as unconcerned about money as an archduchess.]


**BRIEF COMMENTARY**

The main interest of this passage lies in the use of tenses. If the basic values of the tenses for the written language were established in the seventeenth century, nineteenth-century authors found new stylistic uses for the past tenses, and notably for the imperfect. While *style indirect libre* had already been employed in the English works of Jane Austen to present the inner life of her characters, Flaubert was innovative in the

---

a The editor has modernized the spelling, but retained the punctuation of the Charpentier edition of 1873. She notes that there are considerable variations in the typography between the manuscripts and the different editions of the work that appeared during Flaubert's lifetime.

extensive use he made of the technique and in exploiting it to create ironic
uncertainty as to whether what was being reported is the character's or
the narrator's viewpoint. Technically, in *style indirect libre* there are
features of direct speech such as direct questions, exclamations, emotive
words and colloquialisms and the deictics of direct speech (note here, for
example, *N'importe!*, l. 12, *Oh! quelle impossibilité!*, l. 19), but these are
reported using the person and tenses appropriate to indirect speech, that
is using the third person and in the imperfect, pluperfect and conditional
tenses. The style is 'free' in the sense that the markers of indirect speech
are absent; there is no introductory main clause containing a verb of saying
or thinking. Thus we may contrast:

> *Direct speech:* He said, 'I am tired. I am going home'.
> *Indirect speech:* He said that he was tired and that he was going
> home.
> *Free indirect speech:* He was tired. He was going home.

Flaubert makes extended use of this style in our passage, beginning from
'Quel calme dans ce temps-là!' (l. 4). When we are faced with a question
like 'D'où venait donc cette insuffisance de la vie, cette pourriture instantanée des choses où elle s'appuyait?' (ll. 12–14), we follow Emma's
thoughts, but are uncertain as to whether the viewpoint is shared by the
narrator. Note that the narration of events is given in the past historic,
which remains vital in the literary language and indeed highlights the innovative uses of the imperfect.

As regards other linguistic features, we may observe that the unmarked
position of the adjective is after the noun (*cette pourriture instantanée*,
ll. 13–14, *une nature valeureuse*, l. 15), but that an adjective may be placed
before its noun for a number of reasons including when it refers to an
inherent quality of the noun (*la blanche neige*) or if the sense is abstract
(*un noir chagrin*). Since the position after the noun is generally the
unmarked one (although in journalism particularly there is something of
a trend towards placing the adjective before or after the noun, without
any distinction of meaning or stylistic value), the prenominal position may
be selected to emphasize the adjective or throw it into relief. Thus in the
following examples – *les ineffables sentiments* (ll. 4–5), *une irréalisable envie*
(ll. 22–23) – Flaubert helps point up the unrealistic and excessive nature
of Emma's dreams by placing the adjectives in the marked position before
the noun. As regards agreement, both the agreement with collectives
(*un infini de passions peut*, ll. 26–27) and *tout* (l. 29) are firmly established
by this period.

A number of terms which originated in the religious domain but have
moved into general usage are employed by Flaubert to great effect since
they keep here, with ironic overtones, the connotations of their original
value (e.g. *exaltation*, l. 16, *ineffables*, l. 4). The use of the rare borrowing
from Latin, *épithalame*, l. 17, also contributes to the impression that Emma

is victim to excessive romantic notions. *Râle* (l. 24), used mostly in medical contexts to denote breathing difficulties or the death rattle, cleverly picks up both the medical themes of the novel and the idea of death and decay expressed in lines 13–14.

## 39  Robert Desnos, *Langage cuit* (1923)

Already in the seventeenth century, poets complained about the restric-
tions placed on French literary usage by Vaugelas and other grammarians
but since then they have constantly exploited the creative possibilities of
French and pushed it to its limits most successfully. This is exemplified by
this short and apparently simple poem by Robert Desnos, who was born
in 1900 in Paris, active in the Resistance, and died of exhaustion in the
Terezin Camp in Czechoslovakia in 1945. Desnos joined André Breton in
the early Surrealist movement, although he broke with the doctrine in
1930. This poem comes from the collection *Langage cuit* of 1923, where
*cuit* of the title contrasts with *vert* or *cru*; it was published again in *Corps
et biens* (1930) which brought together the texts dated 1919–29. The poem
is just one example of Desnos's obsession with language, his playing with
words and experimentation with grammar.

> **Au mocassin le verbe**
> **Tu me suicides, si docilement.**
> **Je te mourrai pourtant un jour.**
> **Je connaîtrons cette femme idéale**
> **et lentement je neigerai sur sa bouche.**
> **Et je pleuvrai sans doute même si je fais tard, même si**    5
> **    je fais beau temps.**
> **Nous aimez si peu nos yeux**
> **et s'écroulerai cette larme sans**
> **raison bien entendu et sans tristesse.**
> **Sans.**    10

> (From Robert Desnos, *Corps et biens*. Préface de
> René Bertelé (Paris, Gallimard, 1968), p. 79.)

[*Let's kick the verb*
You suicide me, so sweetly,
I shall die you, however, one day.
I/we shall know this ideal woman
and slowly I shall snow upon her mouth.
And I shall doubtless rain even if I am late, even if    5
    I am fine weather.
We/you love us so little our eyes
and I this tear will fall in ruin without
reason of course and without sadness.
Without.]    10

### BRIEF COMMENTARY

In this poem Desnos plays with the verb forms by using them ungram-
matically. This disrupts the syntax and delays immediate comprehension,

but also opens up new shifting possibilities of meaning as emotions take precedence over grammar. Toying with language in this way, and placing the verb forms at odds with both themselves and their context, shifts the focus to language itself. There are three main types of breach of the rules governing verb usage. First, there is non-agreement between the personal subject pronoun and the verb, in each case to slightly different effect. In *je connaîtrons* (l. 3) a sense of both the individual and the collective is conveyed, while in *nous aimez* (l. 7) there are resonances of both the imperative and the homophonous construction *nous aimer*. In *s'écroulerai* (l. 8) there is discord between the first person verb ending and the reflexive pronoun, while the verb stem also carries echoes of the verbs *couler* and *(s')écouler* which are intensified by *cette larme* which follows. Second, intransitive verbs are used transitively in *je te mourrai* (l. 2) and *tu me suicides* (l. 1), in which the reflexive verb is used transitively to imply both his and his lover's part in the action. Third, impersonal verbs are used with personal subject pronouns in *je pleuvrai* (l. 5), which sounds similar to *pleurai*, *je neigerai* (l. 4), *je fais tard* (l. 5) and *je fais beau temps* (l. 6). Aside from these exploitations of verbal usage, note how the final preposition *sans* (l. 10), which by definition implies the need for a following term to complete the sense, is left eloquently suspended, emphasizing the sense of lack implied by the meaning of the word itself.

## 40 *Le Monde* (13.4.1961): Gagarin in space

This extract serves a dual purpose: it enables us to look at some of the features of French usage in journalism and also to consider the ways in which the necessary vocabulary is created and diffused for a new science or technology. Journalistic style is often less formal and more direct than literary style; as news comes in rapidly, frequently as here, through an international press agency, terms may be borrowed or calqued from other languages. Today this influx is primarily from English, and may even extend beyond the lexicon: it has been suggested, for example, that the increasing tendency to place adjectives before the noun in newspaper style may in part derive from the rapid translation of news from English into French. In this passage, however, where a breakthrough is made by the USSR in sending the first man into space, Russian is a source of neologism.

**Voici le texte du premier communiqué diffusé mercredi matin par l'agence Tass:**

**'Le 12 avril a été placé sur une orbite autour de la Terre le premier navire cosmique, le Spoutnik "Vostok" (Orient) avec un homme à bord.** 5

**'Le pilote astronaute du vaisseau cosmique est un citoyen de l'U.R.S.S., le pilote major Gagarine Youri Alexeievitch.**

**'Le départ de la fusée cosmique à plusieurs étages s'est effectué normalement, et après le développement de la première vitesse cosmique et la séparation du dernier étage de la fusée** 10 **porteuse le "Vostok" a commencé son vol libre sur orbite autour de la Terre.**

**'D'après les données préliminaires, la période de rotation du vaisseau cosmique autour de la Terre est de 89,1 minutes. L'éloignement minimum de la surface de la Terre (périgée)** 15 **est de 175 kilomètres, et l'éloignement maximum (apogée) est de 382 kilomètres. L'angle d'inclinaison sur le plan de l'équateur est de 65 degrés 4 minutes.**

**'Le poids du vaisseau cosmique avec le pilote est de 4725 kilos sans le poids du dernier étage de la fusée porteuse.** 20

**'Une liaison radio dans les deux sens a été établie et se maintient avec l'astronaute Gagarine. Les fréquences des émetteurs à ondes courtes sont de 9,019 mégahertz et de 20,006 mégahertz, et, dans la bande des ondes ultra-courtes, 143,625 mégahertz.** 25

**'L'observation de l'état physique de l'astronaute s'effectue à l'aide du système radiotélémétrique du système de télévision.**

**'Le pilote Gagarine a supporté de façon satisfaisante la période de passage du vaisseau cosmique "Vostok" (Orient)** 30

**sur l'orbite, et actuellement il se sent bien. Les systèmes qui garantissent les conditions nécessaires vitales dans la cabine du vaisseau-spoutnik fonctionnent normalement.**

**'Le vol du vaisseau-spoutnik "Orient" avec le pilote cosmonaute Gagarine se poursuit sur l'orbite.'** 35

(From *Le Monde*, 13 April 1961, p. 2, cols 1–2.)

[Here is the text of the first communiqué issued Wednesday morning by the Tass agency:

'On 12 April the first spaceship was sent into orbit around the earth, the Sputnik "Vostok" (East) with a man on board.

[6] 'The pilot of the spaceship is a citizen of the USSR, pilot Major Yuri Alexeyevich Gagarin.

'The departure of the space rocket in several stages occurred normally, and after reaching the first cosmic speed and the separation of the last stage of the launch rocket the "Vostok" began its free orbit around the earth.

[13] 'According to preliminary data, the period of revolution of the spaceship around the earth is 89.1 minutes. The minimum distance from the earth's surface (perigee) is 175 kilometres, and the maximum distance (apogee) is 382 kilometres. The inclination of the orbit to the Equator is 65 degrees 4 minutes.

'The weight of the spaceship with the pilot is 4,725 kilos not including the weight of the last stage of the launch rocket.

[21] 'Two-way radio communication has been established and is being maintained with the astronaut Gagarin. The frequency of the short-wave transmission is 9,019 and 20,006 megahertz, and in the band of ultra-short waves, 143,625 megahertz.

[26] 'Observation of the physical condition of the astronaut is carried out with the help of the radio-telemetric system of the television system.

'The pilot Gagarin has withstood in a satisfactory way the passage of the spaceship "Vostok" (East) into orbit, and at the moment he feels well. The systems which guarantee the necessary conditions for life in the cabin of the sputnik are functioning normally.

[34] 'The flight of the sputnik "East" with the cosmonaut Gagarin aboard is continuing in orbit.'

## COMMENTARY

### The use of French in journalism

As in scientific discourse (cf. text 41), newspaper articles reporting news items often favour constructions which suggest impersonality and objectivity: thus we find here use of passive constructions (ll. 3, 21), pronominal passives (*se maintient*, ll. 21–22, *s'effectue*, l. 26), and presentatives (*voici le texte* ..., l. 1).

*Use of past tenses*

According to Engel (1990: 102–7), there is a hierarchy of factors which determine whether in journalism the compound past together with the present and future tenses will be used, as in this report, to relate events, or whether a journalist will rather favour the past historic as the main narrative tense. The factors influencing the choice of tense here include what may be termed the axis of orientation (the event is being narrated from a present viewpoint) and the subject matter (news, information rather than sport, 'faits divers', arts where a past historic might be more likely). However, it is also possible to find examples where a journalist switches between the past historic and the compound past for no apparent reason. It is worth noting the use of the conditional, particularly common in journalism, to report an alleged fact; in the phrase 'le président serait mort' the journalist does not specify whether he believes the veracity of the report or not.

*Nominalization*

Journalism also shares with scientific discourse the tendency to minimize the use of verbs (ll. 1–2) from a desire to communicate information quickly and succinctly and to enhance the impression of objectivity. Allied to this is the preference for conveying information through complex noun phrases (ll. 21, 34), and the use of semantically weak verbs which simply string the information together; so, we may observe, for example, the repetition of *est* in lines 13–20.

**Lexical creativity**

This extract provides a telling example of how a journalist may need to find the necessary vocabulary to convey new information to the general public. The work of Jules Verne, research carried out in France from early in the century by scientists such as Robert Esnault-Pelterie and by others in Europe, had helped shape the field. In order for the information to be readily comprehensible, much of the vocabulary relies on material already available in French and particularly on the transference of words relating to other fields of travel, notably aeronautics. The present commentary is based on the important study by Louis Guilbert (1967) who analysed the descriptions of space missions in the press in the early 1960s.

*Semantic change*

Many of the words relating to space travel were derived from other related semantic fields, particularly other means of transport; thus we find from travel by air: *pilote* (l. 7), *vol* (l. 34); and by water: *navire* (l. 4), *vaisseau*

(l. 14); as well as *orbite* (l. 3) from astronomy. These words may be used on their own as simple terms, or put into new expressions, usually with the general terms being given a specifier, as in *navire cosmique* (l. 4), *fusée cosmique*, (l. 8), *vaisseau cosmique* (l. 14), *vaisseau-spoutnik* (l. 33). Note that whereas complete synonymy is rare in the general lexicon, synonymy – and indeed polysynonymy – is common in technical domains, as these last examples indicate. It is perhaps significant that *astronaute* is first used in the text as a modifying adjective (l. 6) to clarify its sense before being employed as an independent noun (l. 22).

## Borrowings

Since the Russians led the world in sending a man into space, some of the vocabulary is derived from Russian: an example here is *spoutnik* (l. 4). In other technical domains, such as computing and information technology, English has donated a significant number of terms to French.

## Word formation

Some of the derivations rely on well-established suffixes such as *-ique* (*cosmique*, l. 4, *radiotélémétrique*, l. 27), others on newer ones such as *-naute* (*astronaute*, l. 6, *cosmonaute*, l. 34, later spreading to, for instance, *océanaute*) or *-vision*. There is a marked preference in Modern French, particularly in technical and scientific fields, for learned suffixes and prefixes derived from Latin and Greek (e.g. *ultra-courtes*, l. 24), rather than the popular forms which were productive in Old French (*outre*). This dependence on Latin and Greek is shared with many other European languages and permits easy communication between scientists of different nations. Compared with word formation in earlier periods, compound and complex noun phrases have grown in importance: *fusée porteuse*, ll. 10–11, *ondes ultra-courtes*, l. 24, *une liaison radio dans les deux sens*, l. 21.

## The regulation of technical vocabulary

The most striking difference between lexical creation today and that of earlier periods is perhaps the fact that today it is carefully monitored. Technical and scientific vocabulary is under the control of the *Délégation générale de la langue française* (formerly called *Commissariat général de la langue française*) which since 1984 has co-ordinated the various *commissions de terminologie* for each industry and scientific field, and liaised with government committees and other bodies. Other important regulating bodies include the *Comité d'étude des termes techniques français* (see text 43) and FRANTERM established by AFTERM (*Association française de terminologie*) under the control of AFNOR (*Association française de normalisation*) which is roughly comparable to British Standards.

acronyms

# 41 *Annales de l'Institut Pasteur. Microbiologie* (1986)

Following our example of popular medicine in the medieval period (text 10) and the Renaissance medical text by Paré (25), this is an example of modern scientific discourse from a leading journal of microbiology. It is significant that the journal has since been renamed with an English title (*Research in Microbiology*) and that the vast majority of articles are now in English, showing that, despite French government efforts, English is increasingly replacing French in scientific discourse, acting as the *lingua franca* of scientists as Latin did in former times. The text contains many features which are typical of usage in scientific discourse, including the tendency towards impersonality and objectivity (cf. text 40) through a higher frequency of use than in general of passive constructions, the impersonal pronoun *on*, and nominalization. There tend to be few specialized verbs in technical fields, compared with a large number of technical nouns. The sentences may be long and quite complex (ll. 9–15), but there is little tense variation, the basic tenses being the present and the perfect.

The following is the résumé by the authors of their article and the English summary they themselves provide. Comparing the two abstracts highlights the similarities between the French and English technical terminology which is based on the same learned, and principally Greek, elements (e.g. *entérocolite* (l. 3) 'enterocolitis', *anatomopathologique* (l. 4) 'anatomopathological'). Purists worried by the influence of English on French should take note that in general the preferred order of French terms (*déterminé + déterminant*) is maintained: *âge gestationnel* (l. 19) 'gestational age', *cathétérisme ombilical* (l. 25) 'umbilical catheterization'.

**Cent quinze nouveau-nés, âgés de 31 jours au plus et hospitalisés dans deux unités de soins intensifs, ont été groupés en 6 classes d'après le diagnostic clinique (entérocolite avec ou sans examen anatomopathologique et avec ou sans pneumatose radiologique, 'colites hémorragiques', diarrhée aiguë, absence de troubles diges-**   5
**tifs). Le nombre total de bactéries cultivables et le nombre de *Clostridium* ont été déterminés dans leurs selles. Dans certaines selles, on a également recherché la présence de rota- et/ou de coronavirus. Les effectifs de nouveau-nés souffrant d'entéro-colites, avec ou sans pneumatose, ou de colites hémorragiques**   10
**dont les selles contiennent des *Clostridium* ne sont pas significa-tivement différents de ceux des nouveau-nés sans trouble digestif, alors que les selles de nouveau-nés atteints de diarrhée aiguë contiennent moins fréquemment des *Clostridium* que celles des autres nouveau-nés. Les *Clostridium* identifiés appartiennent aux**   15
**espèces *C. butyricum, C. perfringens, C. difficile, C. tertium* et *C. sordellii*. L'analyse des correspondances comparant la variable classe de diagnostic à 23 autres variables suggère que les variables**

suivantes: gémellité, poids de naissance < 1900 g, âge gestationnel
< 35 semaines, détresse respiratoire, pose d'un cathéter ombilical   20
et nombre de *Clostridium* > 10⁷/g de selle à l'apparition des signes
cliniques, soit entre le 8ᵉ et le 12ᵉ jour de vie, sont liées au diagnostic d'entérocolite avec pneumatose. A l'opposé, l'absence de
gémellité, un poids de naissance et un âge gestationnel élevés,
l'absence de troubles respiratoires, de cathétérisme ombilical et   25
de *Clostridium* fécaux, l'apparition des premiers signes cliniques
à un âge inférieur à 8 jours, mais la présence de rota- et/ou de
coronavirus dans les selles, sont liés au diagnostic de diarrhée
aiguë.

(From O. Fontaine and others, 'Comparaison entre le nombre et la
nature des *Clostridium* fécaux et d'autres facteurs de risque impliqués
dans la pathologie intestinale des nouveau-nés', *Annales de l'Institut
Pasteur. Microbiologie*, 137B (1986), pp. 73–74.)

[One hundred and fifteen infants aged 1 to 31 days from two inten-
sive-care units were grouped into 6 classes according to clinical criteria
(enterocolitis with or without anatomopathological examination and
pneumatosis intestinalis, 'haemorrhagic colitis', acute diarrhoea or
absence of intestinal disorders). [6] The total number of viable bacteria,
the number of *Clostridium* and, in some cases, the presence of rota-
and/or coronavirus were determined in their stools. The incidence of
*Clostridium* in the stools of infants with enterocolitis (with or without
pneumatosis intestinalis) or haemorrhagic colitis was not significantly
different from that of infants without intestinal disorders, whereas stools
of infants with acute diarrhoea less often contained *Clostridium* than
those of other infants.
[15] *C. butyricum, C. difficile, C. perfringens, C. tertium*, and *C. sordellii*
were identified. Correspondence analysis comparing the variable, 'clinical profile', with 23 other variables, suggested that the variables of
gemellity, a birthweight below 1900 g, a gestational age of less than 35
weeks, respiratory distress, umbilical catheterization and a *Clostridium*
count above 10⁷/g at the onset of clinical signs, *i.e.* between 8 to 12
days of age, were linked to the clinical profile of necrotizing enterocolitis with pneumatosis intestinalis. [23] Conversely, the absence of
gemellity, a high birthweight and gestational age, the absence of respiratory distress or umbilical catheterization, the onset of diarrhoea
within 8 days, and the presence of rota- and/or coronavirus in the stools
were linked with a clinical profile of acute diarrhoea.

(ibid., pp. 61–62)]

## BRIEF COMMENTARY

Since the main interest of this text is lexical, we shall comment on some
of the key terms, providing notes on their history and usage. Note the

high incidence of learned material, particularly elements derived from Greek (sometimes via Latin as is the case with *hémorragique*, l. 5), and of compound formations.

**anatomopathologique** (l. 4) While the noun *anatomie* dates from the fourteenth century and the adjective *anatomique* from the sixteenth century, it was really in the nineteenth century with the increasingly scientific and technical nature of medicine that a whole range of nouns and adjectives were created with *anatomo-* as their first element.

**cathéter** (l. 20)/**cathétérisme** (l. 25) The noun *cathéter* was derived from Greek in the sixteenth century; *cathétérisme* is a seventeenth-century derivation, but the verb *cathétériser* was not formed until the 1830s. Thus a family of related terms was gradually created over a period of some 300 years.

**diagnostic** (l. 3) In the sixteenth century *diagnostique* with a Greek root and a French suffix was introduced; however, *diagnostic*, dating from the 1730s gradually came to replace it and is used in a number of twentieth-century compounds such as *radiodiagnostic, électrodiagnostic*.

**entérocolites** (l. 9) The learned prefixes *entér-* and *entéro-* from Greek have been used in a number of specialized medical terms from the nineteenth century on and relate to the intestines; the former is no longer productive. *Colite* (first attested 1824), calqued on the learned Latin *colitis*, may be an independent noun or, as here, used as the second element of a compound.

**gémellité** (l. 24) The French lexicon is sometimes described as having a 'double keyboard' because of the co-existence of popular and learned terms, which may obscure the relationship between cognate forms. While *jumeau* from *gemellus* has undergone a number of sound changes, the learned form *gémellité* which was first attested in 1866 entered French long after these had been completed.

**ombilical** (l. 25) The adjective *ombilical* is already attested in Middle French and has remained largely in the specialized medical domain in such phrases as *cordon ombilical*. The related adjective *ombiliqué* means 'umbilicate, navel-shaped'.

**pneumatose** (l. 4) Whereas in the case of *entér(o)-* only one of the two forms is now productive, in the case of *pneum(o)* and *pneumat(o)*, derived from Greek, the different possibilities are all still exploited with the forms ending in *-o* used before words beginning with a consonant and the others elsewhere.

**radiologique** (l. 4) This early twentieth-century formation is composed of two elements (*radio-/-logique*) both of which are widely used in medical terminology, thus allowing easy comprehension of new formations.

**rotavirus/coronavirus** (ll. 8–9) *Virus* is a good example of how the meaning of a word may change as scientific knowledge deepens. The term is already attested in the fifteenth century to refer to an organic substance, such as pus, capable of transmitting disease. In the seventeenth century there is reference to the *virus de la rage*, but it was not until the twentieth century with the development of the scientific study of micro-organisms that the modern meaning evolved.

## 42 Decree of the National Assembly, 20 July 1790

The text of this decree made during the Revolution by the National Assembly may be compared with that of the Strasbourg Oaths (text 1). Like the Oaths, it is conservative in its usage, particularly as regards morphology, formulaic (e.g. *ainsi qu'il appartiendra*, l. 18, *à titre onéreux*, l. 20) and repetitious, for example in the reiteration of the verbs *abolir* and *supprimer*. In short, the authors are concerned not with stylistic niceties but with the clear and unambiguous expression in well-tried formulae of a decree with legal and binding status.

**Décret du 20 Juillet 1790**
**L'Assemblée Nationale, considérant que la protection de la force publique est due à tous les habitans du royaume indistinctement, sans autre condition que celle d'en acquitter les contributions communes:**
    **Après avoir ouï le rapport de son comité des domaines,**   5
    **A décrété & décrète que la redevance annuelle de 20,000 liv., levée sur les Juifs de Metz & du pays Messin, sous la dénomination de** *droit d'habitation, protection & tolérance,* **est & demeure supprimée & abolie, sans aucune indemnité pour le concessionnaire & possesseur actuel de ladite rede-**   10
**vance;**
    **Décrète en outre que les redevances de même nature, qui se lèvent partout ailleurs sur les Juifs, sous quelque dénomination que ce soit, sont abolies & supprimées, sans indemnité de la part des débiteurs, soit que lesdites rede-**   15
**vances se perçoivent au profit du trésor public, soit qu'elles soient possédées par des villes, par des communautés, ou par des particuliers, sauf à statuer ainsi qu'il appartiendra, sur les indemnités qui pourroient être dues par la Nation aux concessionnaires du gouvernement, à titre onéreux, d'après l'avis**   20
**des directoires de département, dans le territoire desquels lesdites redevances se perçoivent: à l'effet de quoi, les titres leur en seront représentés, dans l'année, par les possesseurs & concessionnaires.**
    **Décrète enfin qu'il ne pourra être exigé aucuns arrérages**   25
**desdites redevances, & que les poursuites qui seroient exercées, pour raison d'icelles, sont & demeurent éteintes.**

(From 'Rapport fait au nom du comité des domaines, Le 20 Juillet 1790, sur le droit de protection levé sur les Juifs. Par M. de Visme, Député du Vermandois. Et Décret rendu sur ce rapport' (Paris, Imprimerie Nationale), pp. 15–16.[a])

a  Also available as a facsimile reprint in *La Révolution française et l'émancipation des juifs*, Vol. 7: L'Assemblée Nationale constituante. Motions, discours & rapports. La législation nouvelle 1789–1791 (Paris, Éditions d'histoire sociale, 1968), unpaginated.

[Decree dated 20 July 1790
The National Assembly, considering that the protection of the power of
the state is due to all the inhabitants of the kingdom without distinction,
without any other condition than that of paying the common contributions:

Having heard the report of its estates committee,

[6] Has decreed and decrees that the annual dues of 20,000 francs, levied
on the Jews of Metz and the surrounding region, under the name of the
'right of habitation, protection and tolerance', is and remains suppressed
and abolished, without any indemnity for the grantee and present owner
of the said dues;

[12] Decrees in addition that dues of the same nature which are everywhere else levied on the Jews, whatever they may be called, are abolished
and suppressed, without indemnity from the debtors, whether the said
dues are levied for the profit of the public treasury or whether they are
owned by towns, communities or by individuals, reserving the right to rule,
as it shall be deemed advisable, on the indemnities which might be owed
by the Nation to the grantees of the government, subject to certain liabil-
ities, according to the directory of the department in whose territory the
said dues are levied; for which purpose their titles will be restored to them
during the year by the owners and grantees.

[25] Decrees finally that no arrears can be demanded on the said dues
and that the legal actions which might be conducted on account of them
are, and remain, cancelled.]

*revolution – standardization of French*

## BRIEF COMMENTARY

### Orthography

Aside from the replacement of *oi* by *ai*, the Academy dictionary of 1835
introduced another important reform in recommending that the plurals
of words ending in *-ent* or *-ant* should be spelt *-ents* or *-ants* and not *-ens*
or *-ans*, thereby bringing the plural formation of these words into line
with the regular pattern of adding *s*. In this text the author still follows
D'Olivet's recommendation of the 1740 edition that *t* should be omitted
between *n* and *s* in plurals such as *les habitans* (l. 2).

### Morphology

Certain forms which have long disappeared from general usage have
survived in the specialized domain of legal language; these include the
determiners *ladite* (l. 10), *lesdites* (l. 15), *desdites* (l. 26), etc. There is also
an example here of one of the demonstrative pronouns beginning with
*i-*, fossilized in the expression *pour raison d'icelles* (l. 27).

**Syntax**

The syntactic structure of sentences in legal language is frequently of a complexity more reminiscent of sixteenth- than of seventeenth-century usage. In the first sentence of our text, for example, the nominal subject (*L'Assemblée Nationale*, l. 1) is separated from the main verb (*a décrété & décrète*, l. 6) by a series of non-finite clauses. The initial subject also suffices for each of the different things decreed and is not repeated or picked up with a personal subject pronoun before the repeated verb *décrète* (ll. 12, 25). If the clausal links are at times somewhat cumbersome (*à l'effet de quoi*, l. 22), they nevertheless serve to convey the meaning unambiguously.

journalist

# 43 Jacques Cellard, *Chroniques de langage* (1972)

In much the same way as Vaugelas in the seventeenth century discussed points of doubtful usage (text 28), so in the twentieth century writers and linguists have debated in newspaper columns contentious and difficult linguistic issues and innovations. Perhaps the best known of these is Jacques Cellard, who for many years contributed a regular language column to *Le Monde*; many of these were then subsequently collected and published in book form.

This is the opening of the *chronique* entitled *Anglicismes et logologie*, which treats perhaps the most discussed and contentious linguistic issue of the century, the question of the borrowing of English words into French and possible alternatives to them. The style is fairly informal, and immediately involves the readers through use of the pronoun *nous* (l. 1).

**Nous n'aurons plus d'excuses à parler du dispatching des départs en vacances, d'un effet de feed-back, ou (ceci est pour mon écot) des conducteurs de bulldozer. C'est *répartition*, effet de *rétro-action* et *boutoir à lame* qu'il faut nous efforcer d'employer maintenant que le comité d'étude des termes techniques français** 5
**vient de publier une première série de recommandations. Ce comité d'étude est bien connu des lecteurs du *Monde*, et R. Le Bidois, qui participait activement à ses travaux, lui avait consacré plusieurs de ses chroniques. Scientifiques et techniciens s'y retrouvent depuis 1954 avec des universitaires, les premiers beaucoup** 10
**plus nombreux, pour créer et proposer des équivalents nationaux aux termes techniques anglais dont certaines industries se laisseraient trop facilement saturer, et veiller au meilleur emploi de termes français dévoyés. Ce que le comité nomme, avec une modestie et un réalisme bien sympathiques, un 'essai d'orienta-** 15
**tion de la terminologie' est en fait un véritable dictionnaire de francisations heureuses.**

**Celles-ci dans le cas le plus simple, se font par un simple changement de suffixation: *coding* devient codage, *cracking* → craquage, *zoning* → zonage, etc. Le plus souvent, le radical est commun aux** 20
**deux langues, qu'il soit grec, latin ou même germanique: ainsi de *listing* → *listage*, ce dernier amorçant, à partir de *liste*, une série morphologique qui amènera un jour ou l'autre dans la langue *lister*, établir la liste de ... ou inscrire sur une liste. La transcription est parfois à peine sensible: de *computer* et *tester* (l'un,** 25
**cercle de calcul pour la navigation aérienne, l'autre préleveur d'échantillons) on tire aux moindres frais *computeur* et *testeur*. Plus simplement encore, on aligne la prononciation du mot sur sa graphie, qui reste inchangée: ainsi de *dragline* (une) et *pipeline* (un), qu'il suffit de prononcer à la française pour les faire entrer** 30

**dans la langue. La même utilisation judicieuse et parfaitement justifiée des suffixations disponibles amène à faire de *fan in* et *fan out* (qui désignent en électronique les maximums d'entrées ou de sorties tolérés par des microstructures) *entrance* et *sortance*, sur le modèle endurer/endurance, résister/résistance.** 35

(From J. Cellard, 'Anglicismes et logologie (3 juillet 1972)', *La Vie du langage. Chroniques 1971–1975 Le Monde* (Paris, Le Robert, 1979), p. 50.)

[We will no longer have any excuse for talking about *dispatching des départs en vacances* ('the staggering of holiday departures', i.e. central control by zone of holiday departures), *un effet de feed-back* ('a feed-back effect'), or (and this is my contribution) of *conducteurs de bulldozer* ('bull-dozer drivers'). It is *répartition, effet de rétroaction* and *boutoir à lame* which we must try to use now that the Committee for the Study of Technical Terms has just published a first set of recommendations. [6] This Committee is well-known to readers of *Le Monde*, and R. Le Bidois, who was actively involved with its work, devoted several of his columns to it. Scientists and technicians have met at it since 1954 with university academics, with the former in the majority, to create and propose national equivalents for English technical terms with which certain industries would allow themselves to be too readily saturated, and to oversee the better use of misused French terms. What the committee calls, with a very pleasing modesty and sense of realism, an 'attempt to guide terminology' is in fact a veritable dictionary of felicitous gallicized forms.
[18] In the simplest case, these are created through a simple change of suffix: *coding* becomes *codage, cracking* → *craquage, zoning* → *zonage*, etc. Usually the root is common to both languages, whether Greek, Latin or even Germanic: so from *listing* → *listage*, this last one leading, from the root *liste*, to a morphological series which will one day or other bring into the language *lister* meaning 'to establish the list of . . . or to write down in a list'. Sometimes the change is barely percep-tible: from *computer* and *tester* (the one referring to the computational circle for aerial navigation, the other to someone who takes samples) *computeur* and *testeur* are derived at little cost. [28] Even more simply, the pronunciation of the word is aligned to its written form, which remains unchanged: thus with *dragline* (fem.) and *pipeline* (masc.) which can be assimilated into the language merely by pronouncing them in a French way. The same judicious and perfectly justified use of available suffixes leads to the replacement of *fan in* and *fan out* (which designate in elec-tronics the maximum inputs and outputs tolerated by microstructures) by *entrance* and *sortance* on the analogy of *endurer/endurance, résister/ résistance*.]

## COMMENTARY

### Borrowings from English

Borrowing in any quantity from English really dates from the seventeenth century, but in that early period, loanwords were still relatively few and were assimilated as far as possible not only in terms of pronunciation but also as regards their form and orthography (*boulingrin, contredanse, paquebot*). The number of English loanwords increased in the eighteenth century when there was an influx of words denoting English institutions and eccentricities (*club, rosbif,* and *budget,* this last derived from French *bougette,* 'petit sac de cuir'); the rate of borrowing further accelerated in the nineteenth century with England taking the lead notably in industry, commerce and transport (*tramway, truck, cab, break*).

The twentieth century has, however, witnessed an explosion in the influence of English on French; throughout the century links between England and France have become closer, whether in political and economic terms or as regards tourism and communications, and the countries have been allies in war. Added to this, of course, is the vital factor of the rise of the USA as a world power.

While some borrowings seem to be used merely out of snobbery (*en vente au men's department*), other loanwords have come in with an object or concept for which no French term is available (*rugby*).[a] They tend to cluster in certain semantic fields including sport (*tennis,*[b] *basket, catch*), entertainment and popular culture; as a result they are likely to feature much more prominently in the popular speech of young people than in more formal registers. It is important, in the face of the often hostile reaction to English loanwords, to remember that estimates suggest that no more than about 4 per cent of the contemporary lexicon is of English origin.[c]

### Assimilation of borrowed forms

The vast majority of borrowed terms are nouns which, in terms of their morphology, need relatively little adaptation to fit into French patterns; they are given masculine gender unless there is a good semantic reason (*la girl*) or formal pressure (*la vaseline*) for doing otherwise; all the nouns mentioned by Cellard are masculine with the exception of *dragline* (1. 29). Most plurals are formed simply by adding -*s* although words like *baby* or *rugbyman* cause hesitation. Derivatives may be formed using French means, thereby helping the assimilation of a whole family of words (*boxeur, catcheur*); in other cases French may use English elements to form a

---

a   Although even here the purist Étiemble (1964: 283) supplies the alternative (*partie de*) *ballon ovale.*
b   English *tennis* was itself originally derived from French *tenez.*
c   About 3 per cent of the entries of the *Petit Larousse* for 1975 (Picoche and Marchello-Nizia 1989: 356).

derivative or compound, which may not exist in the donating language (*rugbyman*, *babyfoot* 'table football').

In terms of pronunciation, differences between the English and French phonological systems cause uncertainty as to how to pronounce English loanwords. So, for example, the pronunciation of words containing diphthongs (*pipeline* (l. 29) [pajplajn]/[piplin]) or ending in -*ing* [ŋ], a phoneme previously unknown to French (*cracking* (l. 19) [krakiŋ]/[krakiɲ]/ [krakiɲɲ]), tends to vary from speaker to speaker (see Martinet and Walter 1973, which gives six different pronunciations for *bulldozer* (l. 3)).

As regards orthography, the majority of terms enter unchanged, although a French suffix may replace an English one, as suggested in this text. The meaning of a borrowed form is frequently modified as it fills a particular gap in the lexicon. Thus, for example, *pipeline* (l. 29) has specialized its meaning and denotes a gas or oil pipeline. An English term may then be borrowed alongside a related French word, and each have slightly different meanings (*épreuve/test*). Since the loanwords do not fit into established French lexical series, they are unmotivated and can therefore not only be given different meanings, but also be used elliptically (*le skating* for 'skating rink').

So far we have considered only the borrowing of individual lexical items, but the influence of English may be felt in other ways. An English expression may be translated literally (*col blanc*, *poids mouche*, *Lille a gagné chez lui*), thereby extending the range of the existing terms. This is also seen where the meaning of a French term is 'contaminated' by that of a formally similar English one; in this way *réaliser* has acquired the meaning formerly expressed only by *se rendre compte de/que*. Occasionally literal translation of an English expression results in a compound in which the traditional elements of the terms are reversed (e.g. *tennis club* rather than *club de tennis*). On the whole, however, with the possible exception of the positioning of the adjective, it is difficult to find conclusive instances of the impact of English on French syntax, which would surely be of much greater concern to purists.

### Reaction to English borrowings and the threat of *franglais*

Cellard discusses one of the different types of reaction to English borrowings – the work of the *Comité d'étude des termes techniques français* – while at the same time illustrating another – discussion by individuals whether in books or in newspaper columns. Other examples of individual responses include Étiemble's well-known satire *Parlez-vous franglais?* (1964). While reaction to English loanwords and the suggestion of alternatives was earlier in the century often the work of private organizations such as the *Office du vocabulaire français*, this role has since the mid-1960s been increasingly taken over by government organizations and indeed by legislation. The *Académie française* now plays a primarily symbolic role as protector of the purity of French; real power lies with such governmental bodies as the *Délégation générale de la langue française* and the *Conseil international de la langue française*. The issue of protecting French against what is seen as the threat of being overtaken by English has become associated with the promotion of French as a major world language, or *la francophonie*, and since 1988 there has been a *Ministre délégué à la francophonie*. The strength of feeling may be measured by the fact that it has been felt necessary to introduce legislation to protect French (see Introduction, p. 14).

As is clear from Cellard's text, a number of different bodies have concentrated on specific domains and various *commissions de terminologie* have, since 1972, recommended which terms they consider correct in different areas of the lexicon.

### The fate of the terms recommended as alternatives to the English borrowings

Some of the possible alternatives for English borrowings are outlined by Cellard; these include pronouncing the word in a French way (e.g. *pipeline*), substituting a French suffix for an English one (e.g. *listage*), creating a new French term on the basis of existing models (e.g. *sortance*) or trying to find native equivalents (e.g. *boutoir à lame*). Reaction to the alternatives proposed has been mixed, as discussion of the subsequent fate of the English loanwords and the alternatives proposed suggests. In the case of *bulldozer* (dating from 1927) this has become well-established and the alternative has not caught on; indeed the ninth edition of the Academy's dictionary includes it as a new accession to the dictionary. Similarly the *Trésor de la langue française (TLF)* only includes *cracking* not *crackage*. In other cases the *TLF* includes both the borrowed term and its alternative (e.g. *dispatching/répartition*, *feed-back/rétroaction*, *zoning/zonage*. Both *listing* and *listage* feature, as indeed does the verb *lister* which, however, is given specific technical meanings. Again, both *tester* and *testeur* are included in the *Grand Larousse de la langue française*, with identical recommended pronunciations but with different meanings, the former having the specialized sense of a machine used for testing oil seams. *Pipeline* is still listed in the *TLF* as a synonym for *gazoduc/oléoduc*; this latter term indicates that the French have fewer qualms about relying on Greek and Latin forms (in this case a hybrid) than on English, perhaps because they fear the cultural or technical supremacy of other nations which borrowing may imply. Some of the English borrowings discussed by Cellard do not appear in the *TLF*, having failed to become established in usage (e.g. *dragline*, *fan in/fan out*). *Codage* not *coding* is listed, but neither *computer* or *computeur* are included. All this testifies to the unpredictable nature of the lexicon and the difficulty of trying to regulate and control its development.

## 44 Regional French: Spoken Midi French

Of the different parameters of variation which affect the contemporary French language, regional variation is of prime importance; there is more difference generally between speakers of different regions than between speakers of different socio-economic status within the same region. The dialects of the *langue d'oïl* area are now in a state of advanced decline; they had largely disappeared from towns by the beginning of the century, and have lost much ground in rural communities since, holding on strongest perhaps in north and north-eastern regions. As the dialects have declined, they have nevertheless left their mark on the speech of the area, giving rise to what is usually termed *français régional,* that is essentially standard French coloured with local traits. Unlike the dialects and patois, regional French is not apparently considered inferior to the standard language and allows intercomprehension between speakers of different regions. The main differences concern pronunciation (for example, the number of nasalized vowels varies between regions) and the lexis, with the regional varieties having local terms and giving different meanings to words common to the standard lexicon. On the whole, grammatical differences are few, although we may mention the main clause use of the *surcomposés*, which is broadly confined to the *franco-provençal* and southern French regions.

In the case of this text we are dealing with a slightly different situation since of course in medieval times it was Occitan, not French, that was spoken in Provence. In the twelfth century, Provençal had enjoyed an important prose and verse literary tradition. In the thirteenth century, with the fall of the Toulousain dynasty, the South was subjected to the royal authority of the North; this made little difference to the use of Occitan as an everyday spoken language, but was a crippling blow for the written language. Thus by about 1300 French was already gaining ground in the South as a literary language, and from the fifteenth century on it increasingly replaced Occitan in written contexts. In the sixteenth century the *Ordonnances de Villers-Cotterêts* (see Introduction) dealt a further blow to the prestige of Occitan, although both Occitan and French continued to be found in administrative documents and records for some time. Nevertheless, such was the infiltration of French into the South in the second half of the century that by the seventeenth century Occitan was rarely written, although it was of course still widely spoken. An attempt was made to revive the language and literature of Provence in the nineteenth century led by Frédéric Mistral and known as the Félibrige movement (1854–); while it helped reawaken interest in Provençal culture, it did not result in a permanent and widespread adoption of Occitan as a literary language. Today Occitan is understood by about 7–8 million people, with perhaps about a quarter of these using it as their everyday language. As with the dialects of the North, it is best preserved in rural areas by older speakers. But here too, it has left a strong impression on the regional French of the Midi.

The speaker of our extract is an artisan aged 45 living on the outskirts of Marseilles. Like most Marseillais of his generation, he knows a few words of Occitan, more of dialectal French, but does not speak the *patois marseillais*. Rather, he speaks French with a Midi accent and a few local terms, in short the *français régional* of the area.

The advent of recording has made it possible to transcribe accurately spoken usages, and for the first seven lines we have included a phonetic transcription, thereby enabling discussion of the regional accent. The written transcription has not attempted to 'tidy up' the speech, so we can also identify features typical of spontaneous spoken language.

In this extract the speaker recounts the capture and raising of decoy birds which he subsequently uses to catch thrushes.

Voilà // Par exemple / je ... je me fais d'abord une petite cabane //
[vwala  par ezaãmplə  ʒə    ʒə mə fe    dabɔr   ønə pətitə kabanə

(rires) hein // Toute en ... en   broussailles quoi // Voyez / et je
εε̃:ʔ  tutə  aã    aãm brusajə    kwa    vwaje  e ʒə

plante   des petits 'arbustres' / tout 'le' tour // Alors à
plaãntə de pətiz  arbystrə   tu   lə  tur    alɔrə a

l'intérieur / je me fais des petites ... 'fenestrons' (sous ce) ...
lε̃nterjœr  ʒə mə fe  de  pətitə   fənεstrɔ̃ŋ  su  sə

toujours à l'intérieur / je regarde que 'j'y' avais mis sous          5
tuʒur   a lε̃nterjœr  ʒə rəgardə kə  ʒi  ave  mi su

ces petits arbustres / des ... des verguettes // C'est des ... des
se pətiz arbystrə  de    de vergεtə     se   de    de

bâtons quoi / p(l)acés tout(t) autour / avec du ... de la glue //
batɔ̃ŋ kwa   pase    tu     otur   avεkə dy    də la glyə ...]

Voyez // Et je laisse ça // Je rentre à l'intérieur / je prends mes appelants / Auparavant quoi / toujours / et je les mets autour // Ces bêtes elles chantent // Mais i(l) faut faire heu ... aucun bruit   10 hein / pa(r)ce que sinon ... elles sont là / e(lles) regardent à droite / e(lles) regardent à gauche mais heu ... (rire) elles chantent pas // Quand une bête passe / d'un arbr(e) à ... à l'autre elles se mettent à crier //Et pfst elles se jettent / sur le b... premier bâton qu'elles 'voyent' // C'est là que ... / vous restez heu / plus attentif   15 à ... à voir la bête que ... / vous vous dites / est-c(e) qu'elle va y rester / ou est-ce que e(lle) veut pas y rester // Le premier geste de la bête / c'est de se tourner sur la branche ... que vous la voyez faire / toujours / e(lle) regard(e) à droit(e) e(lle) regard(e)

à gauche // Tout d'un coup son instinct / elle lève une patte // hun /    20
hop / (e)lle lève l'autre / elle se sent prise // C'est authentique de
la voir faire la bête èh pa(r)ce que ... vous y êtes dessus / quoi
// Qu'est-ce qu'elle fait? // Elle se sent prise // Son instinct c'est
de ... d'envoyer les ailes /ou de se laisser tomber // Alors / (il)
y en a qui se laissent tomber // Mai(s) elles pensent pas / qu'elles    25
ont la queue longue // En se laissant tomber elles s'accrochent la
queue // Ave(c) la queue / quand elles se sentent prises / qu'est-
c(e) qu'elles font? / elles envoyent les ailes / et elles se prennent
les deux ailes et la queue //

(From F. Carton and others, *Les Accents des Français*
(Paris, Hachette, 1983, pp. 50–51[a])

[There, for example, I ... I make first of all a little hut (laughs) eh? all
from brushwood, you see, and I plant little bushes all round. Then inside
I make myself some little ... windows (under this) ... anyway inside I
see that I had put under these little bushes some little sticks, it's ... sticks
like placed all around with ... birdlime, [8] you see. And I leave that, I
go inside, I take my decoy birds, before that, anyway I put them round,
these birds sing, but you mustn't make, um ... any sound because otherwise ... they are there, they look right, they look left, but um ... (laughs)
they don't sing. When an animal passes from one tree to the next, they
begin to call, [14] and psst they fall onto the first stick they see. It's there
that ... you keep um more attentive to ... to see the animal that ... you
say to yourself, is it going to stay there, or isn't it going to stay there?
The first movement of the animal, it's to turn round on the branch ...
which you see it do, anyway, it looks right, it looks left, suddenly its
instinct, it lifts a foot, hey, hup, it lifts the other, it senses it is caught. It's
natural to see the animal behave like that, eh, because ... you are above,
right. [23] What does it do? It senses it is caught. Its instinct is to ...
spread its wings or to drop. So there are some which drop but they don't
think that they have a long tail. In falling they get caught on their tail.
With their tail, when they feel caught, what do they do? They spread their
wings and they are caught by both wings and the tail.]

---

a    In the transcription the symbol $\infty$ over a vowel is used to indicate a lightly nasalized
vowel sound. Note that / marks the end of a rhythmic group or a short pause, // the end
of a breath group or a longer pause. The authors also provide a useful outline of the
phonology of the text, some of which has been incorporated here.

## COMMENTARY

### Midi French

*Phonetics and phonology*

Mid vowels

Whereas in the standard language there are four distinctive degrees of opening in the vocalic system, in the Midi there are only three. So, for example, there is no phonological opposition in this speaker's usage between [e] and [ɛ]; in open syllables, whether in word-final position or elsewhere, it is always the vowel [e] which occurs: *fais* (l. 1) [fe] (Standard French (SF) [fɛ]); *avais* (l. 5) [ave] (SF [avɛ]); *c'est* (l. 6) [se] (SF [sɛ][b]). Similarly there is no phonological opposition between [o] and [ɔ] in closed syllables in Midi French, and only [ɔ] appears. In short, use of the mid vowels in this regional variety is simply conditioned by the syllable type. Note that in *une* (l. 1) the speaker uses half-closed [ø] in initial position, rather than standard [y].

/a/ ~ /ɑ/

This opposition, exemplified for instance by *tache* [taʃ] and *tâche* [tɑʃ], is increasingly fragile in many areas of northern France. In the South the opposition does not exist and only [a] occurs as in *bâtons* (l. 7) [batɔ̃ŋ]. Thus the system of oral vowels in Midi French is reduced compared with that of SF:

| Midi French | | | | SF | | |
|---|---|---|---|---|---|---|
| i | y | u | | i | y | u |
| E | Ø | O | | e | ø | o |
| | A | | | ɛ | œ | ɔ |
| | | | | a | | ɑ |

Use of *e muet* or schwa

The mid central vowel schwa [ə] is used in a number of contexts in Midi French where it would not occur in SF. Here, for instance, it appears:

- in word-final position after a consonant as in *plante* (l. 3) [plaã̃ntə]
- in final position after a vowel as in *glue* (l. 7) [glyə]
- word internally where it is preceded by only one consonant as in *appelants* (l. 9), whereas in SF it only occurs if preceded by two consonants

b  Although note that, for example, the opposition between *je mangeai* [e] and *je mangeais* [ɛ] is no longer made by a considerable number of French speakers.

– in final position after a consonant where it does not feature in the orthography as in *alors* (l. 3) [alɔrə], *avec* (l. 7) [avɛkə]

### Nasalized vowels

In Midi French, vowels are partially nasalized[c] and one of the nasal consonants is generally sounded after them depending on the place of articulation of the following consonant; thus [n] before [t] or [d] ([lɛɛ̃nterjœr], l. 4), [m] before [p] or [b] ([ezaãmplə], l. 1), [ŋ] before [g] or [k] or in final position ([batɔ̃ɔ̃ŋ], l. 7). No nasal consonant is heard at the end of *hein* (l. 2) or of the first occurrence of *en* (l. 2). There is also a tendency for the Midi nasalized vowels to be slightly more closed than their SF counterparts. Note, however, that the opposition between [ɛ̃] and [œ̃], which is tending to disappear for instance from Parisian French, is well maintained in the South.

### Consonant groups

There is a tendency for consonant groups to be simplified as in *exemple* (l. 1) in which [gz] is simplified to [z], and *p(l)acés* (l. 7). In the case of *arbustres* (l. 3), however, an [r] has been inserted (SF *arbustes*), perhaps influenced by the related term *arbre*.

### Liaison

In this rapid speech the speaker makes few liaisons and no liaison consonant is heard, for example in [tu otur] (l. 7).

### *Vocabulary*

A number of diminutive suffixes were productive in Old French, but today the modern language generally prefers to note the idea of smallness through the adjective *petit*. Regional vocabularies typically conserve features which have disappeared from general usage; so here we find two local terms with diminutive suffixes, *verguettes* (l. 6) to refer to short flexible rods, and *fenestrons* (l. 4) for 'little windows' (cf. Provençal *fenestroun*).

### Spoken French

This text exemplifies spontaneous spoken usage. In general we may speak of the economy and brevity of the spoken word compared with the

c  I have followed Carton and consistently transcribed the nasal vowels, for example as [aãn] rather than [ãn], even though in the rapid speech we have there is something of a tendency for the vowels to be nasalized throughout.

tendency towards redundancy and duplicative marking in writing to ensure that the meaning is conveyed unambiguously in a situation where there is not the potential for feedback, as in conversation, nor the aid of such paralinguistic features as gesture. The spontaneous nature of the discourse is indicated by the pauses, false starts and self-corrections, hesitations and repetitions. The speaker also uses a number of interjections and fillers while he is structuring his thoughts such as *hein* (l. 2), *quoi* (l. 2), *èh* (l. 22), and onomatopoeic and expressive terms which would be inappropriate in more formal contexts (*pfst*, l. 14, *hun hop*, ll. 20–21).

## Discourse markers

Informal speech typically employs a number of discourse markers which have little semantic content but serve to structure the discourse. So, for example, *voilà* (l. 1) marks the opening of the utterance, whilst *voyez* (l. 2) maintains contact with the listener. Words which normally have a temporal value are also often used in this way in speech (*alors*, l. 24, *toujours*, l. 5).

## Syntax

In informal discourse of this kind it is, of course, almost impossible to talk of sentences, as the utterances are composed of a mixture of correctly constructed phrases, false starts, hesitations, etc. Features typical of informal spoken usage include the increased use of presentatives (*voilà*, l. 1, *c'est*, l. 23), the non-use of *ne* in negative constructions (*elles chantent pas*, l. 12), the avoidance of inversion in questions, with the speaker here using the register-neutral *est-ce que* (ll. 16–17), and a preference for co-ordination rather than complex subordination. The speaker does, however, retain the impersonal subject pronoun *il* (l. 10) which is frequently dropped in informal conversation. Of course, speech is not homogeneous either and displays considerable variation according to register. In our extract there are equally features associated with the lower register style of *français populaire* such as the reduplication of a nominal subject by a pronoun subject, which is in terms of normative grammar incorrect (*ces bêtes elles chantent*, l. 10) or the extensive use of *que* as a kind of passe-partout connector (l. 18).

## Vocabulary

In the twentieth century there has been something of a narrowing of the gap between the lexicons deemed appropriate for speech and writing as authors such as Céline have felt increasingly free to open up literary usage to different registers. In general, however, we may observe that spoken usages tend to employ lower register items (note here the use of *ça* not *cela*) and a more limited range of terms, including function words such as conjunctions. Thus in speech use of *quand* (ll. 13, 27) greatly outweighs that of other conjunctions meaning 'when'.

Quebecois
New France
normandy

# 45 Antonine Maillet, *La Sagouine* (1971)

Antonine Maillet was born at Buctouche in New Brunswick in 1929; she
is one of the first Acadian authors, and certainly the greatest. *La Sagouine*,
described as a 'pièce pour une femme seule', was first published in 1971
and revolves around a 72-year-old woman of whom Maillet writes: 'Je
vous la livre comme elle est, sans retouches à ses rides, ses gerçures, ou
sa langue. Elle ne parle ni joual [lower-class speech of Quebec], ni chiac
[a kind of *franglais* spoken by the younger generation of Acadian
speakers], ni français international. Elle parle la langue populaire de ses
pères descendus à cru du XVI<sup>e</sup> siècle' (Maillet 1976: 15). Although this
is a literary work with all the hazards that implies, as we have seen, for
the linguist trying to analyse spoken usage, the work nevertheless provides
an excellent example of rather conservative Acadian usage which, because
of the history of settlement patterns, contains dialectal features notably
from Poitou, archaisms, and traits of the *français populaire* spoken in
sixteenth-century France.

In this extract the old woman is reminiscing on the effect of the war
on her life and on the region.

> Par chance, qu'y a eu la guerre! Quoi c'est que j'arions fait, nous
> autres, sans ça? Ah! les temps étiont rendus point aisés. Entre la
> dépression et la guerre, y a eu un temps mort où c'est qu'i' se
> passait pus rien entoute. Pus rien qu'i' se passait, en ce temps-là,
> et j'arions été capables de corver coume des bêtes abandounées,      5
> droite là dans nos trous. Ben y a eu la guerre. A' s'en a venu par
> icitte juste à temps, c't'elle-là. Juste au bon temps pour nous
> sauver de la misère. Parce que si j'avions pas pu nous rendre
> jusqu'à la guerre et que j'avions corvé en chemin, pas parsoune
> s'en arait aparçu. Parce que ce temps-là, apparence que même les    10
> riches en arrachiont pour attraper les deux boutes. Ça fait que
> nous autres ... ben nous autres, je tchenions même pas un boute
> dans nos mains. Je tchenions pus rien entoute. Par chance, y a eu
> la guerre.
>
> Ouais ... une ben boune guerre, que je vous dis. Avant qu'a'     15
> s'amenit, la guerre, je crois ben que le Bon Djeu en parsoune
> arait été dans l'embarras si je l'avions questiouné sus les genses
> d'en bas. Je crois ben qu'il arait point été capable de toute nous
> noumer. Y a pus parsoune qu'avait l'air de saouère que dans notre
> boute y avait encore du monde en vie. Parce que les darniéres     20
> ânnées, tout ce qui sortait d'en bas, c'était des sarcueils d'enfants.
> Ceuses-là qu'arriviont pas à mouri' restiont terrés coume des
> marmottes dans leu trou jusqu'à ça que le printemps erssoude.
> Ben notre printemps, ç'a été la guerre.
>
> Là, j'avons erssoudu, nous autres itou. Ils veniont même nous     25

qu'ri' chus nous. Ça faisait point trois mois que la guerre était coumencée, qu'ils saviont déjà le nom de tous les houmes d'en bas, avec leur âge, leu pesanteur, leu couleur de cheveux, les maladies qu'ils aviont pis ceuses-là qu'ils aviont pas; ils saviont itou ça que chacun pouvait faire, et pis le nombre de leux femmes    30
et de leux enfants. Tout ça était écrit sus leux papiers coume si le gouvarnement en parsoune avait l'étention à l'avenir de s'occuper de nos affaires. C'était tchurieux, ben je nous plaignions pas. Par rapport que ça faisait pas de diffarence qui c'est qui pornait nos affaires en main, il pouvait pas en prendre plusse que    35
j'en avions et j'en avions point.

   La darniére chouse que j'avions lâchée, je me souviens, c'était nos lits pis nos matelas. Ah! c'était point des matelas à ressorts ni des lits de plumes, faut pas se faire des accrouères. Souvent je nous fabriquions des lits avec des planches de goélettes échouées    40
sus les côtes. Ça sentait un petit brin l'étchume et pis le goémon, ben ça pornait pas l'eau, toujou' ben. Et je les faisions assez hauts sus pattes pour pas partir à la d'rive au temps des marées hautes et à la fonte des neiges. Ben à la fin, j'avons dû quitter partir nos lits avec le reste. Par rapport qu'un soumier pis des plumes, ça se    45
mange point. Une parsoune peut dormir deboute ou dans la place, ben a' peut point manger du bois ... Pas longtemps, toujou' ben ... Pas toute sa vie ... Par chance, y a eu la guerre.

From A. Maillet, *La Sagouine, pièce pour une femme seule* (Paris, Grasset, 1976), pp. 97–99.)

[It was lucky there was the war. What would we have done without it? Ah! times weren't easy. Between the Depression and the war, there was a dead period when nothing at all happened. Nothing happened at that time and we could have died like abandoned animals, right there in our holes. [6] Well there was the war. It came here just in time, it did. Just at the right time to save us from destitution. Because if we hadn't been able to go to war and we had died on the way, nobody would have noticed it. Because at that time, seems that even the rich were having difficulty making ends meet ... well we didn't even have an end in our hands. We had nothing at all. It was lucky there was the war.
[15] Yes ... a damn fine war I tell you. Before the war came, I truly believe that the good Lord himself would have been in difficulty if we had asked him about the people here. I truly believe he wouldn't have been able to name us at all. Nobody seemed to know that in our neck of the woods there were still people living. Because in the previous years, all that came from there were children's coffins. Those who didn't manage to die remained dug in like marmots in their holes until spring arrived. Well, our spring, that was the war.
[25] Then we also arrived. They even came to look for us here. It was

not three months after the war had begun when they already knew the names of all the men here together with their age, weight, hair colour, the illnesses they had had or hadn't had; and they also knew what each one could do and then the number of their wives and children. All that was written on their papers as if the government itself intended in future to take an interest in our affairs. It was curious, but well we didn't complain. Because it didn't make any difference who it was who took charge of our affairs since they couldn't take more of it than we had and we had nothing.

[37] The last thing we gave up, I remember, were our beds and our mattresses. Oh! they weren't spring mattresses or feather beds, don't have any illusions. Often we made beds from planks from wrecked coasters on the shore. It smelt a bit of foam and wrack, but well that didn't let in water, after all. And we made them quite high on feet so that they didn't get carried away at high tides or snow thaws. Well in the end we had to let our beds go with the rest. Because a mattress and feathers, they can't be eaten. [46] A person can sleep standing up or on the floor, but, well, he can't eat wood ... Not for long, anyway ... Not all his life ... It was lucky there was the war.]

## COMMENTARY

### Brief history of Acadia

Acadia as such no longer exists geographically or politically, and Acadians today live principally in New Brunswick, Nova Scotia and on Prince Edward Island, each of the provinces having its own linguistic peculiarities. In 1524 the Italian navigator Verrazzano went for France to the New World and gave the name Arcadia, later Acadia, to a region stretching along the Atlantic coast near Delaware. The first settlement in Acadia occurred in 1604 and in the following year moved to Port Royal (now Annapolis Royal, Nova Scotia). During the seventeenth century the colony continually passed back and forth between British and French rule. The French-speaking settlers arrived mostly in the 1630s, 1640s and 1670s and came principally from regions south of the Loire, and especially Poitou. Under the Treaty of Utrecht (1713) Nova Scotia passed definitively into British hands; then in 1755 many of the French speakers were deported when the threat of imminent war with France raised the spectre of a possible revolt. By the Treaty of Paris (1763) France ceded to Britain the entire Maritime region together with all of New England, but from 1765 to 1770 the French gradually returned to Acadia. In 1784 New Brunswick was separated from Nova Scotia, and the resettled Acadians took an oath of allegiance. Gradually at the end of the nineteenth century and at the beginning of the twentieth century, the Acadians managed to gain their own schools and colleges, a national flag and song, and French-language newspapers. By the 1969 Official Languages Act, Canada became officially bilingual, in 1972 the *Parti Acadien* was founded and in 1981 a guarantee was given for the equal status of French and English. There is now French-language television and radio available, a university at Moncton, and something of a social and literary revival of Acadian through the work of authors such as Maillet.

## The vitality of French in Canada

Estimates vary as to the number of French speakers in Canada, but it is clear that there is a significant proportion of French speakers only in Quebec, where approximately 80 per cent of the population are French-speaking, and New Brunswick, where about one-third are. The next highest proportions are found in Ontario, Manitoba and on Prince Edward Island; in each case probably less than 5 per cent of the population now use French on a daily basis. The *Canadian Encyclopedia* (1988) gives the following numbers of French speakers in former Acadia for 1982:

|  | French origin | French mother tongue | Use French language |
|---|---|---|---|
| New Brunswick | 251,070 | 234,030 | 216,410 |
| Nova Scotia | 71,350 | 36,030 | 24,450 |
| Prince Edward Island | 14,770 | 6,090 | 2,360 |

These figures indicate clearly that, apart from in New Brunswick, the rate of transference of speakers from French to English is very high, leaving very small numbers of French speakers. In Nova Scotia and on Prince Edward Island therefore the future of French looks fairly bleak. If French is to survive in Canada its greatest hope is surely in Quebec, which is of course officially monolingual in French, followed by New Brunswick.

## Acadian French

Our account of the Acadian French of New Brunswick is greatly indebted to the work of Péronnet (1989), and is necessarily somewhat simplified. First, compared with *québécois*, Acadian French seems to have become fixed earlier, and to have shown greater resistance to standardization. It is therefore rather conservative, for example, in the use of *ici* rather than *ci*, in the plural verb endings, and in the loss of final *r* in such words as *leur*. Second, whilst Acadian French shares regional peculiarities with areas south of the Loire, especially Poitou, Quebec displays features of more northern usage and particularly that of Normandy and the Île-de-France. These differences are borne out by a study of patronymics: of New Brunswick names some 36 per cent derive from Loudun, and another 15 per cent from other western central areas. As regards grammar, few of the peculiarities of Acadian speech are precisely located in these areas, however: for example, use of *a* or *al* in place of *elle* is common to Poitou and Normandy as well as to other regions. Third, Acadian speech, at least as used by the older generation, seems to have preserved a number of features which are attested in the *usage populaire* of sixteenth- and seventeenth-century France. This includes use of [st . . .] for demonstrative adjectives and pronouns and the form [ʒ(ə) . . . ɔ̃] for the first person plural verb endings.

*Phonology*

This is a brief summary of some of the features typical of the Acadian French of New Brunswick as exemplified in Maillet's transcription:

- the affricates [tʃ] and [dʒ] replace respectively standard [k] and [g], at least in the speech of the older generation, so here we find *tchurieux* (l. 33), *étchume* (l. 41). The affricate is also represented here in *tchenions* (l. 12).
- final *-r* is often not pronounced, except in liaison, as was common in sixteenth- and seventeenth-century popular usage. This affects, for instance, *leur* (l. 28) and the ending of *-ir* verbs (*qu'ri'*, l. 26). On the other hand, the spelling used seems to suggest the pronunciation of final [s] and [t] (e.g. *genses*, l. 17, *boutes*, l. 11).
- the opposition between [ɔ]/[u] (and indeed [o]) is neutralized in closed syllables before a nasal consonant, as is suggested by the spellings of *coume*, l. 5, *boune*, l. 15, *coumencée*, l. 27, etc.
- as is attested in popular texts of the sixteenth and seventeenth centuries, [ɛ] opens to [a] before [r]; there are numerous examples here, including *parsoune*, l. 9, *sarcueils*, l. 21, and *gouvarnement*, l. 32.
- there is neutralization of the opposition between [ɔ] and [œ] before [r], perhaps reflected in *corvé* (l. 9) for *crevé*.
- the pronunciation [wɛ] has remained as in *saouère*, l. 19 and *accrouères*, l. 39. Less common, although also attested, are [wa] and [wɑ].

In addition, we may note features which are shared with popular usages in France, such as the syncopation of unstressed vowels (*qu'ri'*, l. 26, *d'rive*, l. 43) and glides (*ben*, l. 42). There are also instances of metathesis in *corvé* (for *crevé*, l. 9) and *pornait* (l. 35).

*Morphology*

The morphology of Acadian French tends to be extremely conservative; we may note, for example in the case of demonstratives, the use of *icette* in the expression *par icette* (here *par icitte*, ll. 6–7) for standard 'par ici'. In some cases, as with *leur*, Acadian morphology is influenced by phonetic habits. We will focus here on personal pronouns and verb morphology.

## Personal pronouns

The typical Acadian unstressed personal pronouns are as follows:

| | |
|---|---|
| 1 | : *je* [ʒə]/[ʒ] (l. 15) |
| 2 | : *tu* [ty]/[t] |
| 3 masc. | : *i(l)* [i] ([j, il]) (l. 4) |
| 3 fem. | : *a, al* [a, al] (l. 6); these forms are also widespread in much of western and northern France, although not in Brittany. |
| 4 | : *je* [ʒ(ə)] together with the verb ending *-ons* [ɔ̃] (ll. 1, 25, etc.); this seems to have been common in lower-register French usage of the sixteenth century, and is still occasionally attested in some seventeenth- and eighteenth-century texts. It is found in a number of central dialects of the *langue d'oïl*. In the speech of younger Acadians *on* may be used as in lower-register hexagonal French. |
| 5 | : *vous* [vu]/[vuz] |
| 6 masc./fem. | : *ils* [i] ([j, il]) (l. 25); as in the case of the first person plural, the loss of gender distinction in third person plural pronouns is still found in certain northern dialects; attested first in Anglo-Norman, there are examples of more widespread usage of this dating from the fourteenth and fifteenth centuries. |

As for the stressed forms, the first and second person plural forms are always *nous autres* (ll. 1–2), *vous autres*.

## Verb morphology

Two verb endings are of interest: the first person plural *-ons* ([ɔ̃]) which combines with the subject pronoun *je* (*j'arions*, l. 1), and the third person plural ending *-ont* ([ɔ̃]) which is generalized from the third person plural present indicative of *avoir* (*ont*) and the future tense ending for the third person plural to use with all third person plural verbs (*ils veniont*, l. 25, *ils saviont*, l. 27). According to Nyrop (Péronnet 1989: 148), this popular usage appeared early on in the history of French, but especially from the thirteenth century; it survives in a number of modern patois of the southern and eastern parts of the *langue d'oïl* area. Note the future stem of *avoir* is *ar-*, so for example *j'arions fait* (l. 1) is a future perfect form.

*Syntax*

The majority of syntactic peculiarities exemplified here are shared with *français populaire*. We may note, for instance, the tendency to generalize the use of *avoir* as an auxiliary verb at the expense of *être* (*a' s'en a venu*, l. 6), the omission of the impersonal subject pronoun *il* (*faut pas*, l. 39), the use of dislocated structures (*avant qu'a' s'amenit, la guerre*, ll. 15–16), the insertion of *que* as a generalized clausal connector (*que je vous dis*, l. 15),[a] and hesitation about the conjugation and use of the subjunctive (*avant qu'a' s'amenit*, ll. 15–16). The form of the interrogative, *quoi c'est que* . . . (l. 1), avoiding inversion is also typical of lower-register European French. We have seen that *ne* is frequently omitted in spoken French; in Canadian French this omission appears to be virtually categorical (e.g. *ça faisait point trois mois que* . . ., l. 26). A study by Sankoff and Vincent (1977) has shown that in the Montreal corpus non-use of *ne* occurs in 99.5 per cent of cases.

*Vocabulary*

The lexicon of Acadian French is equally marked by the preservation of archaic, regional and popular features. There are no anglicisms in this extract since this would be inappropriate for the character; however, the speech of younger Acadians makes liberal use of these.

In a number of cases the text uses words which are common to standard French, but with a different meaning; these include *bout(es)* (l. 11) used to refer to the region one lives in, *patte* (l. 43) to denote the foot of a piece of furniture, *soumier* (l. 45) for a horse-hair mattress, *goélette* (l. 40) for a coaster of small tonnage, *en arracher* (l. 11) meaning 'to experience great difficulty', and *quitter partir* (l. 44) for *laisser partir. Pis* (l. 38) for standard *puis* is used not only as a temporal conjunction and adverb, but also as the simple co-ordinator 'and'.

Other terms are associated with familiar and popular registers in France, such as the verb *s'amener* (l. 16) meaning 'to come', the adverb *itou* (l. 25) meaning 'also', *par rapport que* (l. 34) with the sense 'because', *brin* (l. 41) to refer to 'a touch of, a bit of something', and *questionner* (l. 17), which typifies the preference in lower registers for regular *-er* verbs.

Finally, we may note the following peculiarities of Canadian usage: *entoute* for standard 'du tout', and *erssoudre* (l. 23) for 'apparaître' or 'sortir'.

---

a  This contrasts with usage in *québécois* where *que* is frequently omitted. Note that whereas *que* is used in line 1 (*qu'y a eu la guerre!*), it is omitted in a similar context in line 13.

# Appendix I:
# Summary of main linguistic features

The purpose of this Appendix is first to provide a summary of the principal sound changes which occurred during the history of French, since these have not been dealt with systematically in the textual commentaries (Section 1), and second to list for easy reference places in the text where discussion of the principal orthographical, morphological, syntactic and lexical features of Old French, Middle French and Modern French may be found (Section 2). We have selected three very broad periods for these résumés (each roughly encompassing two of the sections of the main text), since they are intended simply as a means of introduction to the history of French and as an *aide-mémoire*. It is, however, vital to remember not only that the French language evolved constantly within each of these periods, but that the language was in no sense as unified as such summaries may wrongly imply.

## 1 PHONOLOGICAL CHANGES

*Pre-textual phonological changes: Latin into French*

### Vulgar Latin (up to the fifth century)

*Vowels*

(a) In Classical Latin (CL), there were five phonemic vowels (their precise phonetic quality is uncertain), each of which could be phonemically long or short, giving the following vocalic phonemes /ĭ, ī, ĕ, ē, ă, ā, ŭ, ū, ŏ, ō/. In addition, there were three diphthongs /ae, au, oe/. In Vulgar Latin (VL), vowel length ceased to be phonemic and was replaced by differences of vowel quality; long vowels tended to become (or stay) closed, while short vowels tended to become open. This transformation is given below, with the CL system in the middle and the VL system outside:

*nīdum* > [nidu]   [i] — ī                          ū — [u] *dūrum*  >  [duru]

*fĭdem* > [fede]           ĭ               ŭ            *gŭtta*  >  [gota]
                    [e]⟨                     ⟩ [o]
*vēla*  > [vela]           ē               ō            *flōrem*  >  [flore]

*pĕdem* > [pɛde]  [ɛ]—ĕ                     ŏ — [ɔ] *nŏvem*  >  [nɔwe]

                           ă        ā

                              [a]

*mălus, mālus* > [malu]

Of the three diphthongs, two simplified to monophthongs (oe > e,
*poena* > [pena], ae > ɛ, *caelum* > [kɛlu]), leaving only [au], which in
the Gallo-Roman period reduced to [ɔ] (*aurum* > [ɔr]).

(b) The first wave of diphthongization occurred in the third and
fourth centuries and affected the half-open vowels [ɛ] and [ɔ]. When
tonic and in an open syllable, these two vowels lengthened and
diphthongized giving ɛ > iE (*feru(m)* > *fier*), ɔ > uɔ (*nove(m)* > [nuɔwe]
> *neuf*).

(c) Unstressed vowels weakened and fell, beginning with those in penultimate and pretonic position; this loss of internal unstressed vowels
resulted in the reduction of proparoxytones (words with stress on the
antepenultimate syllable): *pérdere* > *perdre*, *vívere* > *vivre*.

(d) When *e* or *i* appeared in hiatus with another following vowel, they
closed in the second and third centuries resulting in [j]: *filia* > [filja];
*vinea* > [vinja].

(e) Initial consonant clusters composed of [s] followed by [p], [t], or [k]
developed a prosthetic vowel during Vulgar Latin. This probably
began as a faint initial [i] or [ə], but subsequently developed into [e]:
*scutum* > *escu* (> *écu*).

*Consonants*

(a) The first wave of palatalization also occurred in the second and third
centuries: this affected an initial [k] or [g] followed by [i] or [e].
Anticipation of the following front vowel caused the [k] and [g] to be
articulated further forward in the mouth at the palate, giving palatalized [t'] and [d']; these then modified to [ts] and [dʒ] respectively:
*centum* > [t'ɛntu] > [tsɛntu]; *gentem* > [d'ɛnte] > [dʒɛnte]. The presence of yod [j] following a consonant also had a palatalizing effect as
the tongue moved too early to the palate in anticipation of the place
of articulation of [j]; in the case of [nj] and [lj], this resulted in two
new consonant phonemes, the palatal nasal /ɲ/, and the palatal lateral

/ʎ/, which finally disappeared from French only at the beginning of the nineteenth century: *filia* [filja] > [fiʎə] (later [fij], *fille*); *vinea* [vinja] > [viɲə].

(b) Latin [h] disappeared from pronunciation in all positions in Vulgar Latin, *habere* > [abere] > *avoir*.

(c) Final [-m] was lost probably in the first century AD – which of course had important repercussions for the declension system of nouns – except in certain monosyllables (*rem* > *rien*, *meum* > *mien*).

(d) The articulation of consonants in intervocalic position (or when between a vowel and [r]) evolved. While [l, m, n, r] remained stable, [p, t, k, b, d, g] began to modify through a process of partial or total assimilation to the surrounding vowels. The unvoiced consonants acquired voicing through assimilation and then the voiced consonants went through a further stage of assimilation as speakers failed to make the full closure required for stops, the result being the corresponding fricatives (p > b > β; t > d > ð; k > g > ɣ). The bilabial fricative [β] was lost when it preceded (or occasionally followed) a vowel with lip-rounding (*nuba* > [nu βa] > *nue*), but elsewhere became the labiodental [v] (*ripa* > [riba] > [rivə] > *rive*). Likewise the velar fricative [ɣ] was only fully assimilated when there was a neighbouring velar or back vowel (*locare* > [logare] > [loɣare] > *louer*); in other positions it moved forward to become the palatal fricative [j] (*baca* > [baga] > [baɣa] > *baie*). The dental fricative [ð] survived into early Old French, but then fell in all contexts (*nuda* > [nuða] > [ny], *nue*). Intervocalic [s] voiced to [z] (*causa* > *chose*).

## Gallo-Romance (fifth to ninth centuries)

*Vowels*

(a) During this period, perhaps under the influence of the strong expiratory stress of Germanic speech, the second wave of diphthongization took place in Northern France, this time affecting [e] and [o], so that [e] > [ei] and [o] > [ou]; thus *fidem* [fede] > [feiθ], *flōrem* [flore] > [flour].

(b) Tonic free [a] also modified to [ɛ], perhaps passing through a stage of diphthongization *[aj]: *mare* > [mɛr]. When this vowel followed a palatal consonant, it became [iɛ] (*caru* > [tʃiɛr]) (= Bartsch's Law).

(c) Final vowels all weakened and fell (*muru* > *mur*) with the exception of [a], which became [ə] (*porta* > *porte* [pɔrtə]); a schwa was also introduced when it was required as a 'supporting' vowel for a final consonant cluster which would otherwise be difficult to pronounce (*merlu* > [merlə]); this also affected third person plural verb endings, where a [ə] was inserted to break up a sequence of C(onsonant) + *nt* (*vendunt* > *vendent*).

(d) Unstressed vowels in paroxytones (words stressed on the penultimate syllable) equally fell (*múrus* > *murs*).

(e) Towards the end of the period the articulation of [u] moved forward to [y]; there is no satisfactory explanation for this change, which has been attributed by some scholars to Celtic substrate influence (*murum* > [myr]).

## Consonants

(a) A second wave of palatalization occurred, although not in the most northern regions (e.g. Picardy); this time [k] and [g] palatalized when followed by [a] resulting in [tʃ] and [dʒ]: *campum* > [t'ampu] > [tʃamp]; *gamba* > [d'amba] > [dʒambə].

(b) [h] and [w] (> [gw]) were re-introduced into French in words borrowed from Germanic. Germanic [h] in words such as *honte*, *haïr* did not finally cease to be pronounced until the eighteenth century, although as early as the sixteenth century we find grammarians criticizing those who drop their *h*s.

(c) Geminate consonants simplified (*gutta* > *goute*), with the exception of *rr*.

## Old French

A striking feature of Old French is the large number of phonemes it had. We may note the following changes during the Old French period.

## Vowels

(a) Nasalization is the regressive, assimilative influence of a nasal conso-nant on a preceding vowel sound. According to traditional accounts, before nasalization took place, [ɛ] and [ɔ] were raised to [e] and [o] respectively before a nasal consonant; all five other vowels were nasal-ized [a, e, i, o, y], starting with the most open vowel, [a], in the tenth century and finishing with [i, y] in the thirteenth century. Thus, when followed by a nasal consonant, [a] > [ã] (tenth century); [e] > [ẽ] (eleventh century); [o] > [õ] (twelfth century); [i] > [ĩ], [y] > [ỹ]. At this stage the nasal consonant continued to be pronounced. Nasalization appears to have had an opening effect on the quality of the vowel, so that already by the end of the eleventh century [ẽ] > [ã] (*tempus* > [tãms]). Where the vowel preceding the nasal conso-nant occurred in a tonic open syllable, diphthongization also occurred, creating a series of nasal diphthongs, which subsequently reduced to simple vowels. For more recent accounts of nasalization, see above, pp. 63–65.

(b) In Early Old French the diphthong [uɔ] had differentiated to [ue], and [ou] to [eu]. Old French witnessed the reduction of many of the diphthongs; this seems to have been associated with a change of syllabification. While at the beginning of the twelfth century, French had falling diphthongs (i.e. diphthongs accented on the first element), the accent shifted to the second element, thus [íE] > [jÉ]. Through assimilation of the lip-rounding of the [e] to that of the back rounded vowel, the diphthong [ue] became [wœ] and then reduced to give a new front rounded vowel, as in *cœur* [kœr] (in Modern French the presence of [ø] or [œ] is largely dependent on syllable type; see below). A similar development occurred in the case of [eu] (*fleur* > [flœr]). On the other hand, [ei] differentiated to [oi] but evolved to [wɛ] only in the thirteenth century. Finally, the diphthong [au], created as a result of the vocalization of [l] before a consonant, remained until the sixteenth century: *alter* > [autrə].

(c) [u] was re-introduced into French when [o] in initial unstressed syllable or tonic blocked syllable raised to [u]: *bucca* > *boche* > *bouche*; *nutrire* > *nourir*.

(d) In initial syllables, the opposition between [e] and [ɛ] was neutralized; the subsequent evolution of this /E/ depended on the syllable type, with [ɛ] resulting in closed syllables, but [ə] in open syllables (*venire* > [vənir]).

*Consonants*

(a) During the Early Old French period, [l] in preconsonantal position vocalized to give [u]; this joined with the preceding vowel to form a diphthong: *alter* > [autrə].

(b) Old French witnessed the simplification of certain consonant groups. The loss of implosive consonants began in Early Old French; [s] before a consonant other than [p, t, k] was lost first, bringing with it lengthening of the preceding vowel *isle* > [iːlə]. The cluster [gw] of Germanic words also simplified to [g], and [kw] to [k] as in *qui* ([kwi] > [ki]). During Old French it was the turn of affricates to simplify [ts] > [s], [dz] > [z], [tʃ] > [ʃ], [dʒ] > [ʒ].

(c) From Early Old French, unsupported final consonants had devoiced as happens in many other languages (e.g. Modern German). From about the twelfth century, final consonants, starting with [s] and [t], began to fall if the next word began with a consonant. This left two different pronunciations for words ending in a consonant, one with the final consonant pronounced when they were followed by a pause or a word beginning with a vowel (*lit*, [lit], *drap*, [drap], etc.), the other without the final consonant, used elsewhere ([li], [dra]). If the final consonant was [f] or [s] there were indeed three different pronunciations, for the final consonant voiced to [v] or [z] when followed by a vowel; this survives today in the three-fold pronunciation of *six* and *dix*: *j'en ai six* [sis], *six femmes* [si fam], *six hommes* [siz ɔm].

## Middle French (including the sixteenth century)

*Vowels*

(a) The reduction of vowels in hiatus is one of the key features distinguishing Middle French from Old French: thus we find for instance [əy] > [y] (*sëur > sûr*), [əɔ̃] > [ɔ̃] (*rëond > rond*).

Middle French also witnessed the loss of [ə] after another vowel; this occurred earlier internally, for example in future verb forms, but more slowly in final position; the orthography is, however, often slow to indicate these changes with, for example, both the spellings *suppliera* and *supplira* occurring in the period.

(b) According to traditional accounts, during Middle French the remaining nasalized vowels opened, giving [ĩ] > [ɛ̃], [õ] > [ɔ̃], and [y] > [œ̃]. Perhaps more important still was the loss, from the end of the sixteenth century on, of the double nasal articulation, that is, when the nasal consonant was followed by a consonant, it fell, leaving phonemic nasal vowels ([tʃãmp > ʃã(p), põnt > põ(t)]). Where the nasal consonant was intervocalic, it did not, however, fall; rather, the vowel denasalized (*fina(m)* [fĩnə > fin], contrasting with *finu(m)* [fĩn] > [fɛ̃n] > [fɛ̃]).

(c) The diphthong still represented by *oi* had moved to [wɛ] at the end of the thirteenth century. During Middle French there was considerable variation between the pronunciations [wɛ] and [ɛ]; [wa], a popular pronunciation, was also used from the fourteenth century on. In the sixteenth century, grammarians still advocated [wɛ], but in the following century [ɛ] came to be accepted in a number of words, as well as imperfect and conditional verb endings. [wa] continued to be censured but nevertheless persisted, and seems finally to have become established as acceptable at the Revolution.

(d) From the thirteenth century on, another popular pronunciation was the opening of [ɛr] to [ar], and this appears to have been very common in the sixteenth century. Most of the words in which this occurred, such as *guarir* for *guerir*, did not retain this pronunciation, but a few, including *larme* for *lerme*, did.

(e) While [o] seems to have generally raised to [u] in initial syllables in Old French, there appears to have been in Middle French a learned movement to restore [o] or even [ɔ] in these words, culminating in the sixteenth century with the hard-fought debate between the *ouïstes* supporting [u] and the *non-ouïstes*, favouring [o]. This explains the presence of [o] in words such as *soleil* and *colonne*.

(f)  In the sixteenth century the triphthong [əau] of *eau* reduced to [əo], finally becoming [o] in the following century.


## Consonants

(a)  By the sixteenth century we find clear indication that the pronunciation of [h] was weakening.

(b)  Intervocalically there was a tendency for [r] > [z] in the fifteenth and sixteenth centuries; this has survived in *chaise*, which forms an etymological doublet with *chaire*. On the other hand, final [-r] was slowly restored to the infinitives of *-ir* and *-oir* verbs from the sixteenth century onwards.


## Modern French

*Vowels*

(a)  From at least the sixteenth century on, and probably much earlier in the case of the opposition /e/ ~ /ɛ/, there are signs of a tendency to prefer the half-closed vowels [e, ø, o] in open syllables and the half-open vowels [ɛ, œ, ɔ] in closed syllables; this seems to have become established in the seventeenth and eighteenth centuries. The front unrounded mid-vowels now only contrast in final open syllables (*pré* [pre]/*près* [prɛ]), and many speakers fail to make this opposition systematically, particularly in the case of the verb endings *-ai* [e] and *-ais* [ɛ]. In the case of the other two pairs, oppositions occur only in final closed syllables; if, however, the opposition between /o/ and /ɔ/ is evidenced in a number of minimal pairs (*saute* [so:t]/*sotte* [sɔt], *paume/pomme*, etc.), the opposition between /ø/ and /œ/ only occurs in two pairs (*jeûne* [ʒø:n]/*jeune* [ʒœn] and *veule* [vø:l]/*veulent* [vœl]).

(b)  Vowel length has ceased to be phonemic, with the possible exception of /ɛ:/, since some speakers continue to make an opposition between pairs such as *mettre* [mɛtr] and *maître* [mɛ:tr].

(c)  The vowel [ɑ] has become phonemic in Modern French, whereas in Old French it was probably an allophonic variant of /a/ before [s] and [z]. When the affricate [ts] simplified to [s], there were thus created minimal pairs of the type *chasse* ([tʃatsə] > [ʃas]) and *châsse* ([ʃɑ:s]). The presence of [ɑ] is associated particularly with the loss of implosive [s] before a consonant (*pâte*), but also with such factors as the loss of vowels in hiatus (*âge*). Note, however, that few Parisians now differentiate between pairs such as *tache* and *tâche*, both of which they pronounce with [a].

(d) Similarly, many speakers, particularly in Paris, no longer make an opposition between [œ̃] and [ɛ̃], and instead have generalized the latter nasal; thus pronunciations such as [lɛ̃di] (*lundi*) and [ɛ̃ lapɛ̃] (*un lapin*) are extremely common in Parisian speech.

*Consonants*

(a) *r* was probably pronounced as a trill produced by the vibration of the tip of the tongue right up to the seventeenth century, and not supplanted by the characteristic uvular fricative of Parisian pronunciation until the eighteenth century. This change may be associated with the simplification of geminate *rr* which occurred between the fifteenth and seventeenth centuries, thereby eradicating the difference in pronunciation between pairs such as *guère* and *guerre*. It has been suggested that in order to continue an opposition here, there may have been pressure to change the point of articulation of simplified *rr* to the uvular fricative. However, this pronunciation soon generalized with the result that the phonemic opposition was lost.

(b) Loss of [h] was finally accepted in the eighteenth century. Although the replacement of [ʎ] by [j] is attested in seventeenth-century metalinguistic texts, the palatal lateral lingered on until the beginning of the nineteenth century.

(c) The velar nasal [ŋ] has entered French in a number of English borrowings in the twentieth century. On the other hand, there is a tendency for some speakers today to replace [ɲ] by [nj] except in word-final position.

## 2 GUIDE TO THE LOCATION OF DISCUSSION OF THE PRINCIPAL LINGUISTIC FEATURES OF EACH PERIOD (EXCLUDING PHONOLOGY)

For each period, the main discussions in the text of the different features are listed.

### Old French

### Orthography

**Morphosyntax**

(a) Nouns
   *Noun morphology:* text 1, pp. 27–28; *Decline of the case system:* text 4, pp. 51–52; text 5, p. 63; text 11, p. 90.
(b) Adjectives
   *Adjective morphology:* text 2, pp. 36–37; *Comparative and superlative forms:* text 3, p. 44; text 4, p. 53; *Analogical reworking:* text 4, p. 52; text 10, p. 86; *Position of:* text 5, p. 67.
(c) Articles (definite, indefinite, partitive)
   *Morphology:* text 2, p. 37; *Use of articles:* text 4, pp. 53–54.
(d) Personal pronouns
   *Morphology:* text 1, pp. 28–29; *tu/vous:* text 4, p. 54; *Use of subject pronouns:* text 5, p. 66; text 11, pp. 92–93; text 12, p. 97; *Use of impersonal 'il':* text 10, p. 86.
(e) Demonstrative pronouns and adjectives
   *Morphology:* text 1, p. 29; text 5, p. 65; text 8, pp. 76–77.
(f) Possessive pronouns and adjectives
   *Morphology:* text 1, p. 29.
(g) Relative pronouns
   *'que' for 'qui':* text 10, p. 86.
(h) Verbs
   *Verb morphology: Present indicative:* text 5, p. 65; text 11, pp. 91–92; *Past historic:* text 8, pp. 77–78; text 12, p. 96; *Future:* text 1, p. 29; text 4, p. 53; *Conditional:* text 2, p. 38; *auret, etc.:* text 2, p. 38; *Passive:* text 2, p. 38; *Anglo-Norman:* text 4, p. 52.
   *Use of tenses:* text 2, p. 38; text 4, p. 54; text 5, p. 66; text 9, p. 82.
   *Use of subjunctive:* text 2, p. 38; text 4, p. 54; text 5, p. 66; *Conditional clauses:* text 11, p. 93.
(i) Adverbs
   *Morphology:* text 4, p. 53; text 5, p. 65.
(j) Prepositions
   text 1, p. 28; text 11, p. 92.

**Sentence structure and word order**

(a) Negation
   text 4, p. 55; text 6, p. 71.
(b) Agreement
   *Subject and verb:* text 4, p. 55; *Collectives:* text 4, p. 55; *Past participle:* text 4, p. 55.
(c) Co-ordination
   text 11, pp. 92–93.

(d) Parataxis/hypotaxis
   text 5, pp. 66–67; text 6, p. 71.
(e) Word order
   text 1, p. 30; text 2, p. 39; text 3, p. 45; text 4, p. 56; text 11, p. 93; text 12, p. 97.

## Vocabulary

(a) Learned and semi-learned terms
   text 1, p. 30; text 4, p. 56.
(b) Lexical creativity
   text 5, p. 67; text 11, p. 93; *Infinitives as substantives:* text 1, p. 30; text 6, p. 71.
(c) *Mots-clés*
   text 1, p. 30; text 5, p. 67.
(d) Germanic words
   text 4, p. 56; text 5, p. 67.
(e) Colloquial, *argot* terms
   text 7, p. 73.
(f) Technical terms
   text 10, p. 87.
(g) Semantic change
   text 4, pp. 56–57; text 8, p. 79; text 11, pp. 93–94.
(h) Loss of words
   text 6, p. 71.

## *Middle French*

## Orthography and typography

*Orthography:* text 13, p. 102; text 14, p. 109; text 17, p. 125; text 18, pp. 129–30; text 21, p. 145; text 25, p. 163; text 26, p. 169; *Reform:* text 27, pp. 173–74.
*Typography:* text 25, pp. 162–63; text 26, pp. 168–69.

## Morphosyntax

(a) Nouns
   *Loss of case system:* text 13, p. 105; *Gender:* text 21, p. 145.
(b) Adjectives
   *Adjective morphology:* text 14, p. 110; text 17, p. 125; text 23, p. 155.
(c) Articles (definite, indefinite, partitive)
   *Morphology:* text 13, p. 105; text 18, p. 130; *Use of articles:* text 13, p. 105; text 14, p. 111.

(d) Personal pronouns
*Morphology:* text 13, p. 104; text 19, p. 133; *tu/vous:* text 17, p. 126; *Use of subject pronouns:* text 13, p. 106; text 17, pp. 125–26; *Use of tonic forms:* text 13, p. 106; text 17, p. 126; text 20, pp. 138–39; *Use of impersonal 'il':* text 14, p. 111; text 20, p. 139.

(e) Demonstrative pronouns and adjectives
*Morphology:* text 14, p. 110; text 18, pp. 130–31; text 21, pp. 145–46; text 23, pp. 154–55; text 25, p. 164.

(f) Possessive pronouns and adjectives
*Morphology:* text 21, p. 145.

(g) Relative pronouns
*lequel, laquelle, etc.:* text 13, p. 106; text 21, p. 145; *'que' for 'qui':* text 21, p. 145.

(h) Verbs
*Verb morphology: Stem levelling:* text 17, p. 125; text 22, p. 151; text 27, pp. 176–77; *Present indicative:* text 13, p. 104; *Past historic:* text 13, pp. 104–5; *Future:* text 16, p. 121; *Conditional:* text 13, p. 104; *Imperfect:* text 13, p. 104; *Present subjunctive:* text 16, p. 121; text 22, p. 151; *Imperative:* text 13, p. 104; *Verbal periphrases:* text 22, p. 151.
*Use of subjunctive:* text 15, p. 117; text 17, p. 126; text 25, p. 165.

(i) Adverbs
*Morphology:* text 18, p. 130.

(j) Prepositions
text 21, p. 146.

## Sentence structure and word order

(a) Negation
text 13, p. 106; text 17, p. 126; text 21, p. 146–47.

(b) Interrogation
text 14, p. 112; text 22, p. 152.

(c) Agreement
*Subject and verb:* text 21, p. 146; *Past participle:* text 14, p. 111; text 26, p. 170; *Present participle:* text 26, p. 170.

(d) Government
text 25, p. 164.

(e) Co-ordination
text 17, p. 126; text 18, p. 131; text 22, p. 152; text 25, p. 165.

(f) Subordination
text 17, p. 126; text 23, p. 155.

(g) Use of *si*
text 14, p. 111; text 19, p. 134; text 20, p. 139.

(h) Latinate constructions
text 14, p. 111; text 17, p. 126; text 18, p. 131; text 21, p. 146; text 23, p. 155.

(i)  Word order
 text 13, p. 106; text 14, p. 112; text 15, pp. 117–18; text 17, p. 127; text
 21, p. 147; text 25, pp. 165–66.

## Vocabulary

(a) Influence of Latin
 text 14, pp. 112–13; text 21, p. 147.
(b) Lexical creativity
 text 14, p. 112; *Derivation and composition:* text 21, p. 148; text 22,
 p. 152.
(c) Italian borrowings
 text 21, p. 148.
(d) Low-register, familiar terms
 text 16, pp. 121–22; text 20, p. 139.
(e) Technical terms
 text 19, pp. 134–35; text 25, p. 166; *Metalinguistic terms:* text 27, p. 177.
(f) Binomial synonyms or near-synonyms
 text 14, p. 113; text 17, p. 127; text 18, p. 131.
(g) Semantic change
 text 13, p. 107; *Historical causes:* text 20, p. 139; *Metonymy:* text 15,
 p. 118.
(h) Loss of words
 text 13, p. 107; text 21, p. 148; text 22, p. 152.

## *Modern French*

## Orthography

text 28, pp. 185–86; text 29, p. 190; text 30, pp. 195–96; text 33, p. 209;
text 37, p. 235; text 42, p. 253.

## Morphosyntax

(a) Nouns
 *Gender:* text 33, p. 209.
(b) Adjectives
 *Comparative and superlative:* text 30, p. 196; *Position of:* text 30,
 p. 196; text 37, p. 236; text 38, p. 240.
(c) Articles (definite, indefinite, partitive)
 *Morphology:* text 29, p. 190; *Use of articles:* text 29, p. 191; text 37,
 p. 235; text 42, p. 253; *Creole:* text 36, p. 226.
(d) Personal pronouns
 *Use of personal pronouns:* text 31, p. 201; text 32, p. 205; text 35,
 p. 220; *Creole:* text 36, p. 226; *Acadian:* text 45, p. 272.

(e) Demonstrative pronouns and adjectives
    *Morphology:* text 29, p. 191; text 42, p. 253.
(f) Relative pronouns
    *lequel, laquelle, etc.:* text 29, p. 191. *Use of:* text 31, p. 200.
(g) Verbs
    *Verb morphology:* text 28, pp. 184, 186; *Present indicative:* text 32, p. 205; *Future:* text 31, p. 201; *Imperative:* text 32, p. 205; *Surcomposés:* text 31, pp. 200–1; *Creole:* text 36, p. 227; *Acadian:* text 45, p. 272.
    *Use of tenses:* text 33, p. 210; text 37, p. 236; text 40, p. 246; *In 'Style indirect libre':* text 38, pp. 239–40; *Use of pronominal verbs:* text 28, p. 187; *Use of subjunctive:* text 28, p. 187; text 31, pp. 201–2; text 37, pp. 235–36.
(h) Adverbs
    *Morphology:* text 29, pp. 190–91.
(i) Conjunctions
    text 29, p. 192.

## Sentence structure and word order

(a) Negation
    text 28, p. 187; text 29, p. 192; text 33, p. 210; text 35, p. 221; *Creole:* text 36, p. 227; *Acadian:* text 45, p. 273.
(b) Interrogation
    text 44, p. 265; text 45, p. 273.
(c) Agreement
    text 28, pp. 186–87; text 31, p. 202; text 38, p. 240; *Past participle:* text 29, p. 191; *Present participle:* text 29, p. 191; text 33, p. 210.
(d) Government
    text 33, p. 210.
(e) Co-ordination
    text 28, pp. 184–85.
(f) Non-finite clauses
    text 33, p. 210.
(g) Latinisms
    text 29, p. 192.
(h) Word order
    text 28, p. 187; text 31, p. 202; text 37, p. 236; *Creole:* text 36, p. 227.

## Vocabulary

(a) Influence of Latin
    text 33, p. 211; text 37, pp. 236–37.
(b) Lexical creativity
    text 30, p. 196; text 40, pp. 246–47.

(c) Borrowings
   *Italian:* text 31, p. 203; *Russian:* text 40, p. 247; *English:* text 43, pp. 257–59.
(d) Low-register, familiar terms
   text 31, p. 202; text 44, pp. 265–66
(e) Technical terms
   text 34, pp. 214–15; text 40, pp. 246–47; text 41, pp. 249–51.
(f) Abstract nouns
   text 32, p. 205; text 37, p. 237.
(g) *Pureté*
   text 28, p. 185.
(h) Loss of words
   text 30, pp. 196–97.
(i) Creole
   text 36, p. 228.
(j) Acadian
   text 45, p. 273.

# Appendix II:
# Glossary of selected technical terms and guide to the sounds of Modern French

## TECHNICAL TERMS

There are a number of dictionaries of linguistics available for help with other terms, such as D. Crystal, *A Dictionary of Linguistics and Phonetics*, 3rd edition, Oxford, Blackwell, 1991.

**analogy**: a process of regularization whereby a form or pattern is aligned with another form or pattern of the language.

**antonyms**: two or more words which are opposite in meaning.

**aspiration**: a period of voicelessness (audible breath) after the release of an articulation, before the voicing starts for the following vowel, as in the articulation of the plosive of English *pie* [pʰaɪ].

**assimilation**: the process whereby a sound takes on some or all of the qualities of a sound preceding or following it.

**assonance**: a sort of rhyming of one word with another used in Old French verse in which the final stressed vowels are the same but not the consonants. A modern French example is *sombre/rompre*.

**clitic**: a form whose behaviour falls between that of a word and an affix, i.e. a form which resembles a word but which in normal speech does not stand on its own but rather depends on a nearby noun or verb (e.g. *il* and *me* of *il me voit*).

**declension**: either variation of a noun, pronoun or adjective for case, gender or number, or the class into which a noun, pronoun or adjective is placed according to its variation for these categories.

**deixis**: refers to linguistic features which relate directly to the person, place or time of the utterance, and whose meaning is therefore related to these, e.g. now/then, here/there, this/that.

**dialect**: a regional or social variety of a language which has its own phonetic, morpho-syntactic and lexical peculiarities.

**diglossia**: two different varieties used throughout a speech community each with a different set of uses; sociolinguists often distinguish between a high (H) variety used for formal contexts and a low (L) variety used in informal situations.

**diphthong/monophthong/triphthong**: in the case of a diphthong a single perceptual change in vowel quality is heard during a syllable, whereas with monophthongs no such change is heard, and with triphthongs two such changes may be heard. Old French possessed a range of diphthongs and triphthongs which have not survived into Modern French. A distinction may be made between **primary diphthongs** which are the result of **diphthongization**, and **secondary diphthongs** which are the by-product of another process, such as palatalization, or the vocalization of [ł] > [u].

**enclisis**: refers to the process whereby a clitic is bound to a preceding word. For example, when an unstressed vowel in a monosyllable is dropped before a following consonant and the rest of the word is joined to the preceding word ending in a vowel (*a le > al*; *en les > es*).

**glide consonant**: a weak transitional consonant produced as the speaker moves from one sound to another. For example in pronouncing *cam'ra* the speaker anticipates the closing of the nasal passage for the following [r] and the non-nasal counterpart of [m], i.e. [b], is heard, giving *chambre*.

**hiatus**: a gap or pause in a group of two or more continuous vowels which do not fall in the same syllable.

**homonyms**: words sharing the same form, but having different meanings. We may distinguish **homophones**, which share the same pronunciation but have different meanings (*saint, sein, sain*), and **homographs**, which have the same spelling but have different meanings (*voler* 'to fly', *voler* 'to steal').

**hypotaxis**: see parataxis.

**imparisyllabic**: having an unequal number of syllables; refers in the history of French to nouns which had an extra syllable in the non-nominative singular forms (e.g. *ber, baron*).

**imperfective/perfective; durative/punctual**: aspectual labels which refer to the internal temporal structure of a situation. **Imperfective/perfective** refer respectively to actions which are incomplete and completed; **durative** forms express an action perceived as having a certain duration, as opposed to the **punctual** expressing an action which happened at a given point in time, without reference to its duration.

**interrogation, partial/total**: in **partial interrogation** the focus of the question bears on a particular element of the utterance, e.g. *quels livres voulez-vous? quand pars-tu?*. In the case of **total interrogation**, also referred to as yes/no questions, the question rather bears on the predicate as a whole, and assumes the answer to be either 'yes' or 'no', e.g. *pleut-il? votre sœur vient-elle demain?*.

**labialization**: the process whereby lip-rounding is added to a sound.

**lenition**: the process whereby a **fortis** (a sound articulated with a relatively strong degree of muscular effort and breath force) becomes a **lenis** (a sound articulated with a relatively weak degree of muscular effort and breath force). An example of **lenition** in the history of French is the voicing of unvoiced stops in intervocalic position ([p > b; t > d; k > g]).

**metathesis**: alteration of the normal sequence, usually of sounds.

**metonymy**: a process of semantic change whereby the name of an object or concept is applied to another object or concept with which it has some real and constant association; for instance, the name of a part may denote the whole (*le bas-bleu*) or the place a product produced there (*le camembert*).

**metalanguage/metalinguistic**: **metalanguage** refers to the form of language used to discuss and describe language itself.

**nasalization/denasalization**: **nasalization** is the process whereby the soft palate is lowered, allowing the audible escape of air through the nose. In the history of French, nasal vowels are created as a result of the nasalization of oral vowels followed by a nasal consonant when the lowering of the soft palate required for the nasal consonant is anticipated. **Denasalization** refers to the loss of nasal quality.

**palatalization**: the process whereby the articulation of a sound shifts to the palate, say back from the teeth or forward from the velum.

**parataxis/hypotaxis**: **parataxis** refers to constructions which are simply juxtaposed or linked through intonation or punctuation; in **hypotactic** structures, on the other hand, subordinating conjunctions are used to join clauses.

**patois**: the meaning of this term is much debated; it is used typically to refer to a local version of a dialect which lacks status in relation to a more prestigious variety.

**stress, tonic, countertonic, atonic**: **stress** refers to the degree of force used in producing a syllable, and is usually due to an increase in loudness, but may also be associated with greater length and higher pitch. Different syllables in a word may receive different degrees of stress: the main or **tonic** stress; secondary stress (**countertonic**), borne in Latin by the first or initial syllable; and weak stress (**atonic**).

**synonyms**: two or more words having the same meaning. In general, natural languages have few complete synonyms, that is words which are interchangeable in all contexts. Partial synonymy, that is interchangeability in some contexts, is more usual.

**syllable, open/closed**: a **closed syllable** is one ending in a consonant (e.g. CVC [Consonant Vowel Consonant]), an **open** (or **free**) **syllable** is a syllable ending in a vowel (e.g. CV).

## THE SOUNDS OF FRENCH

Since there is not a one-to-one relationship between the orthographic symbols of Modern French and their pronunciation (see p. 235), linguists rely rather on the International Phonetic Alphabet to transcribe sounds. The table below gives the sounds of a standardized variety of contemporary French; earlier periods of French used, for example, a range of diphthongs and triphthongs, and a number of other fricatives and affricates, as well as [h].

### Vowels and glides

| | | front | | back | |
|---|---|---|---|---|---|
| | | unrounded | rounded | unrounded | rounded |
| oral vowels | closed | i (*il*, [il]) | y (*une*, [yn]) | | u (*où* [u]) |
| | ½ closed | e (*école*, [ekɔl]) | ø (*peu*, [pø]) | | o (*mot*, [mo]) |
| | ½ open | ɛ (*mère*, [mɛr]) | œ (*peur*, [pœr]) | | ɔ (*vol*, [vɔl]) |
| | open | a (*patte*, [pat]) | | ɑ (*pâte*, [pɑt]) | |
| nasal vowels | | ɛ̃ (*vin*, [vɛ̃]) | œ̃ (*un*, [œ̃]) | ɑ̃ (*blanc*, [blɑ̃]) | ɔ̃ (*bon*, [bɔ̃]) |
| glides | | j (*pied*, [pje]) | ɥ (*lui*, [lɥi]) | | w (*oui*, [wi]) |

There is also the central rounded vowel [ə], variously termed *e muet, e instable, e caduc, e féminin* or schwa.

### Consonants

| place of articulation / manner of articulation | | | bilabial | labiodental | dental | alveolar | alveolar-palatal | palatal | velar | uvular | |
|---|---|---|---|---|---|---|---|---|---|---|---|
| stops | oral | voiceless | p | | t | | | | k | | *père* [pɛr], *très* [trɛ], *car* [kar] |
| | | voiced | b | | d | | | | g | | *balle* [bal], *danse* [dɑ̃s], *golf* [gɔlf] |
| | nasal | | m | | n | | | ɲ | | | *mère* [mɛr], *nez* [ne] *agneau* [aɲo] |
| fricatives | | voiceless | | f | | s | ʃ | | | | *frère* [frɛr], *sac* [sak], *cher* [ʃɛr] |
| | | voiced | | v | | z | ʒ | | | | *vrai* [vrɛ], *zone* [zon], *joue* [ʒu] |
| approximants | | lateral | | | | l | | | | | *lit* [li] |
| | | central | | | | | · | | | ʁ* | *rond* [ʁɔ̃] |

* This is the typical Parisian uvular *r* of Modern French; since the precise quality of the *r* is not generally relevant to the discussion we have generally used [r] instead for typographical simplicity, which strictly speaking denotes a dental, alveolar or postalveolar trill.

Modern French words borrowed from English have introduced another sound into French which, however, only features in word-final position, [ŋ] as in *parking* [parkiŋ].

# Appendix III:
# Suggestions for further reading

This is a brief selection of further reading; full details of the works may be found in the references at the end of the book. Wherever possible, at least one work in English on each topic has been included; other suggestions for reading are given in the individual commentaries.

## General histories of French

The standard history of French is still that by Brunot (1905–59, reprinted 1966–79), of which the last two volumes (XII and XIII) were written by Charles Bruneau. A further volume covering the period 1880–1914 has subsequently appeared (Antoine and Martin (eds) 1985).

There are a number of good one-volume histories of French written in English, notably those of Rickard (1974, [2]1989) and Price (1971); two older studies, but still of considerable value, are Ewert (1933, 1966) and Pope (1952). Lodge (1993) adopts a sociolinguistic framework.

An excellent one-volume history written in French is Picoche and Marchello-Nizia (1989), which has strong coverage of French beyond France. Other useful surveys in French are Caput (1972), Cohen (1947, [4]1973), François (1959) and Wartburg (1934, [10]1971).

## Dictionaries

The standard etymological dictionary is Wartburg (1922–) which is in German, but there are a number of smaller, more manageable ones available including Bloch and Wartburg (1932, [6]1975), Rey (1992) and Picoche (1992). For individual periods the following are especially useful; Old French: Godefroy (1880–1902), Greimas (1980); Renaissance: Huguet (1925–67), Greimas and Keane (1992). The *Trésor de la langue française* (1971–94), the *Grand Larousse de la langue française* (1971–78) and the *Grand Robert de la langue française* (1985) all contain valuable historical information as well as serving as dictionaries of the modern language.

**The history of different aspects of French**

Of the numerous studies available, we recommend the following as starting points for further investigation.
Orthography: Beaulieux (1927), Catch (1978).
Phonetics: Fouché, (1958–61), Zink (1986).
Morphology: Lanly (1977), Picoche (1979).
Syntax: Harris (1978), Nyrop (vols V and VI, 1925, 1930).
Vocabulary and semantics: Chaurand (1977), Ullmann ($^3$1965).

**Old French**

For the earliest period Allières (1982) is a helpful introduction. There are a number of accessible introductions to the study of Old French including Anglade (1965), Foulet (1919, $^3$1970), Einhorn (1974) and Zink (1987). A mine of information on Old French dialects is Dees (1980). For Old French morphology, see Chaussée (1977), Zink (1989); syntax, Ménard (1968, $^2$1976); vocabulary, Matoré (1985). Further collections of Old French texts may be found in Aspland (1979) and Studer and Waters (1924).

**Middle French**

The best single-volume account of this period is Marchello-Nizia (1979). Also useful are Zink (1990) and Martin and Wilmet (1980). Rickard (1976) offers an extensive collection of fifteenth-century texts.

**Renaissance**

Gougenheim (1974) is invaluable; a shorter overview of the period may be found in Huchon (1988). Rickard (1968) not only includes a wide-ranging selection of sixteenth-century texts, but also has a detailed introduction.

**Classical and Neo-classical French**

For the history of French grammar and syntax in the seventeenth century, see Haase (1898) and Spillebout (1985). An introduction to the linguistic thought of the period can be found in Rickard (1992). An excellent study of the eighteenth century is Seguin (1972).

**Modern French**

For the period 1880–1914, see Antoine and Martin (1985). There is a plethora of material on the modern language; among the general discussions we will mention Désirat and Hordé (1983), Battye and Hintze (1992) and Walter (1988). Some of the many varieties of French are surveyed in Muller (1985), Offord (1990) and Ager (1990); an insight into *la francophonie* may be gained from Valdman (1979), while Chaudenson (1979) provides an introduction to 'French' creoles. Grevisse (1993) is a comprehensive reference grammar of the modern language in French; for a somewhat shorter English one, see Price (1993a). Further details about French phonetics and phonology may be found in Tranel (1987).

# References

In references where more than one date is given, the first date is that of the first edition. Numerical superscripts denote edition numbers. The publication details relate to the most recent edition cited, which is also generally the edition used for citations in the text.

Académie Française (1694, $^2$1718, $^3$1740, $^4$1762, $^5$1798, $^6$1835, $^7$1878, $^8$1931–35, $^9$1986– [Vol. I: A–Enz complete]) *Dictionnaire de l'Académie française*, Paris: Imprimerie Nationale.

Adam, A. (ed.) (1966) see Voltaire (1966).

Ager, D. (1990) *Sociolinguistics and Contemporary French*, Cambridge: Cambridge University Press.

Albouy, P. (ed.) (1973) see Hugo (1973).

Allières, J. (1982) *La Formation de la langue française*, Paris: Presses Universitaires de France (Que sais-je?).

Andrieux, N. and Baumgartner, E. (1983) *Manuel du français du Moyen Âge: Systèmes morphologiques de l'ancien français. A. Le verbe*, Bordeaux: Sobodi.

Anglade, J. (1965) *Grammaire élémentaire de l'ancien français*, Paris: A. Colin.

Antoine, G. and Martin, R. (eds) (1985) *Histoire de la langue française 1880–1914*, Paris: Éditions du Centre National de la Recherche Scientifique.

Aspland, C.W. (ed.) (1979) *A Medieval French Reader*, Oxford: Clarendon Press.

Ayres-Bennett, W. (1994) 'Quelques considérations sur l'usage des formes surcomposées en francais du XVIe au XVIIIe siècle', in *Opérateurs et constructions syntaxiques: Évolution des marques et des distributions du XV$^e$ au XX$^e$ siècle*, Paris: Presses de l'École Normale Supérieure, pp. 149–75.

Balibar, R. (1985) *L'Institution du français: Essai sur le colinguisme, des Carolingiens à la République*, Paris: Presses Universitaires de France.

Barnett, F.J. (1961) 'Some Notes to the *Sequence of Saint Eulalia*' in *Studies in Medieval French Presented to Alfred Ewert in Honour of his Seventieth Birthday*, Oxford: Clarendon Press, pp. 1–25.

Battye, A. and Hintze, M.-A. (1992) *The French Language Today*, London and New York: Routledge.

Beaulieux, Ch. (1927) *Histoire de l'orthographe française*, 2 vols, Paris: Champion.

Bédier, J. (1927) *La Chanson de Roland* commentée par Joseph Bédier, Paris: L'édition d'art.

Beer, J.M. (1992) *Early Prose in France: Contexts of Bilingualism and Authority*, Kalamazoo: Medieval Institute Publications, Western Michigan University.

Benoît, J.-D. (ed.) (1957) see Calvin (1957).

Bertelé, R. (ed.) (1968) see Desnos (1968).

Billot, C. (1984) *Chartes et documents de la Sainte-Chapelle de Vincennes (XIV<sup>e</sup> et XV<sup>e</sup> siècles)* par Claudine Billot avec le concours de Josiane di Crescenzo, 2 vols, Paris: Éditions du Centre National de la Recherche Scientifique.

Bloch, O. and Wartburg, W. von (1932, <sup>6</sup>1975) *Dictionnaire étymologique de la langue française*, Paris: Presses Universitaires de France.

Bodel, J. (1962) *Le 'Jeu de saint Nicolas' de Jehan Bodel*. Introduction, édition, traduction, notes, glossaire complet, tables par A. Henry, Brussels: Presses Universitaires de Bruxelles, Paris: Presses Universitaires de France.

Bodel, J. (1981) *Le Jeu de saint Nicolas*, édité par A. Henry, Geneva: Droz.

Brereton, G.E. and Ferrier, J.M. (eds) (1981) *Le Menagier de Paris*, Oxford: Clarendon Press.

Brunot, F. (1891) *La Doctrine de Malherbe d'après son commentaire sur Desportes*, Paris: Masson (reprinted Paris: A. Colin, 1969).

Brunot, F. (1905–59, <sup>2</sup>1966–79) *Histoire de la langue française des origines à nos jours*, 13 vols in 23 parts, Paris: A. Colin.

Burney, P. (1955, <sup>4</sup>1967) *L'Orthographe*, Paris: Presses Universitaires de France (Que sais-je?).

Burnley, D. (1992) *The History of the English Language: A Source Book*, London: Longman.

Calder, R., Screech, M.A., and Saulnier, V.-L. (eds) (1970) see Rabelais (1970).

Calvin, J. (1539) *Institutio christianae religionis*, Strasbourg: V. Rihelium.

Calvin, J. (1936) *Institution de la religion chrestienne*. Texte établi et présenté par J. Pannier, vol. 1, Paris: Les Belles Lettres.

Calvin, J. (1957) *Institution de la religion chrestienne*. Livre premier. Édition critique avec introduction, notes et variantes publiée par J.-D. Benoît, Paris: Vrin.

*The Canadian Encyclopedia* (1988), editor in chief J.H. Marsh, 4 vols, Edmonton: Hurtig.

Caput, J.-P. (1972) *La Langue française: Histoire d'une institution*, 2 vols, Paris: Larousse.

Carruthers, J.K. (1993) 'The *formes surcomposées:* The discourse function and linguistic status of a rare form in contemporary French', unpublished Ph.D. dissertation, University of Cambridge.

Carton, F. and others (1983) *Les Accents des Français*, Paris: Hachette (book and cassette).

Castellani, A. (1969) 'L'Ancien Poitevin et le problème linguistique des Serments de Strasbourg', *Cultura neolatina*, 29: 201–34.

Castellani, A. (1978) 'Nouvelles Remarques au sujet de la langue des Serments de Strasbourg', *Travaux de linguistique et de littérature*, 16.1 (= *Mélanges Rychner*): 61–73.

Catach, N. (1978) *L'Orthographe*, Paris: Presses Universitaires de France (Que sais-je?).

Cellard, J. (1979) *La Vie du langage: Chroniques 1971–1975 'Le Monde'*, Paris: Le Robert.

Cerquiglini, B. (1989) *Éloge de la variante: Histoire critique de la philologie*, Paris: Seuil.

Cerquiglini, B. (1991) *La Naissance du français*, Paris: Presses Universitaires de France (Que sais-je?).

Champion, P. (ed.) (1928) *Les cent nouvelles nouvelles*, Paris: Droz.

Chaudenson, R. (1979) *Les Créoles français*, Paris: F. Nathan.

Chaurand, J. (1977) *Introduction à l'histoire du vocabulaire français*, Paris: Bordas.

Chaussée, F. de la (1977) *Initiation à la morphologie historique de l'ancien français*, Paris: Klincksieck.

Chrétien de Troyes (1989) *Le Chevalier de la charrette (Lancelot)*. Texte établi, traduit, annoté et présenté avec variantes par A. Foulet et K.D. Uitti, Paris: Bordas.

Cohen, M. (1947, [4]1973) *Histoire d'une langue: le français (des lointaines origines à nos jours)*, Paris: Éditions sociales.

Conseil supérieur de la langue française (1990) 'Les Rectifications de l'Orthographe', *Journal officiel de la République française. Édition des documents administratifs, 8 décembre 1990*, Paris: Direction des journaux officiels.

Cotgrave, R. (1611) *A Dictionarie of the French and English Tongues*, London: A. Islip (facsimile reprint, Menston: Scolar, 1968).

Dees, A. (1980) *Atlas des formes et des constructions des chartes françaises du XIIIe siècle*, Tübingen: Niemeyer.

De Poerck, G. (1955) 'Le Sermon bilingue sur Jonas du ms. Valenciennes 521 (475)', *Romanica gandensia*, 4: 31–66.

De Poerck, G. (1956) 'Le MS. B.N. lat. 9768 et les Serments de Strasbourg', *Vox Romanica*, 15, 2: 188–214.

De Poerck, G. (1963) 'Les Plus Anciens Textes de la langue française comme témoins de l'époque', in Straka, G. (ed.) *Les Anciens Textes romans non littéraires: Leur apport à la connaissance de la langue au Moyen Âge*, Paris: Klincksieck, pp. 129–62.

De Poerck, G. (1964) 'Sainte Eulalie', in Bossuat, R., Pichard, L. and Raynaud de Lage, G. (eds) *Dictionnaire des lettres françaises: Le Moyen Âge*, Paris: Arthème Fayard, p. 675.

Désirat, C. and Hordé, T. (1983) *La Langue française au 20e siècle*, Paris: Bordas.

Desnos, R. (1968) *Corps et biens*. Préface de R. Bertelé, Paris: Gallimard.

Diderot, D. and Alembert, J. le Rond d' (1751–65) *Encyclopédie, ou Dictionnaire raisonné des sciences, des arts et des métiers, par une société de gens de lettres*, 17 vols, Paris: Briasson, David, Le Breton, Durand, Geneva: Samuel Faulche.

Dufournet, J. (ed.) (1986) *La Farce de Maître Pierre Pathelin*. Texte établi et traduit, introduction, notes, bibliographie et chronologie par Jean Dufournet, Paris: Flammarion.

Einhorn, E. (1974) *Old French: A Concise Handbook*, Cambridge: Cambridge University Press.

*Encyclopédie* (1751–65) see Diderot and d'Alembert (1751–65).

Engel, D.M. (1990) *Tense and Text: A Study of French Past Tenses*, London and New York: Routledge.

Ernst, G. (1985) *Gesprochenes Französisch zu Beginn des 17. Jahrhunderts. Direkte Rede in Jean Héroards 'Histoire particulière de Louis XIII' (1605–1610)*, Tübingen: Niemeyer.

Estang, L. (ed.) (1962) see Racine (1962).

Estienne, R. (1539/40) *Dictionaire francoislatin*, Paris: R. Estienne.

Étiemble, R. (1964) *Parlez-vous franglais?*, Paris: Gallimard.

Ewert, A. (1933, [2]1943 [reprinted 1966]) *The French Language*, London: Faber.

Ewert, A. (1935) 'The Strasbourg Oaths', *Transactions of the Philological Society*, 16–35.

Faral, E. (ed.) (1938–39) see Villehardouin (1938–39).

Fisher, J.H. and Bornstein, D. (1984) *In Forme of Speche is Chaunge: Readings in the History of the English Language*, Lanham, London: University Press of America.

Flaubert, G. (1971) *Madame Bovary*. Sommaire biographique, introduction, note bibliographique, relevé des variantes et notes par C. Gothot-Mersch, Paris: Garnier.

Flegg, G., Hay, C., Moss, B. (1985) *Nicolas Chuquet, Renaissance Mathematician: A Study with Extensive Translation of Chuquet's Mathematical Manuscript completed in 1484*, Dordrecht: D. Reidel.

Fleischman, S. (1985) 'Discourse Functions of Tense-Aspect Oppositions in Narrative: Toward a Theory of Grounding', *Linguistics*, 23: 851–82.

Fleischman, S. (1986) 'Evaluation in Narrative: The Present Tense in Medieval "Performed Stories" ', *Yale French Studies*, 70: 199–251.

Fleischman, S. (1990a) 'Philology, Linguistics, and the Discourse of the Medieval Text', *Speculum*, 65: 19–37.

Fleischman, S. (1990b) *Tense and Narrativity. From Medieval Performance to Modern Fiction*, London: Routledge.

Fontaine, O. and others (1986) 'Comparaison entre le nombre et la nature des *Clostridium* fécaux et d'autres facteurs de risque impliqués dans la pathologie intestinale des nouveau-nés', *Annales de l'Institut Pasteur: Microbiologie*, 137B: 61–75.

Fouché, P. (1952–61) *Phonétique historique du français*, 3 vols, Paris: Klincksieck.

Foulet, A. and Uitti, K.D. (1989) see Chrétien de Troyes (1989).

Foulet, A.L. (ed.) (1924) see Sarrasin (1924).

Foulet, L. (1911, ³1970) *Petite syntaxe de l'ancien français*, Paris: Champion.

François, A. (1959) *Histoire de la langue française cultivée (des origines à nos jours)*, 2 vols, Geneva: Jullien.

François de Sales (1630) *Introduction à la vie deuote; du bien-heureux François de Sales, Euesque de Geneue . . . Derniere edition. Reueüe, corrigée, & augmentée par l'Autheur, auant son decez . . .*, Lyon: Chez la vefue de Claude Rigaud & Claude Obert.

Freeborn, D. (1992) *From Old English to Standard English: A Course Book in Language Variation across Time*, Basingstoke: Macmillan.

Galet, Y. (1971) *L'Évolution de l'ordre des mots dans la phrase française de 1600 à 1700: La Place du pronom personnel complément d'un infinitif régime*, Paris: Presses Universitaires de France.

Gessler, J. (ed.) (1934) *La Manière de langage qui enseigne à bien parler et écrire le français: Modèles de conversations composés en Angleterre à la fin du XIVᵉ siècle*. Nouvelle édition avec introduction et glossaire publiée par J. Gessler, Brussels: Édition universelle, Paris: Droz.

Gigot, J.-G. (ed.) (1974) see Monfrin (ed.) (1974).

Gilliéron, J. and Edmont, E. (1902–10) *Atlas linguistique de la France*, 35 fascicules, Paris: Champion.

Godefroy, F. (1880–1902) *Dictionnaire de l'ancienne langue et de tous ses dialectes, du IXᵉ au XVᵉ siècle*, 10 vols, Paris: F. Vieweg, É. Bouillon.

Gothot-Mersch, C. (1971) see Flaubert (1971).

Gougenheim, G. (1951, ²1974) *Grammaire de la langue française du seizième siècle*, Nouvelle édition, entièrement refondue, Paris: Picard.

*Grand Larousse de la langue française* (1971–78), 7 vols, Paris: Larousse.

*Grand Robert de la langue française – Dictionnaire alphabétique et analogique de la langue française* (1985), 2ᵉ édition entièrement revue et enrichie par A. Rey, 9 vols, Paris: Le Robert.

Greimas, A.-J. (1980) *Dictionnaire de l'ancien français jusqu'au milieu du XIVᵉ siècle*, Paris: Larousse.

Greimas, A.-J. and Keane, T.M. (1992) *Dictionnaire du moyen français: La Renaissance*, Paris: Larousse.

Grevisse, M. (1993) *Le Bon Usage: Grammaire française refondue par André Goosse*. Treizième édition revue, Paris, Louvain-la-Neuve: Duculot.

Guilbert, L. (1967) *Le Vocabulaire de l'astronautique*, Rouen: Publications de l'Université de Rouen.

Guiraud, P. (1986) *Les Structures étymologiques du lexique français*, Paris: Payot.

Haase, A. (1898) *Syntaxe française du XVIIᵉ siècle*, traduit par M. Obert, Paris:

Alphonse Picard et fils.

Harris, M.B. (1978) *The Evolution of French Syntax: A Comparative Approach*, London: Longman.

Henry, A. (ed.) (1962) see Bodel (1962).

Henry, A. (ed.) (1981) see Bodel (1981).

Hilty, G. (1978) 'Les Serments de Strasbourg et la Séquence de Sainte Eulalie', *Vox Romanica*, 37: 126–50.

Hilty, G. (1990) 'La Cantilène de sainte Eulalie: analyse linguistique et stylistique', in Dion, M.-P. (ed.) *La Cantilène de sainte Eulalie: Actes du colloque de Valenciennes, 21 mars 1989*, Lille: ACCES, Valenciennes: Bibliothèque municipale de Valenciennes, pp. 73–79.

Huchon, M. (1988) *Le Français de la Renaissance*, Paris: Presses Universitaires de France (Que sais-je?).

Huguet, E. (1894) *Étude sur la syntaxe de Rabelais comparée à celle des autres prosateurs de 1450 à 1550*, Paris: Hachette.

Huguet, E. (1925–67) *Dictionnaire de la langue française du XVIe siècle*, 7 vols, Paris: Champion, Didier.

Hugo, V. (1973) *Les Contemplations*. Édition établie, présentée et annotée par Pierre Albouy, Paris: Gallimard.

Hunt, T. (1990) *Popular Medicine in Thirteenth-Century England: Introduction and Texts*, Cambridge: D. S. Brewer.

Jourda, P. (ed.) (1965) *Conteurs français du XVIᵉ siècle*. Textes présentés et annotés par P. Jourda, Paris: Gallimard.

Kristol, A.M. (1989) 'Le Début du rayonnement parisien et l'unité du français au moyen âge: le témoignage des manuels d'enseignement du français écrits en Angleterre entre le XIIIᵉ et le début du XVᵉ siècle', *Revue de linguistique romane*, 53: 335–67.

La Bruyère, J. de (1965) *Les Caractères de Théophraste traduits du grec, avec les Caractères de ce siècle*, edited by R. Pignarre, Paris: Garnier-Flammarion.

Laclos, P.-A.-F. Choderlos de (1782) *Les Liaisons dangereuses, ou lettres recueillies dans une Société, & publiées pour l'instruction de quelques autres. Par M.C. . . . .de L. . .*, vol. 1, Amsterdam, Paris: Durand.

Lanly, A. (1977) *Morphologie historique des verbes français*, Paris: Bordas.

Lodge, R.A. (1993) *French: From Dialect to Standard*, London: Routledge.

Lote, G. (1949) *Histoire des vers français*, tome 1, première partie: *Le Moyen Âge*, Paris: Boivin.

Maillet, A. (1976) *La Sagouine, pièce pour une femme seule*, Paris: Grasset.

Marchello-Nizia, C. (1979) *Histoire de la langue française aux XIVᵉ et XVᵉ siècles*, Paris: Bordas.

Marchello-Nizia, C. (1985) *Dire le vrai: L'adverbe 'si' en français médiéval: Essai de linguistique historique*, Geneva: Droz.

Martin, R. and Wilmet, M. (1980) *Manuel du français du Moyen Âge: Syntaxe du moyen français*, Bordeaux: Sobodi.

Martinet, A. and Walter, H. (1973) *Dictionnaire de la prononciation française dans son usage réel*, Paris: France-Expansion.

Marzys, Z. (1993) 'Rabelais et la norme lexicale', *Travaux neuchâtelois de linguistique*, 20 (*Le Traitement des données linguistiques non standard: Actes des Rencontres Besançon-Neuchâtel, Neuchâtel, 29–30 janvier 1993*): 177–90.

Matoré, G. (1985) *Le Vocabulaire et la société médiévale*, Paris: Presses Universitaires de France.

Matte, E.J. (1984) 'Réexamen de la doctrine traditionnelle sur les voyelles nasales du français', *Romance Philology*, 38: 15–31.

Meigret, L. (1542) *Traité touchant le commun usage de l'escriture françoise . . .*,

Paris: D. Janot (facsimile reprint, Geneva: Slatkine, 1972).

Meigret, L. (1550) *Le Trętté de la grammęre françoęze*, Paris: C. Wechel (facsimile reprint, Menston: Scolar, 1969).

Ménard, Ph. (1968, ²1976) *Manuel du français du Moyen Âge*, vol. 1: *Syntaxe de l'ancien français*, Bordeaux: Sobodi.

*Mercure de France, dédié au Roy. Septembre. 1732.*, Paris: G. Cavelier, La Veuve Pissot, J. de Nully (reprint, Geneva: Slatkine, 1968).

Meunier, J.-M. (ed.) (1933) *La Vie de saint Alexis: Poème français du XIᵉ siècle.* Texte du manuscrit de Hildesheim, traduction littérale, étude grammaticale, glossaire par J.-M. Meunier, Paris: Droz.

Mirabeau, V.R. Marquis de and Quesnay F. (1764) *Philosophie rurale ou économie générale et politique de l'agriculture, Réduite à l'ordre immuable des Loix physiques & morales, qui assurent la prospérité des Empires*, vol. 1, Amsterdam: Les Libraires associés.

*Le Monde*, 13 April 1961.

Monfrin, J. (ed.) (1974) *Documents linguistiques de la France (série française)*, publiés par Jacques Monfrin avec le concours de Lucie Fossier, vol. 1: *Chartes en langue française antérieures à 1271 conservées dans le département de la Haute-Marne*. Volume préparé par Jean-Gabriel Gigot, Paris: Éditions du Centre National de la Recherche Scientifique.

Montaigne, M. de (1965, ³1978) *Les Essais de Michel de Montaigne*. Édition conforme au texte de l'exemplaire de Bordeaux ... par Pierre Villey, rééditée sous la direction et avec une préface de V.-L. Saulnier, Paris: Presses Universitaires de France.

Muller, B. (1985) *Le Français d'aujourd'hui*, Paris: Klincksieck (original German edition, 1975).

Nyrop, K. (1899–1930) *Grammaire historique de la langue française*, 6 vols, Copenhagen: Gyldendalske Boghandel, Nordisk Forlag.

Offord, M. (1990) *Varieties of Contemporary French*, London: Macmillan.

Olivétan, R. (1535) *La Bible. Qui est toute la Saincte escripture. En laquelle sont contenus/ le Vieil Testament & le Nouueau/ translatez en Francoys*, Neuchâtel: P. de Wingle.

Pannier, J. (ed.) (1936) see Calvin (1936).

Paré, A. (1545) *La Methode de traicter les playes faictes par hacquebutes et aultres bastons à feu ...*, Paris: V. Gaulterot.

Péronnet, L. (1989) *Le Parler acadien du Sud-Est du Nouveau-Brunswick: Éléments grammaticaux et lexicaux*, New York etc.: Peter Lang.

Picoche, J. (1979) *Précis de morphologie historique du français*, Paris: Nathan.

Picoche, J. (1992) *Dictionnaire étymologique du français*. Nouvelle édition revue, Paris: Le Robert.

Picoche, J. and Marchello-Nizia, C. (1989) *Histoire de la langue française*, Paris: Nathan.

Picot, É. (ed.) (1907) *Maistre Pierre Pathelin*. Reproduction en fac-similé de l'édition imprimée vers 1485 par Guillaume Le Roy à Lyon, Paris: Société nouvelle de librairie et d'édition.

Pignarre, R. (ed.) (1965) see La Bruyère (1965).

Pope, M.K. (1934, ²1952) *From Latin to Modern French with Especial Consideration of Anglo-Norman Phonology and Morphology*, Manchester: Manchester University Press.

Price, G. (1971) *The French Language: Present and Past*, London: Edward Arnold.

Price, G. (1990) 'La Cantilène de sainte Eulalie et le problème du vers 15', in Dion, M.-P. (ed.) *La Cantilène de sainte Eulalie: Actes du colloque de Valenciennes, 21 mars 1989*, Lille: ACCES, Valenciennes: Bibliothèque municipale de Valenciennes, pp. 81–87.

Price, G. (1993a) *L.S.R. Byrne and E.L. Churchill's A Comprehensive French Grammar*, completely revised and rewritten by Glanville Price, Oxford: Blackwell.
Price, G. (1993b) 'Eulalia, v. 15, Once again', *Romance Philology*, 46: 464–67.
Quereuil, M. (1988) *La Bible française du XIIIᵉ siècle: Édition critique de la Genèse*, Geneva: Droz.
Rabelais, F. (1970) *Gargantua*. Première édition faite sur l'*Editio princeps*. Texte établi par Ruth Calder. Avec introduction, commentaires, tables et glossaire par M.A. Screech. Préface par V.-L. Saulnier, Geneva: Droz.
Racine, J. (1953) *Théâtre de 1668 à 1670*. Texte établi et présenté par G. Truc, Paris: Les Belles Lettres.
Racine, J. (1962) *Œuvres complètes*. Présentation et notes de L. Estang, Paris: Seuil.
'Rapport fait au nom du comité des domaines, Le 20 Juillet 1790, sur le droit de protection levé sur les Juifs. Par M. de Visme, Député du Vermandois. Et Décret rendu sur ce rapport', Paris: Imprimerie Nationale (facsimile reprint in *La Révolution française et l'émancipation des juifs*, 1968).
*La Révolution française et l'émancipation des juifs* (1968), vol. 7: *L'Assemblée Nationale constituante. Motions, discours & rapports. La législation nouvelle 1789–1791*, Paris: Éditions d'histoire sociale.
Rey, A. (ed.) (1992) *Dictionnaire historique de la langue française*, 2 vols, Paris: Le Robert.
Richelet, P. (1680) *Dictionnaire françois, contenant les mots et les choses, plusieurs nouvelles remarques sur la langue Françoise . . .*, Geneva: J.-H. Widerhold.
Rickard, P. (1968) *La Langue française au seizième siècle: Étude suivie de textes*, Cambridge: Cambridge University Press.
Rickard, P. (1974, ²1989) *A History of the French Language*, London: Unwin Hyman.
Rickard, P. (1976) *Chrestomathie de la langue française au quinzième siècle*, Cambridge: Cambridge University Press.
Rickard, P. (1992) *The French Language in the Seventeenth Century: Contemporary Opinion in France*, Cambridge: D.S. Brewer.
Roberts, I. (1993) *Verbs and Diachronic Syntax: A Comparative History of English and French*, Dordrecht: Kluwer.
Rochet, B.L. (1976) *The Formation and Evolution of the French Nasal Vowels*, Tübingen: Niemeyer.
Romaine, S. (1982) *Socio-historical Linguistics, its Status and Methodology*, Cambridge: Cambridge University Press.
Rothwell, W. (1993) 'From Latin to Anglo-French and Middle English: The Role of the Multilingual Gloss', *Modern Language Review*, 88: 581–99.
Rychner, J. and Henry A. (eds) (1974) see Villon (1974).
Saint-Méry, M.L.E. Moreau de (1797) *Description topographique, physique, civile, politique et historique de la partie française de l'Isle Saint-Domingue*, vol. 1, Philadelphia: Chez l'auteur.
Sampson, R. (ed.) (1980) *Early Romance Texts: An Anthology*, Cambridge: Cambridge University Press.
Sankoff, G. and Vincent, D. (1977) 'L'Emploi productif de *ne* dans le français parlé à Montréal', *Français Moderne*, 45: 243–56.
Sarrasin, J. (1924) *Lettre à Nicolas Arrode (1249)* éditée par A.L. Foulet, Paris: Champion.
Segond, L. (1957) *La Sainte Bible qui comprend l'Ancien et le Nouveau Testament traduits sur les textes originaux hébreu et grec*, nouvelle édition revue, Paris: 58 rue de Clichy (reprint of 1910 edition).
Seguin, J.-P. (1972) *La Langue française au XVIIIᵉ siècle*, Paris, Brussels, Montreal: Bordas.

Sgard, J. (ed.) (1991) *Dictionnaire des journaux 1600–1789*, 2 vols, Paris: Universitas, Oxford: Voltaire Foundation.

Sneddon, C.R. (1993) 'A Neglected Mediaeval Bible Translation', *Romance Languages Annual*, 5: 111–16.

Spillebout, G. (1985) *Grammaire de la langue française du XVIIᵉ siècle*, Paris: Picard.

Stefanini, J. (1962) *La Voix pronominale en ancien et en moyen français*, Aix-en-Provence: Publication des Annales de la Faculté des Lettres.

Storey, C. (1968) *La Vie de Saint Alexis: Texte du Manuscrit de Hildesheim (L)*. Publié avec une Introduction historique et linguistique, un Commentaire et un Glossaire complet par Christopher Storey, Geneva: Droz.

Studer, P. and Waters, E.G.R. (1924) *Historical French Reader: Medieval Period*. Oxford: Clarendon Press.

Sweetser, F.P. (ed.) (1966) *Les cent nouvelles nouvelles*, Geneva: Droz.

Tabachovitz, A. (1932) *Étude sur la langue de la version française des Serments de Strasbourg*, Uppsala: Almqvist & Wiksells Boktryckeri-A.-B.

Thevet, A. (1558) *Les Singularitez de la France Antarctique, autrement nommée Amerique: & de plusieurs Terres & Isles decouuertes de nostre temps*, Paris: Héritiers de Maurice de la Porte (facsimile reprint, Paris: Le Temps, 1982).

Thurot, C. (1881–83) *De la prononciation française depuis le commencement du XVIᵉ siècle, d'après les témoignages des grammairiens*, 2 vols, Paris: Imprimerie Nationale.

Tournier, M. (1980) *Gaspard, Melchior & Balthazar*, Paris: Gallimard.

Tranel, B. (1987) *The Sounds of French: An Introduction*, Cambridge: Cambridge University Press.

*Trésor de la langue française: Dictionnaire de la langue du XIXᵉ et du XXᵉ siècle (1789–1960)* (1971–94), Paris: Éditions du Centre National de la Recherche Scientifique, Gallimard.

Truc, G. (ed.) (1953) See Racine (1953).

Ullmann, S. (1952, ³1965) *Précis de sémantique française*, Berne: Francke.

Valdman, A. (ed.) (1979) *Le Français hors de France*, Paris: Champion.

Vaugelas, C. Favre de (1647) *Remarques sur la langue françoise vtiles à ceux qui veulent bien parler et bien escrire*, Paris, Veuve Jean Camusat et Pierre le Petit (reprint edited by J. Streicher, Geneva: Slatkine, 1970).

Villehardouin, G. de (1938–39) *La Conquête de Constantinople*, éditée et traduite par Edmond Faral, 2 vols, Paris: Les Belles Lettres.

Villehardouin, G. de (1978) *Josfroi de Vileharduyn, La Conqueste de Costentinoble d'après le manuscrit nᵒ 2137 de la B.N.* par la section de traitement automatique des textes d'ancien français du C.R.A.L., Laboratoire associé au C.N.R.S., Nancy: Centre de Recherches et d'Applications Linguistiques, Université de Nancy II.

Villey, P. and Saulnier, V.-L. (eds) (1978) see Montaigne (1978).

Villon (1974) *Le Testament Villon. I: Texte. II: Commentaire*, édité par J. Rychner et A. Henry, Geneva: Droz.

Voltaire (1759) *Candide, ou l'Optimisme, traduit de l'allemand de Mr. le Docteur Ralph*, [no place], [no publisher].

Voltaire (1966) *Le Siècle de Louis XIV*. Chronologie et préface par Antoine Adam, 2 vols, Paris: Garnier-Flammarion.

Walter, H. (1988) *Le Français dans tous les sens*, Paris: Robert Laffont.

Wartburg, W. von (1922–) *Französisches Etymologisches Wörterbuch*, Bonn: F. Klopp, Leipzig–Berlin: Teubner, Basel: Helbig and Lichtenhohn, Basel: Zbinden.

Wartburg, W. von (1934, ¹⁰1971) *Évolution et structure de la langue française*, Berne: Francke.

Whitehead, F. (ed) (1942, ²1946 [reprinted 1988]) *La Chanson de Roland*, Oxford: Blackwell.

Woledge, B. and Clive, H.P. (1964) *Répertoire des plus anciens textes en prose française depuis 842 jusqu'aux premières années du XIII^e siècle*, Geneva: Droz.

Woledge, B. and others (1967–69) 'La Déclinaison des substantifs dans la *Chanson de Roland*', *Romanica*, 88: 145–74, and 90: 174–201.

Wright, R. (1982) *Late Latin and Early Romance, in Spain and Carolingian France*, Liverpool: Cairns.

Zink, G. (1986) *Phonétique historique du français*, Paris: Presses Universitaires de France.

Zink, G. (1987) *L'Ancien Français (XI^e–XIII^e siècle)*, Paris: Presses Universitaires de France (Que sais-je?).

Zink, G. (1989) *Morphologie du français médiéval*, Paris: Presses Universitaires de France.

Zink, G. (1990) *Le Moyen Français (XIV^e et XV^e siècles)*, Paris: Presses Universitaires de France (Que sais-je?).

Zumthor, P. (1960) 'Document et monument. A propos des plus anciens textes de langue française', *Revue des sciences humaines*, fascicule 97: 5–19.